D.I.Y. MANUAL

D.I.Y. MANUAL

p

This is a Parragon Book
This edition published 2004

Parragon
Queen Street House
4 Queen Street
Bath BA1 1HE, UK

Copyright © Parragon 2002

ISBN: 1-40542-823-6

A copy of the CIP data for this book is available from the British Library upon request.

Written by Maria Costantino
Project Editor Gill Paul

The right of Maria Costantino to be identified as the author of this work has been asserted in accordance with Section 77 of the Copyright, Designs and Patents Act of 1988.

Printed and bound in China

CONTENTS

CONTENTS

CONTENTS

ABOUT THIS BOOK

From small beginnings, DIY has grown into a way of life with an industry ready to supply our every material need. This book provides information on a wide range of subjects, from interior decorating and projects in the garden to working on the structure of your home, and services such as plumbing and electrics. Most of the jobs described can be done by someone who is 'handy', who has the time and patience to see a job through to the end, and who is willing to pay attention to detail. As you read through the step-by-step instructions you may be inspired to try your hand at jobs you previously hesitated about doing yourself. Before you start any of the projects, stop and think how the procedures described relate to your home and to your level of skill.

Jobs that require electrical wiring, plumbing and drainage all need a degree of confidence, and some of the more advanced projects will take a much higher level of expertise because a mistake could prove both costly and dangerous. If you feel uncertain about how to proceed, then stop! Seek and take advice from a professional: there are a number of specialist trade organizations who will be happy to help. If you are planning on

altering the structure of your home in any way, always check first with your local council regarding rules and regulations.

You cannot tackle any home improvements without tools. Good tools make work easier, more accurate and much safer. At the beginning of each chapter you will find information on tools, their use and their maintenance. A good basic toolkit will be enough for general repair jobs around your home. Where specialized tools or equipment are called for, these are noted in each section.

All too often, people take notice of safety warnings after they have had an accident. It cannot be stressed too strongly at this point that before you undertake any DIY job – no matter how small or large – you must stop and think about the tools and materials (including any chemicals) you are going to use, the heights and weights involved, and the possible consequences of your actions. Make sure you read all the instructions supplied and that you carry out the appropriate safety precautions for each job. These are outlined in each chapter and with individual projects, where relevant. Don't ignore these warnings; it's not worth taking risks.

Contents

INTRODUCTION

BE YOUR OWN SURVEYOR

Before you buy a home, it is important that you make yourself completely aware of the state of its structure. At some point before buying, you should obtain a survey from a qualified surveyor or house inspector; in fact, if you are borrowing money, your lender will insist that its is surveyed professionally. But before you engage a surveyor, there are lots of things that you can look out for when you view the property yourself.

Start outside: don't let the agent or occupants hurry you indoors.

- **Foundations:** how do they look? Are there any visible cracks? Is earth banked up against the walls? Are there any large trees nearby whose roots might be undermining the structure? Are the downpipes and overflows channelled away from the property? Is there a damp-proof course?

- **Drains:** Is the drain cover accessible? Is the concrete around the cover cracked? Does water rush or pool below the cover? Are rainwater drains clear of debris?

- **Walls:** Are the walls standing straight? (Look at corners for any tell-tale bulges.) Are there cracks in the stone/brickwork? Is the mortar between the bricks loose? Is the render (stucco) loose? (Tap it to see if it sounds hollow.) Are weatherboards rotting? Are there

any stains on the walls below/behind the guttering, beneath the roof or under the windows? Are the walls covered in moss or ivy?

- **Exterior doors and windows:** Are they warped? Are there traces of rot? Is the putty around frames and caulking around doors in good condition? Do the doors and windows close securely? Are the windows double-glazed?

- **Roof:** Has the roof recently been replaced or renovated? Does the ridge of the roof sag? Are there any loose slates or tiles? Can you see any cracks in the joints around chimneys or dormer windows? Are the chimney stacks straight? Does the guttering look sound?

While you are outside, you may also want to inspect any outbuildings and the garden.

- **Garden:** Are the fences and paths in good condition? Does the water drain properly from terraced areas, patios, driveways and paths? Are steps and railings secure?

Once you've worked your way round the exterior, it's time to start inside.

- **Walls and ceilings:** Are they straight? Are there any cracks? (Look especially in corners.) Are the surfaces in good condition? Are there gaps between the skirting boards and the walls? Are there any stains or bulges?

- **Floors:** Do the floors slope? Are the joists below the floorboards in good condition? (Check in the basement if possible.)

- **Basement:** Does it smell musty? (A sign of dry rot.) Are there any signs of damp? Is the wiring and plumbing tidy? Is there ventilation? (Look for metal grilles or air bricks that allow currents of air to circulate. These must not be covered or damp can set in.)

- **Attic:** Can you see light through the roof? Can you see any signs of damp? (Look especially around chimneys, skylights and along the walls.)

- **Stairs:** Are the stairs too steep or narrow? Can you get your whole foot on the tread? Is there enough headroom above the stairs? Are there light switches at the top and bottom? Are the stairs solid? Does the banister wobble?

- **Fireplaces:** Are there any signs of damp around the fireplace? Are the chimneys open? Does the fire draw properly? (Test by holding a piece of lighted paper in the fireplace to see if the smoke is drawn upwards.) Is there a back boiler (where water is heated)? If there are dampers, do they close properly?

- **Plumbing:** Look for rusting and crusting on pipes and joints: a sign they have been leaking. Turn on taps and flush lavatories – is there a knocking noise? Does water come out of taps? Is the flow adequate? Do taps drip after being turned off? Are the taps sunk into the walls or behind tiles? (Check for damp, loose or recently replaced tiles.) Are there traces of limescale? Is there a water softening system installed? Are any overflows overflowing? Where is the main stop cock?

- **Heating:** How is the property heated? Is there central heating? Is the boiler for the central heating adequately ventilated? When was the boiler last serviced? (Ask to see the service record.) If there is an oil tank, how much does it hold? Is it leaking or rusted? Can you control the heat in each room? Where is the thermostat? Does each radiator heat to the same degree? Are any radiators switched off? Why? Is the house well insulated?

- **Electricity:** Do the lights flicker? Is the wiring old? (Look for messy leads around the distribution box and old round pin sockets.) What are the light fixtures like? (Look for rusty lightbulb sockets.) What are the electrical sockets like? Where is the meter?

- **Kitchens:** Any signs of damp? (Look inside kitchen cupboards and under the sink.) Is the kitchen well ventilated? Do windows open? Where are the electric sockets?

- **Bathroom:** Is the light switch outside? (It should be, unless it is on a pull switch.) Is it well ventilated? (Look for damp around fittings, behind the lavatory cistern and on the floor around basins and lavatories.) Is the grouting between tiles mouldy? Are any tiles cracked?

Where there are problems, you must consider whether they can be easily dealt with or whether they are so significant that they outweigh the advantages of making an offer for the property below the asking price. Check the relevant sections of this book for advice on how much work it would take to fix any problems you have identified.

ADDING VALUE TO YOUR HOME

The golden rule is not to over-improve. The National Federation of Builders advises that your 'improved' home's value should be no more than 20% above the average price for the area. A sure-fire method of adding value is to create an extra room, either by extending into the garden at ground level or converting loft space into an additional bedroom. Off-street parking is desirable in most areas. Think twice before installing new kitchen or bathroom units; you might create an equally good impression by simply redecorating the old ones.

PUTTING YOUR HOME ON THE MARKET: CHECKLIST

- Make sure the windows are clean and free of paint splashes.

- Fix drooping curtains or shutters.

- Wash or repaint the front door and polish door fittings.

- An untidy garden can drop the house price by as much as 10%, so trim hedges, cut lawns and weed flowerbeds. Consider planting some seasonal flowers in bloom.

- An efficient central heating system is always a good investment that adds value.

- Double glazing can be a selling point if your home is situated on a main road.

- Give your kitchen and bathroom units a makeover rather than replacing them completely. A fresh coat of paint, new fittings or just a good clean may be all that is needed.

- If you need to replace particularly shabby floor coverings, choose a neutral colour.

- Repair cracks and wash walls and paintwork. Repaint stained or damaged areas.

- Off-road car parking is always a desirable addition, or make sure potential buyers know if parking permits are available.

ASSESSING AND PLANNING

THE STARTING POINT

By now, you have probably identified a list of jobs that you want to do around your home and you are ready to plan the order in which they should be done. Every DIY project should have a beginning, a middle and an end. It may sound like stating the obvious, but understanding that there is a clear order in which work is done will save you time and energy in the long run. It's no use painting over damp patches, or installing a new bathroom suite if your plumbing needs to be replaced. You'll only have to start again and destroy much of the work you've already done. So, start with the preliminaries, then move on to new constructions and adding services, then end with finishing.

- Make sure you have all the materials you will need to complete the job.
- Clear the decks. Empty the room you are working on of furniture and carpets and protect other areas with dust sheets.
- If your DIY involves demolition then where load-bearing sections are to be altered, you'll need to prop them up (see page 48).
- Demolish the unwanted structures, strip out any redundant plumbing, electrics or fixtures and clean away the rubbish.

If you are installing a new damp proof course, now's the time to put it in. Lift every fifth floorboard for timber treatment if required and carry out timber treatment on all wooden structures – the roof, floors and stairs. Cut out any timber affected by dry rot and spray surrounding brick work. Now's the time also to sweep chimneys and flues and re-line them if necessary.

After you have completed any necessary preliminaries, you are ready to move to the second stage. What you do here will depend on the extent of your DIY project: it may involve building work if you are adding an extension, or it may be that you are adding to or updating the services – the gas, electrical, telephone, plumbing systems, adding new or extra insulation, or replacing worn 'elements' such as floorboards.

The finishing stage of DIY projects can take the longest of the three stages. Attention to detail is vitally important and some finishes just can't be rushed.

- **First finishes:** At this point, walls and ceilings are plastered, tiled, boarded or paneled. It is also when the doors are hung, new glass fitted to window frames, skirting boards and architraves are fitted and wood and floorboards sanded down.

- **Fitting out:** Kitchen and bathroom units, wardrobes and cupboards are built in; bathroom suites are installed and connected to the water supplies and waste pipes; radiators are installed and connected to feed pipes, and kitchen equipment is installed, plumbed in or connected to supplies.

- **Decoration:** This begins with preparing the surfaces: sanding, priming, lining, and applying undercoats for paint. Only when these have been done can you move to the final finishes: wallpapering and painting walls, ceilings and woodwork.

- **Last fittings:** After you've decorated, you can install electrical switch cover plates, fit new door furniture and window catches, and put up curtain poles and tracks.

- **Furnishing:** This is the final stage when carpets are laid, curtains hung, light fixtures fitted, furniture replaced and pictures arranged on walls.

EXTERIOR WORK

Plan to begin exterior work in late summer or early autumn when the warm summer weather will have dried out the fabric of the building. The best weather for working outside is warm but overcast. Avoid working in rain or bright sunshine as paints and adhesives will either become too tacky to work with or won't dry out at all. Follow the sun around the house so morning dew has had time to dry out. Don't work on windy days when working up ladders is risky and dust will get deposited on newly painted surfaces. On dry, still days, sprinkle some water or use a houseplant sprayer to dampen down areas around doorways so that any dust has settled before you prime or paint.

TAKING ACCURATE MEASUREMENTS

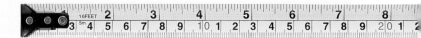

Accurate measurements are essential to ensure that you don't buy too much, or run out before the job is done. Since 1994, most items – with the exception of wood screws – have been sold by metric measure, even though the centimetre is not used in building or allied trades. So always think and measure in metric. There are various types of measures available but a retractable steel measuring tape in its own handy case is a useful tool, which allows you to measure long lengths. The one that measures 8m (26ft) is useful, although you can get longer – and shorter – ones. These measures are very accurate, since the gradations are very fine. For shorter lengths, a folding carpenter's rule made of box, or a metal rule 610mm (24in) long are useful as they also provide a straight edge. In order to ensure accurate right-angles, a try-square with a fixed blade is a valuable addition to any toolbox. A size of 203mm or 228mm (8in or 9in) is useful, or you might want to consider investing in a combination try-square. This enables you to mark out other angles as well as right angles.

A hard-point pencil, well sharpened, is good for marking measurements, but the graphite can leave behind marks, which might show through on wallpaper or paintwork. Avoid 'soft' pencils as these will give you a 'fatter' line and it will be more difficult to make an accurate cut since you'll inevitably wonder which side of the line to make your cut. A slim, marking knife, which marks measurements with greater precision than a pencil, is a much better tool, although it may take a little while to get used to working with one.

See page 372 for metric/imperial conversion charts; see pages 373-4 for advice on buying timber; and see pages 374–7 for the types and standard sizes of nails and screws. On page 308 you will find a table indicating the amount of wallpaper you will need for different-sized rooms. For information on the types of material and tools, as well as the level of difficulty of each job, check the relevant section in the book.

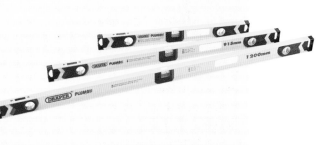

LEFT: A combination try-square allows you to mark out different angles.
TOP, CENTRE AND LEFT: Retractable and folding measuring tapes show metric and imperial measurements.
ABOVE: You'll need a spirit level to check surfaces are level.

WHEN PLANNING PERMISSION IS REQUIRED

Restrictions on what you are allowed to do vary from place to place, but the basic aim of all the official restrictions is to stop you from endangering the stability of a building, from creating a health or fire hazard, or from adversely affecting the surrounding environment.

If you are planning on making structural changes to your house – either by altering its method of support or adding an extra load – it will probably be subject to approval. If you remove an internal wall you may not necessarily be making an alteration that will affect the structural stability of your house; but if you knock through an outside wall to create an extra window or door, then you definitely will be.

Altering the exterior of your home may also need to be approved by the planning or zoning authorities to make sure it does not impact negatively on the neighbourhood and that your improvements are acceptable to your neighbours. You may find that the new window you envisaged letting more light into your room directly overlooks your neighbour's home and infringes their privacy. On the other hand, your planned new extension may block their light and could have to be re-sited.

Every property, as long as it is not a listed building, has an allowance, which is known as Permitted Development. This means you are permitted to extend up to 40 *cubic* metres or 10% of the size of your home without planning permission. But beware: this 40 cubic metres or 10% includes *any previous extensions*. If you, or the previous occupants, have extended the property by adding a garage or another extension, then it's possible that your permitted development allowance has already been used up and you will therefore need planning permission.

You must also check that there are no restrictions contained in the deeds to your house. It may have been built to a specific design by a local landowner a hundred years or more ago, but the restrictions about what the original occupants could do to the property may still remain in force.

If your home is not 'freehold' then you will need to check with the leaseholder to see if you are allowed to carry out any substantial alterations.

Changing the internal layout of your home is subject to laws regarding the size and height of rooms, the treatment of staircases, and the amount of light and ventilation, while fire regulations will stipulate how the structure of the building needs to be protected.

Heating and plumbing installations need to comply with local building regulations: a mistake in the wiring or in the drainage system can put lives at risk from fire or illness.

Buildings that are recognized as historical or of architectural interest, or houses located in designated 'preservation areas', may be listed, and are subject to stringent conditions: you may not even be allowed to re-paint the front of the building, or even the front door, except in an approved colour.

HOW TO APPLY

The Building Inspector's office (in London, it's the District Surveyor) and the Planning Office of your local council are the two most important offices for the self-sufficient do-it-yourselfer.

The Building Inspector is in charge of enforcing your local authority's rules to see that houses are healthy and safe. When you want to knock down a wall between two rooms, the Building Inspector is there to make sure that you do it in such a way that your bedroom doesn't then fall into your lounge.

When you plan a new bathroom you need to know the layout of existing water pipes and sewage outlets and be compliant with water regulations. It is illegal to make any alterations or additions to the plumbing or drainage of a building without reference to the local building inspectorate.

If you are planning on doing any solid building or demolition you need to contact the Building Inspector, tell him what you are planning and, if it comes under his jurisdiction, he will check your plans and tell you what amendments are necessary to comply with the law.

The Planning Officer is responsible for keeping villages, towns, cities and countryside from being 'spoiled' by buildings that are out of character, or by buildings whose use or function may have an adverse effect on our lives. While the Planning Officer doesn't guard against your house falling down, he can insist that you pull down parts of it if it's in breach of planning rules, or if the property is a listed building, or your improvements are not in the same materials or architectural style as the original house.

If you live in a designated preservation area you need to find out what rules and regulations apply before you make any alterations to your home, either internally or externally. While adding a conservatory may be straightforward in one area, in a preservation area you may not be able to site it where it is visible from the road, or even add one at all.

Both the Planning Officer and the Building Inspector are there to help you and you will find them both at your town hall. Applications for planning permission currently cost around £100 and you will need to provide detailed and accurate measured drawings. If you aren't able to draw these up yourself, then you will have to pay someone to do them (see the advice on employing an architect, on page 17).

Your application is made public and anyone who wishes to object to your plans has 21 days in which to lodge their objections. Talk to your neighbours first about your plans so they know what to expect and you'll also find out if they are likely to object. If two objections are lodged, then your planning application has to go before a planning committee. They will take into account your plans and the objections: they may refuse you outright or they may ask you to make changes. If this is the case, you will need to re-submit your amended plans. If you decide to make further changes to your plans, these will also have to be submitted for approval.

Expect the Building Inspector to pay you a visit during the course of your work. He will check that the work is being carried out to standard. If it's not, then you'll have to start all over again. Only when the work is completed to standard will you be given the Building Inspector's Certificate. It's a very valuable certificate: should you wish to sell your home, this will put prospective buyers at ease as it certifies that the work has been done properly.

If you are in any doubt about the legal status of any works you wants to carry out, check with the appropriate authorities first, and ignore their advice at your peril. Be warned that obtaining planning permission can take months.

BELOW: Planning permission is required for knocking through external walls. Any extensions added must not block your neighbours' light or overlook their home.

BUDGETS AND TIMING

It's important to plan your budget in advance for each DIY project and make sure you have enough money to pay for materials, tools or the hire of specialist equipment. Remember that in some hardware stores the prices shown do not include VAT, so you'll need to add on an extra 17.5%. If you are buying any material in large quantities, it's worth asking for a discount.

GRANTS

For some home improvements, such as installing a damp-proof course or insulation, extending a tiny bathroom or kitchen, or modernizing the electrical system, you may be eligible for a local authority grant. Check with your local council. If your home was built before 1919 and requires substantial structural repairs, you may also be eligible for financial assistance. If your home does not have a fixed bath or shower, wash hand basin, or they are not supplied with hot and cold water, you may also be eligible for a grant. The council will inspect your property and inform you what work will have to be done to make you eligible. They may want to see drawn-up plans and you will have to provide them. If they decide you are eligible for a grant, you will then need to get builder's estimates; you may in fact be required to use local contractors approved by the council rather than be permitted to do it yourself. Owners of Listed Buildings may also qualify for certain grants for renovation or restoration. See Useful Addresses, page 377.

LOANS

Your bank or building society may be prepared to 'top up' your mortgage with a loan to cover home improvements provided they are satisfied that what you are planning to do will add value to the property. Alternatively, they may offer you a separate home improvement loan – but remember that this is likely to be a secured loan; your house may be used as collateral and could be at risk if you default on the repayments.

CUTTING COSTS WITHOUT CUTTING CORNERS

You can cut costs on any DIY project by planning ahead and being prepared to modify your 'want' list. Check the local paper for bargains. Investigate the range of tile or floor paints available to rejuvenate old floors before you rip them out. Check out second-hand materials from

CAN YOU AFFORD:

- Materials?
- Tools and tool hire?
- Redecoration and new furnishings?
- Have you costed the basic work?
- Have you allowed some extra money for unseen developments?
- If you are borrowing money, what will the loan cost and how much are the repayments?
- Can you get a grant or tax relief ?
- Will the improvements add to the value of your home? (Ask a local estate agent.)

architectural salvage yards and auctions, particularly if you are trying to match up new additions with the original features of your house.

PLANNING YOUR TIME

Some DIY tasks are quick, while others take more time: undercoats and glues need drying time, cement and mortar need time to 'go off'. How will the weather affect your roof repairs? Furthermore, you may have neighbours to consider. Some management agents for apartment blocks will not allow DIY in the evening or at weekends, so check the house rules first. If you don't have the time to do everything yourself, it's worth considering professional help. See pages 17–19 for advice on hiring professionals. If you really do want to do it yourself, then be prepared to spend time doing it well. All home improvements turn out to be more time-consuming than you first expect.

THE AFTERMATH

There is also the DIY 'aftermath' to consider: how do you dispose of the old windows, doors or drainpipes? Do you need a skip? If so, where will you put it so it doesn't block your – or your neighbour's – drive? If you live in the city centre or have a resident's parking permit scheme, you will have to arrange and pay for a skip license. And if your skip is parked on the road, it will need lights at night. Failing to illuminate it could cost you a fine of up to £1000. Contact your local authority for advice on safe disposal of chemicals and hazardous waste.

WORKING WITH PROFESSIONALS

It's vital to know your own limitations and call in professionals for the trickier jobs, or the ones you don't have time to complete yourself. The most important thing about working with an architect or a builder is that you understand each other. You need to agree plans, drawings, budgets and schedules, and you must be willing to keep an eye on progress yourself. Contact details for all the organizations listed in this section can be found on page 377.

EMPLOYING AN ARCHITECT

The first thing an architect should do is listen. His skill lies in translating your verbal descriptions of your needs and wants for your home into outline drawings. He will be able to advise you on the feasibility of your ideas – whether it is technically possible to do what you'd like – and then draw up draft proposals and budgets.

Once you have agreed with these proposals, your architect will produce a detailed working drawing and a schedule of work. It is also the architect's responsibility to obtain estimates from builders or contractors and to obtain any necessary building and planning permissions (see pages 14–15). (If you are going to do-it-yourself, then you may still want to consider appointing a solicitor or lawyer to handle the legal paperwork on your behalf.)

It is also the architect's job to produce a detailed budget. Remember: it's your money, so ask for everything, right down to the nails and screws, to be itemized and costed. If you think a price is unreasonably expensive, ask your architect why. It could be that he has specified a particularly 'high grade' material, so you'll need to ask him whether a less expensive option is available or practicable. Don't be intimidated: your architect works for you, so ask him questions and make sure you understand his answers.

You have the option of employing your architect to manage the work you have agreed to, or you can find your own builder and other contractors.

The best way to choose an architect is by personal recommendation. If you don't know anyone who has used an architect, then the professional bodies such as the Royal Institute of British Architects (RIBA) and the Architectural Association will give you names and contact numbers for architects in your area.

Always ask to see a portfolio containing images and designs of their work, and ask which ones have been realized and which are 'dream schemes'. A good architect should be able to put you in direct contact with some of his previous clients.

RIBA registered architectural practices are required to undertake continuous professional development, adhere to the RIBA code of conduct and have Professional Indemnity Insurance.

Costs

At the planning stage, most architects will usually charge an hourly fee for their advice. The professional bodies mentioned above will be able to advise you on the recommended scale of fees for the various types of architectural services, so check with them first. For a full architectural service – from start to finish – expect to pay between 10% and 15% of the *total price* of the works.

EMPLOYING A BUILDER

Once again, the best way to find a good builder is by personal recommendation. If a builder has done a good job for someone you know, then chances are he will do a good job for you. It is also highly likely that a good builder is a busy builder. You will need to be patient as it may be some time before he can start working for you.

Ask for details of at least two previous clients, and call them for references. If a builder refuses to give such details, start looking again. You must check your builder's insurance to ensure they are fully covered.

The building industry's professional body, the National Federation of Builders, has nine regional offices and each can provide details of

INTRODUCTION

reputable, professional builders. Builders who are members of the NFB have satisfied stringent entrance criteria. These include providing no fewer than eight references from customers, suppliers and financial institutions. The NFB also operates a code of conduct for its members.

ESTIMATES

In order for your builder to provide you with an estimate, you must give him written specifications of what you want done and to what standard. Ask him to knock down a wall and that's what he'll do. If you didn't originally specify that you wanted the hole 'made good' ready for decorating, don't expect him to do it at no extra cost.

Always get estimates from at least three builders. As well as the total cost of the work, ask when they can start and how long they will take to do the work. A useful tip is to always try to tie estimates to agreed completion dates.

Take a careful note of 'provisional sums'. These are normally for work that a builder would use a sub-contractor to complete – a plasterer, or an electrician perhaps – and for which he does not yet have firm quotes. If your project requires such sub-contracted works, always make sure that your builder consults you before any provisional sum is finally agreed. Make sure that the sub-contractors your builder wishes to employ are also registered members of their trade associations.

ELECTRICIANS AND PLUMBERS

Once again, word of mouth can be the best way to find an electrician or plumber. They should be able to provide references. Don't think that because an advert in the phone book has a trade association logo beside it, they are definitely members; some cowboys are prepared to mislead you from the start. Contact the trade associations to check if they are bona fide members.

The National Inspection Council for Electrical Installation Contracting (NICEIC) will provide you with information about approved contractors. The NICEIC is the electrical industry's independent

GAS SAFETY

- It is very important that gas appliances are installed properly and maintained regularly. Around 30 people die each year due to carbon monoxide produced by faulty gas appliances. A few simple steps could help to save lives!

- Gas appliances should be checked annually for safety to make sure that they are working properly. If you're a tenant, your landlord has the responsibility to make sure that this annual check is carried out. You should ask to see the gas safety check certificate; your landlord is legally obliged to provide this.

- You must ensure that the installer you use is CORGI registered. You can check this by asking to see the ID card that all registered installers carry. If you have concerns about the card's validity call Customer Services on 01256 372300, or log on to HYPERLINK http://www.corgi-gas.com to verify details. Gas is a safe fuel in the hands of an expert so you should never DIY with gas.

- Ventilation is a vital part of the safe operation of gas appliances so never block ventilation and have flues checked annually to ensure that they are working effectively

- To find an installer in your local area, please contact CORGI, the Council for Registered Gas Installers. You can do this by phone (01256 372300) or log on to our website and click on Find an Installer.

- CORGI is the body given the responsibility by the Health and Safety authorities to maintain a register of competent gas installers. Installers must hold valid certificates of competence, which are renewed every 5 years.

safety regulatory body, set up to protect consumers against unsafe and unsound electrical installations. NICEIC Approved Contractors are regularly inspected to confirm that they meet the required national technical standards. The NICEIC also operates a Complaints Procedure and Guarantee of Standards Scheme.

The Institute of Plumbing (IP) has registered members who undertake work to high standards of professionalism, competence and responsibility. The Association of Plumbing and Heating Contractors (APHC) is a guarantor of its member's skills and they operate a Code of Fair Trading and an emergency service.

Any plumber who works on gas-fired central heating must be also be CORGI (Confederation for the Registration of Gas Installers) registered (see box). Regional offices will provide information on local, approved installers from their register of members.

Remember, membership of an organisation does not guarantee good workmanship. Always ask for references.

PAYING UP
If your building project is small scale and isn't expected to last very long,

then most builders and craftsmen will accept payment when the work is completed. The NFB maintains that a reputable builder will not ask for money 'up front', unless specialist materials are required. It is also important that you avoid any 'cash-in-hand' deals from builders or contractors. The chances are they are not VAT registered and not 'above board' – and you won't have a valid, written contract.

On larger jobs, the standard procedure is to make interim payments. These are percentages of the whole cost of the job paid at specified stages of the work. By law you have the right to hold onto 20% of the total cost of the work for six months after your builder has completed the work – but *only* if you have put this in writing at the estimate stage. This money is your insurance: it is to cover the cost of making good any defects that may arise due to faulty work.

The NFB recommends the JCT contract: this is a straightforward, plain-English legal contract, which sets out in writing exactly what is expected of the homeowner and the builder. The JCT contract can be obtained from CIP (Construction Industry Publications) by calling 0121-722 8200.

GETTING ON WITH THE WORK
When your builder turns up to start work on your home, make sure you are prepared. Clear out any rooms he will be working in so he can get on

with the job. Roll up carpets and remove ornaments. Decide on how and when your builder will have access to your home. A secure space for them to leave their tools at the end of the day is a bonus: a builder without tools can't work on another project and has to come back. If you are having substantial alterations made to the structure of your home, you must inform your home insurance company. They will insure you and your home against any accidents or damage caused while work is in progress, including damage to third parties.

TOP: Royal Institute of Chartered Surveyors
ABOVE AND CENTRE: The Guild of Master Craftsmen

PLANNING COLOUR SCHEMES

There are no hard and fast rules about what is the 'right' colour for a room, but understanding the language used to describe colour and how colours work will help to inform your colour decisions.

Natural light, also called 'white light', is made up of all the colours of the spectrum: red, orange, yellow, green, blue, indigo and violet. Light affects the tone, warmth and clarity of a colour. In daylight we are able to see colours for what they are but at night, it becomes harder to see the 'true' colour, as it seems to 'change'.

All colours derive from three basic 'pure' or primary colours: red, blue and yellow. Using these three colours alone, in different proportions, it is possible to mix more than 2,000 distinct colours. Mix equal parts of yellow and blue together and you make green. Mix equal parts of red and yellow and you'll make orange. Equal parts of red and blue will make violet. Green, orange and violet are known as secondary colours. Black and white are known as 'non-colours' or 'neutrals': white reflects light while black absorbs it. That's why a room painted in white or a very pale colour will need less artificial light than one painted in a very dark colour.

A tertiary colour is a primary colour – for example, red – mixed with one of its secondary colours – either orange or violet. The tertiary colour result of mixing red (primary) and orange (secondary) will be a red-orange.

The tertiary colour produced by mixing red (primary) with violet (secondary) will be a red-purple.

COLOUR WHEEL

The colour wheel shows the relationship between primary, secondary and tertiary colours. In general, yellow is placed at the top of the colour wheel. From yellow, the colours proceed in a clockwise direction through the 'cool' colours on the right side of the wheel, to the 'warm' colours on the left side. Notice how the colours are grouped together: this is because they share certain characteristics. The 'warm' colours are red and yellow combinations – colours we associate with fire and sunshine – while the 'cool' colours are blues and greens – colours we associate with water, the sky and vegetation.

The 'warm' colours are 'advancing' colours: they seem to draw surfaces closer and create a cosy comfort. In interior design, advancing colours are often used to transform gloomy, north- or east-facing rooms. The 'cool' colours are receding colours: surfaces painted in them seem further away. Consequently, cool colours create a sense of space, making a room seem bigger than it actually is.

NEUTRALS, TINTS AND SHADES

Subtle colours are made by mixing different proportions of pure colour, or by changing the tone of a colour by adding a neutral. The purest form of neutral is black or white. Neutrals are extensively used in interior design schemes because they do not 'clash' with other colours. However, they can be rather 'bland' or stark, so touches of colour are often added to make neutrals 'warm' or 'cool'.

Adding white to a colour creates pastel colours, or tints. With tints you can play safe – or live dangerously! Whatever tints you use together, there will generally be an overall harmony. You can create more vibrant effects by using a mixture of warm and cool tints. Shades of colours are produced by the addition of black. These are much richer colours and include browns that blend harmoniously into most schemes.

PATTERN AND TEXTURE

A smooth surface appears to shine because it is reflecting light. A coarse or rough surface, because it absorbs light, will create shadows when light falls on it from certain angles. A rough surface will therefore look entirely different to a smooth one, even if they are painted in exactly the same colour.

Texture adds visual interest: use the contrast of rough wood or brickwork against smooth paintwork, or the reflective qualities of glass, metal or ceramics to produce original decorative effects.

Texture also adds to the 'feel' of a room: soft, woven fabrics and furnishings and matt emulsion paints give a sense of warmth and luxury, while highly polished stone, steel, vinyl, and light-reflecting gloss and silk vinyl paints can give a 'clinical' or high tech feel to a room. Texture is most important when a room is all one colour.

Combining patterns can be tricky, so it's worth remembering that strong patterns tend to dominate a room, while small, less definite patterns will merge into the background. Pattern can be used to disguise ugly or intrusive features. Wallpaper applied to door panels to match the walls will make doors seem less obvious. Regular patterns will highlight walls that are 'out of true' or uneven. Floral patterns, which don't allow the eye to settle in one place, are great for use on irregular 'bumpy' walls or for disguising lots of awkward angles – in an attic room perhaps. By linking together soft furnishings and curtains, patterns can also be used to co-ordinate areas of rooms. And don't forget that the same patterns can be used in different colourways.

MANIPULATING SPACE

It is possible to use the properties of colour, texture and pattern to create optical illusions that appear to alter the dimensions of a room. Warm colours, which appear to advance towards the eye, can be used to make a room feel smaller. Cool colours, which appear to recede, will make a room feel more spacious. Tones also reinforce this sense of illusion: dark tones – even of cool colours – will advance towards you, and pale tones will tend to open up the space.

If you paint the ceiling a darker tone than the walls, the ceiling will appear to be lower. A fitted carpet in a matching or similar tone to the dark ceiling will compress the vertical space even further. Make a ceiling appear to be higher by painting it with a light, receding colour.

Long narrow halls and passageways can be 'opened out' by painting them in cool receding colours, which reflect more light. A rectangular room can be made to appear more square if the end walls are decorated with dark, warm colours and the side walls with paler, receding ones.

Using linear patterns – either striped wallpapers or floorboards – is another way to manipulate space. A low ceiling will appear higher if the walls are vertically striped. The horizontal pattern of venetian blinds will make windows appear wider.

Don't forget, too, that using mirrors can add to a sense of space. Position them at an angle to windows to redirect the light in a room.

SAMPLE BOARDS

One of the best ways to start planning a scheme is to collect together things that will help you make decisions. Make a collection of magazine cuttings or items that you really like for their colour, pattern or texture: they may be nuts, flowers, leaves, feathers, jars of spices or items of clothing. Try to think about these objects in relation to your room and see if they are creating a theme. You can now start to make a sample board. Professional designers use these to check the relative proportions of materials and colours they intend to use in a scheme.

Make your own board by gathering, assembling and glueing swatches of wallpaper, painted paper, fabrics and floor coverings onto a piece of stiff card. Start with the largest area – usually the floor. If you can't cut a swatch of the floor covering, take a photograph of it instead and stick it down on a piece of stiff card. Smaller areas of colour such as the wood-work and accessories are represented by 'spots' of colour. Butt the edges of your samples against each other; floors meet walls in real rooms. Avoid leaving borders of white space around the samples as this will alter the colour contrasts and harmonies. Look at your board in both natural light and artificial light.

When you have to incorporate an existing feature such as a bathroom suite into your scheme, try cutting a hole in your sample board to act as a window. Hold up your board and look through the window at the bath: how does your scheme look with the bath inside it?

ENTRANCES, HALLS AND STAIRCASES

We 'pass through' hallways, entrances and staircases, rather than live in them, so these spaces are often relegated to bottom of your list of priorities. Yet this is where visitors to your home cross your threshold and first impressions should be good impressions. It's well worth spending time and energy making these spaces warm and inviting. Don't overlook the possibilities of using the space in your hallway or entrance as workspaces, study areas or even as a temporary dining area.

ENTRANCES, HALLWAYS AND STAIRS CHECKLIST:

- What do you like or dislike about this space?
- What do you use this space for? The telephone? Coats and shoes? Would additional storage be useful?
- Is the hallway warm and inviting? Is it dark, cold and gloomy? Can the lighting be improved?
- Are there any spaces that can be used for other purposes – under the stairs, on the landing?
- What are the doors like that lead off the hallway?
- Does the hallway feel too high? Too low? Too long and narrow? Consider how you can create a feeling of openness with new colour schemes.
- Are the stairs creaky?
- Does the banister wobble?
- Is the stair or hall carpet or floor covering worn out?

The lower parts of walls in entrance halls have to withstand pretty rough treatment from muddy boots, pets, bicycles stored against walls and shopping bags banging against them en route to the kitchen. The Victorians solved this problem by placing tiles or paneling below a dado rail. Both these solutions allow you to re-decorate worn, lower walls without having to re-do the entire height of a hall or stairwell. Finishes should be durable and easy to clean; to avoid accidents, floors should not be slippery and there should be ample lighting.

Most hallways become the dumping ground for outdoor shoes, raincoats and umbrellas. In this case, storage is a priority and it can be built in to 'dead ends' or shallow alcoves. If there is a cupboard under the stairs, consider improving the way the space is used. It's even possible to use the smallest 'wedge-shaped' space right at the back where the stairs meet the floor by adding doors, shelves and drawers to the outside side wall of the stairs.

In even the smallest hallways there seems to be a handy surface for dumping post, shopping and keys but note that home security advisers warn against leaving door and car keys on hall tables, as thieves are able to pass long hooked wires through letter boxes to remove them.

Some hallways have so many doors leading off them that there seems to

be very little wall. If this is the case in your home, make the doors the features. Ugly doors can be improved when old paint is stripped off and new handles added. Wallpapering the panels of doors in the same (or even contrasting) paper as the walls can create exciting effects, and part-glazed doors can allow extra light into halls and the rooms beyond.

Stairs tend to be thought of as simply the means to get from one level of a house to another. Encourage people to linger by displaying paintings or photographs. Stairs can make a very dramatic statement, particularly if they look and feel 'open'. A window letting in natural light can help, but even if the staircase is very confined and has a low ceiling, the illusion of openess can be achieved with light colour schemes.

Lighting is very important so that you can clearly see the risers and the treads of the stairs. Positioning lights on staircases can be tricky as you need to avoid them glaring into people's eyes as they climb up or down. A landing is a space that is all-too-often overlooked. A large landing can be converted into a mini-library or study area, while a small one can be transformed into a comfortable area for talking on the telephone.

RIGHT: Choose light colour schemes to brighten narrow hallways, and select a durable, easy-to-clean paint finish.

LIVING ROOMS

This is likely to be the largest room in your home. It's also the room in which you've probably spent the most money on furniture, fabrics and carpets. You entertain here and spend a lot of time in it, so the living room decor needs lasting appeal.

Living rooms only used for a single function are rare, so it can help to divide out spaces. Make comfortable 'nooks' by using folding screens or divide up a large area with a free-standing set of shelves. Storage in any living room is important: you'll want somewhere to keep books, magazines, CDs and videos, toys,

LIVING ROOM CHECKLIST:

- Is your living room in the right room? Could you relocate it elsewhere?
- Who uses the living room? When is it most used? What is it most used for?
- What do you like/dislike about your living room? What objects are you most fond of and which are you prepared to get rid of?
- Can your living room be 'improved' by moving the furniture? Changing the lights? Changing the colour scheme? Changing the furnishings?
- What type of storage do you need? Do you want built-in storage with doors, or shelves to place objects on display?
- If a room is too dark, consider adding a window or replacing a solid door.
- Consider adding more electrical sockets or lights, or changing to mood lighting with dimmer switches (see page 211).

plus a place for your 'treasures' – souvenirs, ornaments or objects d'art. Real living rooms are never static. Instead, they are always changing with your needs.

If your living room seems isolated from the rest of your home, consider opening up the space by removing a wall, or simply replacing a solid or opaque door with a transparent one. Open-plan living has its benefits but do you have to turn the TV volume up to drown out the sound of kitchen equipment? Do you have to turn the volume down to answer and speak on the phone? Closing off some space with folding doors or by reducing the size of an archway with curtains, or simply re-locating the telephone, can solve a lot of problems. Adding some additional electrical sockets often means that you can relocate the stereo or TV, while changing or adding different lights can help divide up a large area into smaller spaces.

Think about moving your living room. Look at where people in your home 'naturally' congregate. It's generally in the most appealing or welcoming space and often not where you intended. If the view from your present living room window is dull or perhaps looks out at street level, why not move it upstairs so you look out across roofs or treetops? Traditional layouts tended to put living rooms at the front of the house but if this means the room is dark, why not make it your dining room or a bedroom instead?

Unless you have the luxury of more than one living room, this room must feel comfortable during the day and relaxing in the evening. There are some simple decorator's tricks that can help you solve some of the more common living room problems, and they are worth trying before you make any major or expensive alterations.

In many living rooms the fireplace is the focal point – even when central heating has been installed – but it often means that you sit with your back to the window. Try placing a mirror over the fireplace, so the windows and the view through them become incorporated into the room. A mirror placed at right angles to a window will double the image and make a small room feel more open and spacious.

Adding a window to a wall that doesn't have one can improve the quality of light and space, while curtains or blinds are often the solution to creating changes of mood in a living room. In the day, pulled aside, they are unobtrusive elements but in the evening, when drawn, they become a wall of pattern or colour, capable of enhancing and transforming even the simplest of schemes.

RIGHT: Furniture is often grouped around the fireplace but take advantage of good views from a window with blinds that can be opened during the day.

DINING ROOMS

In older houses, which were designed to have separate, self-contained dining rooms, these can often be neglected, under-used spaces. If so, it may be worth considering giving this space a secondary role as an 'quiet' room for study and homework, or as a children's playroom. If the dining room is located close to your kitchen, you could consider opening up the space and extending one room into the other.

There is no single formula for a successful style or layout for a dining room or dining area: a lot will depend on the size of your family and its age span, and also on your eating patterns. Do you 'breakfast and run' then grab a bite to eat for lunch in the kitchen? If so, then your

dining area is most likely used in the evening. If you love giving dinner parties, then your dining area is going to be of great importance to you. The key to planning a successful dining room or eating area scheme is to understand how it works and how to adapt it to your personal needs.

Dining rooms need little in the way of furniture: a table, some chairs and an extra surface – another small table perhaps, or some shelves – to act as a sideboard for storing cutlery, glasses and wine, and for placing dishes prior to serving. All of these the enthusiastic do-it-yourselfer can make or at least transform in some way by stripping, painting or staining and varnishing.

Round tables will accommodate more people than a rectangular one, and they also do away with the formality of having a 'head of the table'. Even the most utilitarian tabletop can be transformed with an elegant tablecloth. Chairs with arms take up more room than those without arms and, if space is limited, stools can be tucked under countertops and tabletops when not in use. Whatever type you choose, seats should be comfortable and there should be enough room for your knees to fit under the table.

Ambience is established through the choice of colours for walls, floors and furnishings and through lighting. Strong, dark colours look soft and rich when tabletops are lit by overhead lights. This creates an

intimate pool of light over the table: glasses and cutlery sparkle, while the rest of the room fades into the shadows. Candlelight adds glamour. Always place candles so the flames are above or just below eye-level: flames directly in people's eye-lines tend to mesmerize them. Tiny, floating candles cast light upwards on diners and have the effect of making their faces look tired.

Pay special attention to windows. Curtains and blinds add to the warmth and friendliness of a room, but if you are fortunate enough to have beautiful windows and stunning views, it's a shame to detract from them or cover them up.

The walls and floors in separate dining rooms will not get as much wear and tear as those in kitchen-dining rooms, so you could consider using fabric to cover the walls, matched with luxurious carpets. In dining areas subject to more use, washable and durable materials would more practical. Even if your kitchen incorporates a dining area, it's worthwhile creating a relaxing space. Soft textures such as cork floor tiles, richly coloured rugs and different wall colourings and patterns and lighting will help define the dining space.

RIGHT: Dark colours look soft and rich when illuminated by overhead lighting. Here a dado rail helps to reduce the height of the ceiling for an intimate feel.

DINING ROOM CHECKLIST

- When do you eat there? Why do you eat there? Could you eat somewhere else?
- What do you like/dislike about your dining area?
- How many people usually eat there? Can you extend the space to accommodate more people?
- Is your dining room self-contained? Can you move easily from the kitchen to the dining room?
- Do you use the space for other purposes? Is the room or space subject to a lot of wear and tear?
- What is your budget? How much time are you willing to spend?

BEDROOMS

The decor and layout of bedrooms should reflect the characters of their occupants. A children's or teenager's bedroom is going to be substantially different to an adult's bedroom. A teenager's room will inevitably double up as a study and a sitting room where friends gather, so it needs to be functional and friendly. The smallest bedroom is usually reserved for guests or infants, but it can be manipulated through use of

BEDROOM CHECKLIST:

• What do you like/dislike about your bedroom?

• Is your bedroom for you alone, or do you share it?

• Does your bedroom have a second function: is it your dressing room or a workspace as well?

• How much storage do you need? What type of storage do you want?

• Do you like to wake up in natural light or do you prefer a darkened room?

• Are you disturbed by noise or car headlights at night? Would heavier curtains help?

• Do you read in bed? Is the lighting sufficient to read by? Do you have to get out of bed to switch the light on/off? Would extra electrical sockets be useful?

• What do you need by your bedside? A clock? Telephone? TV/video remote control?

• What kind of floor would you like to step out of bed onto? Cool stripped floorboards or cork tiles? Cosy, warm carpet?

colour and texture to be a very desirable as well as comfortable and relaxing space.

Lighting is of crucial importance. Bedrooms should be relaxing at night, with soft flattering lights rather than harsh overhead ones. Colour, pattern and texture all play their part in creating gentle, luxurious and seductive moods. A very dark, or even black, colour scheme may look fabulous at night, but could you wake up in it? And could you get to sleep surrounded by acid green or orange walls?

The smaller the space, the more carefully you should plan. Inevitably the bed itself will be the main piece of furniture. Since the average person spends about a third of their life lying in bed, make sure you choose the right type for you.

Don't forget about storage and wardrobe space. Calming bedrooms should not have piles of objects lying around. If you have a lot of clothes to accommodate, would it make sense to build fitted wardrobes (see page 276)? They needn't look as though they are taking over the room if you fit mirrors on the doors to reflect the light, and they can use 'dead space'.

Is the bedroom also your dressing room? Is it also a library? Do you have to get out of bed to turn off the light? What you do in your bedroom will influence its layout and decorative scheme.

Don't clutter bedrooms with too many ornaments and decorative elements. They need to remain calm rather than busy. Another improvement is to re-hang pictures, posters or photographs. People often hang them too high in a room – remember they will appear higher when you are lying down – and make it feel formal and unrelaxed. Pictures hung in pairs are more relaxed and informal than a single one over a bed. Group small pictures together rather than spreading them out across the walls: it's a bedroom, not a museum.

The carpets in bedrooms are often less hard-wearing than those in public rooms, since they don't get walked on so much. Choose soft rugs to warm the floor underfoot and give a more luxurious feel.

Co-ordinate all the fabrics in the room: bed linen, curtains and swags round dressing tables look good in the same fabric and create a feeling of unity. Drape the material in soft, flowing swathes for a romantic look.

Use subtle colourwash effects to add a hint of colour to wooden furniture and windowframes, or try more sophisticated effects like liming.

RIGHT: Create a simple canopy over a bed by attaching a circular curtain rail to the wall and draping hemmed fabric onto it with curtain hooks.

KITCHENS

Kitchens need to be functional areas capable of withstanding a great deal of wear and tear, so in most instances, the materials you choose will be dictated by practicalities. The colours you choose, however, do not have to be restricted. Kitchen sinks and electrical appliances are available in bright colours as well as in the standard stainless steel or white enamel. Coloured melamine or tile worktops and splashbacks, tile or vinyl floor coverings, or even painted floors, are all ways to introduce colour into your kitchen.

Most kitchens are based on the principle of the 'work triangle' drawn between the three main activity areas: water supply, cooking area and food storage. Each area needs to be easily accessible from the other and good lighting and ventilation are essential. The spaces between the

three areas should not be more than a double-arm span: this means you can easily move from stove to sink, or refrigerator to stove.

Few homes actually have a triangular shaped kitchen. Instead, there are a handful of basic kitchen layouts. There is the single-line kitchen, the galley kitchen, the 'L'-shaped and the 'U'-shaped kitchens and what is often known as an 'island kitchen'.

The single-line kitchen has everything – sink, stove, cupboards, appliances – lined up on one wall. This layout is very useful if you have a limited amount of space: head-height cupboards and built-under units will free up work surfaces.

The term 'galley kitchen' describes a kitchen that has been installed in a corridor or other long, narrow space. Cupboards and appliances are arranged on two facing walls with just enough space left in the middle for you to bend down.

The 'L'-shaped kitchen is most often found in small, square rooms and makes for a good, open-plan kitchen. The 'U'-shaped kitchen is most often imagined as wrapping around three walls, but it can also be created within a larger, open space like a kitchen-dining room. This gives all the benefits of the 'triangle' plus maximum work surfaces. In an open plan or through kitchen-dining room scheme, it can mark out the boundary between preparation space and the dining area.

The island kitchen has become popular in recent years, largely due to celebrity cooks. TV companies like them because it makes filming chefs easier. Island plans are great for large spaces where the islands act as room dividers, but they can be expensive.

Whatever layout you decide on, you have to incorporate the essentials. These are work surfaces, cooking equipment, sinks and storage space. Work surfaces need to be close to the stove and the sink, heat resistant, waterproof, and easily cleaned. They also need to be large enough to hold all the ingredients of a meal as it is being prepared as well as all the electrical and other gadgets you use, and they should be the right height for you to work in comfort.

The position of your sink will be determined by the water supply and drain connections, unless you are prepared to do some major plumbing. But the style of sink and of taps can be changed very simply (see pages 152 and 162).

The 'old style' free-standing, all-in-one cooker has in many homes given way to separate built-in ovens and hob units. Inevitably, these new styles are more expensive but they do save space, especially in small areas.

RIGHT: A galley-style kitchen with cooker, cupboards and all appliances arranged on two facing walls. Note the warming stain used on the woodwork.

KITCHEN CHECKLIST

- What are your priorities? A new colour scheme or design style? An efficient working area? A family eating space? More storage space? All of these require different solutions.
- What is your budget? The extent to which you can make major changes will be limited by this. Think carefully about all your options regarding materials.
- How long do you have? Can your kitchen be 'out of service' for a weekend, a week, a month? Plan carefully the stages in which you work.

BATHROOMS

Bathrooms, like kitchens, have to fulfil definite functions, but because they are often the smallest space in the house, making them 'work' takes careful planning. Nevertheless, it's possible to achieve dramatic effects with the minimum effort and money, since they are such small rooms. Bold treatments can work really well in a bathroom.

Many bathrooms tend to have quite high ceilings. Although painting a high ceiling in a dark colour usually has the effect of lowering the ceiling in a larger room, it can make a

BATHROOM CHECKLIST:

• What do you like/dislike about your bathroom? Is it relaxing?

• Is it warm/cold? Is it well ventilated or always full of steam?

• Is your present bathroom conveniently located? Are you prepared to undertake extensive plumbing work to move it?

• Would a new decorative scheme or new bathroom fixtures – taps, mirrors, tiles – give it a face lift? Do you want a completely new bathroom suite?

• Would you like a shower? For details of how to install a shower, and how to build a shower cubicle, see page 174.

• Is storage a problem in your bathroom?

• What type of bathroom would you really like? What style do you want?

bathroom appear like a box. Instead, try 'breaking up' the walls with a dado rail and treating the sections above and below it differently.

While coloured bathroom suites are readily available, think long and hard before you buy, as it will remain for quite some time as the dominant influence over any future colour schemes. If you live in a hard water area, it's best to avoid all but the very palest colours for bathroom suites, to avoid showing up limescale deposits.

Moving your bathroom to another space can be expensive, but a 'convenient convenience' can make a real difference to your life. If you are planning a completely new bathroom, you must make sure you comply with local water board regulations (see page 146). Don't forget to consider the existing layout of water pipes, sewage outlets and ventilation ducts.

All materials used in the bathroom must be moisture-proof, so avoid uncoated wallpapers, matt emulsion paints, corrodible metals or jute-backed carpeting. Joints and cracks should be well sealed with caulks and silicone sealant.

Of paramount importance when planning your bathroom is safety. Not only should floors and bathtubs be non-slip, or fitted with non-slip mats, glass doors must be shatterproof, and medicine cabinets should have childproof catches. Electrical sockets

must be a specific distance from taps and must be fitted with waterproof covers. Electric light bulbs should be enclosed, as they could short-circuit if they become damp, and lights, heaters and ventilators should only be operated by pull switches or from outside the bathroom.

Because bathroom fixtures are permanent – and expensive – it's important that you choose them with care. First, draw an accurate scale plan of your bathroom. Mark the position of windows and doors, and remember to allow enough space for them to open. Plot the location of taps and lights. In this space you need to fit a bath and/or shower, a sink and a lavatory (if this is not in a separate room of its own). Leave room for a bidet, if you like them. You will also need somewhere to store and hang towels, and a place for bubble-bath, soaps, shampoos and so on.

Classic tiled bathrooms can sound like an echo chamber. Choose materials with sound-proofing qualities, such as cork floor tiles, carpet or polystyrene ceiling tiles. Muffling sound can be especially important if your bathroom is just through the wall from a bedroom.

RIGHT: Choose muted colours and introduce bolder splashes to create a warming effect, and remember to allow for storage of essential items.

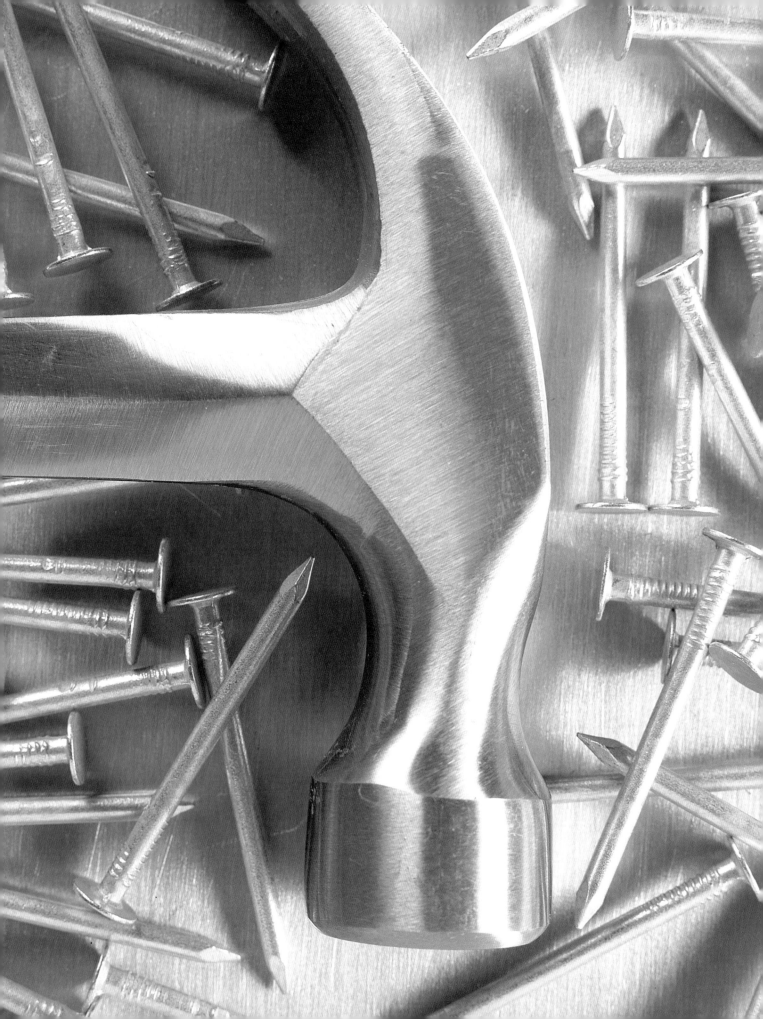

Contents

1

REPAIRS & IMPROVEMENTS

TOOLS & MATERIALS

HAND TOOLS

Basic hand tools are always required, whatever DIY job you undertake. Your toolbox can be added to over time or when you come to do a specialized job, and many specialist tools and powered tools can be hired by the day.

• Measuring accurately is of paramount importance, so for any DIY job it is vital that you have a steel rule, a try square (for marking right angles), a spirit level (to check horizontals and verticals), and a good, hard pencil for making marks. For some jobs it will also be useful to have a chalk line.

• Where high-speed cutting, drilling or sanding are required, it is vital to wear goggles to protect your eyes and a dust mask to stop you breathing in fine particles or fumes. If you are operating power tools for long periods of time, then a pair of ear protectors is a very good idea.

• When you saw wood, you can either saw across the grain (cross-cutting) or along the grain (ripping). A general-purpose hand saw with about 8 teeth per 25mm (1in) will do both types of cutting well. Tenon saws, with square ends and the top of the blade stiffened to keep it straight, are used to make finer, more accurate cuts. Look for one with 12 to 14 points per 25mm (1in).

• A mitre box guide is a useful addition to any toolbox, making 45 degree cuts in timber quicker and easier. For finishing and trimming, a trimming knife with a selection of blades is always needed, while for smoothing wood, a smoothing plane (steel no. 4) or a Surform, and a selection of abrasive papers will be needed.

• Also useful are some files: one fine and one coarse one would be ideal and you can get them flat or half-rounded. These are very useful for rounding off corners, for minor shaping and for smoothing.

• While you work, you will need to be able to hold the material you are working on securely: portable work benches are cheap and very useful, but you may also find that a portable vice and some 'G'-clamps are useful additions to your toolbox.

• A wide selection of hammers is available with wooden or metal handles, and in different weights; try one at around 340g (12oz) for comfort. It is useful to have a cross pein hammer, where one head is rounded and the other flat. This is good for starting small nails. An alternative is a claw hammer (you pull out nails with the claw on the back of the head). A club hammer is useful for heavy work, as is a pin hammer (for driving home fine pins) and a rubber or wooden mallet.

• A selection of chisels and an oilstone with two different grade sides for keeping them sharp will serve you very well. Firmer chisels have square rather than beveled edges and are tougher and easier to keep sharp. Good sizes to have are 25mm (1in), 12.5mm (½in) and 7mm (¼in). Also useful for tackling masonry repairs is a cold chisel.

• A selection of screwdrivers – large, medium and small – is useful but on big jobs you may find a spiral-ratchet screwdriver saves you time and energy. They have three operating positions: ratchet right, ratchet left and locked solid. The spiral ratchet screwdriver – sometimes called a pump screwdriver – has a ratchet action but with a telescopic shaft, which cleverly drives in the screws simply by pushing the handle back and forth.

• A hand drill will work just as well as an electric drill for holes between 1mm (¹⁄₃₂mm) and 6mm (¼in) in diameter. A hand brace with auger bits is ideal for drilling holes between 6mm (¼in) and 25mm (1in), but you can get special expansive bits, which can be adjusted to bore holes between 12mm (½in) and 62mm (2½in) in diameter. But the simplest and quickest way to drill holes is an electric drill and these are well worth the investment. With an electric drill, use the twist bits for small bore holes and the flat bits for larger ones.

• A bradawl is useful for making holes to start screws in. A good pair of scissors is a useful addition to any toolbox, as is an old kitchen knife – one used for spreading butter is ideal! For applying filler to cracks, a filler knife is required.

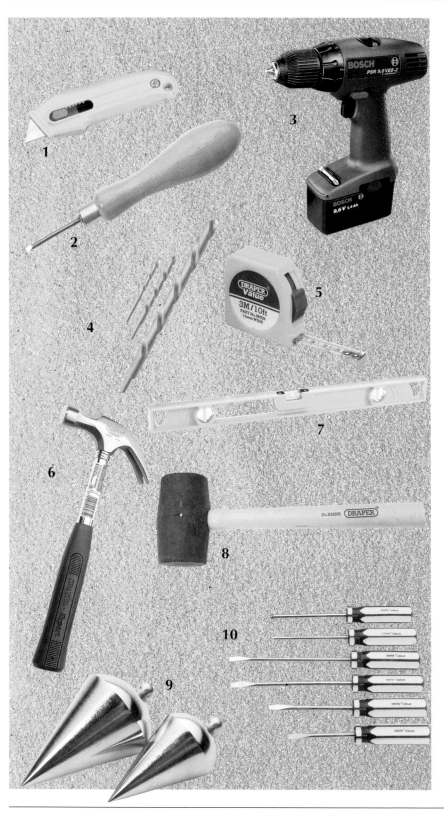

TOOLBOX

1 Trimming knife
2 Bradawl
3 Electric drill
4 Selection of drill bits
5 Steel rule
6 Hammer
7 Spirit level
8 Mallet
9 Plumb bobs
10 Selection of screwdrivers
11 Nails and screws
Try square
Files
Chisels
Goggles
Dust mask
Saw
Long saw
Tenon saw
Smoothing plane
Cold chisel
Oilstone
Floats/plaster

11

POWER TOOLS

Power tools save time and, despite their initial cost, they can save you money too because they enable the amateur enthusiast to undertake a wider range of DIY jobs. Power tools fall into two groups: the purpose-built one-job tool with its self-contained motor, and the power drill with its attachments and accessories. Keen woodworkers may need a purpose-built power saw but, for most of us, a good drill with attachments added as needed is the best buy.

Use power saws for large jobs like cutting floorboards or wall panels.

Most drills are classified by the size of their 'chuck'– the jaws that clasp the twist drill or accessory. The bigger the chuck, the bigger the metal drill it can take, and the bigger the chuck the more power it will need. Because power tools incorporate a fan to keep the motor cool, a drill operating at full speed will not overheat even if it is used for long periods without rest. Beware

drops in motor speed: this could be a sign of overloading, which can lead to overheating and motor burn out.

It is important to remember that different materials have different safe cutting speeds: a single speed drill operating at around 2500 revs a minute is fine for sanding, sawing and drilling holes up to about 1cm (⅜in) in timber. If you are boring bigger holes, or drilling through steel, masonry or concrete, a slower speed is necessary to prevent damage to the drill twist and the material being worked on.

To achieve low speeds you will need a two-speed gear box, which will give you around 2500 rpm in top speed and around 1000 rpm in low gear. Some tools also have a trigger speed control, which gives lower speeds by restricting electricity supply

to the motor. A useful power drill is a 1cm (⅜in) two-speed drill to which you can add a hammer attachment, a circular saw attachment, a jig saw attachment and a sanding attachment.

Check out the power tools available in your local DIY store and always ask for a demonstration and, if possible, a test drive in the store.

NAILS AND PINS

Panel pins are used for fixing thin wood or ply and, rather than using a hammer to drive them home, it's better to use a panel push-pin.

Hardboard pins have tapered heads so when they are driven home, the head disappears almost completely.

Oval wire nails are for general woodwork, especially in thin or short-grained wood, while round wire nails have heads that help the grip and won't spoil the surface appearance.

For roofing felt repairs, sash cords and fencing, galvanized clout nails are the best as these prevent rust, while for quality flooring and work where the heads of nails need to be inconspicuous, lost head nails are the best type.

In floorboards where visible nail heads don't matter but splits in wood do, then the oddly shaped nails called cut floor brads are required.

A very firm grip is given by cut nails. These have a blunt point, which reduces the risk of splitting the wood.

Nails are sold in small quantities in local shops and DIY stores, but they can be bought more cheaply by the kilo from builder's merchants. See page 376–7 for advice on the standard sizes in which they are sold.

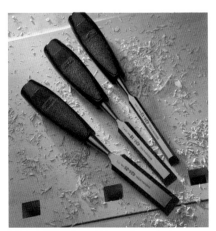

SCREWS

Wood screws are either countersunk, round head or raised head.

Countersunk screws are generally used to fix wood to wood or fixings to wall plugs. Round head screws, which are normally black-painted steel or brass, are for fitting ironmongery to timber, while raised head screws, which are usually brass, are for fixing decorative hardware such as door or window furniture.

Brass screws are ideal if you need to remove them occasionally, because they don't rust or stick. Avoid steel screws in damp conditions because they rust; choose zinc-coated or sheradized screws (which are very strong) or alloy screws (which are slightly less strong).

Star head or cross head screws have a cross-shaped notch on the head. There are also dome-headed screws in steel or brass, which come with 'cups' – screw-on covers, which hide the slotted screw head underneath. These are the type you'll find holding up mirrors or bathroom panels and they give a very professional finish.

There are also a number of special fixings such as rawlnuts and gravity and spring toggles. A rawlnut is a flexible cylinder that expands widthways to grip the hole when the bolt is tightened, while a gravity toggle is used for fixing the skin of a vertical cavity (such as a flush door or wall panel).

Screws are bought by the diameter (or gauge) and length. The higher the gauge, the heavier the screw: a 38mm long screw comes in different gauges from 6 to 14. The most common sizes are 12mm to 50mm long and between 4 and 10 gauge. See page 375 for a complete list of screw sizes.

OTHER TOOLS

For some DIY jobs around the home, such as repairs to brickwork, you will also need more specialized tools such as a brick-laying trowel, a pointing trowel, tingles, a steel float and a wood float or 'hawk' – which you can easily make yourself.

When it comes to renovating, repairing and replacing floorboards, you will find a floorboard saw, floorboard bolster, drill, screwdriver, nail punch, electric sanding machine (which can be hired by the day from most tool hire shops), pad or jigsaw, wood glue and abrasive paper are indispensable to a perfect finish.

For each of the DIY projects in this book, any specialized tools and materials will be itemized. See also the Tools & materials sections at the start of each chapter, where the main tools you will need are explained and instructions on how to use and maintain them are outlined.

TOP AND CENTRE: Firmer chisels have square rather than beveled edges that are easier to keep sharp.

BOTTOM: A panel drill with screwdriver attachment.

WORKING WITH LADDERS

If you are undertaking repairs to external walls, guttering, roofs or any areas above head height, you will need ladders. It is vital that these are in good condition, suitable for the job, anchored securely against movement and used correctly.

Stepladders should stand about 2m (6ft 6in) high so you can reach the ceiling without having to stand on the top step. A second shorter stepladder might be useful for other jobs, and you can use both with scaffold boards to build a platform on which to work. Choose a stepladder with a platform at the top to take paint cans and trays. The most secure stepladders are those that have folding side stays, which lock in the open position and are further secured by a 'fold down' tray or platform.

The main, all-purpose ladder for work outside the house is the **extension ladder**. The upright sections are known as *strings* or *stiles*, while the cross pieces, which are placed at about 255mm (10in) intervals, are called *rounds* or *rungs*.

Wooden ladders are perfectly reliable but always look for stiles of straight-grained fir, pine or spruce. The grain of the wood should run parallel to the edge of the stile and the best (and most expensive) wooden ladders have rounds of ash or oak. Choose a wooden ladder with reinforcing metal rods stretched under the rounds for added security. Wooden ladders should never be painted as this can mask defects. Instead, use varnish or clear wood preservative. Ideally, wooden ladders should be stored in the rafters of a shed or garage, or hung on brackets fixed to a wall, where the air can circulate around them. Never leave a wooden ladder on the ground as it will get damp and may warp. Remember to inspect wooden ladders for signs of rot or woodworm: a few holes or slight sponginess could mean invisible damage just below the surface.

Aluminium ladders weigh significantly less than wooden ladders, and they generally don't warp. However, it is worth remembering that they can conduct electricity so it is vital that they are kept free of any overhead domestic electricity supply. Aluminium is very smooth, so ladders must be firmly secured at the top and bottom and fitted with rubber feet to stop sliding.

A **double extension ladder** comes in two sections allowing you to reach up to the eaves of a typical two-storey house. The second piece of the ladder has clips, which fit onto the rounds of the first section. These ladders come in various sizes: a 4.27m (14ft), which extends to around 7.3m (24ft) is about the right height for the average home. To estimate the length of ladder you'll need, add together all the ceiling heights in your house then add at least 1m (3ft 3in) to allow for the angle. Triple extension ladders are

The best stepladders have a folding side that stays locked in the open position.

If your ladder is 4.27m (14ft) long, the feet should be 38cm (1.25ft) from the wall.

Ladder stays hold the ladder away from the wall.

also available; these are normally operated by a rope and pulley so they can be extended singled-handed.

Raising an **extending ladder** is a two-person job. Get a friend to put their foot on the first rung, then raise the ladder, working your hands along the rungs. Carry the ladder in the vertical position to the job and erect it so that the base is placed one quarter of the height of the ladder from the wall.

Make sure the base is on something firm: if it has to stand on bare earth, then make a simple board 'floor' first. If the surface is smooth concrete, lash the base to something secure, such as a stake driven into the ground, or, best of all, get another person to stand at the bottom and hold the ladder steady for you. Secure the top of the ladder with rope to a gutter bracket or to an eye screw driven into a fascia board.

The safest ladders are **scaffold towers**, which can be built up to different heights. It is a lot easier to work from a scaffold tower than from a ladder, and two scaffold towers with intermediate staging or decking will let you carry out repairs over a span or distance.

Major roof repairs will require **cat ladders**, which can be hired. Cat ladders are wooden ladders with an angled lip at the top, which sits over the ridge tiles. These ladders must be anchored securely, usually by a rope fastened to one stile, which is then threaded around the chimney stack a couple of times, and tied to the stile further up the ladder.

There are a number of **ladder accessories** available. Ladder stays hold the ladder away from the wall. This is vital when you are painting overhanging eaves or guttering, where you might be forced to lean backwards and possibly overbalance and fall. Clip-on platforms are wide, flat boards, which clamp to the rounds. These are much more comfortable to stand on for long periods than rounds. Adjustable legs, which bolt onto the bottom of the stiles, allow you to level the foot of the ladder on sloping or uneven ground. Because you should always have one hand on the ladder, a metal 'S'-hook means you can hang a can of paint from a round. You can also get clamps that fasten to the stiles so you can have your paint can handy at your side, but most useful is a clip-on tray on which you can place a small selection of tools.

SAFETY FIRST

Safety on Ladders

- It's better to wear shoes on ladders as heavy boots don't let you feel the rungs through the soles. On the other hand, shoes with too soft a sole will bend over the rungs and you'll be taking all your weight on the arches of your feet.

- Before you climb up any ladder, make sure your shoes are free of mud or grease so your feet don't slip.

- Make sure your shoelaces are tied securely and tuck trouser hems into your socks or use bicycle clips.

- Cloths, brushes and abrasive papers can be carried in your pockets, but sharp tools must be carried in the hand so you can throw them clear in the event of a mishap.

- When you start to climb the ladder, keep your eyes on the wall immediately in front of you. Don't look up or down in case you get dizzy and when you get to the top, only look at the job you are doing.

- Never, ever, stand on the very top rung of a ladder: the minimum safety position is about four rungs down from the top. And always leave a minimum two-rung overlap between sections of a 4.27m (14ft) extension ladder (three rungs on a 4.9m/16ft extension ladder).

- Never lean out from either side of, or backwards from, the ladder. Always keep your centre of gravity inside the ladder stiles and only work on those parts of the structure you can reach.

WALLS

EXTERNAL WALLS

The colours and textures of external walls form the 'public face' of a home, and they also play a vital structural role. External walls are load-bearing, supporting the weight of the roof, floors and internal walls. Depending on the age of your home, external walls will either be of solid or cavity construction. Houses built before 1914, and many that were constructed between 1914 and 1945, have solid walls. The best way to find out which type of external wall your home has is to measure the thickness of the wall at a window or door opening; the size of cavity and solid walls are different.

Cavity Walls

A cavity wall consists of two separate walls known as 'leaves'. Each wall is the width of a single brick with a 50mm (2in) space between. A modern leaf, built with metric size bricks would be 100mm (4in) thick. A leaf built prior to metrication, using imperial sized bricks, would be slightly larger, at 113mm (4½in) thick. Lightweight aerated concrete blocks are increasingly used to construct the inner leaf as they are cheaper and more efficient at conserving heat.

Cavity construction provides a building that is warmer and drier than one with a single solid wall. The cavity between the leaves stops rainwater that penetrates the outer leaf from soaking through to the inner one, and gives a 'cushion' of air that acts as insulation. Cavity wall insulation can be added to this inner gap. To make the whole structure stronger, the two leaves of cavity walls are held together by wall ties that are bedded into the mortar on both sides. These ties are often flat strips of metal that have been twisted so any moisture that collects on them is thrown off before it reaches the inner leaf.

DRILLING

If you carry out work on a cavity wall that requires drilling or cutting through one of the two leaves, it is vital that you don't let any debris fall into the cavity. It could collect in a small pile or land on one of the wall ties, forming a bridge that may cause damp on the inner leaf. If you have a mystery damp patch on the upper part of a cavity wall this is the most likely cause,

Solid Walls

Solid walls are usually as thick as the length of a brick, about 225mm (9in), although some houses were built with what are called 'brick-and-a-half' walls, making their thickness around 345mm (13½in). This type of solid wall construction is most common in three- or four-storey houses where the lower-floor walls were built in 'brick-and-a-half' for extra strength, and the upper-floor walls were lighter, single brick construction.

Solid walls offer limited protection against the weather because rainwater can soak through the brickwork, causing dampness on the interior plaster. The insulation of solid walls can be improved by timber or tile cladding, or by adding a rendering.

INTERNAL WALLS

Some internal walls are load-bearing, supporting the weight of the house, while others are simply partition walls dividing the space into rooms. It's not always easy to tell the difference, but there are some guidelines. However, if you are in any doubt, alway ask the advice of a professional.

• A lath-and-plaster or plasterboard wall is likely to be a partition. A brick or block wall, however, is more likely to be load-bearing.
• If the wall is in the middle of the house, running parallel to the floorboards in an upstairs room, then the wall is at right angles to the joists, and will be load-bearing.
• A wall that stands to one side of the house and runs at right angles to the floorboards in the room above it (and is therefore parallel to the joists) is likely to be a partition wall.

Solid Internal Walls

An internal, load-bearing wall will generally be constructed like an exterior solid wall and will be around 225mm (9in) thick. However, if it is of lesser constructional significance – i.e. the weight it is bearing is not enormous – you may find that the wall is only half this thickness (the width rather than the length of a brick).

In many modern homes, building blocks are used instead of bricks to construct solid, load-bearing internal walls. These walls are often dry-lined: plasterboard is nailed to a framework of wooden battens screwed into wall plugs. Not all solid internal walls are load-bearing: partition walls are sometimes solid as well.

Hollow Partition Walls

In most instances, partition walls are hollow structures built on a framework of timber with an outer covering of lath-and-plaster in older homes, or plasterboard in more modern constructions. The hollow middle of a partition wall is most often used to carry and conceal electric cables around your home.

A lath-and-plaster wall is constructed on a timber framework with a horizontal member (ceiling plate) at the top and a corresponding floor plate at the bottom. Between these is a series of vertical members called 'studs' and, to strengthen the framework further, there may also be horizontal members called 'noggins', placed about halfway up the studs. Across the studs are nailed thin, narrow timbers – the laths – which act as a key for the plaster that is skimmed onto them.

Plasterboard walls have a similar framework except that the vertical studs are usually spaced wider apart. The sheets of plasterboard are fixed to one or both sides of the wooden framework. Factory-built sections are also available: these are plasterboard sheets attached to an inner core, which slot together to form non-load-bearing partition walls.

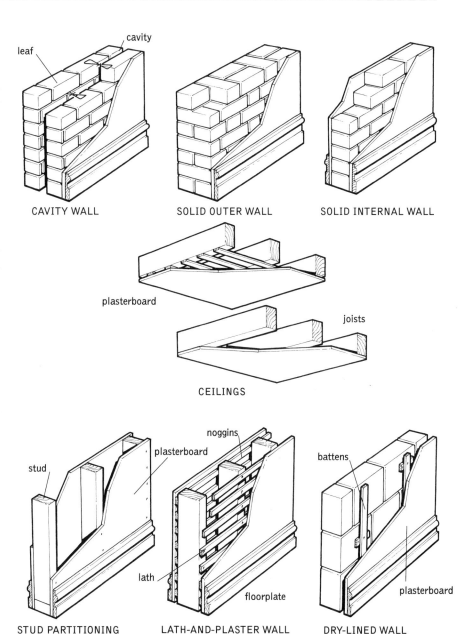

CAVITY WALL   SOLID OUTER WALL   SOLID INTERNAL WALL

CEILINGS

STUD PARTITIONING   LATH-AND-PLASTER WALL   DRY-LINED WALL

CEILINGS

Domestic ceilings are usually covered with plaster. Where the floor above is made of concrete – such as in a block of flats – the plaster is applied to the underside of the concrete. Where the floor above is laid on joists, the ceilings are also fixed to joists.

Traditionally, ceilings were made using lath-and-plaster, but in most modern homes, the ceiling is more likely to be made from plasterboard. You may come across another type of ceiling in your loft or basement: a hollow-joisted ceiling, where the joists are on view. If there is a room above, you can also see the underside of its floor.

On top storeys, such as lofts (see pages 106–11), plasterboard may be fixed over the joists, while on lower floors the space between the joists on the underside of the floor may be lined with plasterboard.

REPAIRS TO MASONRY

Brightening up brickwork can give a new lease of life to its appearance, but it is also important to repair or replace damaged bricks and mortar, and to cure flaws and deterioration to bricks, joints and surfaces.

Smartening up old brickwork often requires no more than cleaning it down with a stiff broom and water. Mould and lichen growth can be removed with a mix of one part household bleach to four parts water. Don't use detergents as these can affect the face of the brick. Remove stubborn patches of dirt with a wire brush but avoid rubbing too hard or you could damage the brick's face. Faded brickwork can be treated with brick dyes, but these lighten after a time and will need renewing.

One of the most common faults in brick walls is efflorescence – the white, powdery substance that appears on the surface. In modern homes this is caused by the salts in the bricks drying out and crystallizing as they come to the surface and can be removed with a stiff brush. Don't use water – you'll slow down the whole drying and crystallization process.

On older properties, an 'outbreak' of efflorescence could indicate that the wall is damp, so remedy the cause of this before cleaning the brickwork.

Rust can occur around ironwork embedded in brickwork and joints. This causes bricks to flake and crack, so any mortar around ironwork should be raked out and replaced. Clean the metal thoroughly and then prime it – you may also need to use a rust inhibitor. Rust in the joints between bricks is caused by the ironstone in the sand. Where this occurs, you have to rake out the mortar and repoint.

REPOINTING AND WATERPROOFING

Repoint walls by pushing mortar into the joints in the brickwork.

Paint on clear, repellent fluids to waterproof brickwork.

REPOINTING
The mortar in brick walls is affected by wind and rain, causing it to loosen, crumble and wear down below the level of the brickwork. Repointing means adding new mortar on top of the old to bring it to the correct level. It's not a difficult job and needs only a few tools, but if you have to repoint in high areas, then it's worth hiring a scaffold tower for safe access.

Use an old chisel or screwdriver for raking out any loose mortar and a club hammer to clear out stubborn bits. Working on about 1m sq. (1sq.yd) at a time, first clear out the vertical joints, then the horizontal ones. Clear them to about 15mm (¾in): any deeper and you may damage the wall. Brush down the joints to remove dust and mortar and then soak the brickwork so that it doesn't absorb moisture from the new mortar. Mix up enough mortar for about two hours' work.

With the trowel, push the mortar into the joints, first into the uprights, then the horizontals, the top and then the bottom. Make sure that you match the new joints to the existing ones. Once the mortar has set, brush gently – an old broom head is ideal. Wash off any mortar stains; if necessary, rub them with a piece of old brick. When you repoint brickwork, you can add colourants to the mortar to produce matching effects. The colour will be altered somewhat if you use ordinary sand, so white sand is better.

WATERPROOFING
Old, soft bricks can become porous so applying a water repellent is a good method of preventing water infusion and improving insulation. Clear, repellent fluids can be painted on easily, but this should be done only after damaged bricks are replaced and faulty joints repointed.

REPLACING A BRICK

SPALLED BRICKS

Because bricks are porous, they absorb moisture in wet weather, which then evaporates when the weather is dry. On old houses, the faces or edges of bricks can begin to crumble or 'spall' because in very cold weather the water in them freezes and then expands, cracking and shattering the brick. The brick then stops being weatherproof and moisture can pass to the inside wall. The only solution is to replace the brick. Remember that your home may have been built with imperial-sized bricks, which were slightly larger than metric sized ones (see page 373). If you can't find matching bricks of the same size, you could turn the old brick the other way round and clean up the face now on view. If you need to replace it with a new brick, compensate for any size difference by adding a little more mortar in joints.

1 Removing old bricks

Rake out the pointing surrounding the damaged brick using a club hammer and a bolster or cold chisel. Next, chop out the brick. If it's very difficult to remove, try drilling into it several times with a large-diameter masonry bit before working on it with the chisel. The brick should crumble away in pieces. Clean out the debris from the opening and then dampen the opening and surrounding bricks so that they don't absorb the moisture from the new mortar.

2 Mortaring new bricks

Dampen the new, replacement brick. Place new mortar on the bottom and sides of the opening. Apply mortar to the top of the new brick – this is called 'buttering'. If you are replacing a single brick, then apply mortar to the bottom and one side of the hole, and butter the top and opposite side of the brick. Slot the new brick into place and clean off any mortar that oozes out.

3 Pointing

Place some mortar on a hawk and smooth it into a pat. Holding the hawk close to the wall, scoop up some mortar onto the back of the trowel and push the trowel forwards, tilting the front of the hawk upwards at the same time so that the mortar is lifted clear. Point the vertical joints first, pressing the mortar well into the joints. Chop off any surplus mortar with the side of the trowel or straight edge. Point the horizontal joints, filling each joint roughly before drawing the trowel across it to form a smooth, continuous band of mortar and cut off the surplus at the bottom of the joint.

4 Horizontal joints

The horizontal joints must be formed so that rainwater doesn't collect in them. Three types of joint shapes are common: flush, keyed and weatherstruck. To create a flush joint, scrape away the excess and let the mortar become semi-stiff. Working in one direction, rub a piece of heavy sackcloth along the joint to flush it with the brickwork. Keyed joints are concave and can be achieved by pressing a length of metal or plastic tube along the joint as shown above. The concave should be about 6mm (¼in) in depth. Weatherstruck joints have sloped surfaces to shed rainwater: verticals slope to one side and horizontals are recessed beneath the top brick and overhang the lower. Once the mortar has set, brush off and clean any mortar stains. You can do this by rubbing a piece of old brick onto the mortar so that brick fragments colour it.

REPAIRING EXTERIOR RENDER

SMOOTH RENDER

Rendering is a mix of cement, lime and sand (or other aggregate) that is applied to external walls either to make them more weatherproof, or to cover up less attractive construction materials such as cement blocks. The main problems with a rendered surface are that sand and cement mixes shrink and, because all buildings move, cracks can occur. Rainwater can penetrate even the finest hairline cracks, work under the surface of the render and weaken the bond between it and the wall. Blisters of loose material appear and large patches of the surface can fall away. Damage can be especially severe if the water beneath the render freezes.

Good-quality exterior wall paints can provide protection and cover hairline cracks but paint will not help if the cracks are wider than 1.5mm (1/16in), and any larger cracks will need to be filled using an exterior-grade filler. On very large cracks, a sand and cement mix is better and more economical. You can buy small packs of ready-mixed mortar, or mix your own, using one part cement to three parts sharp sand. Clean out the crack with the point of a trowel and remove any loose dust and debris. Push the filler into the crack – you may need to make a couple of applications if it is a big one – and smooth it off flush with the surrounding surface area.

If a patch of rendering becomes loose, repair it immediately. Hack away the loose material back to the underlying brickwork or blockwork with a bolster chisel and hammer. Start at the centre of blisters and work out to the edges until you reach sound material. With a bare patch, hack away around the edge of the hole until you reach sound rendering.

Treat the bare blocks or bricks with a PVA building adhesive. You can mix your own mortar: one part cement to five to six parts sharp sand with a proprietary plasticizer added, or buy ready-mixed and add water. The mortar should be of stiff consistency and is applied in two stages.

1 Applying scratch coat with a float
Place some mortar on a hawk and hold it close to the wall. Push the mortar into the damaged area with a float. Repeat until the hole is filled. Just before it hardens, scratch the surface in a criss-cross pattern with a knife or the point of a trowel to provide a 'key' for the finishing coat. Leave to dry for 24 hours.

2 Finishing coat
Choose a finishing coat that is as similar as possible to the rest of the wall. If the wall is smooth, spread the topcoat until it is slightly proud of the surrounding area, then draw a batten across the surface in a gentle sawing motion to remove surplus mortar. Leave for about an hour, dampen with water, and smooth off with a float.

3 Painting
Rendered surfaces can be enhanced by applying a coat of paint. Masonry paint is waterproof, so it offers protection as well as decoration. Exterior-grade emulsion paints, which are available in a wide range of colours, provide a solely decorative finish and have no waterproofing qualities.

SHINGLE DASHING

Walls can be left smooth or decorated with many other finishes: roughcast, scraped and textured finishes are just a few. Scraped finish is achieved by leaving the final coat to harden for several hours before scraping it with a sharp tool, such as an old saw blade.

Textured finishes can be achieved by stippling the topcoat with an old dustpan brush, dabbing with a fabric pad, or, by running a piece of ribbed rubber over the surface to create a wavy effect. Pebble dashing and shingle dashing are often confused.

With pebble dashing, pea gravel is mixed with the topcoat to form a wet, sloppy consistency and applied directly from a bucket. With shingle dashing, shown below, dry shingle is flicked onto a fatty butter coat to give a speckled, textured finish.

1 Applying a scratch and floating coat
Carry out repairs as for smooth rendering by applying a first 'scratch' coat (see step 1, opposite). Next, apply a 'floating' coat comprising one part cement to three parts soft sand with a small quantity of plasticizer added to the mix. Scratch the surface with horizontal lines then leave to dry for 24 hours.

2 Applying a butter coat
After 24 hours, the floating coat should be dry and the butter coat can be applied. This is made of three parts sand, half a part cement, and one part lime. Working on a small area at a time – about 500mm sq. (7sq.in) – apply the butter coat and smooth it evenly across the surface to a depth of about 6mm (¼in).

3 Adding the shingle
Flick the thoroughly washed shingle onto the butter coat. The idea is to apply the shingle as evenly as possible. The ideal tool for this is a laying-on trowel: one trowel load will cover an area one-third greater than the area of the trowel. Don't pick up too much shingle or you won't be able to flick your wrist to apply it evenly. Put a dust sheet or sheet of polythene down under the area you are working on to catch any shingle that doesn't stick. Move on to the next area, and apply the butter coat and shingles. When you have shingle dashed about 2m sq. (2sq.yds) take a dry, wooden float and tap the shingle very gently into the butter coat. Wipe the float clean and dry it off.

SAFETY FIRST

- Wear a hard hat and protective goggles to protect you from loose pieces of shingle.
- Loose shingle on a ground can be a trip hazard, so take care.

- If working on a ladder, follow the safety advice on page 41. It is worth hiring a scaffolding tower if you need to do a lot of work in high areas.

REMOVING A WALL

Even though they look solid and some walls are load bearing, you don't have to live with them forever. It's possible to knock two small rooms into one large one, but it's a messy job. And before you reach for the sledge-hammer, check with your local authority. Your plans must be approved first by the Buildings Inspector (see page 14) and you must include drawings – not necessarily architect-standard drawings, but they must be clear and give precise measurements. It is an offence to proceed without the inspector's approval, but it may take a little time for his office to check, visit and tell you if your plans breach current regulations or undermine the structural stability of your home.

If your home is leasehold or mortgaged, you'll need to check with your leaser or mortgage company: you may need their approval, and you'll need it in writing.

Removing outer walls, which carry the weight of the roof and upper floors, is a job for experts. Party walls between semi-detached houses, terraced houses and flats, cannot be touched. Internal partition walls, which carry no weight and merely divide internal space, can easily be demolished. However, load-bearing internal walls can only be removed after you have built a 'bridge' to carry the load in its place.

Pre-cast concrete beams and RSJs (rolled steel joints) are available in standard lengths from good building merchants, but hauling up a concrete beam or RSJ into position is hard work and you can't do it alone. You'll need the help of at least three fit, strong and willing assistants.

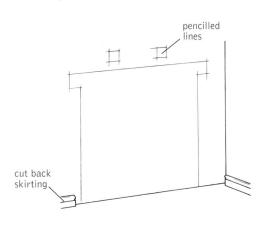
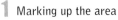

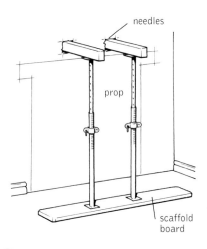

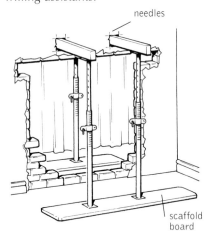

1 Marking up the area

On the wall to be demolished, pencil the area to be removed, leaving at least 300mm (12in) at each side to carry the beam or RSJ. This will rest on shoulders at least 150mm (6in) wide and about 450mm (18in) of wall below the ceiling. About 150mm (6in) above where the top of your new beam or RSJ will be, cut two 127mm (5in) square holes through the wall using a club hammer and chisel.

2 Setting up

Lay the scaffold boards on the floor on each side of the wall. Put the 100mm x 100mm (4in x 4in) lengths of timber (known as 'needles') through the holes. Set the adjustable steel props on the scaffold board – two on each side of the wall – and tighten them well between the scaffold boards and the needles. If the wall carries the joists of the floor above, place a length of 100mm x 50mm (4in x 2in) timber on the ceiling and wedge it in place from the top of the needles.

3 Breaking down the wall

Use a bolster to cut the plaster from the wall along the pencil line, exposing the underlying bricks or blockwork. Next, beginning low down and in the centre of the wall, with a hammer, bolster and a chisel, carefully break down the wall. Use the bolster to trim back bricks near to the pencil line to clear the opening. Now clear away all the debris.

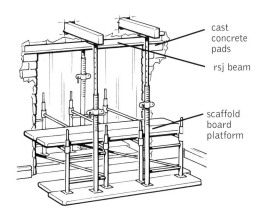

cast concrete pads

rsj beam

scaffold board platform

Create a bridge to carry the load with an RSJ (rolled steel joint) beam and concrete pads.

5 Finishing off

Reposition the wooden strips level with the old, surrounding plaster. Apply a coat of plaster and smooth with a steel float. When this is dry, remove the strips and carefully nail them to the face of the new plaster so they now make a straight edge on the cut edge of the wall and the underside of the beam. You may wish to cut some skirting board to fit round the edges of the remaining sections of the wall (see page 66).

4 Positioning the RSJ

If you are using an RSJ, wrap it in the expanded metal lathing. Lift the beam or RSJ into place so that it rests on the shoulders cut into the wall. Spread a mix of one part cement and three parts sand all over the top of the beam, about 12.5mm (½in) thick. Jack the beam up until the cement and sand mix squeezes out. Make sure the beam is perfectly horizontal, and then wedge the ends up with the two concrete preformed pads. Fill any cracks and joints above and below the beam with the cement and sand mix. Leave to set for a minimum of

12 hours. When the cement and sand mix is dry, remove the adjustable props. Take out the needles and fill the holes with brick and a mix of cement and sand. To provide straight edges for making good plaster edges on the wall opening, run strips of 75mm x 12.5mm (3in x ½in) timber below the beam and against the cut of the wall. Set the strips back about 6mm (¼in) from the level of the existing plaster. With a 1:3 cement-sand mix, fill in the face of the wall and the vertical edge of the beam to the level of the strips. Leave this to dry for a minimum of 12 hours.

TOOLS & MATERIALS

Special tools and materials for removing a load-bearing wall:

- four adjustable steel props (these can be hired and come with a jack)
- a couple of scaffold boards
- cement and sand
- plaster
- pieces of slate
- two short lengths of timber 100mm x 100mm (4in x 4in), and some pieces 75mm x 12.5mm (3in x ½in) long enough to frame the hole
- either a pre-cast concrete beam or a 75mm (3in) or 100mm (4in) RSJ (rolled steel joist) with expanded metal lathing to wrap it in
- two concrete preformed pads

SAFETY FIRST

- Get an architect or structural engineer to calculate the depth of beam required and where it must be positioned to carry the load safely. If your floor springs when you jump on it, it may not be able to take the extra weight; seek professional advice.

- Make sure your props are spaced no more than 900mm (3ft) apart across the width of the opening.

- Hard hats, protective goggles and gloves should be worn at all times by everyone in the vicinity as this work is carried out.

- Wear a dust mask to prevent dust being inhaled.

CONSTRUCTING WALLS

The main skill in building a solid wall – whether it's an external wall, internal partition or a garden wall – is bricklaying. While bricklaying takes time and practice to do well, it is worth the effort. But, unless you are already an experienced bricklayer, forget about trying to build a high wall – anything over 1m (3ft 3in) or thirteen courses of bricks high is not easy and it's better to call in an expert.

Not all walls need to be solidly constructed of brick. Some partition walls are made of lightweight concrete blocks or hollow clay blocks, which are constructed in the same way as a brick wall, so understanding the principle is invaluable. You can also construct partition walls in stud partition (instructions are provided on pages 52–3).

The first step in building a wall is the same as for any other building job: make sure what you are planning to do is legal and safe. Extensions to the structure of your home and dividing rooms will need planning permission and the work carried out must be approved by the Building Inspector.

SINGLE- AND DOUBLE-THICKNESS WALLS

Brick and block walls can be either one or two courses thick. In double-thickness walls, bricks are laid across the depth of the walls ('headers') as well as along the length of the wall ('stretchers'). A simple wall, such as one for a barbecue in the garden, need only be a single course, because it is not likely to be subjected to sideways forces. Retaining walls, which have to withstand greater pressure, should be double thickness.

Single-thickness solid brick or block walls are laid in what is called a 'stretcher' bond, where each brick overlaps the one above and below by exactly half a brick (as shown below left). Because the width of a brick or block is exactly half its length, making corners in stretcher bond is very easy (see below). At the ends of walls, however, bricks have to be cut in half to fill the gaps. Professionals make this look so easy – a single blow of the trowel and their brick is cut. Beginners inevitably struggle, but an easy way to cut a brick is to first score a line all the

way around, and then sever it using a bolster chisel and a club hammer. Lay the half brick so that the cut end is within the wall.

Double-thickness walls are often constructed from two common bonds: English bond, with alternate courses of stretchers and headers, and Flemish bond, with alternating headers and stretchers in each course. These bonds produce beautiful, strong walls, but they do require some bricks to be cut in half lengthways, into what are called 'queen closers', on alternate courses as the wall is built.

FOUNDATIONS

Unless you are building a low wall that is only one brick thick onto existing paving, all exterior walls need proper concrete foundations. A 1m (3ft 3in) high, single-thickness wall needs foundations that are 300mm (12in) wide and 150mm (6in) deep.

A double-thickness wall of the same height will need foundations that are 225–300mm (9–12in) deep and 450mm (18in) wide. In gardens, where there is a flower bed next to a wall, you will generally find that the foundations are buried at least two courses deep.

When it comes to building a house, the exact nature of the foundations depends on the size and construction

A single-brick wall laid in stretcher bond.

Laying a corner in stretcher bond.

TYPES OF BRICK

The cheapest bricks, known as 'commons', are used for the main structure and on areas that won't be damaged by frost, unless they are covered by render or plaster. 'Facing bricks' are widely used for external work because they are durable and weather resistant as well as decorative. 'Seconds' are 'second-hand' bricks that have been reclaimed and cleaned. These are useful if you need to replace bricks on a period property or match the colour of your existing weathered brickwork. Structural blocks, made of cast concrete, are grey or white in colour and rectangular. These are often used as the structural core of a wall that will be rendered over or plastered. Facing blocks, which have one decorative face and often resemble natural stone, can be used in place of bricks to construct the external leaf of a cavity wall while the inner leaf is made of cheaper, and less attractive, structural blocks.

of the building and on the type of sub-soil the house is built on. The most common type of foundation for a small building is known as a 'strip foundation'. This is used where the soil is firm and it consists of a trench all around the perimeter of the house. In modern houses, the trench is filled with concrete, while in older houses, brick or stone is used. The trench serves as a 'footing' on which the external walls rest. In older houses, you may find that the walls are thicker, or 'stepped', at their base. For the internal walls and for 'sleeper' walls – brick walls or piers only a few courses high – that support the joists of a suspended timber floor, less substantial foundations are constructed. Where the underlying sub-soil is soft and sandy, the foundation may be a large concrete 'raft' with an extra-deep perimeter and a central spine or spines to support internal and sleeper walls.

In order to keep the house's substructure ventilated, dry and rot-free, air bricks are situated low down in external walls, while internal walls, sleeper walls and walls below ground-floor level are built in a honeycomb pattern, with bricks omitted in places so the air can circulate freely. If any air bricks in your home have been covered up – either accidentally by leaves or plant debris, or deliberately to prevent draughts – they should be unblocked immediately, otherwise your home is at risk from damp.

LAYING COURSES

The starting point in constructing a brick wall is to lay a bed of mortar on top of the concrete foundation. The mortar should end up about 10mm (⅜in) thick, and the more practice you have, the sooner you will be able to judge just how much mortar to scoop up with your trowel. It helps to make a gauge stick – a length of timber marked out with brick or block courses, with the correct thickness of mortar allowed for. From time to time, you can hold the gauge stick against the wall to check that your mortar is the right thickness and that the bricks are laid correctly.

After you've placed the scoop of mortar onto the surface, use the point of the trowel to make a series of 'V'-shaped grooves in the surface of the mortar. The first brick is laid onto the mortar course, and pressed into place so that mortar is squeezed out underneath. The second brick has one end 'buttered' (mortar applied) to make the vertical joint between the two bricks. Press the brick into position so it lines up with the first and remove any excess mortar with a scraping action by working the edge of the trowel along the horizontal joint, then up the vertical joint. Subsequent bricks in the course are laid in the same way, but after you've laid three or four bricks, use a spirit level to check that the bricks are horizontal and in a straight line. As the wall increases in height, you will also need to check that it is vertical. Do this in several places along the length of the wall to check that it's not bowing or bulging.

DAMP BARRIER

Where a garden wall meets a house wall, there must be a damp barrier or it could bridge the house's damp-proof course (DPC) and introduce damp. Take account of this at construction stage because inserting a DPC afterwards is a major task.

CONSTRUCTING INTERIOR WALLS

The easiest way to divide a room in two is to construct a partition wall. This is made of plasterboard over a framework of timber. You can place a door anywhere you wish in the length of the wall, or it can have a 'window' or serving hatch.

Don't forget that your plans will have to be structurally safe and must comply with regulations regarding fire hazards, light and air. Before you start construction, examine the existing room and find out where the electricity cables and water pipes run (see pages 190–1 and 147). If possible, mark their course on the floor: this will stop you accidentally nailing the partition platform into them.

Plasterboard is available in two thicknesses: 9mm (around ⅜in) and 12mm (½in). While the thinner board is cheaper, you will need more timber supports, so you may not save money in the long run. Additionally, the thicker plasterboard offers better sound insulation, and this may be something you'll need to consider. Plasterboard sheets are available in a range of sizes. For the full height of a room partition, you'll need the large size, which is 1200mm (47½in) wide x 2400mm (94½in) long. Use tapered edge boards to help disguise the joins.

1 Positioning the ceiling plate

Mark where the top of the wall is to go. Cut the ceiling plate (the frame top) the length you require from wall to wall. If the ceiling plate runs at right angles to the ceiling joists, it can be nailed directly into them. If it runs parallel to the ceiling joists, rather than raising the floorboards in the room above, try to move the position of your stud partition so it's right below a joist. Cut the ceiling plate from 75 x 50mm (3 x 2in) unplaned softwood using a fine-toothed woodworking saw. Fit it and then drop a plumb line and bob from it down to the floor to get the vertical. The ivory-coloured side should face into the room.

2 Cutting and fitting the sole plate

Measure and cut the sole plate (the bottom of the frame) from the 75 x 50mm (3 x 2in) unplaned softwood remembering that it will not extend across doorways. Check the position of the sole plate using the plumb line and bob to make sure it lies exactly beneath the ceiling plate. Take time here to ensure the position is accurate. Nail the sole plate to the floor with 100mm, 75mm or 60mm round wire nails, or use screws to fix it if vibrations would cause damage to a ceiling below.

3 Fitting the studs

Measure and cut studs (vertical members) for the sides of the frame. These are nailed to the sole and ceiling plate and fixed to the wall. Measure and cut studs at each side of any openings then, working from one end, fit studs in between these so that the centres are 600mm (2ft) apart for 12.7mm-thick plasterboard, or 400mm (15¾in) apart for 9.5mm-thick plasterboard. Fix the studs by driving a nail into the side of a stud at an angle so it goes into the plate below or above. This nailing technique is called 'skewing' and makes strong, secure joints.

PLASTERBOARD

Plasterboard is fairly easy to cut, but don't rush. Use a fine-toothed woodworking saw to cut long lengths. Short lengths can be cut by scoring the face with a sharp knife and then snapping off the waste over a straight edge.

You'll probably have to cut a hole somewhere in the plasterboard for an electrical socket or light switch. First draw the shape on the board in pencil, then drill a small hole using an ordinary twist bit at each corner, and saw out with a pad saw. Lightly sand the cut edges to smooth them off.

For the timber framework, use 75mm x 50mm (3in x 2in) unplaned softwood. Unplaned material is not only cheaper, but it's also thicker than prepared softwood, so offers more support and strength. It doesn't need to be finished wood because it will be hidden behind the plasterboard panels in the finished wall.

To fix the framework and the plasterboards, you'll need nails (or screws if nailing causes too much vibration on a ceiling below). Use 100mm, 75mm and 60mm round wire nails for the frame, and 40mm jagged plasterboard nails. Finish by applying some joint scrim and plasterboard joint filler.

4 Supporting the framework

To give the framework support, horizontal members called 'noggins' are needed. These are skew nailed to the studs. Always check with a spirit level that each stud has remained vertical. If you are planning to fix items to the finished wall, such as shelving (see pages 256–62), then try to plot the exact position at this stage. If you fit a noggin now, there will be something to receive screws later. Pre-drilling the nail holes into the studs will make nailing easier and stop the studs from slipping out of true vertical. Use a drill bit that is slightly smaller than the nail diameter.

5 Fitting the boards

Cut the plasterboard to a length 25mm (1in) less than the height of the room. Place the cut edge at the bottom of the wall and hold it up against the frame. Now lift the board and jam it up against the ceiling, using a footlifter (a wedge-shaped piece of wood); one end goes under the board and you press the other end with your foot, thus lifting the plasterboard upwards. Fix the board to the frame with galvanized plasterboard nails spaced at 150mm (6in) along every member and about 12.5mm (½in) from the edges. Butt the boards tightly against each other along the edges.

6 Creating a smooth finish

Fill any indentations in the boards using a filling knife. When this has set, apply a thin coat of finish and 'feather' it off with a damp sponge. To make good the tapered edges of the boards, apply a band of filler about 60mm (2½in) wide down the joint, and press in well. Press paper scrim into the filler using a filling knife, squeezing out air bubbles. Apply more filler over the scrim. When this filler is just about to 'go off' (set), smooth its edges with a damp sponge. When all the filler has set, coat it with a thin layer of joint finish, feather the edges with a damp sponge and allow to dry. Repeat to create a smooth finish.

REPAIRING OLD AND NEW PLASTER

OLD PLASTER

To achieve a smooth, well-plastered surface needs skill and patience. Nevertheless, carrying out repairs to plaster is something that an able do-it-yourselfer can quite easily undertake. Cracks and holes look unsightly, and they can also be signs of deterioration in the fabric of your home, and should be attended to immediately.

Cracks are generally caused by slight settlement of the building; vibrations from traffic; a heavy knock, for instance when furniture is moved; damp penetrating the walls; and sometimes because of the impurities in the original plaster itself. There are two kinds of cracks: cheque cracking is caused when the plaster shrinks, and is generally a minor problem; map cracking produces deeper and wider cracks, which may be caused by the building settling or by timber beams shrinking.

Before you begin any large repairs, take a good look at the existing plaster to help determine what type of plaster you need to 'make good' (see also page 57). In many older properties, the plaster used was a lime-hair plaster, which has a soft finish. If you are repairing this type of plaster, then a proprietary ready-mixed, soft plaster, called a 'retarded hemi-hydrate', would be best. Retarded hemi-hydrate plasters set in about 1½ hours, so, they can only be worked during the first 60 minutes or so. Once it starts to harden, it is not possible to soften it, although a little water can be used to lubricate the finishing trowel during final polishing. The short setting time means that it can be difficult to work on large areas unless you are an experienced plasterer.

If the existing plaster surface is hard and grey in colour, then you need a slow-setting, hard, anhydrous plaster. This has a continuous setting time of around 3 hours, and it can be softened with water at the end so you can polish out any irregularities with a steel finishing trowel. This is easier to work with for the less experienced.

RIGHT: Small cracks can be filled with decorator's filler, applied with a filling knife. Don't confuse this tool with a scraper; the filling knife has a flexible blade whereas the scraper is rigid. Begin by running one corner of the blade down the length of the crack to dislodge loose material and to make the crack a wedge shape, which is narrower at the surface of the wall. Brush out any debris from the crevice, and dampen it with water using a brush so it penetrates right into the crack. (Some cellulose fillers do not need damp to bond with the wall, so check the manufacturer's instructions.) Next, use the knife to spread a little filler across the width of the crack, flexing the blade so the filler is pushed well into the crack. Draw the knife lengthways along the crack, flexing the blade to wipe the filler flush with the surface and smooth it down. Don't paint for at least 24 hours.

ABOVE RIGHT: Cracks that are more than 6mm (¼in) deep are filled in two stages. After cleaning the crack and 'under cutting' the edges to make a wedge shape, fill to within 3mm (⅛in) of the surface. When this has set, damp it down a little, and fill to the surface with fresh filler, flushing it off level with the surrounding surface using a finishing float. If the crack is larger than 20mm (¾in) wide, or there are several cracks in one area, it's better to put in one large patch than to fill each crack individually. In this case, the whole damaged area must be cut away with a bolster and hammer and then the edges tidied with a cold chisel. For further advice on patching plaster, see page 56.

NEW PLASTER

Plaster is used as a coating for interior walls because of its capacity to take decorative treatments. At one time, new plaster had to dry out for several months before it could be decorated, but modern plaster settles much more quickly: around two months after application new plaster is ready to receive paint, wallpaper, or any other decorative finish. In a brand new home, the plaster will have dried out completely before you move in but, if you are having a wall plastered – perhaps in a newly built extension to your home – you should leave it to dry out for a couple of months before you begin to decorate.

If you can't stand the sight of bare plaster, paint it with a very thin emulsion paint, so that moisture can escape from the wall. Never heat plaster to try and speed the drying process as this can cause it to crack. As new plaster dries, you'll find efflorescence – a powdery substance caused by salt crystals – forming on the surface. Wipe this off with a dry coarse cloth, and continue to do so until the efflorescence stops forming.

1 Achieving a smooth finish

As new plaster dries out, small circles can break away over the heads of the nails that fix plasterboards in place. Use a nail punch (to avoid causing further damage with a hammer head) and gently tap the nails home. Next, fill the hole with a proprietary filler, letting it harden a little slightly proud of the surface. Sand it down when dry. Use a piece of fine abrasive paper wrapped over a wood block. This gives even pressure and ensures a flush, smooth finish.

2 Preparing the finished surface

To clean any particles of plaster or filler dust on the wall, gently wipe the surface with a barely damp sponge. Allow to dry thoroughly. New, absorbent plaster will need priming before painting: a thinned coat of emulsion works for emulsion paint. If you are using oil-based paints then you'll need an alkali-resistant primer. Before wallpapering, apply size to the plaster so it does not absorb water too quickly from the paste, resulting in poor adhesion, especially at the edges.

PLASTER PROBLEMS

- **Uneven surfaces**

If you try to level a surface after the plaster has set, you will just create a lot of dust and the result will look untidy. Try for a smooth surface as you apply plaster. Shine a light obliquely across the wall to check for irregularites and smooth them with a filling knife before the plaster sets.

- **Crazing**

Fine cracks in finished plaster can be caused by a sand and cement undercoat shrinking as it dries, or by trying to dry plaster too quickly by heating it. So long as the plaster is sound, you can wallpaper on top of it, but for a perfect finish you will have to strip the wall and start all over again.

- **Setting too quickly**

Don't try to rework plaster that has begun to set by adding more water. Discard it and make a fresh batch. Make sure you clean old plaster off your tools, as this can reduce the strength of new plaster. Only mix small batches – about as much as you can apply in 20 minutes. Take care to get the consistency correct, following the manufacturers' instructions.

- **Loss of strength**

If the gypsum and cement dry out before setting takes place, they will not develop their full strength. Spray plaster lightly with water then trowel the surface to produce a smooth finish.

PATCHING PLASTER

Before you decorate any room, there will always be some filling to do. In addition to cracks (see page 54), you may find that there is a hollow patch where the plaster has 'blown' – in other words, it is no longer bonded to the wall. You can recognize blown areas of plaster very easily by tapping the wall gently. Listen for the difference in sound: a blown area will sound hollow. Unless these hollow spots are cut out, they will soon craze and, if wallpaper is applied on top, they will cause it to split.

BONDING AGENTS

Once plaster is removed, the masonry surface beneath needs cleaning and priming with a bonding agent. These 'regulate' the amount of moisture the surface bricks or blocks 'suck' from the new plaster and help the plaster to bond (adhere) to the wall surface. When you use a bonding agent, the basecoat (known as a 'floating coat') of plaster should not be more than 10mm (⅜in) thick. If the 'hole' is deeper than this, you will have to build up the plaster in layers.

Scratch the surface of each layer of plaster with the point of the trowel to provide a key for the subsequent layer and allow at least 24 hours for it to dry before applying the next coat. Check manufacturers' instructions for the number of coats necessary.

1 Removing damaged plaster
Where there is a blown area, all the damaged plaster must be removed with a bolster, chisel and hammer. First, cut a line around the edge of the damage with the bolster, then remove the plaster inside this area, right back to the underlying brick or blockwork.

SAFETY FIRST

Always wear safety goggles and protective gloves when chipping out old plaster.

2 Testing the surface
Clean up the edge by cutting back a further 25mm (1in), then undercut with a corner of the bolster. Clean the area with a damp brush. Remove as much loose material as possible, both around the undercut edge of the plaster and from the joints and surface of the underlying wall. Test the absorption of the underlying masonry by splashing water on it: if it stays wet, then the absorption is normal and it won't absorb water from the plaster too quickly. Highly absorbent surfaces will leach the moisture from the plaster making it difficult to work with.

3 Priming the masonry surface
Low-absorbency smooth brickwork or concrete should be primed with a solution of one part bonding agent to three to five parts water. Apply and allow to dry, then apply a second coat of three to five parts bonding agent to one part water. Absorbent surfaces, such as aerated concrete blocks, should be primed with one part PVA bonding agent to three to five parts water. The second coat should be a mix of three parts bonding agent to one part water. When the second coat is tacky (don't leave any more than 24 hours), apply the plaster.

TYPES OF PLASTER

There are two grades of plaster: a base plaster (known as a 'floating' coat) and a finishing plaster. The most common type of plaster is produced from gypsum, which is processed to remove most of the moisture and ground into a powder, which will set hard when mixed with water again.

How quickly the plaster goes off (sets) is determined by the retarding additives. Plaster of Paris has no retardant added, which is why it sets so quickly. Consequently, it can't be used for general plastering but is useful for casting and repairs to decorative mouldings (see page 96). In many period properties, a mix of lime and sand was used for the floating coat, sometimes with animal hairs added to act as a binder, and neat lime used for the finish. Lime is still used as an additive to plaster to improve the handling, but special care must be taken (and protective clothing and goggles worn) during its handling as it is highly irritant.

There are a number of plasters available for domestic work: Carlite Plaster is a pre-mixed retarded gypsum plaster mixed with a lightweight aggregate – about half the weight of plaster mixed with sand. This sets in about one to two hours. A range of floating coat plasters are available, designed to suit different background surfaces and absorption rates, as well as a finishing plaster. Thistle also produce a wide range of plasters, including a finish plaster for use over floating coats, a finish for use over plasterboard surfaces, and a renovating plaster containing

fungicide for use on walls with residual damp. This is most often used in old houses where a new damp-proof course has been installed. Sirapite B is a finish coat plaster. Used by many professionals, it has a gradual set and can be brought to a very high quality finish – although it cannot be used over plasterboard.

Also available, and popular with the DIY market, are one-coat plasters.

These are mixed with water and can be built up to a thickness of 50mm (2in) in one coat. This saves a great deal of time, but this type of plaster is more expensive and is generally only used for small-scale repairs. If you are uncertain about the type or quality of plaster you need to use, describe the wall you are plastering to your builders' merchant or materials supplier and ask them for advice.

1 Applying plaster

Pick up some plaster using the hawk or mortarboard, tip the board towards you and, in one movement, cut away about half of the plaster with the trowel, scraping and lifting it off the board onto the face of the trowel. Hold the loaded trowel tilted at a slight angle to the face of the wall and apply the plaster using a vertical, upwards stroke, pressing firmly so the plaster is fed onto the wall surface. Flatten the angle of the trowel as you go but don't lay it completely flat or the suction created will simply pull the plaster off the wall again.

2 Creating an even surface

Add more plaster, using upward strokes, as evenly as possible. Build up the plaster until it is slightly proud of the surrounding old plasterwork. Start at the bottom of the wall and use a plasterer's rule (a straight wood batten) to level the surface. Work the rule upwards, moving it from side to side then carefully lift it away, taking the excess plaster off as well. Trowel on more plaster to fill any hollows, then level again. Let it stiffen up before finally smoothing over with the trowel. Once the floating coat has set, a finishing coat can be applied where appropriate.

DAMP-PROOF COURSE

Check the walls inside and out to locate the cause of damp patches. Patches at wall junctions could be caused by damaged flashing at a roof junction (see page 104) or faulty pointing between bricks (see page 44 for advice on repointing). General damp patches at skirting level indicate rising damp and a damp-proof course should be installed or an existing one repaired. Use an electronic moisture meter to check the areas of your wall that are damp.

There are three types of damp: rising damp, which as its name suggests is damp rising up in the house structure from the ground; penetrating damp, which is caused by rainwater entering the house through a defective roof, for example, but can also be caused by plumbing defects; and condensation, which originates inside the house. Caused by cooking, laundering and bathing, condensation is aggravated by poor ventilation (see pages 62–3). Sometimes it is hard to tell which type of damp your home is suffering, and you may need to seek expert advice.

While condensation can be treated with improved ventilation, and penetrating damp by making appropriate repairs to the fabric of the house, rising damp is a little more difficult to cure. Rising damp is a problem common to many older homes as damp-proof courses weren't adopted until the late 19th century, and cavity walls were a 20th-century solution. The incidence of rising damp has increased since open fires were abandoned, as these kept up a sufficient draught to evaporate moisture from inside rooms and sweep it up the chimney.

Modern houses are built with moisture barriers to prevent damp from entering the house. Damp-proof membranes are usually a thin plastic sheet below the ground floor, which stops moisture rising up through the concrete 'raft' foundation. A damp-proof course (DPC) is a thin, impervious layer that is built into the lower part of a brick wall to prevent the bricks sucking up moisture from the ground. You can find a DPC near ground level: look for a thicker horizontal mortar course, with a thin – usually black – line in it going all the way round the house. In older houses, the DPC may be made of slate, lead, mastic, asphalt or bituminous felt. In most modern homes the DPC is made of PVC.

There are several ways for the practical do-it-yourselfer to keep back the rising tide of damp. The most widely used method is to inject a proprietary silicone-based waterproofing chemical through the entire thickness of the wall to form a continuous barrier. This can be used on both stone and brick walls up to 600mm (2ft) thick. You'll need a pressure injection machine; these can be hired from good DIY centres. Most of these machines have three hoses, which are connected to nozzles. The nozzles come in different lengths: you'll need the shorter ones first, and the longer ones later. The three nozzles, attached to their hoses, are inserted into drill holes in the wall and the pump, which maintains pressure at about 100 PSI (pounds per square inch), circulates the chemical. Fluid is injected into the wall until it wets the brick. You then move on to the next three holes and repeat the procedure. Always follow the manufacturer's instructions and don't hire a machine if it doesn't come with complete operating instructions.

You'll also need to calculate how much DPC fluid you need: between 70–90 litres (around 15–20 gallons) per 30m (100ft) of 225mm (9in) thickness of brick or stone wall.

SAFETY FIRST

- **Protective clothing**
  The chemicals in DPC fluid are highly toxic and goggles, protective gloves and a mask should be worn at all times.

- **Using professionals**
  Reputable damp-proofing companies will normally supply a 30-year guarantee of the work, which could help when you come to sell the property.

1 Preparing the wall

Remove skirting boards and hack off the plaster to a height of about 450mm (18in) above the level of the damp. Repair any damaged brickwork. Next, you need to measure the level of the internal floor. If it is a suspended wooden floor, your external drill holes should be about 150mm (6in) above ground level, but below the level of the floor inside. If the floor inside is solid concrete, then the drill holes should be positioned above ground level and above the level of this floor. If the wall has an existing DPC, set the level for the new drill holes just above it, but make sure you don't perforate the old PVC when you drill later. On a 225mm (9in) solid brick wall, mark the positions of the drill holes at the correct level and at 113mm (4½in) centres, positioning them about 25mm (1in) below the upper edge of a brick course. If the wall is impervious stone, mark the position of the drill holes at the required level and spaced at 75mm (3in) intervals. If a wall is thicker than 225mm (9in), then you'll need to mark the positions for identical drill holes on the interior side of the wall to ensure a continuous DPC.

SPECIAL TOOLS FOR THE JOB

- Any good tool-hire firm will be able to supply the pressure-injection pump and DPC fluids.

- An inexpensive moisture meter will let you determine the level the rising damp has reached in your walls, so you know how far up to inject the DPC.

- Drilling a large number of holes into solid masonry may overload the average DIY drill, so it might be worth hiring a more suitable masonry drill.

2 Drilling the injection holes

Use a masonry bit about 15–25mm (¾–1in) but before drilling, double-check the size of the nozzle on the injection machine: the diameter should not be less than that of the nozzle. Place a piece of tape on the drill bit to give you your drilling depth: on a 225mm (9in) thick wall you need to drill in to a depth of 75mm (3in) at first and, later, to a depth of 190mm (7½in). Wearing protective goggles, angle the drill downwards very slightly and drill to 75mm (3in). Repeat on the other side of the wall, as appropriate. Treat each part of a cavity wall separately, drilling to a depth of 75mm (3in) in each leaf.

3 Injecting the DPC

Following the instructions on the injection pump, inject the chemical DPC into the wall. When you reach the other end of the wall, switch off the pump and return to the starting point. Now mark the depth on the drill bit at 190mm (7½in). Drill into each hole again. Remove the short injection nozzles and replace them with longer ones; you may find you have to wrap some PTFE sealing tape (see page 171) around the threads. Insert the nozzles into the wall and repeat the injection procedure. When you have finished, you will need to clean out the pump by flushing it through with white spirit to remove chemical residue.

INSULATING WALLS

EXTERNAL WALLS

Everyone knows that insulating a house saves energy and money but there are also other benefits: chilly corners in underused rooms are eliminated and, combined with a warmer atmosphere, this helps to reduce condensation. If you are planning on installing central heating, think first about your insulation: fully insulating your house means that you could reduce the area of radiators by up to half and reduce the size of the boiler by up to one third. Good insulation also means you could save up to six weeks' worth of heating each year, as heat created inside the house will be trapped for longer. Finally, a fully insulated house is more valuable and easier to sell. Some grants may be available from your local authority to help with the costs. Check with your local council or local benefits agency for details.

Although figures vary from house to house and depend on the type, design, location and construction materials, in general, in an uninsulated house, three-quarters of the heat generated inside will be lost. About one-third of this will disappear through the walls, a quarter through the roof, another quarter through the windows and doors, and about one-sixth through the floor. While it is impossible to eliminate heat loss completely – and undesirable, as currents of cooler air are needed to circulate through a house to keep damp at bay – insulating the roof, walls and windows plus some simple draughtproofing can reduce heat loss by up to 50%.

CAVITY INFILL

While cavity walls prevent damp from crossing the air gap to reach the inner wall, the air gap itself is ventilated, allowing a constant stream of cold air to circulate through the cavity, thus cooling the inner wall. Cavity wall insulation effectively seals the air inside the cavity but without causing a bridge across which moisture could travel.

There are three forms of cavity insulants: urea formaldehyde foam injected into the wall cavity, mineral or glass fibre treated with water repellent, and expanded polystyrene beads, which are blown in. Cavity infill is not a DIY job and should only be carried out by approved, accredited contractors. You will need local authority permission before you proceed – a good contractor will do this for you, but remember to get a copy of the approval notice for your own records. Always check that that the work is fully guaranteed – and get it in writing.

Insulate solid external walls by applying wall cladding over a wooden framework, which incorporates blanket or slab insulation. Other methods include a render of cement and polystyrene beads laid 80mm (3¼in) thick, or polystyrene and glass fibre or mineral slabs glued to the walls, and covered with a mesh before rendering.

During cavity infill, the air gap between the two leafs is filled to seal in the air. Holes are drilled at regular intervals in the exterior brickwork and the insulant is injected or blown through these holes. The holes are then plugged, and should not be noticeable except under close scrutiny. This job should be carried out by professionals.

SOLID WALLS

These walls are more difficult to insulate: wrapping the outside of a house with insulation means adding a waterproof skin: tiles, weatherboard, or even bricks. Consequently, the external appearance of a house will be dramatically altered and you will need planning permission.

Fitting reflective radiator foil.

Applying expanded polystyrene veneer.

Dry-lining with furring strips.

INTERNAL WALLS

The simplest way to insulate internal walls is to reduce the heat lost through them at the hot points just behind radiators. Up to 25% of the radiant heat from a radiator on an outside wall is lost into the wall behind it. Fitting reflective radiator foil means that around 90% of this otherwise lost heat is reflected back into the room. You don't have to take the radiators off the wall to fit it, but you do need to switch them off and allow them and the wall to cool.

The material is available in rolls, sheets and tiles and fits any size or shape of radiator. All you have to do is measure the radiator, marking the position of the wall brackets, and, using a sharp knife or scissors, cut the foil to a slightly smaller size all round. Cut slots to fit over the brackets. Some foils are self adhesive, while others require a coating of heavy-duty fungicidal wallpaper paste. For both, you will need a smooth batten with a clean duster wrapped around it to smooth the foil against the wall. Make

sure that the foil has adhered thoroughly to the wall before you turn the radiator back on again.

A second simple method of insulating walls is to apply expanded polystyrene veneer. This is available in rolls in various thicknesses from 2mm to 5mm (⅒in to ⅕in). You paint the wall surface with a heavy-duty fungicidal wallpaper paste and apply the veneer as you would wallpaper (see pages 308–19). Straight edges can be butt-jointed, but where this is impossible, allow the edges to overlap a little and, using a sharp knife, cut away the overlap. Pull away the surplus edge and apply a little more paste to the wall and roll the two edges together. You can hang wallpaper directly onto the veneer, but if the paper is heavy, it's best to put lining paper horizontally across it first. This insulation is not a cure for damp, and should not be used to hide damp patches, which will only get worse.

The most effective way to insulate a solid exterior wall is by dry-lining: the inside wall is lined with insulating material and covered in plasterboard.

While this can result in considerable heat savings, it is costly and time-consuming to do, and it slightly reduces the floor area. Check with your local authority to see if you need permission. Begin the process by removing skirting boards, door and window trims and picture rails, and then remount electrical accessories.

There are several methods of dry lining but most common is a system of light timber battens, or furring strips, treated with wood preservative and fixed to the walls with screws or wall plugs. Insulation board is nailed to the battens or insulating material is placed between the battens. A polythene vapour barrier is fixed over the insulation by stapling it to the furring strips before the panelling is attached. Alternatively, use a metallized, plastic-backed plasterboard, which does not require the polythene vapour barrier. The plasterboard is nailed to the furring strips and the joints finished. Finally, the skirting boards, door and window trims are refitted. A rough edge between the wall and the ceiling can be disguised with cove.

VENTILATION

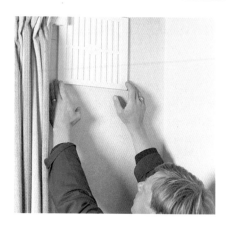

Ventilating our homes is vital, particularly if time, energy and money have been invested in insulation. When houses were heated with open fires, fresh air was drawn in through the natural openings, but with central heating, draughtproofing and insulation installed, rooms can become stuffy.

While the battle against rising and penetrating damp is being won, a new front has opened up: condensation. The simple fact is that the warmer the air is, the more moisture it can hold. Air picks up more moisture in some rooms than others: the kitchen and bathroom are especially vulnerable because of all the water that is used in them on a daily basis.

Warming a room causes air to move around, and when warm air meets cold surfaces – such as glass, tiles, laminates and plaster walls – it sheds some of its moisture. Bathrooms are comparatively small, and when a bath is run a great deal of steam is produced. One solution would be to run the cold water first, and then use a hose to run hot water under the cold water but most people would consider this unnecessarily fussy.

Apart from buying a dehumidifier, there are two ways in which you can fight condensation. One is to reduce the amount of moisture in the air. Ventilation lets in more air, bringing the humidity inside in line with that outdoors, where it is less humid. Whenever the outdoor temperature permits, throw open doors and windows. A fixed louvre ventilator installed in a wall, window or doorway (see left) may be enough to provide a continuous trickle of air without causing a draught. You can buy 'hit and miss' ventilator grilles, which you can open and close.

In kitchens and bathrooms, consider installing a cooker hood with a fan ducted to the outside, or extractor fans. An open fire needs oxygen to burn, but if that supply is reduced because of insulation through double glazing and draughtproofing, the fire won't burn properly; note that an unused fireplace that has been sealed by bricks, blocks or plasterboard also needs ventilation. Air must be able to flow up the chimney to keep out penetrating damp and condensation. If the chimney has not been capped, then this is not a problem, but when most chimneys were sealed off, the chimney pots usually found their way into the garden as planters. The safest bet is to insert a ventilator grille.

EXTRACTOR FANS

An extractor fan keeps the air moving and removes heavy concentrations of moist air. For maximum efficiency, the fan should be positioned very high up in the room – in the kitchen it should be near the cooker or other source of steam. It is important to fit the correct size of fan: it must be able to produce enough force to drive against an oncoming wind. As a rough guide, multiply the volume of the room by 15 (air in a kitchen should be changed around 15 times per hour).

There are extractor fans available for wall or window fitting, as well as for mounting in pitched roofs, roof lights and in ceilings directly below attic spaces. Extractor fans should have back-draught shutters built into them, which prevent draughts of cold air entering the room when the fan is switched off.

SAFETY FIRST

If you intend to fit an extractor fan into a window, get advice from your glass merchant: the glass must be strong enough to carry the weight of the fan. If your central heating boiler is in your kitchen, get expert advice first in order to ensure that the appropriate ventilation mechanisms have been installed – an extractor fan could starve the boiler of vital combustion air and cause dangerous fumes.

FIXING WALL BOARDS

A second way to combat condensation is to transform cold wall surfaces into warm ones. Soft, dull paints such as emulsions are better than hard, shiny gloss paints. There are specialized kitchen and bathroom paints available that provide thermal insulation, and these also absorb moisture when humidity is high, and release it when the air is drier.

Cladding may be a little more expensive to apply, but it is worth considering even if only on the coldest, external walls. Cladding can be fixed directly onto the bare brickwork of a wall in the place of plaster, or it can go on top of existing plaster. (New plaster should not be directly clad for at least two months to allow it dry out thoroughly.) Cladding is available in a wide range of decorative styles and materials, and in standard-sized sheets or panels.

If you are planning on cladding walls, take the opportunity to add a damp-proof membrane and some insulation material, such as expanded polystyrene sheeting, glass-fibre or mineral wool (see page 61), between the wall surface and the panelling.

  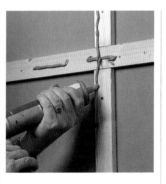 

1 Fix battens

Remove skirting boards and picture rails. Measure and cut timber for battens: you will need four (one on each edge of the wall) to make a frame, plus at least one intermediate vertical batten (how many you need depends on the size of the room and the wall panels). You will also need at least two intermediate horizontal battens. Where there is a power point or light switch, fix a square of battening around it so the panel can be fixed once a hole is cut out for the switch or point. Check the level of the battens with a spirit level then fix them to the walls using masonry nails or non-rusting screws.

2 Cut panels to fit

Before fixing the panels, arrange them along the wall to check the effect and to find out if any will need cutting to size. Cut panels face-side upwards with an eight- to ten-point hand saw, having first scored the cutting line on the face with a sharp marking knife. Cover the cutting line with masking tape to ensure a split-free edge. Depending on the decorative finish of your panels, you can attach them to the battens using lost head pins or use a proprietary adhesive. Adhesive should be applied to both the battens and the panels. It can also be used in addition to pins for extra support.

3 Attach panels

Starting at one corner, fix the panels along the surface area, allowing a 3mm (⅛in) gap for ventilation at the ceiling and floor. Position the first panel, and check it with a spirit level. The remaining panels should then be true when fixed. Panels should meet in the centre of a vertical batten. If you have to clad around a power point, unscrew and lift it out, position the panel and drill a hole to align with the switch. Pull the wires through, enlarge the hole then reconnect and position the panel around the square batten support. Screw the face plate of the unit back on (see also page 65).

4 Finishing

There are small gaps at the floor and ceiling to provide ventilation. Both gaps can be disguised behind skirting board and ceiling cove.

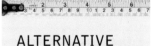

ALTERNATIVE

Panels can be fixed directly to a wall surface as long as it is sound and level. Make sure the walls are clean and dry then apply adhesive to the wall surface and the back of each panel with a notched spreader and allow it to become tacky.

TIMBER CLADDING

Solid timber lining in the form of wood strips is one of the most popular types of wall cladding. This can be used to clad an entire wall from floor to ceiling, or to clad just part way up a wall to the height of a dado rail. There is a wide range of colours available in both soft and hard woods and in various 'profiles'. One of the most popular is 'tongue and groove'. These planks have a tongue along one edge and a matching groove on the other. The 'meeting edges' can be left with square sides so that when two planks are joined they fit snugly together. Others have their meeting edges machined into decorative profiles, the most popular being 'V' shaped. When two boards are fitted together, a 'V'-shaped groove is formed. This is known as TGV (tongued, grooved and 'V'-jointed) and is sold by timber merchants in various lengths up to 3m (10ft). You can also buy pre-packed kits; these come with metal clips, which fit in the groove leaving a tab, which takes the pin. These kits are more expensive, and they have only six panels in pre-cut standard lengths of either 2.4m or 2.7m (8ft or 9ft). Carefully calculate the amount you need and see what savings, if any, are to be had.

Make sure you buy enough TGV boards to complete the job, and buy them from the same batch. If you have to buy more later, you may find that the profile of the tongues and groove is different and the joints won't fit.

TONGUE AND GROOVE

1 Measuring and marking up
TGV boards are not attached directly to the wall, but to a frame of soft wood battens called furring strips. The first step is to remove existing skirting boards and dado rails (plus picture rails and coving if you are panelling the whole wall). Measure and mark the position of the furring strips across the walls, using a spirit level to guide you. It's a good idea to line external walls with a polythene vapour barrier before you fix the strips.

2 Fixing the furring strips
For the battens, use 50 x 25mm (2 x 1in) soft wood, treated with wood preservative. With TGV panelling, the furring strips run horizontally: the lowest strip should be level with the top of the skirting board, with short vertical strips below it to fix the skirting to later. Space the furring strips horizontally at 400mm (1ft 4in) apart and fix them to the wall with 50mm (2in) masonry nails, or non-rust screws and wallplugs.

3 Fixing the boards
Once the furring strips have been fixed, mark out and cut the TGV boards to length. Unless they came in a kit, the boards must be sanded as well. Start at the corner, with the grooved edge against the left hand wall, and plumb the first board with a spirit level. Nail the panel to the furring strip, through the centre of the face, using 25mm (1in) panel pins.

4 Secret nailing

Slide the next TGV board onto the tongue, protecting the top edge of the panel with an off-cut of wood if necessary to tap it into position. The second and subsequent boards are attached to the furring strips by 'secret nailing': drive a pin through the inner corner of the tongue at an angle and sink the head below the surface of the panel using a nail punch. Slide on the next board to cover the fixing and repeat secret nailing. At the end of the wall, you may have to cut a TGV panel down its length so it fits in the space. If it is a tight fit, 'spring' the last two boards into place at the same time: first, slot the two final boards together, then fit the groove of the penultimate panel onto the tongue of the exposed board. Push the 'double panel' into the wall. Fix the panels in place by nailing through the face of the grooves. Punch down the heads and fill the holes with filler if necessary.

PANELLING AROUND YOUR ELECTRICAL SOCKET

1 Remove socket

Turn off the power at the mains. Unscrew the face plate and draw it forwards, away from the wall. Remove the screws that attach the metal mounting box to the wall. There should be enough slack in the cables for you to refix the box flush with the new wall surface. Alternatively, it can be fixed using metal box mounting flanges for use on partition walls. To do this, batten around the fitting, but allow for a narrow margin of panelling all the way round. Fit the flanges.

2 Cut hole and refit

Measure and mark the position and size of the socket on the TGV panels. Cut the 'hole' for the socket in the panels using a pad saw. Offer up the TGV panels and fix to the furring strips using the secret nailing technique. Refit the face plate. If flanges have been fitted, they will pull the box against the margin.

ALIGNMENT

Electrical socket outlets and light switches must be brought up to the level of the new wall surface. If these are surface mounted, simply panel around them and they'll become flush with the new wall. If they are flush mounted already, you will need to bring them forwards to set them flush with the new wall. For more on electrical sockets and wiring, see Chapter 3.

SAFETY FIRST

If you are in any doubt about disconnecting and reconnecting electrical switches and power sockets, you must consult a qualified electrician (see page 18).

SKIRTING BOARDS AND DADO RAILS

SKIRTING BOARDS

Skirtings vary according to their age, from the older 375mm (15in) high ones with ornamental mouldings to 75mm (3in) high modern champfered ones. Renewing a section of heavily moulded skirting can be quite expensive: you may have to look for lengths at specialist architectural salvage merchants, or have them purpose made.

When you remove existing skirting boards, prise them off carefully to avoid splitting them. Start in the corner with a board that overlaps and use a hammer and bolster to prise it off. Place a thin strip of wood behind the tip of the bolster to protect the wall, and tap the bolster in further to loosen the nails. Work your way along the board. If you need to replace a damaged middle section of skirting, lever away enough of the board to cut a mitre at either side of the damage: make a vertical cut at about 45 degrees to the face of the board.

1 Fitting skirting board

Fitting skirting board is a simple job if you know that the fixing will be done by nails into breeze walls, or in 'grounds' (small pieces of wood fitted to the underlying wall). If you are replacing older skirting with smaller modern skirting, the plaster on the wall above will need lowering so the new skirting neatly covers the edge. To fix skirtings, first mark the position of the timber grounds on the face of the skirting board. Place the board in position and nail home with cut nails into brick work, lost head nails into wooden grounds. Don't split the board. Use a punch to drive the nails below the surface and then fill any nail holes with filler. If you intend to paint the skirtings a dark colour, the filler may show up light underneath, so mix a little of the dark paint into the filler, so it dries a matching tone to the eventual paint.

2 Cutting internal mitre corners

For a really neat and professional finish, where lengths of skirting meet along the wall, they are joined with a mitred joint. On the bottom edge of the board, mark a 45 degree angle on the edge and square it across the face of the board. Clamp the board on edge in a vice and carefully cut down the line of the angle. Where boards meet at corners, they are scribed and butt-jointed. To achieve the profile, place a length of skirting with a square cut end against the return wall. Place skirting at a right angle and pencil the shape of the profile. Using a coping saw, carefully cut along the contour line on the moulded face of the board so that it will slot against its neighbour like a jigsaw piece (see below).

DADO RAIL

When you are redecorating your home, attention to detail makes all the difference. As well as being decorative, many period features also have a functional role. Cornices strengthen the junction between ceilings and walls. Dado rails are useful in areas subject to heavy 'traffic' where the walls become scuffed or dirty; treating the wall in two sections means you can choose a less costly, more durable material for the lower portion, and you only have to redecorate half the wall at a time. You can also use a dado rail to good effect if you want to optically lower the height of a tall room or corridor.

There are kits available, which come with patent fixing clips and concealed fixings but it's as easy, and cheaper, to install a dado rail yourself. When you buy architectural mouldings, unwrap them and store them in the room they will be used in for a day or so, so they can become conditioned to the room's temperature and humidity. Treat the back faces of mouldings with wood preservative before you install them, especially if they are going on an external wall.

LONG DADO RAILS

Fix a long length of dado rail by its two outermost fixings first, then add intermediate ones. This will stop the rail being forced away from its guideline as you fix it to the wall.

1 Measuring up

To estimate the material needed for a dado rail running right around a room, divide the perimeter by the standard length of the moulding you want to use. Round up the answer to the next whole number, to allow for cutting mitred joints. Use a spirit level and a long straight edge to draw a pencil guideline around the room at the level you want to fix the rail. If the walls are stud partitions, you will need to locate the studs to ensure a firm fixing. Start on the longest wall: if one length of moulding will span the wall, cut it to the required length on the face side, using a steady sawing action. Fix the rail to the wall with screws and wall plugs. If the walls are solid masonry, use lost head nails to timber stud partition walls.

2 Matching joints

If you need more than one length to span the wall, cut a 45-degree mitre on the 'open' end of the length so it faces out into the room. Butt the square end of the first length into the corner and fix it into place along the pencil line on the wall. On the end of the next length, cut a 45-degree mitre facing the other way, so the two cut ends join precisely. This prevents the joint from opening up visibly if the timber shrinks. Cut the other end square to length so it will run into the corner of the room. Fix the rail in place as before, carefully aligning the mitre joint.

3 Cutting mitre corners

Internal corners are usually cut at 45 degrees. Measure the moulding in the usual way. Scribe the end of the first length on the next (second) wall to fit over the face of the board on the first wall. Use a bit of off-cut moulding as a template to draw around on the back of the length and then cut it with a mitre saw or coping saw. Always cut into the face of the moulding as this will ensure that any splintering will be on the back, flat face, which will not be seen when fixed to the wall. Internal corners are rarely square, so you may find you have to disguise a very small gap in a mitred joint with an appropriate filler. Complete the second wall with a square ended board and scribe the end of the first length on the third wall as before. Carry on scribing corner joints to complete any further internal angles. Where the final length of moulding joins the first length, scribe both corner joints.

4 External corners

To cut an external mitre, measure and mark the moulding to the correct length. Again these are cut at a 45-degree angle. Set the mitre saw to 45 degrees (a mitre box only gives 45-degree settings) and cut to length, cutting into the moulded face to avoid splintering it. Fix the rail in place by glueing and pinning the joint through the corner, from the side of the mitre joint, so it won't open up if the moulding shrinks. You can paint, stain or varnish timber mouldings to suit your decor. Fill all nail holes and then sand the filler down flush with the wood. Decorator's mastic, which is flexible and won't crack, can be used to fill any irregularities between the moulding and the wall.

SAFETY FIRST

Make sure your saws are sharp, so they cut properly. Blunt saws cause accidents – replace them immediately.

PICTURE RAILS

Measure, mark and cut the picture rail to length.

Use a low speed on a power drill.

A picture rail attached to a wall adds visual interest to a room.

PERIOD STYLE

Picture rails, like dado rails, can be used to create the effect of lowering a high ceiling. They are also functional. True picture rails have a P-shaped profile onto which 'S'-shaped hooks can be attached. Attached to these hooks is a length of cord from which a picture or mirror hangs. The beauty of using a picture rail is that pictures or mirrors can be easily moved and the underlying wall and its decorative covering is not damaged by being 'nailed' into.

The Victorians' taste in interior decoration included expensive wall coverings such as ornate wallpapers, and deeply embossed relief papers such as Lincrusta. This is a solid film of linseed oil and fillers – wood pulp or cotton fibres – fused onto a backing paper, which is then engraved with a steel roller. These 'whites' or relief papers imitated the delicately moulded plasterwork found in very grand houses. With these expensive new wall coverings, the Victorians found use for picture rails and even the most modest houses built in the 19th century would have them.

Traditionally, they would have been painted or wood-grained to resemble exotic hard woods such as mahogany.

Nowadays, original architectural mouldings are seen as 'period details' and can raise the value of a house. But often renovation or modernization over the years has led to many of these period details being stripped out. They are easy to replace but care should be taken in selecting mouldings to match the style of the room in which they are to be installed. Main living rooms and hallways traditionally had the most ornate mouldings. Stair landings and the main bedroom would be less ornate, while those in the remainder of the house were relatively plain.

TYPES OF WALL

There are lots of different styles and profiles available. If you want a functioning picture rail, then you must use one with a P-profile. However, it is not advisable to fit a P-profile picture rail to a plasterboard wall. While it will probably support the rail, it won't stand the weight of pictures or mirrors hung from it. You could install a 'decorative' picture rail

instead; this is a good idea if a stud partition wall is built in a room that already has one. It will unify the new room decoratively and the new wall won't look like it's just been erected. Locate the studs first by tapping along the wall with your finger; where the sound is duller, that's where a stud is located, and you can fix the moulding to it with nails.

FITTING

Picture rails are installed in the same way you install skirting boards or dado rails (see pages 66–7) but if you are working in a room that has already been decorated, it's easier to paint, stain or varnish the moulding before you fix it to the wall.

Decide on the height – the usual location is about 45cm (18in) below ceiling or cornice level. Use a spirit level and straight edge to draw a pencil line across the wall. Watch out for any hidden electric cables. Measure and cut the moulding to length. Long lengths that will be fixed high on a wall can be difficult to handle, so you may find that pre-drilling holes in the moulding helps.

FLOOR TYPES: PROS AND CONS

PARQUET

PROS
Smooth, beautifully finished parquet provides a durable floor and blends in well with any colour scheme. Parquet floors can be laid using 450mm (18in) square panels to which thin veneers of either softwood or hardwood have been glued into herringbone or basketweave patterns. The panels are easy to cut, are pre-sanded and come with a bitumen based backing to protect them from rising damp – although the floor must incorporate a damp-proof membrane.

CONS
Parquet must be laid on an absolutely level sub-floor. Durability is high, but stiletto heels and cigarette burns will leave bad marks. The harder and thicker the veneer, the more expensive the panel will be. Too much dry heat may cause shrinkage and butt-jointed boards may shrink and twist. Frequent wetting will cause swelling and warping, so parquet is not suitable for bathrooms.

FLOORBOARDS

PROS
Floorboards provide tough flooring that can be stripped and left bare or painted, stained, varnished – in fact a whole range of decorative finishes can be applied. Floorboards come as standard sized (125mm x 25mm/5in x 1in) softwood planks that are planed all round (PAR) and are available with square edges or tongued and grooved, making the replacement of damaged boards easy. In some older houses, you may find narrower or wider boards – these can be more costly to match up with new boards.

CONS
Old floorboards need to be in good condition. If left exposed they get dirty, damaged and splintery and you can expect draughts unless gaps are sealed between boards. Gap-filling material may be a different colour to the boards when stained or sealed. Bare boards are noisier and, if you live in a flat, your tenancy agreement or lease may not allow them.

WOOD STRIP/ LAMINATE

PROS
Tongue and grooved strips that constitute woodstrip floors are easy to assemble and create the effect of wooden flooring. They can be fixed as parallel strips, or laid in different arrangements to decorative effect. Woodstrip floors, made from solid strips of timber, will take decorative finishes and paint effects. Laminate floors are relatively cheap per square meter. Their surface resembles solid wood strip but is in fact a very thin, photo-mechanically produced 'wood image' with the surface sealed onto a composite backing.

CONS
Woodstrip floors can suffer from the same 'problems' as any other wooden flooring: noise, shrinkage, warping. It can be expensive, depending on the quality of the wood used. Laminated strips are very thin and not durable. Once the laminated surface is scratched, the 'photo' of the wood is exposed and will inevitably degrade.

CERAMIC

PROS

Ceramic floor tiles come in a huge range of colours and styles: sizes range from the tiny to 300mm (1ft) square, and they can be square, rectangular, hexagonal or 'provençal' in shape. Hand-made tiles are charming because of their irregular shape, while machine-made ones are more accurately shaped.

CONS

While tiles are durable, any surface patterns under a thin glaze can be worn away. They are cool, can be noisy, and are slippery when wet. Ceramic tiles must be laid on level, solid floors as they can place strain on suspended timber sub-floors. Timber floors must be covered first with hardboard and the load-bearing capacities of non-concrete sub-floors should be checked by a surveyor. Ceramic tiles are difficult to cut, and set out: poorly laid tiles look awful, may lift up and lead to water seepage, which could damage the sub-floor.

SHEET VINYL

PROS

A semi-hard flooring, sheet vinyl is easy to clean, waterproof, resistant to oil, fat and most domestic chemicals. It is available in various degrees of flexibility, and there is a vast range of thicknesses, colours, patterns, and textures. There are even industrial grades of sheet vinyl available, which are impregnated with quartz crystals or shards of other minerals to make unusual stippled finishes. It's easy to cut and lightweight, can be loose laid or stuck down to a prepared sub-floor with proprietary adhesives. Large spaces can be covered without seams, and it is also available as tiles.

CONS

While thicker or 'cushioned' types are quiet, resilient and warm underfoot, thinner vinyls are colder and harder. Once fitted with glue, vinyl is nearly impossible to lift. It can be damaged by abrasion by dirt or grit particles, and is not immune to burns. It can also be a slip hazard when wet.

CORK TILES

PROS

Cork is a versatile, lightweight but hard-wearing floor covering. It's warm, resilient and quiet, and is available striped, gridded or patterned. Thicker grades give the most resilience and there is even a 'tough' version, bonded with an impervious vinyl surface. Cork tiles are easy to cut to size and can be laid using a proprietary adhesive.

CONS

Cork tiles come only in a narrow range of colours – from 'honey' to dark brown. They must be laid on a smooth, even floor, using an adhesive recommended by the manufacturer, applied to the correct depth with a serrated spreader. Cork tiles are absorbent: in bathrooms this is a bonus, but elsewhere they must be sealed with an acid catalyst sealer, which also requires a face mask. Pre-sealed tiles, and those finished with plastic or wax coatings, must be closely butted together.

LAYING AND LEVELLING FLOORS

There are two types of floor laid in a house: solid, and suspended or hollow floors. Solid floors, sometimes called 'direct to earth' floors, are laid directly on the ground and consist of a concrete sub-floor over a bed of rubble or hard core. The sub-floor is covered with a damp-proof membrane and then surfaced with a layer of screed made of sand and cement. On top of this type of floor you can lay parquet, quarry tiles or vinyl floor coverings. Solid floors are usually found at ground level in houses, but there may be solid floors at all levels in purpose-built blocks of flats.

Suspended or 'hollow' floors are found in nearly all homes, and at ground level in some older properties. These consist of timber floorboards laid on timber joists. At ground-floor level, the joists are usually supported by low brick walls called 'sleeper walls' that run beneath the floor, but the joints may also be built into the walls and supported on timber or metal wall plates, which evenly distribute the load. More recently built homes may have the joists suspended in galvanized metal hangers built into the walls. The joists in any upper floors are supported in similar ways.

The joists of a suspended ground floor are generally made from 100mm x 50mm (4 x 2in) softwood. Usually suspended floors are boarded with

A suspended, or 'hollow' floor.

tongue-and-grooved or plane-edged planks, known as floorboards. In many modern houses, however, especially in 'new builds', flooring-grade chipboard is more commonly used in place of traditional (and more expensive) floorboards.

CLEANING A CONCRETE FLOOR

Concrete can be cleaned in the same way as brickwork – with a stiff brush to remove loose dirt and efflores-cence. Grease spots need to be removed with a degreasing agent (see below). There are a number of proprietory cleaners available, but before you buy, try cleaning the grease away first with a little white spirit. Concrete is trowelled when laid to

give it a smooth surface, but overworking the screed can cause the cement to rise to the surface and when the floor dries, it breaks down into loose dust. There are now many concrete floor paints available that range from 'traditional' colours like cardinal red to metallic and 'sparkly' effects but the floor must first be treated with two coats of PVA bonding

agent. Like many other building materials, concrete is subject to shrinkage and this can lead to cracks in the surface. Holes and cracks deeper than 3mm (⅛in) must be raked out, under cut, and the debris swept clean. Self levelling compound, supplied as a powder, is mixed with water. Pour some of mixture into the corner furthest away from the door and spread the compound with a trowel until it is about 3mm (⅛in) thick (see left). Leave the compound to find its own level. Continue pouring and spreading, joining up the areas of compound, until the entire floor surface is covered. In a little over an hour, the floor can be walked on, but wait two or three days before you lay a permanent floor covering.

LEVELLING A WOODEN FLOOR WITH HARDBOARD

Where timber floorboards are in a poor condition, they can be levelled by covering with sheets of 3mm (⅛in) flooring grade hardboard or 6mm (¼in) plywood to produce a hard, smooth floor surface. Ceramic tiles are best laid onto solid concrete, but if you choose to lay them onto a timber floor use 12mm (½in) plywood or hardboard, screwed down every 300mm (1ft) to make sure that the surface is level and the joists are rigid (see pages 84–5 for advice on laying floor tiles). It is not advisable to lay ceramic tiles on suspended upper floors; if you wish to do so, having calculated the amount and weight of the tiles, you must have the load-bearing capacity of the joist assessed by a surveyor or structural engineer.

Once you seal a floor with hardboard, remember that you won't have access to underfloor cables or pipes. This could be a problem later if you want to upgrade or make repairs to electrical cables and central heating pipes. It's a good idea anyway to mark the location and run of water pipes and electrical cables on the hardboard with a thick, indelible marker pen, so you know where they are in future. You must also ensure that underfloor ventilation is sufficient to prevent damp and dry rot. Doors need to open cleanly so you may have to plane some wood from the bottoms: take the door off its hinges and plane towards the centre of the door from each end (see also pages 114–15).

To prevent the boards buckling after they have been laid, the textured backs are sprinkled with water and stacked back to back for 24 hours in

A solid or 'direct-to-earth' floor.

the room you are working on. If the room has been regularly centrally heated, however, the boards only need to be placed on their edges and exposed to the air in the room for 48 hours so they adjust to the temperature and humidity levels.

As soon as the boards are 'conditioned' they can be laid. Start in the middle of the room and work outwards, so that only the sheets at the edges of the room will need trimming. Lay the sheets in 'brickwork' pattern, with the joints staggered. Nail the first board to the floor using 20mm (¾in) hardboard pins, starting in the centre of the board and fixing every 150mm (6in) until you get to about 25mm (1in) of the edge. Then nail around the edge at 100mm (4in) intervals. Nail the other boards butted up against the first. Scribe narrow edge strips to fit against the skirting boards.

If you have a large area of floor to cover, it might be worth hiring a heavy-duty stapler and mallet to fix the hardboard panels down onto the floorboards.

FLOOR PROBLEMS

• Damaged concrete floors

If concrete is cracking or crumbling across a widespread area of a floor, it is best to resurface the concrete before you lay a decorative floor covering. Remember to leave a sufficient length of time for the concrete to dry out fully before you lay your new flooring.

• Testing for damp

If you suspect that a concrete floor is damp, tape a small piece of polythene to the floor and leave it for a few days, then check for moisture underneath. If damp appears, coat the floor in heavy-duty polyurethane sealant (it may be necessary for you to use up to three coats of sealant).

• Underfloor ventilation

Before sealing a hollow floor with plywood or hardboard, make sure there is enough underfloor ventilation or you could encourage problems with damp or rot.

• Levelling

Always use a spirit level to check that your floor is level before laying tiles, sheet vinyl or carpet. Undulations could cause tiles to lift or crack and carpet, vinyl and other types of flooring to buckle.

STRIPPING FLOORBOARDS

Fill minor imperfections in floorboards with wood filler, using a filling knife to press it into the holes or cracks.

REPAIRING DAMAGED BOARDS WITH FILLER

Wooden floorboards are very durable, but constant traffic over the years, along with changes in temperature and humidity, can cause boards to split along their length. Holes, chips and splinters from heavy furniture or hard items dropped onto them all leave their mark.

Small imperfections are easily dealt with by using wood filler. Press the filler into the hole or crack with a filling knife, leaving it slightly proud of the surface. The filler will shrink a little as it dries – you may even have to add some more to bring the level up.

When it is completely dry, the excess should be sanded off using a fine-grade abrasive paper. Always sand in the direction of the wood grain.

Wood filler is available in a range of different shades to match the natural colours of wood. If you used ordinary 'white' filler, it would show through some decorative finishes as a light area, since filler won't accept stain completely. If you are planning on staining the boards, it would be worth mixing a tiny amount of the stain with the filler to 'pre-colour' it in order to achieve a neat finished effect.

ABOVE: Square-edged floorboards can be lifted by inserting a bolster or cold chisel into the gap near the end.

RIGHT: Slide a rod under the board and press your foot on the loose end to release the nails.

LIFTING BOARDS

Floor boards may have to be lifted if you need to inspect under-floor pipes or cables. If a floorboard is badly damaged, it can easily be removed and replaced. If the boards are old and you want to find a replacement in the same wood and colour, check underneath the carpets in other rooms. If you find a match, remove it and fix it in the room you want, then fit a new board under the carpet where it won't be seen.

Square-edged floorboards, often found in older homes, are relatively easy to lift by inserting a bolster or cold chisel into the gap near the end of the board. Prise the end up, taking care not to split the board, until the end of a claw hammer or other lever can be inserted underneath the board.

Work along the board with the two levers until the board comes free. Alternatively, slide a rod under the board to hold up the end and gently press your foot onto the loose board. The nails beyond the rod will slowly start to give.

REPLACING BOARDS

In many modern homes, the floorboards are T&G (tongued and grooved). To replace these, you will first have to remove them. They are a little more tricky to shift than square-edged boards, as you'll have to cut through the tongue on at least one board. Cut along the length of the joint with a convex-blade flooring saw, a pad saw or circular saw set to cut about 20mm (¾in) deep. With the tongue cut along the length of the floorboard, the board can be levered up and lifted out.

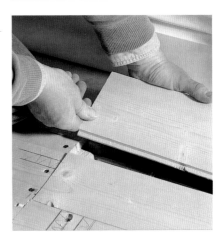

1 Cutting and measuring

Lay a few loose floorboards together to act as a work platform – never stand on or between the joists. Measure the length or width of the room – whichever runs at right angles to the joists. Cut the floorboard to length but so that it stops 10mm (⅜in) short of the walls at each side. Lay the first board parallel to the wall but not directly against it: the grooved edge should be no more than 10mm (⅜in) away from the wall. Nail it into place with cut floor brads or lost head nails that are at least twice as long as the thickness of the board. Position the nails in pairs, 25mm (1in) from the edge of the board and centred on the joists. Punch them home with a hole punch to a depth of about 2mm (¹⁄₁₆in).

2 Laying the boards

Lay the other cut boards in place and cramp them up to the fixed board in order to close the edge joints. Some floorboard kits come with cramps, but they are simply two equal-sized wedge-shaped pieces of wood, which can be cut from 400mm (1ft 4in) off-cut of board. To cramp, temporarily nail another floor-board just less than a board's width away and insert a pair of wedges into the gap – as though you were 'forming' a rectangle from them. Tap the wedges' broad ends together by hammering them at both sides. As the cramps are pushed together to make the rectangle shape, the loose floorboard will be pushed into place against the first fixed floorboard. Nail the second board in place and

remove the temporary nails from the other floor board. At the far wall, you may have to cut a board to fit the gap. Cut this final board with the tongue on the waste side (i.e. it will be cut off). If the board is still tricky to slot into place, cut away the bottom lip of the grooved edge. The final board now only sits on top of its neighbour's tongue, so it will have to be nailed securely into place.

SMALL AREAS

Don't remove all the boards in a floor if only one or two are damaged. Just take up the ones that need to be replaced then work from step 2 above.

PREPARING, SANDING AND VARNISHING

Sealing bare floorboards with polish, stain or varnish allows the beauty of the natural wood to show. To bring old floorboards up to a high-quality finish is a noisy, dusty task. The boards must first be in good condition. If necessary, apply a proprietary woodworm treatment to the floorboards and underlying joists. Any boards with more than a few holes in them should be replaced: the sander will remove a lot of the top surface of the timber and could reveal widespread damage underneath.

Ignore gaps between boards if they don't bother you, or close them up. A few narrow gaps can be filled using wood filler or even *papier mâché*, which is cheap and easy to make. It dries a greyish white colour, but it will accept colour well. Tear the paper into scraps and wet with boiling water while pounding with a piece of timber to make a thick paste, When it is cool, add a little cellulose-based wallpaper adhesive powder. Press it firmly into the gaps and sand it smooth when it has dried out in about 2–3 days. Fill wide gaps – 6mm (¼in) or more – with strips of wood, planed to form a slight wedge. Apply glue to both sides of the wedge and tap it into the gap. When the glue has dried, level with a plane.

To sand a floor, you'll need to hire an industrial sanding machine. You'll need three grades of abrasive paper: coarse, to level the floor; medium and fine to sand to a smooth finish. Large upright sanders are for sanding the bulk of a large floor, but use an edging sander to sand up to the walls, and a hook scraper for corners.

SAFETY FIRST

- **Protection equipment**

  Protect yourself by wearing a dust mask, goggles and ear defenders.

- **Ventilation**

  Open the windows to let fresh air circulate during sanding and when applying varnish, stain or sealer.

- **Electric cable**

  Drape the cable over your shoulder before switching on the machine to keep it out of the way.

- **Knee protection**

  Use knee protectors or cushions when kneeling for long periods on hard surfaces.

2 Prepare the floorboards
Check each floorboard in turn and, where necessary, remove any overlooked carpet tacks with a claw hammer and drive home any nail heads well below the surface using a nail punch. Any raised nail heads will rip the abrasive paper on the sander's drum.

1 Seal up the room
Clear the room of furnishings, open the windows, and seal over the doors with plastic sheeting. Sweep the floor to remove grit and loose dirt. Although most sanders come with a vacuum cleaner type fitting, the fine dust will still spread everywhere.

3 Fit the abrasive paper
With most drum sanders, the paper wraps around the drum and is held in place with a screw down bar. Make sure the paper is tightly fitted: any slack can cause it to slip off and it will get torn to pieces. Start the sanding process with the coarse grade paper.

4 Sanding

Put on a face mask to avoid inhaling dust, and it is advisable to wear ear protection as sanders make a great deal of noise. Tilt the drum of the sander back so it is clear of the floor. Switch on the power and gently lower the sander onto the floor. Keep a firm hold because the machine will propel itself forward. Work across the boards first in a diagonal direction, keeping the drum moving, then make a second run parallel to the first. When you reach the edge of the room, tilt the sander backwards to lift the sanding drum clear of the floor. When you have covered the floor, sweep up the dust, and sand it again on the opposite diagonal. Switch off the power and unplug the sander. Next, change to a medium-grain abrasive paper and sand in overlapping parallel runs along the lengths of the boards. Then sweep up the dust and install fine-grade paper onto the drum. This will remove any scratches and give the floorboards a smooth finish.

5 Sand the edges with a rotary sander

Edging sanders generally use discs of abrasive paper clamped by a central nut to the sole plate. Sand the edges with all three grades of abrasive paper. Use hook scrapers, or a flexible abrasive disc attachment on a power tool, to reach into corners and up to skirting boards.

6 Finishing the floorboards

Dust window ledges, above doors and on top of mouldings and architraves. Vacuum. Wipe over the boards with a dampened cloth and allow to dry. Repeat, but this time wipe the floorboards with a cloth dampened with white spirit. Apply your finish (see box).

VARNISHING

• Once sanded, floorboards can be painted, bleached or stained. You don't need specialized paints provided that the floor is well protected with sufficient coats of varnish. Experiment first on a piece of scrap wood to check the effects of your chosen finish.

• Varnish should be applied with a clean, good-quality brush in a dust-free environment. Clear varnish (water- or oil-based) is available in a range of finishes: matt; satin for subtle sheen; and gloss for a harder, brighter-looking surface. Water-based varnishes are milky but dry to a clear finish. Oil-based polyurethane varnishes are the most durable, but they dry yellowish in colour. Tinted varnishes both colour and protect the wood, but they can chip easily. Always start varnishing at the furthest point from the door and sand lightly between coats to remove visible brushstrokes. For advice on decorative wood finishes, see page 244.

• When using oil- or solvent-based paints and varnishes, always work in a well-ventilated area. Do not allow naked flames or cigarettes nearby. Always wear a face mask to protect you from fumes.

LAYING WOOD STRIP

Wood strip flooring, consisting of tongue and groove boards that slot together and are held in place with adhesive, can be laid over a solid floor. They produce what is called a 'floating floor' because they are not fixed directly to the sub-floor but are held in place by their own weight. This type of flooring is readily available in a wide range of qualities, wood and finishes.

If your boards do not stretch the entire length of the room, stagger them so that all the joins at the end of strips do not run in a straight line. If you are using laminate boards with a photo-mechanically produced surface (see page 70), the same patterns of knots and grains will be repeated over and over. Make sure you arrange them so that the patterns match up evenly.

You can sweep woodstrip floors and mop them with water to keep them clean. Do not use strong detergents that could damage the finish or even loosen the adhesive.

If individual strips get damaged, you can replace them, but you will have to saw through the tongues and stick down replacement strips with adhesive. Buy extra strips in case of this eventuality.

1 Preparing the sub-floor

Some form of insulating material, such as rigid polystyrene or fibre board, is first laid over the top of the screed layer on a solid, concrete floor. A polythene sheet should be fitted on top of the insulating material to form a vapour barrier. This must be a continuous sheet with the edges turned up and trapped behind the skirting boards. Before you start, ensure that the floor is completely level, as any distortions will cause the wood strip to lift and split. See pages 72–3 for advice on how to level a floor.

2 Lay the first board

Make sure your knees are well padded to prevent injury – use knee protectors or kneel on a cushion or rolled-up towel. Lay the first board with its grooved edge on the floor. If you have purchased your flooring in 'kit' form, there will be spacers provided, or you can make your own. Spacers ensure that the board is positioned no more than 10mm (⅜in) from the wall, at its long side and at the edges. This 10mm (⅜in) gap will allow for any expansion of the strips across the floor and will be hidden either behind skirting boards or by using an edge moulding (see page 66).

3 Butt up boards

Wood strip is not nailed to the floor: instead a little proprietary adhesive is added to the tongue of the laid board and into the groove of the next board. The board is then slotted into place. In order to butt the boards – to close up the gap between the boards tightly – place a small block of wood along the length and tap this gently with a hammer. This pushes the tongue and groove together while ensuring that you don't damage the edge of the boards with blows from the hammer head. Wipe off any excess adhesive that has oozed from the joint.

SAFETY FIRST

- Always wear safety goggles when you cut wood strip in case of flying splinters.

- When varnishing, work in a well-ventilated room, wear a face mask and don't allow naked flames.

KEEPING IT STRAIGHT

- Decide the direction in which you want your strips to run. Hammer a nail in the centre of the room at one edge and then the other and stretch a piece of chalked string tightly between the nails. Snap the string to leave a chalk mark on the floor. Lay your strips parallel to this.

- Use a spirit level from time to time to check the boards are level and not bulging.

- Use a straight edge to ensure that any joins between boards are completely accurate.

4 Cutting boards short of skirting

When you reach the walls running at right angles to the boards, the wood strip should be cut so it is 10mm (⅜in) short of the skirting. Don't assume that the boards will be cut straight across at a perfect 90-degree angle: walls are never completely straight, so it's best to scribe the board first so the correct line is cut and the board edge runs parallel to the wall. Measure the board, lay it flat in a vice and cut it across its face so that any splinters will be on the back, out of view. Glue the appropriate tongue and groove and slot the cut board into position then butt the boards together as before, wiping away any excess glue.

5 Fitting around a pipe

If you reach an obstruction, you'll have to cut the board so it fits around it. Measure and mark the position of the pipe. You could use a profile gauge here, or make a template out of a piece of thin card. It's better to spend time and be accurate than spoil a board or the finished look of your new floor. Cut a hole in your board that is slightly larger than the pipe diameter then carefully cut out a tapered or triangular section so it looks a little like a keyhole. Keep hold of the tapered off-cut. Glue, position and butt the board into place and then fit the off-cut behind the pipe with glue to form a neat finish.

6 Fitting moulding and varnishing

If you removed skirting boards before laying the wood strip, they can now be replaced. Alternatively, the 10mm (⅜in) gap that is between the edge of the wood strip and the skirting can be hidden behind an edge strip of quadrant moulding. This can be painted, stained or varnished to match your floor, but it's easier to do this before you fix the moulding into place. The wood strip can be finished with a clear varnish, which will enhance the appearance of the wood and provide a strong, protective covering (see page 77 for advice about different varnishes). Sweep the floor to remove dust before applying varnish.

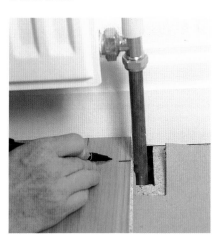

LAYING PARQUET PANELS

The most common form of parquet flooring uses thin, 8mm (⅜in) wooden strips of decorative timber laid in basketweave or herringbone patterns to form 450mm (1ft 6in) square panels. The panels are available in a range of pre-sanded hardwoods such as oak, cherry, mahogany and teak and they can be enhanced by wax, polish and varnished finishes.

The panels have a bitumen-impregnated backing, but the floor itself must also have a damp-proof membrane and it must be clean and level before parquet is laid. Wooden floors should be levelled with hardboard panels (see page 73), and solid floors should be screed with a self-levelling compound (see page 72). The parquet panels are glued to wooden or concrete floors with the edges butted like floor tiles.

Parquet panels can be very expensive. A cheaper alternative is to use timber-faced cork tiles, made from a layer of cork backed with vinyl and surfaced with a thin veneer of hardwood protected by a thin vinyl coating. These are laid in the same way as cork tiles (see page 84).

1 Marking out the floor

Leave the panels to condition in the room where they will be laid for two to three days. Mark out the floor as you would for soft floor tiles (see page 84) and lay out the loose tiles in order to achieve wide border panels around the edges of the floor. You need to allow for a 12mm (½in) expansion gap all around the floor against the skirtings. Few walls are completely straight, so don't rely on them to provide an accurate line. Instead, drive a nail into the skirting at each end of a line marking the edge of the last whole panels along the walls and stretch a piece of string tightly between the nails to form your guideline.

2 Laying out first panel

It is a good idea to wear knee protectors when spending a long period working on your knees. Use the notched trowel to spread the recommended adhesive onto the floor. Follow the manufacturer's instructions, and make the adhesive to the correct thickness. Cover the strip of floor next to the string guideline. Align the first panel with the string and place it in position. Guide the second panel along its edge until it is snug against the first panel, then lower it onto the adhesive. Level the panels using a soft wood block and hammer to avoid damaging the surface of the panels. Check level and alignment with a spirit level and a straight edge.

3 Butting edges

Subsequent panels are butted up against previously laid panels. In order that there are no gaps between the panels, they must be laid absolutely square with the corners meeting precisely. This takes a little practice, but is best achieved by positioning the panel with one hand resting firmly on the previously laid panel. This will stop your hand from shaking. Start by 'matching' one corner, then slowly glide your hand down the side of the panel so the edge lowers into position. Once this edge is in place, the other edge of the panel can be lowered gently into place. Level with a soft wood block and hammer, as in step 2.

OLD PARQUET FLOORING

The harder and thicker the veneer, the more expensive it will be. In older homes, you may find parquet that has been constructed from solid blocks of wood that were cut into 25mm sq (1 sq in) to expose the grain end. If this type of parquet gets marked, it can be difficult to find matching replacement panels. One solution would be to swap sections that lie out of sight.

Parquet is not suitable for bathrooms, as frequent wetting will cause it to warp and swell. It can also be damaged if it is exposed to too much dry heat and it can be marked by stiletto heels and burns. Highly polished parquet flooring can be a slip hazard and any loose rugs or mats should be firmly stuck down. There are special adhesive strips designed for this purpose.

4 Cutting edge panels

On at least one edge of the floor, the panels will have to be cut to fit into the gap against the skirting board. Ideally, the cut panels should be as wide as possible and ideally the cut should be sliced between strips of wood within the panel, as this makes it easier to cut. Lay the panel exactly over the adjacent panel in the row previously laid. Take a second panel and butt it up against the wall, so that it lies on top of the tile to be cut – but remember to allow for the 12.5mm (½in) expansion gap if the panel is to fit next to skirting. Scribe a line onto the panel to be cut using the upper panel as a template. Cut along the line with a coping saw.

5 Cutting into door posts

When the parquetry is to run between two rooms, rather than cut a difficult shape out of the panel to it around the moulded architrave of the door – which is nearly impossible to do – professional parquet fitters cut off the bottom of the door frame. To do this, use a spare piece or off-cut of the flooring to guide the blade of the saw. Place the off-cut on the floor, position the saw on top, and saw away the bottom of the door post. You will then be able to slide the parquet panel neatly under the door frame.

6 Finishing the floor

When the parquet panels have been laid, the floor is ready for finishing. First, sand out any irregularities between the panels, vacuum the floor and then wipe it over with a very lightly dampened cloth. Conceal the expansion gap around the edge of the floor by nailing quadrant moulding to the skirting (see page 66). Varnish the panels with two to three coats of clear varnish to seal and protect the floor (see page 77). Select the finish – matt, silk or gloss – and treat the quadrant moulding in the same way so it matches the parquet panels. Follow manufacturer's instructions when varnishing: wear knee pads and a face mask and ventilate the room well.

LAYING SHEET VINYL

1 Prepare the sub-floor

Before you lay a sheet covering, the sub-floor surface must be level. Wooden floors can be levelled with sheets of floor grade hardboard or plywood and must have adequate ventilation (see page 73). Don't lay vinyl floor covering over timber that has been recently treated with preservatives. Concrete floors should be levelled with a self-levelling screed and must incorporate a damp-proof membrane (see page 72). Check the floor with a spirit level before you start work to ensure it is level. Sweep the floor thoroughly to remove grit, which can puncture the vinyl, and check that any nail heads are driven in well below the surface of the wood. Condition the vinyl by leaving it in the room in which it is to be laid for 48 hours. If possible, leave it opened flat; if not, it should be loosely rolled and standing on its end. Levelling floors and laying sheet vinyl – or any other floor covering – will require you to be on your knees for long periods. Make sure you wear knee pads or kneel on a rolled-up towel to prevent injury.

FITTING AROUND PIPES

To fit a sheet of vinyl around a central heating radiator pipe, first measure and mark the position of the pipe on the vinyl using a compass. Cut or punch a hole in the vinyl for the pipe. From the perimeter of the hole, draw parallel lines to the edge of the vinyl. Halfway between these lines, cut a straight slit. Fold back the slit gently and slide the sheet of vinyl into place. Press the join firmly. You can apply adhesive to seal it if you wish (see step 5). This principle applies for any obstacles you have to lay vinyl around, such as WCs and wash basins. For more complex shapes, you should make a template from thin cardboard and scribe it onto the vinyl.

2 Scribing along the skirting

If the sheet vinyl is to cover the floor in one piece with no seams, start by fitting it at the longest wall first. Remember that walls are rarely straight. In order to lay the vinyl squarely – which is particularly important if there is a geometric-style pattern – drive a nail through a block of wood about 50mm (2in) from the end. Pull the vinyl away from the wall by about 35mm (1½in). Make sure it is parallel to the wall. Butt the end of the block of wood against the wall and scribe a line onto the vinyl following the skirting.

3 Cutting along the scribed line

For clarity, use a ruler or straight edge and draw a pencil line along the line you scribed in step 2. Cut along the line using a lino-cutting tool, a very sharp knife or scissors. This removes the overlap at the end of the wall and the vinyl will now slide up against the wall. Don't worry if your scribing and subsequent trimming is less than perfect: You can always hide flaws behind some decorative quadrant moulding nailed to the skirting board (see page 66).

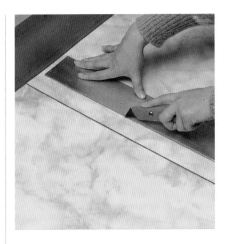

ADHESIVES

While ceramic floor tiles are generally laid using a sand-and-cement mortar with a PVA bonding agent added, there are two other types of flooring adhesives suitable for fixing a wide range of flooring such as vinyl and cork to wood, hardboard, concrete or cement screed sub floors: rubber-resin and synthetic latex. There are brand-name adhesives, but many of the large DIY chains will also stock their 'own brands'. When laying floor coverings that are not 'loose laid' but need glueing down, check with the floor covering supplier who will recommend the correct adhesive. This must be applied to the correct thickness and notched with a spreader, following the manufacturer's instructions.

JOINING VINYL

4 Trimming around edges

So the rest of the sheet lies as flat as possible, you should cut triangular notches at any internal corners and straight cuts at external corners – such as in and around alcoves, window bays, kitchen units or bathroom fittings. Carefully bend back the sheet vinyl and pierce it with the knife just above floor level. Draw the blade up the sheet towards the edge – don't cut downwards into the main field of the sheet. Make triangular cuts around the base of the obstacle until the sheet lies flat on the floor. Crease and cut off waste 'flaps'.

5 Securing with adhesive

Many sheet vinyls are loose laid – they're not stuck directly onto the sub floor. However, in some areas – such as along a door opening – it's a good idea to glue the edges. Carefully lift the edge and bend the sheet back taking care not to crease it or crack the surface finish. Spread a 50mm (2in) band of the appropriate flooring adhesive with a notched spreader. Alternatively, you can also use a 50mm (2in) wide double-sided tape. Replace the edge of the vinyl and immediately wipe away any excess adhesive that may have oozed out.

1 Scribe on edge of the join

Where a large floor is covered with two sheets of vinyl, scribe one edge as described in step 2, left, and overlap the free edge with the second sheet. This will allow you to match up any pattern. Cut through both sheets with a sharp knife, and remove the waste edges.

2 Glueing the join

Bend back the edges to be joined. Apply the adhesive or double-sided tape. Place the edges in position and press together. Wipe off excess adhesive. Weight the join with hard-backed books until it sets.

LAYING 'SOFT' FLOOR TILES: CORK, VINYL, RUBBER

If your tiles have a directional pattern, the backing will have an arrow indicating the direction and you should lay the tiles in this way. Non self-adhesive tiles require glue: spread the adhesive on the floor according to the manufacturer's instructions, using a notched applicator. Only lay enough adhesive to stick two or three tiles at a time, or you'll find that the adhesive has 'gone off' before you've laid the tiles.

1 Marking centre lines

Mark centre lines down the room using chalked strings stretched tightly between two nails. Loose lay a row of tiles along one line, from the centre of the room to the wall. If the space between the end tile and the wall is less than half a tile, move the chalk line half a tile width to the right or left. Find the mid point of this line and use a carpenters' square to draw a pencil line at right angles to the chalk line. Extend this line to 'quarter' the room. Check the border width and if necessary, move the second line away from the wall.

2 Spread adhesive

If you are using self-adhesive tiles, remove the protective paper backing.

3 Lay the first tile

Working from the centre of the room – where the chalk lines cross – align the first tile into one of the intersecting angles of the chalk line. Lower the tile to the floor and press it down firmly but gently. Spread the adhesive with the notched spreader and carefully position the second tile in the next-door angle of the chalk line – to the right or left of the first tile – and press it down. Form a square with two more tiles, and then lay subsequent tiles around the square to form a pyramid shape. Lay all full tiles first, and continue filling half of the room before you tile the other half.

4 Trimming border tiles

At the edges near the wall, lay the tile to be cut exactly on top of the last full tile. Place another tile on top with its edge against the wall. Scribe or draw a line along the edge of this tile, marking the tile below, then cut along the line, using a straight edge and sharp knife. Fit the cut-off border tile into the gap.

5 Cutting irregular shapes

To fit tiles around the curved base of a WC or other built-in obstacle, make a template for each tile out of thin cardboard. Cut slits in the template so you can fit it against the object to reproduce its shape, and then transfer the template outline to the tile.

LAYING CERAMIC TILES

1 Dry setting out

Mark out the floor as for 'soft' tiles (see page 84) and dry lay out the tiles. Work out the spacing so that the floor will have fairly wide border tiles. Nail two softwood battens to the floor, aligned with the last row of whole tiles on two adjacent walls. Use a carpenter's rule to set the battens at right angles. Make a final check and dry lay a square of tiles in the angle. Remember that ceramic tiles will have grout between them, so you need to space the tiles about 2mm (⅛in) apart all round using spacers or pieces of card.

2 Laying onto adhesive

Ceramic tiles are fixed using a thin layer of cement-based adhesive. It is best to choose an adhesive that is waterproof and slightly flexible when dry. Spread the adhesive according to the manufacturers' instructions and with the correct spreading tool – some adhesives specify notched or plain spreaders. Apply enough adhesive to the floor to lay about 5 or 6 tiles; don't cover the floor with more than you can manage, or the adhesive will dry out. Position and press the first tile into place, working between the battens. Lay a 'square' of tiles and check the alignment with a straight edge. Lay subsequent tiles in the pyramid form, laying all whole tiles first until you have filled half of the room. Remove the batten and tile the other half, constantly checking the alignment and level of the tiles with a straight edge and spirit level.

3 Measuring and cutting border tiles

Ceramic floor tiles will need to be measured and cut to fit into the gaps between the edges of the 'field' of tiles and the walls. Place the tile to be cut face down on top of the last full tile. Slide the tile to be cut gently against the wall. Make an allowance for the 2mm (⅛in) spacing between the tiles and mark the position of the cut on the tile using a felt-tipped pen. Because of the thickness of ceramic floor tiles, they are not easy to cut by hand and its best to hire a cutting jig.

4 Grouting

To fill the gaps between the tiles use a ready-made grout. This comes in standard colours such as white, grey and brown, but is also available in a range of colours. Waterproof grout is needed for kitchens and bathrooms. Leave the tile adhesive to set for the required period before pressing the grout between the tiles with a squeegee or plastic scraper. Spread the grout, making sure the joins are well filled and flush with the surface of the tiles so dirt does not get trapped in any 'hollows'. Wipe away the grout from the tile faces with a sponge before it sets. When the grout has dried, polish the tiles with a dry cloth.

SAFETY FIRST

Follow the instructions when using adhesives and always wear safety goggles when cutting ceramic tiles, in case of flying splinters.

CHOOSING AND LAYING CARPET AND CARPET TILES

There is a huge range of carpet types and qualities available in a variety of colours and patterns to suit your home and budget. A rough idea of how durable a carpet is can be gained by pressing your thumb into the pile. The quicker the pile recovers, the denser and more resilient the carpet – unless it's a 'shag pile' with long hairs. For durability, short dense-fibre carpets are the best, while long strand and loops, which may look bulky, in fact weigh less.

Choose a carpet that is right for the situation in which you want to use it: don't put lightweight carpets in living rooms or on stairs. Before you buy, decide roughly how much you'll need so you can compare prices. Ask if the retailer offers a measuring service – if not then draw a rough floor plan and mark the measurements on it. Remember that you will need to allow extra carpet to match patterns, but check estimates to avoid over-ordering and subsequent waste.

Unless the carpet is foam-backed, you'll also need underlay. Choose a good one: animal fibre underlay is tough and should have a weight of about 1kg per square metre (2½lbs per square yard). Rub foam between your fingers with a medium pressure – if it crumbles, reject it. Foam should be laid over paper, felt or hardboard to stop it sticking to the floor. Don't use foam on stairs: use special stair pads or jute-backed crumb rubber.

Carpet tiles, which generally come with an integrated underlay, have long been used for 'contract carpeting' in offices because they are hardwearing and there is no length or width of space that can't be covered. They are easy to lay, and it's easy to cut a single tile to fit. Because they are loose laid, a worn, damaged or stained tile can be easily replaced, so it's worth having a few spares. However, like any carpet, the colours will change over time, so any new tile added to an 'old' field will be apparent. Swapping the positions of tiles to even out wear can minimize this a little. Carpet tiles are laid and cut as for vinyl tiles (see page 84).

2 Laying underlay
Rubber or foam-backed carpets don't need underlay, but lay some brown paper on the sub-floor to stop it sticking and prevent dust rising from the floorboards. The side facing upwards on underlay is clearly marked by the manufacturer. Foam underlay is normally 1.37m (4ft 6in) wide and joins can be sealed with carpet tape. Lay the underlay about 50mm (2in) short of the skirting so the carpet will lie flat along the edge.

1 Prepare the sub-floor
Make sure the floor is clean and dry. Fix carpets to a wooden floor with tacks; rubber-backed carpets can be stuck down with 50mm (2in) wide double-sided tape around the edge of the room. Woven-backed carpets can be held with gripper strips (wooden or metal strips with fine metal teeth). Nail (or glue them if the floor is concrete) about 6mm (¼in) from the skirting with the teeth angled towards the wall. Cut short strips to fit in alcoves, window bays and doorways.

3 Laying out the carpet
Roll out the carpet to room length and position it: the pile should sweep away from the window. This avoids shading in

daylight. If you are laying a patterned carpet, it should run parallel to the main axis of the room. Start at a corner of the room where there are two plain walls. Butt one machine-cut edge against a wall and fix the edge. Tuck the edge down between the gripper strip and the skirting using a bolster.

4 Use the knee-kicker

Knee-kickers are used to stretch the carpet taut. They can be hired from DIY stores. Start at the centre of the wall stretching alternately towards both corners. Use some tacks to temporarily hold down the stretched areas. When you reach the far wall, use the knee gripper to stretch the carpet onto the gripper

strip's teeth and a bolster to tuck the edge down between the strip and the skirting board.

5 Cutting to fit

Cut and fit carpet into doorways, alcoves and window bays as for sheet vinyl (see page 83). Use a pair of heavy scissors or a sharp trimming knife to cut out the shape allowing a margin of about 6mm (¼in) for tucking into the edge between the gripper strips and skirting board. Let the cut carpet lie flat on the floor and adjust it until it is stretched evenly then attach it to the gripper teeth and tuck in the edges. Carpet can be laid to fit snugly around small obstructions such as radiator pipes simply by cutting a slit in

the carpet edge and slotting the carpet around the pipe. Add a little PVA adhesive to the reverse of the carpet to stop it from lifting, and prevent cut edges from fraying or fibres from being shed after the backing has been cut.

CARPET TILES

Carpet tiles are available in a range of durabilities and textures, from natural fibres to tough synthetic ones that can be washed under a tap. Nearly all have a built-in underlay that cushions the tread and prevents them moving around. Some synthetic fibre carpet tiles are treated with dirt repellents. See pages 88–9 for laying advice.

CARPET TYPES

The British Carpet Classification Scheme rates floor coverings according to their durability:

Light Domestic: Suitable for areas of light traffic, such as bedrooms

Medium Domestic: Suitable for areas of light traffic, such as a dining room, or well-used bedroom

General Domestic: For use in living rooms

Heavy Domestic: For use in hallways and stairs

CARPET CARE

New carpets tend to produce fluff: for the first few weeks after laying, don't vacuum, but sweep lightly with a hand brush. Thereafter, vacuum regularly to stop dirt and grit becoming embedded at the base of the pile where it can rub and cut the fibres.

To shampoo, follow the carpet manufacturer's instructions precisely to avoid shrinkage and colour runs. Spray-extraction cleaning – erroneously called 'steam cleaning' – should be left to reputable, professional carpet cleaners.

LAYING CARPET TILES

Carpet tiles are fairly large and they're loose laid, so it's possible to complete a floor quite quickly. Furthermore, they are easy to cut with a sharp trimming knife so fitting irregular corners is easy – and you can create your own patterns of colour: chequerboard, stripes, chevrons – whatever you wish. If you're doing this, it's a good idea to work out your pattern on graph paper first. Note that the tiles treated with dirt repellent are difficult to dye so are limited to a narrow range of plain colours.

CARPET TERMS

Body carpet: Carpet that is less than 1.8 m (6ft) wide that is used for runners in corridors, as stair carpet or seamed to fit awkward spaces.

Broadloom: Carpet wider than 1.8m (6 ft). Common broadloom widths are 2.74m (9ft), 3.66 m (12ft) and 4m (13ft 1in).

Cut pile: Strands of yarn are cut rather than looped into a carpet.

Cord: Hardwearing cord is woven in a wide range or colours, in artificial fibres or non-sheep animal hair.

Looped pile: Uncut loops in the surface with short or shaggy pile.

Shag pile: Pile that is 25–50mm (1–2in) long. Not for use on stairs!

Tufted: Individual fibres are punched into the base material and sealed with a waterproof backing.

1 Measuring and marking out

Even when laying a plain field of tiles, start by finding the centre of two opposite walls and snap a chalk line between them to mark a line across the floor. Lay loose tiles at right angles to the line up to one wall: if the gap at the wall is less than half a tile width, move the chalk line sideways to give a wider margin at the edge. Snap a second chalk line at right angles to the first. Lay loose tiles at right angles to the second line and adjust so that border tiles are at least half a width.

2 Directional arrows

Carpet tiles have a pile like any other carpet, and must be laid in the correct direction, which is usually indicated by arrows printed on the reverse. The arrows indicate the non-slip direction and it's usual to lay carpet tiles in pairs so that one stops the other from moving. For extra security, you can stick down every third row of tiles using double-sided tape. Start at the 'centre' laying the tiles in the angles of the intersecting chalk lines and build up into a pyramid shape, filling half the room.

3 Laying out

Then lay the tiles in the other half. Lay all the whole tiles first then cut and measure border tiles by laying the tile to be cut face down, exactly over the previous full tile. Take another whole tile and lay it over, butting its edge against the wall. Use the overlying edge to draw a line. Cut the tile along the line with a sharp trimming knife and fit it into the gap. In order to even out wear and tear, particularly where there is 'through traffic', rotate the tiles once in a while, swapping their positions.

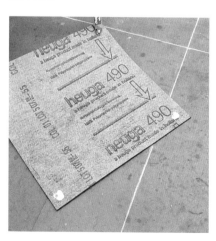
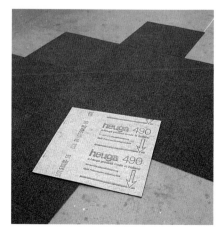

PATCHING/REPAIRING A CARPET

1 Repairing a burn

Small patches of worn carpet and burns are easily repaired, especially if you kept the spare pieces after the carpet was first laid. Remove scorched fibres with a sharp trimming knife or safety razor blade to expose the backing beneath. Cut sufficient matching tufts from the spare piece to fill the hole. Dab the hole and tuft ends with a suitable latex adhesive and insert the tufts into the hole. Leave them to dry and then trim, if necessary, and brush to blend with the pile. If the pile is woven into the carpet, turn the carpet back and mark a square on the backing over the damaged area. If the carpet is foam-backed, the damaged area will be cut from the tufted side.

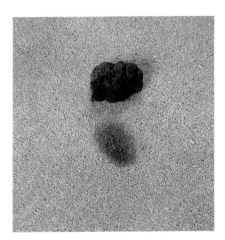

2 Fitting a patch to a damaged carpet

If the carpet to be repaired is foam-backed: cut a square of new carpet larger than the area of damage and temporarily tack it into place to cover the damage. Cut exactly round the new patch and through the carpet underneath. Remove the tacks, the new patch and the damaged square. If the carpet has a woven back: on the reverse side, coat the marked, square area plus about 25mm

(1in) extra on all sides with latex adhesive and rub it into the backing. This will stop the carpet from fraying when you cut it. Using a sharp trimming knife cut out the marked square. Cover the hole in the backing with strips of hessian tape, overlapping the edges by 50mm (2in). Use the damaged square as a template, and cut a new square from a spare piece of carpet. Place the spare piece of carpet over the hole and carefully trim it to fit.

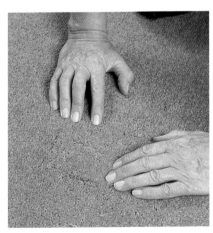

3 Finishing the repair

For a foam-backed carpet: turn back the carpet and stick strips of adhesive tape over the foam-backed side of the hole.

Roll the carpet face up, and press the new patch into place on the adhesive tape. Lightly hammer down to flush. For a woven-backed carpet: coat the back and edges of the new square with adhesive, taking care not to get it on the tufts. Press it firmly onto the hessian strips, making sure that the pile on the patch runs in the same direction as the rest of the carpet. Tap the edges lightly with a hammer to make the patch flush.

SPECIAL CASES

Axminster: The loom inserts pile tufts into the weave from above so the strand need not run along the back. The surface is cut pile, but may be long/shaggy; short/smooth; stubbly or even carved into sculpted relief.

Berber: Originally a carpet with a looped pile in natural, un-dyed wool made by Berber tribes people in North Africa. Now a term for nubby, flecked carpets in a range of natural colours.

Wilton: The loom weaves yarn in a continuous strand. While only a limited number of colours can be used in the weave, Wiltons are famous for their smooth, velvet-like surface.

Repairing Axminster and Wilton: After cutting away the damaged square, remove two or three strands from the edge of the hole and paste the fringed ends now left onto the back of the carpet to prevent fraying then proceed to patch as in step 2.

CEILINGS

FITTING A PLASTERBOARD CEILING

Ceilings have to withstand a lot of stresses. If there is a room above the ceiling, feet passing across the floor above cause the joists to move, even if only slightly, putting a strain on the fixings of the ceiling. Consequently, ceilings are even more likely to develop cracks than walls (see page 54). Small areas of damage can be patched, but a ceiling in very poor condition should be replaced completely. Modern ceilings are almost always made of plasterboard and this is the obvious choice for the replacement. The first stage however, is to remove the old ceiling.

1 Strip away old/damaged plaster
Open the windows and prepare for huge amounts of dust and debris. Warn your neighbours so they understand it's only dust and not your house catching on fire! Wear goggles and a mask and push an old, stout chisel, screwdriver or crowbar up through the old plaster to locate the joists. When you've found them, wrench the old laths free, letting them and the plaster fall to the floor. When all the old lath and plaster is down, carefully and thoroughly inspect the joists for any remaining nails, damage or decay. See page 243 for advice on dealing with woodwork problems, such as woodworm, and wet or dry rot.

2 Start at the corner of the ceiling
Plasterboard comes in two thicknesses: for joists spaced with centres up to 450mm (18in) apart use 9.5mm (⅜in) board. If they are wider apart – up to 600mm (24in) – use 12.7mm (½in) board. Plasterboard that incorporates insulation material is available and is particularly suitable for top-storey ceilings. It is a heavy material, so get a strong friend to help you lift the boards. You must also have proper access so you can reach the ceiling. Start in one corner. Turn the first board flat and hoist it up – both people using their heads and hands to support the board until a 'T'-shaped floor to ceiling prop can be installed. Drive in enough galvanized plasterboard nails to keep the board securely in place.

3 Measuring and cutting boards
When you come to the end of a row of full boards, you will most likely have to cut a board to fit. To cut plasterboard, score it first with a sharp pointed knife on the 'ivory' side and then cut with a sharp trimming knife or a panel saw. Use the off-cut of this panel of plasterboard to start the next row of boards on the ceiling, so that the cross joins of the boards are staggered. Even if an exact number of whole boards makes up a row, start off the second row with half a board so the joins are staggered. Allow for a 3mm (⅛in) gap between each board. This gap will be filled later.

4 Using galvanized plasterboard nails

If you are using 9.5mm (⅜in) plasterboard, fix the boards to the centres of the joists with 30mm (1¼in) galvanized plasterboard nails. These have a jagged shank for extra grip and a coating of zinc to provide protection from corrosion. For 12.7mm (½in) boards, use 40mm (1½in) nails. Start nailing at the joist nearest the centre of the board and work towards the edges. This will stop the board sagging in the middle, which could happen if you nailed the edges first. Each end of the board must be nailed to the middle of a joist. The nails should be driven in at 150mm (6in) centres and no closer than 13mm (½in) from the edge. Leave a 3mm (⅛in) gap between subsequent boards.

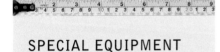

SPECIAL EQUIPMENT

Use support battens and 'T'-shaped props to hold the boards in place. These are sometimes known as 'deadmen'. They should be slightly taller than the height of the room.

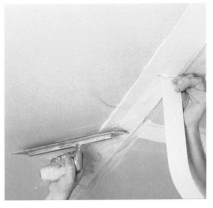

5 Filling the joints

Fill the joints between boards using joint filler and 53mm (2⅛in) paper jointing tape. Mix the filler with water and apply a continuous band about 60mm (2¼in) wide down the joint. Press in the paper tape, smoothing it out to exclude air bubbles. Repeat with another layer of filler over the tape.

6 Applying the finish

When the filler has stiffened slightly, smooth its edges with a damp sponge then let it set completely. When it is set hard, coat it with a thin layer of joint finish. Mix the finish to a thick, creamy consistency and apply it in a wide band along the length of the joint using a plasterer's trowel.

7 Finishing off

Before the finish goes off (sets), feather off its edges. Professional plasterers use a purpose-made tool for finishing joints, but you can also use a close-textured, plastic sponge. Dampen the sponge and feather the edges of the finish using a circular motion. This spreads the finish very thinly to create a smooth finish. Let the finish set, and then repeat, adding a thin, but slightly wider band over the first. Feather off the edges once again.

8 Using filler to hide nail heads

Fill any indentations left after nailing by applying filler with a filling knife. Smooth it out and, when it has set, apply a thin coating of finish and feather off with a damp sponge.

FITTING A WOODEN CEILING

1 Mark the height of the new ceiling

On one wall, mark the height of the new ceiling: don't forget to include the thickness of the boarding in your measurement. Using a straight edge and spirit level, draw a horizontal line across the wall at the proposed height. Continue the drawn line around the perimeter of the room, but be aware that the existing ceiling height may itself not be level.

2 Cut and fix battens to walls

Measure and cut all the battens from 50 x 25mm (2 x 1in) timber. Nail or screw them to the wall at 400mm (1ft 4in) intervals. The lower edges should be level with the drawn line. Check for true horizontals with a spirit level. Lay a straight length of timber on the battens to span the opposite walls and check they are in line with the ones opposite.

3 Cut and nail joists

Measure and cut the ceiling joists to length from the 75 x 50mm (3 x 2in) timber. Cut a notch in each end so that they sit over the wall battens, bringing the bottom edges of the joists flush with the edges of the battens. Skew nail the joists to the wall battens. Cut and fit any hangers and ties required if the joists span a distance of over 2.4m (8ft).

4 Cut and nail noggins

Measure and cut 75 x 50mm (3 x 2in) timber to make noggins. Nail them between the edges of the joists to suit the width of the plasterboard, so the edges of the boards fall along the centre line of the noggins. Check the level of the noggins and joists with a spirit level.

POINTS TO REMEMBER

Before you install a new lowered ceiling consider the following points:

- the proportions of the room will be altered;
- a new ceiling will cover any decorative features of the old one;
- the official recommended ceiling heights must be considered, and the height of existing window openings may limit the ceiling height;
- the cost of materials and ease of installation – a considerable amount of timber is need for the framework and boarding to cover it;
- some materials may constitute a fire hazard; consult your local Fire Officer for advice and information regarding currrent safety regulations;
- lighting circuits will need to be extended;
- new light fittings will be needed;
- you must have proper access so you can reach the ceiling: don't try to balance on a pair of household steps. Instead use a strong, stable working platform;
- you will need a strong person to help you.

FALSE CEILINGS

Pulling down an old ceiling is an extremely messy task. If the ceiling height permits, it might be better to erect a false ceiling just below the existing one. In a top storey room, where there is no accessible attic space above, you can place useful insulation material above the plasterboard to make the house warmer and reduce heating bills.

Lowering a ceiling even by a small amount will alter the character of a room. Furthermore, although you won't need planning permission, such an alteration is subject to minimum standards of construction required by the Building Regulations to safeguard health and safety. Your local Building Control Officer, commonly called the District Surveyor, enforces these standards (see page 14).

The height of a new ceiling should be no less than 2.3 m (7ft 6in) – although in some instances a lower height of 2m (6ft 6in) is acceptable under beams and bay windows. In roof spaces, however, the minimum height must be 2.3m (7ft 6in) for at least half the area of the room.

MATERIALS

Calculate the quantities of timber and plasterboard required and draw up a cutting list:

- 75 x 50mm (3 x 2in) sawn soft wood for timber joists. These should span the room in the shortest direction and be spaced at 400mm (1ft 4in) if you intend to use 12.7mm plasterboard (½in) or 600mm (2ft) if you use 9.5mm (⅜in) plasterboard.

- Room spans of over 2.4m (8ft) should be supported by hangers and ties made from timber not less than 50 x 50mm (2 x 2in) which are fixed to the ceiling above. The hangers are placed at about the middle of the joists' span.

- Extra timber is needed for the noggins fitted between the joists. This is nailed between the joists to suit the width of the plasterboards.

- 50 x 25mm (2 x 1in) sawn soft wood for the wall battens to run around the room's perimeter.

- Plasterboard dimensions will depend on the type of board you use: standard, baseboard, thermal insulated, or vapour-check.

- Nails and screws for fixing frame to the masonry walls; galvanized plasterboard nails of a length appropriate to the thickness of the board; filler, finish and jointing tape.

5 Nailing the plasterboard
Support the first board in place with a 'T'-shaped floor to ceiling prop. Starting in the corner, use galvanized plasterboard nails to fix it in place. Work from the joist nearest the board's centre and nail at 150mm (6in) centres. Nails should be 13mm (½in) from the edge of the board. Leave a 3mm (⅛in) gap at the end of each board. Start the second row with a cut piece so the joins are staggered.

6 Finishing joints
The joints between boards and any indentations left after hammering in nails are filled and smoothed with filler, jointing tape and finish. This is done in the same way as for finishing plaster-board walls and ceilings (see page 91). The joint between the new ceiling and the walls can be covered by coving (see pages 94–5) for a professional and decorative finish.

FITTING COVING

Coving is a 'ready-made' moulding that is used to make a cornice – the continuous, horizontal band of moulding that runs in the angle between walls and ceilings. In many period houses, the cornice can be very elaborately moulded. Not only does cornice add a decorative feature to the room, but it also strengthens the joint between the wall and ceiling.

It is possible to buy new cornice moulding made from casts taken from old patterns. These are best when the style of the house and interiors are in keeping with its use. A more contemporary look can be achieved with plain coving. Plaster coving is made of a hard, gypsum core moulded into a curved section. It is available in a wide variety of styles – from the plain to the highly elaborate –

and in different lengths. Two girth (width) sizes are generally available for use in the DIY market: 100mm (4in) and 127mm (5in) and manufacturers also provide cardboard templates making cutting internal and external mitre joints very easy.

To fix coving you will need a proprietary coving adhesive, which can be purchased in dry powder form or ready-mixed. Coving adhesive 'goes off' (sets) very quickly, so make all your measurements and cuts first, then number each section of coving so you know which piece is fitted first and you avoid having to move sections around.

Good preparation is vital for a neat finished effect. Make sure your walls and ceilings have been stripped and the plaster primed before you fix the coving.

1 Measuring and marking
Make sure you have safe access to the ceiling: don't try balancing on a single pair of household steps. Instead use two pairs and sling some scaffold planks between them to give you a level working platform. Start by marking parallel lines along the wall and ceiling. These should be set off from the angle of the join at the distance recommended by the manufacturer of the coving. Use a straight edge and a spirit level to guide you.

2 Key the surface
Using the point of an old screwdriver or the point of a trowel, scratch the plastered surface between the lines you have drawn on the walls and ceiling. This 'keys' the surface to provide a better grip for the adhesive. After you have abraded the surface, clean away any loose dust.

3 Measure and cut coving
Carefully measure the walls, then measure out the coving and cut it to fit. Use the manufacturer's cardboard templates to help you cut any mitres. Remember that when you mitre-cut the coving for an external corner, the coving must be longer than the wall and must extend up to the line on the return angle drawn on the ceiling. Use a fine-tooth saw and cut through the coving from the face side, support the lengths from underneath.

4 Sand the cut edges
Plaster coving is backed with a thick paper – rather like plasterboard. Any ragged edges on the paper should be removed by gently sanding with a fine abrasive paper. Don't apply too much pressure or you'll sand away the straight edge you've just cut. Gently wipe away any dust.

TOOLS & MATERIALS

- Coving with cardboard templates
- Cove adhesive: dry powder or ready mixed
- 2 pairs of steps
- Scaffold planks
- Measure
- Pencil
- Straight edge
- Spirit level
- Fine-tooth saw
- Fine abrasive paper
- Screwdriver, or another sharp, pointed implement
- Paintbrush or sponge
- Filling knife

PREPARATION

- Measure twice, cut once! It's always worth double-checking your measurements.

- Before fitting mouldings in position, strip off wall and ceiling coverings and make good any defects in the surfaces beneath.

- If you are working in a room that has already been decorated, it may be easier to prime and paint the coving before it is applied. Use an appropriate primer for plaster so that the surface is prepared to accept its finish.

5 Coving adhesive

Coving adhesive is available in dry powder form or ready-mixed. In either instance, follow the manufacturer's instructions regarding application amounts and thickness. In most instances, the adhesive remains workable for about 25–30 minutes, so it's a good idea to work on one length of coving at a time. Use a filling knife to apply the adhesive to both back faces of the coving.

6 Dampen dry, bare plaster

So that it does not leach the moisture out of the adhesive too quickly, dry, bare plaster needs to be dampened down a little before the coving is pressed into place. Use a clean, slightly dampened paintbrush or sponge and dampen the scratched plaster between the drawn lines.

7 Press the coving into place

Offer the length of coving and level it with the guidelines. Press it into the angle between the wall and ceiling. Long lengths of plaster can be difficult to handle on your own, so get a friend to support one end. You could also tap a few nails in the wall along the drawn line to rest the coving on. This will stop it sagging in the middle. Immediately scrape away any filler that has oozed out.

8 Filling the gaps in corners

Use any excess adhesive that has oozed out to fill the gaps in mitred corners. Use a filling knife to get a sharp edge. With internal corners, it's easier to use your finger to apply the adhesive to the join. Wipe along the edges of the coving with a damp sponge to remove any traces of glue. Remove the 'temporary' nails if used and fill any holes. The coving is now ready for priming prior to painting.

REPAIRING CORNICE

In some instances – depending on the style of the cornice – it may be possible to replace a damaged section with a new piece. However, with many elaborate mouldings in older properties, the cornice may not be a standard design and a replacement piece that matches might only exist in another room of your house. An architectural salvage yard or a company that specializes in the restoration of such period details may either have a length of original cornice, or a reproduction taken from a mould of an original. In either case, these would be expensive.

There is however a way that you can repair a cornice yourself, using a device known as a 'craftsman's ride'. Professional restorers use one of these – often placed *in situ* on the wall. A craftsman's ride consists of a sheet of zinc cut to the shape of the cornice. This is fixed to a wooden frame called a 'horse', which 'rides' along a wooden batten nailed temporarily to the wall. Plaster is laid on with a trowel to the damaged area and the horse slid along the batten, scraping off the excess. The process is repeated until the whole area has been built up and the zinc plate has made the shaped profile of the cornice match the rest.

Working high up at ceiling level can be difficult, tiring and dangerous, so it can be easier to use a variation on the craftsman's ride to make a new piece of moulded cornice at 'ground level' that can be used to replace the damaged piece completely.

1 Taking a cornice profile
Use a needle template tool to take the profile shape of an undamaged stretch of cornice. Needle templates are available at larger DIY stores and are invaluable tools for providing accurate templates of complicated forms.

2 Transfer the outline
Transfer the shape to a piece of thin but stiff metal sheet, or laminate. Cut out the shape using a saw file blade fitted to a hacksaw and finish off the profile with shaped files. Check for an accurate fit by placing the profile into a section of undamaged cornice.

3 Attaching the profile
The profile will make the new cornice the correct shape. To make sure it is the right size, measure the height of the existing cornice. Attach the profile to a piece of sturdy board. Position it at a height to match that of the existing cornice, allowing for the height of the baseboard on which the plaster is formed.

4 Attaching support battens
The baseboard is where the plaster will be 'laid up'. To give the plaster something to set around, nail two narrow parallel strips of wood along the length. So the finished cornice slips off the baseboard easily, paint it and then wax it. To stop it moving, you could temporarily nail it to a larger flat surface.

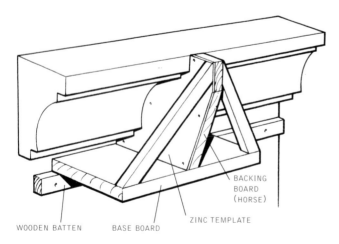

WOODEN BATTEN   BASE BOARD   ZINC TEMPLATE   BACKING BOARD (HORSE)

CRAFTSMAN'S RIDE

5 Working the 'ride' across the plaster
Plaster of Paris dries extremely quickly, so it allows you to build up the cornice in successive layers. Mix the plaster to a thick, creamy consistency. Don't mix too much in one batch or it will set hard before you have a chance to use it. Pour the plaster along the baseboard and then slide the 'horse' along the board. The profile will shape and shave the plaster to the correct form and size. Repeat this step several times, until the profile has been built up to the correct height. A particularly thick moulding can be reinforced by inserting pieces of jute scrim between applications of plaster.

6 Removing new moulding
When the new piece of moulding is hard and dry, it can be lifted from the base-board. Using a fine-tooth saw, cut away the ragged plaster ends. The wax applied to the board should allow the moulding to slip away. Glue the new moulding into position with a proprietary plaster adhesive. Subsequent lengths of new moulding can be made, but remember to clean off and wax the baseboard each time.

REINFORCING

Ceilings have to withstand stresses, especially if there is a room above. The vibrations caused by feet passing overhead means that adhesive alone is not enough to hold even a small ceiling rose in place. Most reproduction ceiling roses have pre-made screw holes. When the adhesive is set, use a long brass screws to attach the rose to a joist or noggin. The screw heads can be disguised with filler.

ADDING A CEILING ROSE

1 Drilling hole for wiring
Reproduction mouldings of decorative ceiling 'roses' made from fibrous plaster are available in a wide range of styles and sizes. In many cases, these mouldings need a hole drilled through their centres for the lighting cable to pass through.

2 Applying adhesive
Small ceiling roses that are to sit on flat ceilings can be fixed in place with a commercial plaster adhesive applied to the back of the moulding. There should be enough suction on the adhesive but you can also use a pair of screw props to hold them in position until they are fixed by screws (see Reinforcing box).

3 Positioning
If there is no existing centre light, find the centre by stretching string diagonally across the corners of the room. Mark and drill a hole to pull the lighting cable through. Using a damp sponge, wipe away any surplus adhesive round the edge of the moulding. Attach the light fixture (see page 208).

SAFETY FIRST

Where there is an existing light fitting in place on the ceiling, turn off the power supply and remove the whole fitting. If you are in doubt about re-wiring the fitting or installing a new one, always consult a qualified electrician.

ROOFS

PITCHED AND FLAT

Steeply sloping roofs are known as 'pitched' roofs. Rainwater drains most easily from this type of roof and snow slides off before it overloads the structure. Pitched roofs are expensive to build so it is standard practice on constructions such as garages and home extensions to fit flat roofs – but even these are made to slope slightly so that water drains off. There are several different types of pitched roofs. 'Two-way' pitched, probably the most common, has a simple slope on each side, meeting in a ridge like a tent (as shown above). The walls at each end are gable walls and are triangular in shape at the top. On a 'hipped roof' the roof also rises from the end walls to the top like the side of a pyramid. Some houses may be built with a combination of both, and the floor plan of the building would be 'L' or 'T'-shaped. A 'mansard' roof is pitched at two angles: a gentle one at the top and a steep one below, while most 'lean-to' buildings and porches have a single-sloped roof known as a 'mono-pitch'.

THATCH

Pitched roofs are normally clad with slates or tiles. In some regions, however, where these materials were not available locally, other roof coverings were used. Straw and reeds have been used for centuries to make thatched roofs, and in many homes they continue to provide a magnificent insulation that is not only weatherproof, but also keeps the interior of the house warm in winter and cool in summer. Over the centuries, thatched roofs were gradually replaced as other materials became available. Many people think that having a thatched roof means sharing your home with assorted wildlife, but in fact the thatch is covered with a netting to stop birds and mice making nests. Spiders are common – but they are a sign of a good dry roof and should, therefore, be a welcome sight. As for bats nesting in the eaves, they are to be encouraged in any roof as they are a protected species!

DREAM COTTAGES

The irony of 17th- and 18th-century thatched-roof cottages, those 'dream cottages' in the country that are so highly valued today, is that they were originally occupied by the poorest rural labourers who were never in a position to afford to replace the thatching with different materials.

Today, if a house has a thatched roof it is automatically a listed building, and the thatch cannot be replaced with tiles or slates – even if it is attached to another house with a slate or tile roof.

There is nothing more magical than watching rain drip off thatch or seeing steam rise as the sun shines on it after a shower of rain. But, there are some drawbacks to thatched roofing too: repairs can be extremely expensive and must be carried out by professional thatchers. As there are few people who practice this craft today, they are inevitably always busy and have long waiting lists of jobs to be done. Often this means having to live with a tarpaulin on the roof for some time.

SAFETY FIRST

If you are working on a ladder while repairing a roof, follow the safety advice on pages 40–1. If you have a large area to work on, it would be best to hire a scaffolding tower.

SLATES AND TILES

Roof coverings for domestic buildings follow long-established traditions, which are, in many cases, based on regional building practices. Despite modern developments in manufacture, many of the materials and the ways of using them have not altered very much. Slate roofs glisten when wet and come in a range of beautiful colours including blue, grey and green. But slate is an expensive material, a heavy one and it is difficult to replace a missing slate because the nails that fix them are covered by the next slate up. An alternative 'slate' – machine-made from non-asbestos cement – is cheaper and lighter, but is available in colours to simulate the real thing. Tiles made of clay will vary in colour depending on either the region in which they were made originally, if they are old, or on the ingredients used in manufacture if they are new. In many modern houses, clay roof tiles have been replaced by concrete tiles, which can also be moulded into various profiles.

ASPHALT AND FELT

These roofing materials are most commonly found on flat roofs and have replaced the lead, zinc or copper that were traditionally used. Both asphalt and felt are bituminous-based coverings. Laying asphalt is a highly skilled job: the asphalt is melted in a cauldron and two layers, separated by a layer of sheathing felt, are spread 'hot' over the roof to a thickness of 18mm (¾in). Roofing felts are bituminous-impregnated sheet materials applied in layers to build up roofing, which is then bonded with hot or cold bitumen. Several grades of felt are available, and their qualities are reflected in their prices.

REPAIRING FLAT ROOFS

When making repairs, use fungicide to get rid of any lichen or moss before applying self-adhesive repairing tapes. These won't be seen from street level. Apply liquid waterproofing to seal.

CORRUGATED PLASTIC

The roofs of many home extensions designed as sun rooms and conservatories are made of plastic. While modern conservatories and sun lounges are roofed in transparent UPVC, many older homes have additions or extensions not intended as habitable rooms that are covered in corrugated plastic. While it is a long-lasting material, leaks can develop and moss tends to grow in the 'valleys'. Cracks can be caused by heavy snowfalls – and even by seagulls dropping stones. The most common defects, however, are corroded sealing washers: sheets of corrugated plastic are fixed to wooden rafters with screws or nails with a nail cap and there are rubber or plastic washers between the nail head and the sheet to stop the rain getting through. In some cases the sealing washers were never fitted. A further problem can occur around the flashing: but this can also be easily remedied and flashing specifically made for corrugated materials is available from builders' merchants (see pages 104–5).

ROOF TILES

REPAIRS TO ROOF SLATES AND TILES

Many roofs are inaccessible or out of view, so we tend to think about them only during periods of bad weather when defects become apparent. It's a good idea to check your roof from time to time. Ask your neighbours; they may have a better view of your roof from their upstairs window than you have from the ground. Use a pair of binoculars and take a good look for missing or cracked tiles or slates, damage to ridge tiles along the 'spine' of the roof and for defects around chimney stacks. Have a look at the inside of the roof structure through the trap door in the attic space: there might not be any visible signs of dampness in the habitable rooms but a defective roof could be causing damage to the structural timbers of the roof itself.

Ignoring your roof can result in serious damage and costly repairs (although substantial re-roofing may qualify for a discretionary grant from your local authority). If you live in a listed building or conservation area, re-roofing will have to be carried out using approved materials – whether thatch, tiles or slate. Check first with the appropriate authorities before you proceed to ensure you are meeting with planning regulations.

BROKEN SLATES

The first task in repairing a broken slate is to remove it. You must have safe access to the roof, so work from an access tower. These are safer than ladders and the extra expense of hiring one is easily justified.

The offending slate may be so loose that you can simply pull it away, but chances are it will still be held in place by at least one of the two non-corroding nails used to fix it to the roof battens. In this case, you'll need a slater's ripper. This is a long, flat blade with a handle at one end and one or two hooks at the other. Push the blade up under the slate and engage the nail into the hook. Give the ripper a good, short sharp tug and the nail should break free. Repeat for the other nail – if there is one – then pull the broken slate clear.

You can't nail a replacement slate into position because the batten it is nailed to is hidden under neighbouring slates. Instead, secure the slate with a clip. This is made from a thin strip of copper, aluminium or

lead about 23mm (1in) wide and the length of the slate plus an extra 25mm (1in) to bend over. Slightly bend one end of the strip to form a lip. Slip the lip onto the batten and fix it in place with a galvanized nail through it and the batten. Keeping the slate flat, ease it into position, lying on top of the strip. Bend the lower end of the strip up and back over the slate to hold it into position.

To cut a slate to size, mark out the correct size on the back of the slate. Place the slate bevel side down onto a workbench with the marked cutting line level with the edge of the bench. Wear protective goggles and chop the edge of the slate with a bricklayer's trowel. Work from both edges towards the centre of the slate to cut to the correct size.

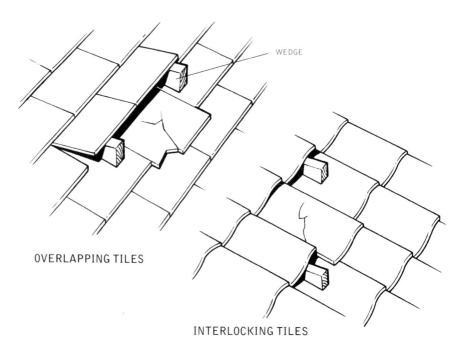

OVERLAPPING TILES

WEDGE

INTERLOCKING TILES

REMOVING OR REPLACING A BROKEN TILE

In some older properties, you may find that slates and tiles have been fixed to battens with mortar. This process was called 'torching'. It should only be used where torching already exists.

This is a straightforward task once it is understood that tiles (and slates) overlap each other by an amount determined by the spacing of the roof battens. The spacing is a crucial part of roof design and should not be increased. The overlap is normally between 60–90mm (2½–3½in).

Although tiles are fixed with nails, not every tile is in fact nailed. Instead they have a lip on the underside of the top edge called a 'nib', which is located onto the batten. The weight of the tile on its overlapping neighbours keeps it securely in place. Only every fourth or fifth row of tiles is nailed. If the tile to be replaced is not nailed,

remove it by pushing a trowel underneath it and lifting the nib clear of the batten. Push the new tile into position under the adjacent tiles until the nib engages with the batten. If the defective tile is nailed, loosen it with a slater's ripper.

If you have to cut a number of tiles to size, use an abrasive cutting disc in a power saw or hire an angle grinder. Wear protective goggles and a face mask. A single replacement tile can be cut by hand using a tungsten grit blade in a hacksaw frame, or you can 'nibble' away at small areas with pincers after first scoring the cutting line with a tile cutter.

REPAIRS TO FELT ROOF

1 Cutting the blister
Blisters or bubbles are caused by moisture, which has penetrated a crack or hole and has expanded with heat causing the felt to lift. To repair them, start by making two cuts across each other.

2 Apply bitumen adhesive
Peel back the four triangles formed by the cuts – a little heat from a hot-air stripper makes this easier. Leave the 'flaps' open and let any moisture underneath evaporate. Apply bituminous adhesive to the exposed area.

3 Press the flaps down
When the adhesive has become tacky, press the triangles of cut felt into place and bed them firmly into the adhesive. To secure them flat and make a close seal, nail each point of the triangles with a galvanized clout nail.

4 Cover the repair
To completely seal the repair, apply a top layer of the bituminous adhesive. You can now either sprinkle on small chippings or cover the repair with a patch of roofing felt cut to overlap the repair by 75mm (3in) all round.

FITTING GUTTERING

Gutters and down pipes are collectively known as 'rainwater goods'. They need to be kept in good condition and clear of any obstructions such as leaves, twigs, birds' nests and dirt, or the walls of a house could become wet and the ground waterlogged – which could result in damp in the foundations.

Traditionally, rainwater goods were made of cast iron, which, while strong and tough, is very heavy and does corrode eventually. Stripping off old paint, de-rusting, priming and repainting is both expensive and tedious, and in some instances completely worthless because the insides of cast-iron pipes are equally prone to rust. Today, most rainwater goods are made of UPVC, which is lightweight, non-corroding and can even be painted to look like cast iron.

MAINTENANCE

Regularly inspect and clean out the interiors of gutters as these concentrate the dirt, which can quickly build up trapping leaves and twigs. Before you know it, you've got a wet, weed-filled lawn growing in your gutter, which is a breeding ground for mosquitoes. One of the commonest causes of gutter overflow is that it becomes blocked. Plastic guttering can be distorted by the weight of standing water – sagging gutters are another cause of overflow.

With a large piece of cloth – an old duster or 'T'-shirt is ideal – block up the outlet hole to the down pipe so that the 'gunk' doesn't get swept down it where it could cause a blockage. Wear some rubber gloves and scoop out the 'gunk' with a trowel, an old spoon or your fingers. Put it in a bucket – don't fling it over your shoulder to the ground below. Sweep the gutter clean with a hand brush then take out the cloth bung. Flush the guttering with a bucket of clean water. If leaves are the main cause of the build up, it's a good idea to fit a net cover over the outlet to the down pipe. DIY and plumbing stores supply such 'accessories' or you can use a piece of chicken wire bent over the outlet hole.

Cast-iron rainwater goods should be kept well painted to contain and limit corrosion. Remove rust with abrasive paper or a wire brush, or use a proprietary rust remover/inhibitor. Strip off loose flaking paint by scraping, wire brushing or applying chemical stripper. Don't use hot stripping as the expansion and contraction from heating and cooling the iron can cause it to crack.

Bare metal must be primed: on previously painted cast iron, 'spot prime' any bare patches. Apply an undercoat and finish with two coats of exterior-grade gloss. Don't forget to treat the backs of down pipes: slip a piece of cardboard behind the pipe to mask off the wall when you paint.

Plastic rainwater goods require little maintenance beyond regular inspection and cleaning. To paint them, prime first with an all-purpose primer, apply an undercoat and finish with one or two topcoats of exterior-grade gloss. Remove old flaking paintwork with a suitable chemical stripper – don't abrade as this can cause splits and don't use hot stripping methods, as the pipes will melt.

Remember that water is a valuable commodity and should be conserved. If you have a garden that requires watering in summer, it makes good conservation sense to fit a water butt to collect rainwater.

TYPES OF GUTTERING

Valley gutters

Not a 'true' guttering system but a form of flashing (see page 104–5) used at the junctions between sloping roofs. The valley directs rainwater into eave or parapet gutters and then into downpipes.

Parapet gutters

These gutters are designed and built as part of a modern building's original structure. In general, parapet gutters 'service' a roof (either pitched or flat) that is set between two parapet walls.

Eaves gutters

These are the most familiar type of guttering. The gutters are supported on brackets fixed to fascia boards running at a slight angle along the eaves of the roof, so that rainwater is channelled into down pipes, which are attached to the walls with clips.

1 Fix support brackets

Remove the old length of guttering and carry out any repairs to the fascia board. Screw the first support bracket to the fascia board no more than 50mm (2in) below tile level. At the opposite end of the run, and close to the top of the fascia board, fix a second bracket. The difference in the heights of the brackets is to provide a fall of at least 25mm (1in) in 15m (50ft). Run a piece of string tightly between the two brackets and fix additional brackets at no more than 1m (3ft 3in) intervals. There should be a bracket wherever two lengths of pipe are joined.

2 Fit the replacement length.

Tuck the back edge of the length of gutter under the roofing felt and into the rear lips of the support brackets. Carefully snap the clips from the lips of the brackets over the front edge of the guttering. Subsequent lengths are installed in the same way with the spigot end of one length pushed into the socket of the next length. Adaptors are also available to connect old guttering to new.

3 Fitting a swans' neck

Down pipes are held in position a little distance away from the walls with clips.

To take a down pipe under the eaves, or to connect a down pipe to the outlet hole in the guttering, you may need to make an 'angle' in the pipe work. This is called an 'offset' or 'swans' neck' because of its shape. You may find the shape and length you need exists readymade but you can easily make the right one using offset lengths of pipes. Use a solvent cement to seal any joints. Fit the swans' neck to the outlet spigot in the guttering. Fit the over end of the swans' neck into the top of the length of down pipe. Mark, drill, then plug the wall and affix the down pipe by its clip using plated screws.

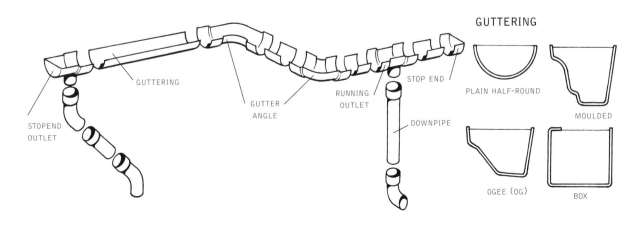

GUTTERING

GUTTERING

STOPEND
OUTLET

GUTTER
ANGLE

RUNNING
OUTLET

STOP END

DOWNPIPE

PLAIN HALF-ROUND

MOULDED

OGEE (OG)

BOX

FLASHING

Aluminium flashing strips.

A moulded flashing unit.

However, it is heavy and expensive and shaping it requires considerable skill. Bitumen felt is used for flashing on felt roofs. It is less durable than metal and is generally used for covering the up-turned edges of roofing felt. Straight horizontal flashing can be repaired with self-adhesive aluminium or bituminous flashing strips and there are special moulded flashing units designed for use with corrugated roofing of plastic or asbestos cement.

Where the line of a roof meets a vertical surface such as a wall or chimney stack, it becomes vulnerable to the weather and must be sealed off to prevent penetrating damp. The usual way to do this is with flashing. Flashing is a strip or sheet of impervious material like bituminous felt or a flexible metal such as lead or zinc. In most instances the upper edge of the flashing is wedged tightly into a raked-out mortar joint. Because it is high up on the roof, and in areas difficult to reach, it's usually best to call in an expert to repair steep flashing beside chimney stacks or where a sloped roof joins a wall. However, replacing a straight horizontal flashing such as on a 'lean-to' or flat roof, is easier and not beyond the scope of a competent do-it-yourselfer.

TYPES

There are a number of different types of flashing used on pitched and flat roofs. Valley flashing is used where two sloping roofs meet. Some tiled roofs use specially curved tiles to fit in the angle, but most roofs will have a flashing of metal. Around chimneys there are generally two types of flashing: apron and abutment. Abutment flashing goes up the side run of a chimney stack and over the ridge of the roof in steps, sealing the join between them. An apron flashing – which is the kind you'll find sealing the join between a lean-to roof and the wall to which it is attached – runs horizontally along the base of the chimney stack, parallel to the roof line. Where the flat roof of an extension meets the wall of a house, this is known as wall abutment. Sealing the join between the flat roof and the internal perimeter edges of the flat roof is a parapet abutment.

MATERIALS

The most common materials used for flashing are lead, zinc and roofing felt, although you will also find that some houses have been flashed with mortar. Lead is considered the best because it is easily shaped and very long lasting.

PROBLEMS WITH FLASHINGS

- Metal flashings can sometimes work loose when the mortar is badly weathered. To fix them, rake out the mortar, tuck the metal back in, wedge it with rolled strips of lead then repoint the joint with mortar or apply a proprietary mastic sealant.

- Lead flashings can buckle and split. You can use flashing tape to repair them, or they can be soldered together. For large areas of damage, a specialist should be hired to weld a new piece of lead in place.

- Where cement fillets are shrinking away from the wall abutments, you can fill the gap with flexible caulking compound applied with a gun.

- For small cracks and imperfections, make repairs using self-adhesive flashing strips.

REPAIRING WITH SELF-ADHESIVE FLASHING

1 Strip away the old flashing
Strip away the old flashing from the walls and roof. Clean and dry surfaces before applying the primer (supplied with the flashing tape). Follow manufacturer's instructions regarding drying times.

2 Cut the tape to length
Measure and cut the flashing tape to the required length and peel away the protective backing as you press the tape into the angle between the roof and the wall.

3 Press the flashing firmly into position
Use a dry rolled-up cloth to smooth out any air bubbles under the flashing tape as you apply it. Smooth the air out to the edges of the tape then run a wallpaper seam roller along the tape's edges.

WATERPROOFING A FLAT ROOF

1 Prepare the surface
Clean the roof of dirt and debris and, if necessary, apply a fungicide to remove moss and lichen growth. Follow the manufacturer's instructions regarding drying times.

2 Apply basecoat
The waterproofing liquid is normally in two parts: following instructions, apply the first coat. Lay strips of glass-fibre fabric into the wet surface, overlapping edges by at least 50mm (2in) and stipple it with a brush loaded with the fluid.

3 Apply the second coat
Leave the first coat with the embedded strips to dry then apply the second coat. When this has become tacky, you can finish the roof with a layer of fine chippings or clean sharp sand to add a tough protective layer.

LOFTS

INSULATION

About 20 per cent of the heat lost from an average house goes through the roof. So while you are tackling roof inspections and repairs, you should also consider how well your loft is insulated. There are two ways of insulating this space: between the joists on the floor of the roof space or between the rafters on the ceiling of the area. It doesn't take long to install insulation, or top it up, and the cost is not high, so, in terms of heat saved, it should pay for itself in around three to four years.

The material used for insulation is always the same – air! The different types of insulation material available are just different ways of packaging air. It is important that the packaging is fire-resistant and it shouldn't encourage mice to nest. The choices include glass fibre and mineral wool, in the form of semi-rigid slabs or blankets that can be laid out between the joists, or a loose-fill material such as polystyrene or cork granules and exfoliated vermiculite. All are easy to lay, but if you have an odd-shaped loft with lots of nooks and crannies, then loose-fill insulation can be quicker and easier to install. If you are topping up existing insulation, use the same type as already laid.

LAYING BLANKET INSULATION BETWEEN JOISTS

Be careful to walk on the ceiling joists only – lay two or three planks over the joists and work from these. Wear a face mask and clear out the dirt and dust between joists. Open the roll of blanket insulation in the loft and, starting at the eaves, lay it between the joists, tucking the end of the roll well into the angle made by the ceiling and roof. The blanket should fit between joists with enough to turn up over the sides. If you need to add strips, overlap the ends by about 50mm (2in) so there are no gaps.

1 Laying loose fill insulation

Clean the loft. Working from two or three planks laid across the joists, pour the insulation between the joists. You will need to lay enough of the pellets to cover the loft floor between the joists to a minimum depth of 100mm (4in). To get the same insulation as from a blanket type 100mm (4in) thick, you would need to lay the pellet to 130mm (5¼in) deep, but you may find this spills over the joists. Don't be alarmed, as the insulation will settle a little over time.

2 Level out the insulation

You can make a 'T'-shaped spreader from wood or laminate. The arms rest on the joists while the middle piece fits between the joists leaving a space at the base that is the thickness of the insulation needed. Start at the eaves and, using the spreader, rake the pellets towards the centre of the room to an even depth. Gather up any excess and store it according to the manufacturers' guidelines, so it can be used later to top up the insulation.

INSULATING THE SLOPING PART OF A ROOF

Insulation can also be fixed directly under the roof rafters. Repair any broken slates or tiles first (see page 100). Condensation can become a problem when you install insulation between rafters because the underside of tiles and slates can get very cold. You must leave a 50mm (2in) gap between the tiles and insulation so the air can circulate freely, keeping the surface dry. This gap will inevitably determine what type of insulation you can use: foil-backed blanket or semi-rigid slabs of glass or mineral fibre, fibre insulation board, or thermal insulation plasterboard.

You must also include a vapour barrier on the warm side of the insulation: sheets of polystyrene can be stapled to the lower edges of the rafters to cover any insulation that is not vapour-barrier backed.

Fitting thermal insulation plasterboard will give you both insulation and a final finished surface ready for decoration, but all the other types of insulation can also be covered with plasterboard.

Foil-backed insulation blanket is simple to install: unroll it and staple it to the underside of the rafters with a staple-gun. Overlap the adjacent edges of subsequent rolls to provide a continuous layer of insulation and vapour barrier.

SAFETY FIRST

- Don't be tempted to open rolls of insulation blanket outside the loft. They are specially packed and expand considerably once the cover is removed.

- Never walk or stand between the joists – the floor won't support you. Use two or three planks laid across the joists to distribute your weight.

- Make sure there is sufficient lighting in the roof space for you to see clearly. If there is no permanent light in your loft, rig up a suitable lamp on an extension lead.

- Wear a face mask when cleaning out the space. If you are handling glass-fibre slabs or blanket insulation, wear long sleeves and gloves as these materials can irritate the skin.

- Mind your head! Sloping roofs restrict access: wear a safety helmet or at least a hat to soften any impact.

LOFT INSULATION

- Some local authorities offer discretionary grants to encourage people to insulate their lofts. To be eligible, you must obtain local-authority approval of your plans before buying the materials or starting work.

- Lagging any pipes and storage tanks in your loft will save a considerable amount of heat and prevent pipes bursting in cold weather (see also page 153). You can buy foam-plastic tubes of various thicknesses. Most will have slits pre-cut in them so you can simply slide them over the pipes. Butt the ends of sections together and seal them with PVC adhesive tape.

- To lag your hot-water storage cylinder, you need a jacket. These are made from mineral-fibre insulation wrapped in plastic. The segments of the jacket fit snugly around the cylinder and then straps are placed round to hold them in place (see page 160 for more information).

- When installing insulation, check that you haven't trapped any cables you may need access to, such as the cable running from the hot-water cylinder to the immersion heater.

- For advice on insulating other parts of your home, see pages 60–1.

LOFT CONVERSION

1 Insulate the sloping part of the roof
Decide on the type of insulation you wish to use and fit it between the rafters on the sloping part of the roof. Don't forget to include a vapour-barrier (see pages 106–7). Wear a face mask and gloves when working with glass fibre or mineral wool insulation materials. Brick gable ends can be lined if necessary using the method described for dry-lining walls (see page 52).

2 Covering with plasterboard
The insulated roof can now be covered with plasterboard. Make sure that you select a convenient width and length of board that will pass through the access to the loft. The plasterboard should be positioned over the vapour barrier and nailed or screwed to the rafters. Don't use a heavy hammer to fix boards or insulation to rafters as you can dislodge tiles if you hammer too hard.

3 Finishing plasterboard
Joins between plasterboards are sealed with filler, tape and finish in the same way you would finish plasterboard walls (see page 52). The surface is now ready for a final decorative finish if desired (see Chapter 5 for a range of decorating ideas and instructions on how to carry them out).

CONVERTING SPACE

If you intend to convert the space into usable, living accommodation, you will need planning permission and your plans must comply with Building Regulations (see page 14). Lofts can provide valuable storage space but before you convert your loft for this purpose, you must get an expert to check the strength of the ceiling joists to be sure they are strong enough to support the additional weight.

SAFETY FIRST

- Don't walk or stand between the joists – they won't support your weight. Lay two or three planks across the joists to make a platform from which to work.

- Use the recommended protective equipment and clothing when working in lofts and installing insulation. Protect your lungs from dust and fibres by wearing a face mask and always wear gloves and long sleeves when handling glass fibre and mineral wool insulation as it can cause skin irritation. Goggles will stop loose fibres irritating your eyes.

- Make sure there is sufficient light to work by.

- Be careful when nailing or drilling into joists, rafters and purlins – the horizontal beams that provide intermediate support for the rafters. Vibrations can cause tiles to slip and plaster ceilings could be at risk of cracking.

LAYING A FLOOR IN LOFT

If your joists have passed inspection and are deemed strong enough, you can lay a loft floor. This makes storing and accessing items much easier and neater, but it's a good idea to keep the central floor area as empty as possible and arrange to store heavy items around the perimeter.

A floor can be made from new or reclaimed floorboards but this might be a little costly for a storage area. Instead, you could use tough, flooring grade chipboard, either nailed or screwed to the joists. For more information on laying floors, see pages 72–3.

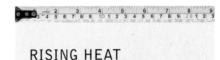

RISING HEAT

If the loft will be used often, insulate the walls but leave the floor uninsulated so that heat can rise through it from the rest of the house.

FIXING WALLS

Unless you have a very tall attic space or you are prepared to pay for a professional loft conversion complete with dormer windows, most of the space is going to be difficult to use because of low roof height and the 'dead space' in the angle between the roof and the floor. Where there is sufficient height, however, it is possible to create a 'room', or even two, using stud partitions to close off the dead space.

1 Construct a timber framework
Measure the length of the 'wall' and the vertical height from the floor to the purlin. Cut and construct a timber frame of studs and noggins according to the dimensions. (See also pages 52–3.)

2 Fix the timber frame
Using a spirit level to check for vertical level, position and fix the wall frame. Secure it to the purlin with nails or screws. Your timber stud partition is now in place.

3 Fixing plasterboard
A 'solid' wall can be made by covering the framework with plasterboard (see page 52). It's a good idea to make a 'hatch' or doorway through at least one of the walls to provide access into the crawl space behind in order to undertake roof inspections or repairs.

FITTING A ROOF WINDOW

1 Strip off the part of the roof
The position of the window will be determined by the position of the rafters. Locate the bottom at the manufacturer's specified distance from the nearest full course of slates so that there are whole or half slates/tiles at each side. Cut through the slating/tiling battens, roof felt and rafters to make the opening.

2 Cut and nail trimmers
Measure, cut and nail horizontal and vertical trimmers. The horizontal trimmers are nailed across the top and bottom of the opening, between the rafters, to set the height of the opening. The vertical trimmer or trimmers – you may need one on either side – set the width of the opening.

3 Screw the window frame into place
Remove the glazed sash part of the window and fix the frame in place using the brackets provided. Manufacturers mark a guideline around the frame so that it is positioned correctly, level with the surface of the roof battens. Measure the two diagonals to check the frame is square. They should be equal.

4 Fit flashing
Working from the bottom of the frame and moving in a clockwise direction, fit the flashing supplied with the window to seal the join between the window and the roof. Different flashing kits are supplied for tile and slate roofs, so make sure you have the correct type.

5 Fit slates/tiles
Finish the exterior work by fitting the tiles/slates. Most roof coverings will be fixed with nails or clips but tiles have an additional nib on their reverse face that hooks over the roof battens. For more information on fixing roof tiles and slates see pages 100–1. Replace the glazed sash in the frame.

6 Finishing the inside
To make good the interior surface, cut and nail plasterboard to the sides of the rafters on the inside and close the gap top and bottom with plasterboard nailed into the groove in the frame and to the timbers of the roof structure. Finish the joints with filler, tape and finish (see page 52), ready for final decoration.

FITTING A LOFT LADDER

1 Locating the joists

The manufacturer of the folding loft ladder will specify the dimensions of the opening you need to make. Don't cut through more than one ceiling joist: these are usually spaced about 400mm (1ft 4in) apart, which gives sufficient width for ladder access. Locate three joists by drilling pilot holes in the ceiling.

2 Mark out the opening

Using the two outer joists as your guideline, mark out the opening to the dimensions specified. Cut an inspection hole inside the marked area to check for obstructions. Be especially vigilant for electrical cabling. Strip away the ceiling plasterwork and then saw through the laths. Wear goggles to protect your eyes.

3 Saw through the middle joist

Climb up into the roof space, being careful to avoid stepping or standing between the joists. Place a board or a couple of planks across the joists to support and distribute your weight. Saw through the middle joist, cutting back to 50mm (2in) from each edge of the hole.

4 Cut and nail trimmers

Measure, cut and nail two lengths of timber to make trimmers to fit between the joists at each end of the opening. 100mm (4in) round wire nails can be used to secure the trimmers to the joists.

5 Insert casing

Ready-to-install folding loft ladders are supplied with a casing and built-in frame. Following the manufacturers' instructions, insert the casing and frame into the opening and screw it securely to the joists. Attach the supplied hinges and mechanisms according to the manufacturers' guidelines.

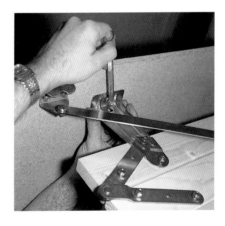

6 Fix ladder in position

Attach the hinges and brackets to the ladder, and fix securely to the ladder casing and frame. Make good damaged areas of plaster on the ceiling side of the opening. Some kits come with a covering door for when the ladder is 'up' and 'stored' but you can make a hinged panel hatch cover from 18mm (¾in) plywood.

DOORS

Patio doors

Glazed door with aluminium frame

Sturdy wooden door

Wherever your 'front' (main) door is located, it should be immediately obvious to callers to your home. If your door is at the side, then pay attention to the path leading up to it. If your door is too rotten or damaged to paint, then replace it. Choose a door that suits the architectural character of your house and that 'fits' with the style of windows. Select furniture – letterbox, door-knocker or bell-pull and door-handle – that is in keeping with the style. House numbers should be clearly evident so that visitors – and the emergency services – can find the right house. If you live in a listed property or in a conservation area, check first that you can replace the door. In some conservation areas, you are only allowed certain colours.

INTERNAL DOORS

Internal doors have a dual role: they make rooms private but also create transitions from one space into another. There are a wide range of door styles and materials available to choose from. Be careful when buying a 'reclaimed' door, particularly for external use: make a careful note of

the measurements of the door opening beforehand. Doors bought from DIY stores are made in several sizes: heights range from 2m (6ft 6in) to 2.03m (6ft 8in), although extra-tall doors at 2.17m (7ft) are also available. Widths range from 600mm (2ft) to 900mm (3ft) with intermediate 'jumps' of about 75mm (3in). Thicknesses also vary: from 35mm (1⅜in) to 45mm (1¾in). Don't assume that all the doors in your home are the same size. In older properties, it was common practice to use bigger doors for the 'important' ground-floor rooms and smaller doors upstairs.

HARDWOOD DOORS

Hardwood doors are more expensive than softwood versions and tend to be reserved for impressive entrances where you can show off the natural features of the wood. Glazed doors traditionally had a wooden frame construction but, increasingly, these have been replaced with double-glazed aluminium frames. If doors are glazed or part-glazed, they must conform to safety standards and be suitable for external and internal use.

Glass doors can add an extra dimension to a room: the patterns and sizes of the panes create their own decorative effects, and bring light into a room. Patio doors and French windows that lead into a garden or patio area fill interiors with light and bring the 'outside in'. Folding or sliding internal doors can not only look good but can also solve space problems in very small rooms.

SAFE AND SOUND

External doors must be secure. Use approved locks and a chain, which allows you to open the door only slightly to strangers. Security needs special consideration in homes with small children, the elderly, disabled or anyone who lives alone or in an isolated place. With small children, the lock on a front door should be out of reach, but they should be able to reach the security glass or see through a 'spy hole'. Internal doors that fit correctly mean fewer draughts and less heat loss. When closed, internal doors should contain fires for a short time, giving vital extra seconds to escape to safety.

INSTALLING AN EXTERNAL DOORFRAME

Exterior doors are heavy and the hinges carry most of the weight and put up with some rough treatment for their size. The weather, wear and tear and lack of maintenance can lead to doorframes splitting or rotting, while a badly fitting frame can come loose from the wall. Because external doorframes are generally built into the fabric of the building, replacing one will cause a little damage to the outside rendering. In older properties, doorframes are recessed into the brickwork with the inside face flush with interior plasterwork, and an architrave covering the joint. In modern homes, the frame may be closer or even flush with the exterior masonry. In either case, work from the side on which the frame is closest.

1 Saw through the jambs

On each jamb, you will find three metal fixings securing the frame into the masonry: one about halfway up, the others about 225mm (9in) from the top and bottom. Cut through these, then saw across the jambs about halfway up.

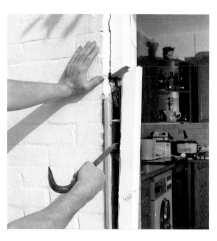

2 Levering frame members

To make removing the frame easier, cut through the head member (the top of the frame) and through the sill (the bottom). Insert a crowbar behind each of the cut members and lever them away from the surrounding walls.

3 Clear away debris

With the old frame removed, clear the dust and debris from the opening. Where the frame was inserted into a cavity wall construction, you'll need to repair the vertical DPC. Use a gun-applied mastic to create a barrier so moisture cannot penetrate between the inner and outer leaves of the cavity wall (see page 58).

4 Position the new frame

At each end of the head member there are 'horns' – 50mm (2in) projections built into the brickwork to hold the frame in place. Fit a new frame with the same shaped horns as the old one. Don't cut off the horns; shape them to fit instead. Wedge the frame in position checking it is central, square and plumb.

5 Drilling clearance holes

Drill three counter-bored clearance holes in each jamb: one halfway up, and the others 300mm (1ft) from the top and bottom. Drill through to mark their positions. Remove the frame, drill the holes and insert no. 12 wall plugs. Re-fit the frame and fix it with 100mm (4in) steel screws, then plug the counter bores.

REPAIRING ROTTEN DOORPOSTS

1 Saw through the jamb
Remove the door. Saw off the rotten piece of the frame, cutting back into good wood. Make the cut at 45 degrees to the face of the post to create half of a scarf joint. If it is useable, keep the metal dowel in the base of the old frame.

2 Measure and cut a new section
Measure and cut a matching section of new timber with one end cut to 45 degrees. Drill a hole in the flat end of the new section and insert the cleaned-off and primed metal dowel. (Or make a new dowel from galvanized steel pipe.)

3 Treat the new timber
The new length of replacement wood should be treated with a proprietary wood preserver. It can then be primed, ready for a final exterior-grade paint finish to match the rest of the frame. Follow the manufacturer's instructions regarding application and drying times.

4 Setting the dowel in mortar
The metal dowel is set into a bed of mortar, and the 'broken' area around the base of the frame made good. Use one part cement to three parts sand with water to form a soft mix. Push it into the hole. Secure all the joints with a waterproof mastic sealant.

DOOR REPAIRS

- Prevention is always better than a cure, so give your doorframes a regular check over. Look for gaps where shrinkage has occurred and apply a mastic sealant.

- Keep pointing in the brickwork around doorframes in good order.

- Keep paintwork on timber in good repair to prevent rot. Properly prime and paint new timber (see page 296).

- Hinges on doors will last longer, work more smoothly and resist rust if they are lightly oiled.

- Correctly fitting hinges have less chance of pulling out of a frame or door and splitting the timber.

- Check weatherboards on external doors: if they are rotten they can cause the bottom rail to swell or rot.

- Always apply a mastic sealant around the outer edge of the frame before hanging a door.

- When drilling holes to hang a doorframe, avoid drilling into the mortar joints.

- When positioning a dowel in mortar, push it down firmly making sure that no air pockets form.

HANGING A DOOR

Doors that creak, don't hang properly or are worn and ugly can be the cause of a great deal of irritation. Whether you are hanging a new door, or re-hanging an existing one, you should plan carefully. Doors must have a clear, all-round expansion allowance. External doors expand in wet weather and changes in temperature and humidity can also affect interior doors. Panelled, solid doors have more 'movement' than doors made of man-made boards, which are inert. Before you hang a new door, leave it in the room in which it is to be fitted for 48 hours to adjust to the humidity.

Panelled or solid, flush doors can be hinged either side; 'cored' flush doors are reinforced at the hinge positions on one side and the lock position on the other, so these types of doors can only be hung one way round. There are usually markers on the doors to indicate the reinforced areas.

To protect doors during storage and transit, manufacturers deliberately make the stiles – the long side rails – over length at the top and bottom. These extension pieces are called 'horns' or 'joggles' and have to be cut off, but leave them on the door until you are ready to hang it.

Exterior doors are hung with what is called a 'kick'. This means that when the door is opened, it is in fact slightly out of vertical so that the clearance at the bottom is increased slightly. This is often necessary for porch doors, which may have a slight fall in the direction of the door. The kick is achieved simply by varying the amount to which the hinges are recessed into the frame.

Most doors are hung on butt hinges, made in a range of sizes. For a heavy door, it's best to use three hinges. This helps to prevent warping and spreads the weight of the door.

1 Saw off the horns

Remove the old door. Start at the top and remove every screw except one from each hinge. Wedge the old door in place or get a helper to hold it so it doesn't fall away from the frame. Remove the last screws and lift the door clear from the frame. Cut off the horns on the new door: lay the door across trestles and cut the horns off flush and then finish with a block plane.

2 'Shoot' the stiles and rails

Try the door for fit. There should be a clearance of about 3mm (⅛in) at the top and sides, and a little more at the bottom if it has to clear floor coverings. Most doors will have to be made to fit: this is done by planing or 'shooting' the door. Use a long plane and 'shoot' from either end to ensure an accurate line free of hollows. If the frame itself is out of true, the door may need to be scribed to fit. Keep fitting and shooting the stiles and rails until the fit is correct.

3 Mark the position of the hinges

Wedge the new door into the frame and hold it steady. Mark the position of the hinge recesses on the frame and transfer these to the door. If the frame is also new, mark on the door and the frame 150mm (5in) from the top and 230mm (9in) from the bottom. These will line up with the standard top and bottom rails. If a third hinge is to be used, position it halfway between the two.

4 Use the hinge as a template
Remove the door from the frame. Use one of the hinges to mark the position on the stile (and on the frame if it is also new). Position the hinges inside the marked line so that the hinge knuckle just clears the door and the frame.

5 Set the marking gauge
Hinges are always hung on the door first, so cut a slot for this recess. Set the marking gauge to the thickness of the hinge flap and mark the front surface of the door for depth.

6 Chiselling the recess
Make a series of wedge-shaped cuts with a chisel to the depth of the hinge, keeping within the profile. Slice crossways and pare away the waste timber to the depth of the hinge. Using the flat of the chisel, clean up the recess.

7 Drilling screw holes
Chisel out the other recess or recesses. The hinges should fit snugly into their slots. Screw holes can now be drilled. Drill pilot holes and screw the first hinge into place on the door using 25mm (1in) screws. Fix the other hinges in the same way as for the first one.

8 Hang the door
Put the door in the frame and insert one screw in each hinge. Make fixing position holes with a bradawl. Check the swing of the door and align it to give uniform clearance all round. Insert a second screw in each hinge and check again. A door should stay open in any position: if it doesn't, adjust the screw positions.

BUYING NEW DOORS

- Before you buy a new door, remember to measure the opening – not the old door – to find the size of replacement you need. The old door may have shrunk over the years.

- Remember, the new door needs to be the correct thickness to fit into the rebate in the frame. With internal doors, the door stop is usually just nailed into place so it can be prised off and repositioned. On external doors, the rebate is an integral part of the moulding. To increase the depth trim a little of it away – not too much or you'll weaken it. To make it shallower, glue and pin extra timber to the frame.

PATIO DOORS

French windows and patio doors give easy access to a garden, patio or terrace. While French windows are hinged and door height, patio doors are tall, horizontal sliding windows. In many instances, patio doors are preferable because they don't blow about in the wind and space isn't required for them to be opened. With slender aluminium frames (lightweight yet strong) and few – if any – mullions, transoms or glazing bars, patio doors offer uninterrupted views. Because one sash slides behind the other when they are opened, access to the outside is only through one opening.

Where patio doors have not been built into the existing structure of a home, installation may involve cutting a new aperture into an external wall.

In order that the structure of the load-bearing wall is not weakened, a lintel must be fitted before the aperture is cut (see pages 48–9). This is a tricky job. It is fairly easy to instal patio doors as a replacement for existing windows or French doors.

Some companies who manufacture patio doors operate on a supply and fit basis only. If you shop around, you might find that a professional installation would work out cheaper than installing them yourself. Finally, even a straightforward replacement will mean living with a gaping hole in your wall, so it's important that you are able to complete the job quickly.

Most patio doors are built to standard sizes and the manufacturers will provide full fitting instructions.

ALUMINIUM

While aluminium does not twist, warp or rust, comes in a range of anodized finishes and requires no maintenance, it has one big drawback: it's an excellent conductor of heat so it will carry the heat from inside the room to the outside very quickly, making the metal as cold inside as it is outside. Warm air condenses on the cold internal frame and can cause slight down draughts. When you buy patio doors, choose a brand that has an insulation barrier in the frame.

1 Installing the frame

Remove the existing windows. Install the new frame and fix the sliding channel to it, following the manufacturer's instructions. Use a spirit level to check the level of the frame and confirm that it is square.

2 Drilling into the frame

In some instances, the patio-door casing is supplied with pre-drilled holes, ready for fixing to the frame. Mark the position of the drill holes on the frame with a bradawl. Follow the manufacturer's instructions regarding the fixings – the necessary screws and plugs should be supplied.

3 Fit the casing into the frame

Clear off any dust or debris from the floor and the bottom of the frame. Although the casing isn't heavy, get a friend to help lift it and position it in the frame to ensure it is not put under strain and the angles knocked out of true.

4 Fix the casing to the frame

Using the screws supplied by the manufacturer, fix the casing to the frame. Always do this in the order specified.

5 Laying the track

On a two-door unit, one must go behind. The other can be fixed, or it can slide as well. Lay at least one length of track at the base of the casing for the glazed unit to slide along.

6 Fitting the glazed units

Follow the manufacturer's instructions to fit the glazed panels. Note that building regulations now require that all fully glazed doors are double-glazed with special insulating glass. Safety glass is advisable if you have children.

7 Fitting locks

Sliding patio doors that aren't properly secured are a burglar's delight. If you didn't buy patio doors with security locks fitted, you will have to add them (see page 122). It's a good idea to have more than one locking system. A single lock at the handle can be forced and the windows simply lifted out.

8 Sealing the edges

With the new patio doors securely in place, it's time to make good any damage to exterior render. The timber frame can be finished with exterior-grade gloss and the gap between the frame and the wall, and the frame and the window casing, should be filled with a proprietary brand of flexible mastic.

MEASURING

Accurate measurements are vital: even if you are installing the doors yourself, it's a good idea to get the door supplier to measure for you – that way they are responsible for errors! However, if you take measurements yourself, measure the length and width at several points. If they vary sharply, work from the smallest measurements. Measure the actual opening – not the existing window frame – from the outside of the house, as you need to know the spacing between brickwork and not the plaster walls inside.

PANELLING AN INTERNAL DOOR

Panel doors are stronger and, many think, more attractive than flush doors. Flush doors are soft wood frames covered in a skin or ply or hardboard and packed with a core material. In the 1970s, such smooth-surfaced doors were very fashionable: many older panel doors were replaced, or simply covered over with an extra skin.

Now panel doors are desirable for their character, but they can be expensive. One solution is to add panelling to a flush door yourself. There are kits available in DIY stores with pre-cut and pre-assembled mouldings. Alternatively, you could buy the mouldings more cheaply by the metre, mitre cut them and make your own instead.

1 Prepare the surface of the door

It's a lot easier to take the door off its hinges and lay it flat on a pair of trestles. Use a proprietary paint or varnish stripper to remove the old finish. Follow the manufacturer's instructions regarding applications and drying times.

2 Lay out the mouldings

Lay out the mouldings in the desired arrangement on the prepared surface. Use a measure: remember that the door may not be square. Mark the positions of the mouldings and apply the recommended adhesive to their backs.

RENOVATING DOORS

- Before you begin, take a close look at the existing flush door to see if it is in fact a panel door with a skin that can be removed to restore the door to its former glory.

- Don't forget the door furniture: replace any unfashionable handles with period-style versions; add a finger plate and an escutcheon to cover the key hole. These are available as coordinating sets in wood, ceramic or brass to suit your door and your pocket. Or check out junk stalls for cast-off originals.

3 Finishing the door

Press the mouldings in position. When the adhesive has set completely, the door and the new mouldings can be finished with a paint effect, stain or varnish of your choice.

4 Re-hang the door

Once dry, re-hang the door (see pages 116–17). Put one screw only in each hinge, tighten and check that the door is aligned and clears the floor. Then fix the remaining screws. Add door furniture of your choice.

HANDLES AND LETTERBOXES

Door knobs, knockers, bell pulls and presses, letterbox flaps, escutcheons, finger plates and house numbers go by the collective name of door furniture. There is a huge variety of styles ranging from contemporary to period styles such as Regency, Georgian and Victorian as well as more 'rustic' ones. Materials include solid brass, stainless steel, plated, cast iron, aluminium and ceramic. With all this choice, any door – whether internal or external – can be given a facelift and new doors made to feel part of the character of your home. Handles are essential and on external doors you will need a letter slot. These should have letter flaps fitted to stop draughts. Letter slots can be placed vertically but are more often horizontal in the middle of the door, at a height that makes it easy for the postman to push letters through without stooping.

ABOVE: Reproduction brass fittings are finished with a clear lacquer to stop them tarnishing. When this wears off, the furniture can be rubbed up with a soft cloth to maintain its shine.

1 Mark the position on the door
Measure the width of the door and find its centre. From this spot, mark out the opening on the middle rail of the door. The opening must be only slightly larger than the hinged flap, so take the dimensions from this. Drill a 12mm (½in) clearance hole in each corner of the marked rectangular area, then cut it out using a pad saw or power jigsaw. Trim the corners of the opening with a chisel then clean up all the cut edges.

2 Fix the letter flap
Mark the centres for the fixing screws – these are close to the edge so be careful when you drill. Drill counter-bored holes on the outside of the door for the threaded bosses on the back of the letter plate, and on the inside to take the screw heads. Drill clearance holes for the screws through the centre of the counter-bored holes. Fix the letter plate in place, shortening the screws if necessary. Plug or fill the counter bores housing the screw heads, or fit an internal flap cover.

FITTING DOOR KNOCKERS AND HOUSE NUMBERS

Door knockers have been replaced in their original function by doorbells and chimes, so are mostly decorative. On a solid panelled exterior door, a period-style door knocker balances and complements the design. The usual position for a knocker is on the central mullion, at about shoulder height. Door numbers are ideally placed just above the knocker so they are clearly visible. Too high or too low and they could be overlooked or obscured by shadows.

FITTING LOCKS

MORTISE

1 Marking the mortise
Determine the position of the lock and hold the casing on the front edge of the door. Mark lines at the top and bottom of the mortise where you will cut.

2 Use a marking gauge
To ensure the mortise is positioned centrally, measure the thickness of the door. Subtract from this the thickness of the lock, set the marking gauge to half the remaining thickness and use it to mark lines from the inside and outside faces of the door.

3 Bore holes
The easiest way to cut out the mortise for the lock casing is to first drill a series of holes, of a diameter equal to the thickness of the lock. The depth of the holes should be the same as that of the lock casing – use a piece of tape to mark the depth on the drill bit.

4 Clean out the mortise
Using a sharp chisel and a mallet, pare out the wood. Push the lock casing into the hole to test for fit. The mortise may need to be eased off a little to fit. Push the casing in again and draw around the face plate. Using a chisel, pare out a recess to take the face and cover plates.

5 Mark the keyhole
Using the lock as a template, mark the location of the keyhole by pushing a pencil or bradawl through the lock. Drill the top part of the hole then complete the lower part with a pad saw. Neaten the keyhole by screwing an escutcheon plate on each side of the door.

6 Fit the lock into the mortise
Push the lock into the mortise and screw it into its recess. Check its operation then screw on the cover plate flush with the stile edge. Hang the door. On the door frame, mark then cut the mortise and recess for the striking plate in the same way as for the lock.

CYLINDER NIGHT LATCH

1 Mark the drill holes

Most cylinder locks come with a paper template, which is taped to the door. Mark, then drill the holes to accept the cylinder. Pass the cylinder through the hole from the outside and connect it to the mounting plate on the inside with the machine screws.

2 Fix the plate to the door

Mark and drill the holes to take the wood screws, which hold the plate to the door. A connecting bar projects from the cylinder through the plate. If necessary, cut the connecting bar to the correct length with a hacksaw. Mark and cut a recess in the door edge for the lock.

3 Attach the lock

Using screws, attach the latch case to the mounting plate and the door. Shut the door and slide the keep onto the latch.

4 Mark the position of the keep

Mark the position of the keep on the door frame. Chisel out a small recess so that the edge of the keep is flush against the frame. Before screwing the keep to the frame, test the lock to see that it runs smoothly in and out of the recess.

HOME SECURITY

- One of the most important functions of an external door is to keep out intruders. Most homes are only secured with a night latch – commonly, and erroneously, called a lock. Locks and latches both have bolts, but the bolt on a latch is sprung automatically. To open a latch, you turn a handle inside or a key outside. A lock, on the other hand, can only be opened and closed with a key. The only advantage of a night latch is the catch that stops the bolt from closing and locking – if you go outside briefly without your keys and accidentally close the door behind you, you won't be locked out. These latches are the easiest of all security devices to force. While they are useful to have, if you are away from your home for extended periods, you should also install more secure mortise locks on external doors.

- Fit a door chain or a spy hole to check the identity of callers before you open the door.

- Don't leave door keys or car keys on hall tables. Determined thieves can easily pass a length of wire through the letterbox, hook up the keys on the end and let themselves in.

WINDOWS

For many years wood was the most common material for window frames but it eventually suffers from the ravages of time and weather. Post-war windows often had steel frames. These were popular because, unlike wood, they didn't rot, shrink or warp. Steel frames were then superseded by aluminium and plastic. Tough and durable, they need little maintenance beyond cleaning. Plastic and aluminium replacement windows come in both contemporary and traditional styles and sizes.

There are four main types of window: casement, sliding sash, pivot and louvre windows. **Casement windows** have hinged sashes so they open outwards like a door. Smaller casements can be hinged at the top. In Britain casement windows open outwards but in most parts of Europe, they open into the room, which makes cleaning easier on upper floors.

Sliding sash windows appear to slide up and down grooves in the window frames. In some, only one of the two sashes slides open; in others,

both open – these are known as 'double-hung'. In original sashes, a pair of weights, which move up and down when the sashes are opened and closed, cleverly counterbalances each sash. Modern versions have spring-assisted spiral balances. These don't need such a deep box construction, because the balances are fitted on the face of the stiles.

Pivot windows are similar to casements but they are held on strong pivoting hinges. This allows the window to be tilted open and right over so the outside can be cleaned. Normally, pivoting windows are fitted with a safety catch to stop them from opening more than 115mm (4½in). Pivoting windows are also available for installation into pitched roofs.

Louvre windows are a form of pivot window. The overlapping boards let in air but keep out the rain. Louvres today are made of unframed 'blades' of glass with the long edges ground and polished smooth. They are held at each end by metal carriers, which pivot on an upright member. Louvres are great ventilators but their design makes them difficult to draught proof.

BUYING NEW WINDOWS

- New windows that suit the architectural style of your home look best e.g. period windows in period-style homes. Changing the window styles can lower the value of your property, so think carefully about this decision.

- New building regulations require that all replacement windows are double-glazed with special insulating glass, which is

more energy efficient. This does not apply to simply replacing a broken pane, only if you are replacing the window.

- Carry out repairs and renovations in autumn after the summer heat has dried out the dampness. Oil the hinges and fasteners on metal casement windows and check they work smoothly. Remove rust immediately (see page 300).

REPLACING WOODEN WINDOW FRAMES

Wooden window frames eventually need to be replaced. Replacements come in standard sizes and if one of these fits your window opening, all you need do is rip out the old frame, prime the new frame – if it isn't supplied ready-primed – and fit the new one after making sure it is upright and square to the wall. You can replace an old window with one of a different style. This comes under the heading of 'house improvements' and does not require planning permission. However, if you live in a listed building or a conservation area, you must check for any restrictions first (see page 14). Remember when you order your new frame to measure the opening, not the old frame.

There are various ways in which a frame can be fixed to the brickwork round its opening. The new frame will probably have projections on the top rail – just like a door (see page 114) – to form horns. These are provided for building into the wall when windows are fitted in a new house while the walls are being constructed.

If you are fitting the window as a replacement you can cut off the horns, or hack out part of the wall to fit them in then make good the brickwork and plaster (see pages 43 and 54). This is the perfectionist's approach, but it isn't strictly necessary. Lower down the frame, screws or nails can be driven through it and into wooden plugs cemented into the mortar courses. Alternatively the screws can go into wall plugs inserted in the brickwork. You can also buy special fixing cramps – a bit like angle brackets – that can be screwed to the side of the frame and embedded in the mortar courses.

Inside, the join between the frame and the wall should be plastered over and can be tidied up further by adding an architrave.

Outside, the join between frame and wall can be pointed with mortar or a flexible, non-setting mastic. This is supplied in tubes, which are held in 'guns'. The trigger mechanism ensures that an evenly sized, continuous 'worm' of mastic is applied to form a perfect seal.

1 Remove the old frame
Take out the sashes and any fixed panes of glass from the old window. Unscrew any exposed fixings. The frame may come out in one piece. If it doesn't, saw through the transoms (the horizontal members) and the mullions (the vertical members) of the window frame.

2 Saw through the jambs
Cut away any external rendering that would prevent the main frame from being easily moved. At each side of the frame near the sill and the head, cut through the jambs and prise them out of the opening.

3 Remove the frame head
Saw through the windowsill and the board and prise these out. Remove the remains of the jambs at the bottom and then prise out the frame head. To do this you will either have to remove the brickwork holding the horns of the old frame in position, or saw them off and leave them there.

4 Clean out the old opening

Remove any dirt and debris from the opening. Wooden plugs in good condition can be reused but rotten ones should be pulled out. If you pull them out, fill the gaps with mortar.

5 Apply a bed of mortar

Place the new frame into the opening to try it for size – adjust it with a plane if it's too big. Re-fit the window and test again for size. Apply a bed of mortar to the bottom of the opening and sit the new frame on it.

6 Drill into the masonry surround

If the wooden plugs were rotten, the window frame will be fixed by screws into wall plugs in the surrounding masonry. Measure and mark the position of the drill holes. Avoid drilling into mortar joints. Drill and plug the holes.

7 Fix the frame

The frame is fixed securely to the masonry of the wall by driving screws through pre-drilled holes in the frame and into the original wooden plugs – if they are sound – or into new wall plugs. Insert the glazed sashes.

8 Making good and finishing

Seal the gap around the sides and the top of the frame with a flexible, gun-applied mastic. Make good any repairs to exterior render and interior plasterwork. The windows are ready for painting using an exterior-grade paint (see page 297).

SAFETY FIRST

- Wear thick gloves when handling glass.

- Handle broken glass carefully: wrap it in several sheets of newspaper, tape it up, and clearly mark it 'Broken Glass' before disposal.

- Replacing a window frame is done from the outside: at ground-floor level, access is not so much of a problem, but at first-floor levels and above, you will need to be able to work safely at a height so hire a scaffold tower.

REPAIRING A SASH WINDOW

Sash windows, correctly called 'double hung sashes' or 'box windows', are operated by cords, pulleys and weights, which counterbalance both the inner and outer sash while sliding up and down. One end of the sash cord is nailed to a groove on the inside of the sash, while the other end is attached to a weight in a hidden shaft inside the frame. Pulley wheels are attached to pulley stiles – the upright sides of the frame that hide the weights. Part of each pulley stile consists of a removable section of timber called a 'pocket'. This fits flush with the stiles and provides an access hatch to the weights. The pockets are usually screwed into place.

Common problems with sashes are sticking, squeaking, rattling and broken sash cords. Sash windows that stick may have absorbed moisture, swollen and become too thick for the channel, causing the beads to hold the sashes in a vice like grip. The immediate remedy is to prise away the affected bead and re-position it. Paint build-up also causes sashes to stick. Every time you repaint you add a layer. Eventually these layers build up and narrow the channel sufficiently to stop the sash sliding. The only remedy is to scrape away the paint or sand it down to an acceptable thickness, then re-decorate. Rattling sashes, on the other hand, are too loose in the channel formed by the beads. The only true solution is to prise out the beads and re-fit them closer to the sash. Squeaky pulleys can be cured with a tiny drop of oil. Sash cords are a bit like light bulbs – they all seem to 'fail' at the same time. If one sash cord is broken, chances are the others are frayed and about to break as well.

1 Prise off the staff beads
Prise off the staff beads from both sides of the window – there is no need to remove the horizontal beads at the top and bottom. Using an old, broad chisel, start in the middle of the bead and gently prise it away from the main frame by about 25mm (1in). Now tap the bead back into place: the pins securing it should pop up through the surface of the bead and can be removed with pliers. If this fails, use a chisel to lever the end off the beads. Try not to damage the beading as you'll need to re-fit it.

2 Swing the lower sash clear
The lower sash can be swung forwards of the frame and rested on the window sill. If the cords are still intact, cut them, but don't let the weight crash to the bottom of its compartment. Remove any remnants of cord and put the sash safely away so the glass doesn't get broken. Label it as the 'lower sash'. Now prise away the parting bead and free the upper sash as before, cutting any intact cords. Label this the 'upper sash' and put it safely away.

3 Retrieve the weights
Each sash cord is replaced in turn with new damp-proof cord and each is done in the same way. Retrieve the weight from the bottom of its compartment. Access to the weights is through the 'pocket', which may be held in place by a screw. Unscrew and lift out the pocket piece – push a thin-bladed knife down its side and prise it away. Lift out the weight and untie the cord. Brush the weights to remove any rust. Remove any dust from the bottom of the compartment with a vacuum cleaner.

4 Fit the cord

Pass a length of the new cord over one of the outer pulleys at the top of the frame. Chances are it won't drop down under its own weight so improvise with a 'mouse' – a small weight tied to the end of a length of string. The mouse must be small enough to pass over the top of the pulley, yet heavy enough to drop down the compartment. Tie the mouse to the string and the string to the cord and then drop the mouse down into the outer weight compartment. Pull the mouse to pull the cord through, and then fasten the cord to the weight in this compart-ment. Pull on the cord until the weight is just clear of the bottom of its compart-ment. Cut the cord about 150mm (6in) from the top of the pulley. Tie a knot in the top of the cord to stop it slipping through the pulley. Deal with the outer weight on the other side in the same way.

SAFETY FIRST

Sash windows are heavy: get someone to help you lift and hold them in position.

5 Replace the upper sash

Bring the upper sash to the window opening. You will probably need a friend to help you lift it. Draw the knotted end of the cord clear of the pulley to give yourself enough cord to work with. Untie the knot, and fix this free end to the top of the side of the sash. There is usually a groove to hold the cord, which is fixed using three or four 25mm (1in) round wire nails. Nail only the bottom 150mm (6in) of cord, not all the way up. The length of the cord should be such that the weight is just clear of the bottom of its compartment. Don't fix the cord right at the top of the sash or it won't close properly: the top fixing nail should be a little further from the top of the sash than the distance between the top of the pulley and the top of the window opening. Fix the cord on the other side in the same way and place the sash carefully in place in the window opening. Test the sash operation by carefully sliding it vertically. If the sash doesn't slide smoothly and quietly, rub a candle on all the sliding surfaces and very lightly oil the pulleys.

6 Renew the cords on the lower sash

Now replace the cords on the lower sash in the same way. When these are done, place them carefully into the window opening. Replace the pocket pieces and the retaining screws and fix the beading back in place. If the beadings are very worn or they got broken when they were prised off, new beading can be fitted easily. Parting bead is plain and fixed to the sides only. The staff bead, however, is usually more ornate and because it is fixed to the sides and the top and bottom, will need to be matched up, or all four pieces replaced. The beading is simply pinned into place.

BEADING

- Beadings are fragile, so, when fitting new lengths, drill pilot holes for fixing pins to stop the timber splitting.

- Don't use glue when re-fitting beading – it will be impossible to renew sash cords in the future without causing extensive damage to the frame.

STOPPING ROT ON WINDOWSILLS

If windowsills are not protected with paint or varnish, they will rot. Drip channels stop rainwater from running over and under windowsills and back onto the wall under the window opening, where it could cause damp. Drenching should be avoided especially under window openings where moisture could be passed to the frames, causing them to rot. One or more grooves formed during manufacture on the underside of a wooden sill or moulded into a concrete one will stop water reaching the wall. These channels must be kept clean otherwise they won't work properly. If you don't have any drip channels under your sills, it is a good

idea to add some. This can be done in two ways: either get a router and cut a couple of grooves in timber sills, or glue and pin a couple of lengths of half-round mouldings close together underneath the sill. The gap between them forms an effective groove. On concrete sills, use a good, waterproof adhesive.

Small patches of rot should be dealt with immediately to prevent them spreading. Test for rot by pushing a sharp knife into the sill. In sound timber, you will meet with resistance. In rotten wood, the point will easily pass through. Concrete windowsills are also vulnerable. Fill any small cracks with decorator's filler suitable

for outdoor use and paint the sill with masonry or gloss paint to conceal the repair. Fill large holes and cracks with cement – but first treat the crack with a PVA building adhesive. Add some of the adhesive to the mortar as well to make it more workable. Fill deep holes in two stages, smoothing the top 'finishing' coat down flush with the edge of the sill, then disguise the repair with paint. If a concrete sill needs extensive repairs, make a stout timber framework – at least 25mm (1in) thick. Hold the framework in place by nailing it to blocks of wood fixed to the wall with masonry nails. Then fill the inside of the framework with cement to form the sill.

REPAIRING WOODEN WINDOWSILLS

1 Strip the paint and expose the wood
Strip off the paint – but don't use a blow torch or hot air stripper anywhere near glass! If sections of the sill are rotten, cut back to sound wood. Fix new sections with dowels driven into the sill at 100mm (4in) intervals and fit a steel brace underneath to support the repair. Brush all the wood of the sill with a good-quality preservative.

2 Fill splits and cracks
Using a proprietary exterior-grade filler, make good any small cracks and splits in the timber. Check and clean out the drip channel (see above). It is important to make sure the damp-proofing of the joint between the underside of the sill and the wall is fit. Use a gun-applied flexible mastic to make good the join.

3 Prime and paint
Finish the sill by lightly sanding any filler that has dried proud of the surface. Sand it flush, working along the grain of the wood. Prime the sill, then paint using exterior-grade paint (see page 297).

WINDOW LOCKS AND GRILLES

Windows are not only vulnerable to the weather; most burglars break into houses through them. They don't often break the glass because it makes too much noise. Instead they usually force

WARNING

Before you fit security grilles (internal or external), check with your local Fire Officer that their location will not impede your exit in an emergency. Only install approved grilles. You must also check with your local Planning Officer: you may need planning permission to erect external security grilles. On a listed building or in a conservation area, this will probably be refused.

the latch and climb inside. Window catches are easy to open: if you've ever locked yourself out of your home, you'll have been grateful for this, but so will intruders.

For just a few pounds and an hour or so spent in fitting them, security devices fitted to windows – especially those at ground-floor level, or accessible from a drainpipe or flat roof – will be time and money well spent. Check with your local Crime Prevention Officer and your Neighbourhood Watch scheme for advice on approved types.

In extreme circumstances, iron bars or security grilles can be fitted either inside or outside. These should always be fixed on a sliding track so they can be opened and closed.

LOCKABLE CATCHES

For casement windows, there are a variety of lockable catches and devices available that fit on the window stays. For vertical sliding sashes, there are devices that lock the window either when closed or just slightly open.

1 Measure up

While security grilles can be fitted easily, it's a good idea to employ a reputable firm to supply them. That way their design, manufacture and installation will conform to British Safety Standards. Remember to measure the opening, not the window.

2 The grilles

Security grilles are available in a range of styles. The 'bars' need to be close enough together to stop an intruder squeezing through. Make sure the grilles supplied are fitted on sliding tracks so they can be opened, and that they can be locked as well.

3 Mark drill holes

The grille framework is secured to the house wall by brackets screwed into the masonry. Mark the position of the drill holes – avoid drilling into the mortar between brick courses. Drill and plug the holes with rawl plugs.

4 Attach the grille

Following the manufacturer's instructions, attach the grill to the framework with the fixings supplied. Check that the grille slides smoothly on its track.

CURTAIN RAILS

POLES

Poles are available in a range of styles in wood, plastic and metal. While they are generally straight, curved ones can be specially made. Poles are held in place with a bracket at each end, with an extra one in the middle if the pole is 2.4m (8ft) or longer.

TRACKS

Tracks are plastic or metal and can be either straight or curved. Tracks can be wall- or ceiling-mounted and are held in place by brackets spaced at about 300mm (1ft) intervals. A few types of track have no brackets but screw direct to the wall or ceiling.

SUPPORTING BRACKETS

For long runs across big windows or where heavy drapes are being hung, tracks require quite large brackets. These are generally hidden by pelmets or valances. Other types of tracks have concealed fittings, and don't require a pelmet or valance.

FIXING A CURTAIN POLE

1 Position the brackets
Draw a pencil guideline at least 50mm (2in) from the top of the window. Align the pole with the ceiling or the window. Mark drilling points on the line 50mm (2in) from each end. Some pole brackets have their fixing holes above centre on the back of the bracket, so allow for this.

2 Drill at the marked points
Using a masonry bit – or a drill with a hammer action if the lintel is concrete – drill at the marked spots. You need to drill about 38mm (1½in) into the masonry to make the pole secure. The fixing screws supplied with the pole are often too short, so you may have to buy replacements.

3 Screw in the brackets
Offer up the first bracket and screw it into place. On a pole with rings and a finial at each end, slide all but two of the rings onto the pole, then fit the pole. Place a remaining ring at each end of the pole and attach the finial.

4 Tighten remaining screws
There is a small hole under the brackets. Insert the correct-sized screw and drive it in until it bites into the curtain pole. This stops the pole sliding sideways when the curtains are moved. Similar drill holes can be found on the finials to fix them to the end of the poles.

FIXING WINDOW SHUTTERS

Before windows were glazed, shutters were fitted to keep out the weather and to secure buildings from intruders. In the countries in Europe and Scandinavia that have to endure extremely hot or cold temperatures, shutters in various local styles endure.

In Britain, shutters were common in Georgian and Victorian homes where they were generally fitted internally, folding back into retaining boxes at the sides of windows, or in some instances, sliding upwards to cover the lower half of a window. External shutters are either casement openings (hinged vertically on the walls) or are held in a metal groove so they slide across the window. Although many of these original period features have disappeared over time, it is possible to find reproductions as replacements.

1 Mark the position of the battens
Make sure you have safe access if you are working above ground-floor level. Shutters that fold back against the outside wall are attached with battens fixed to the masonry. Measure and mark the position of the battens.

2 Fix the battens to the wall
Using a masonry bit at a slow speed, drill into the masonry wall. Withdraw the drill every 5 seconds to let the tip cool down. If the wall is very hard, use a drill with a hammer action. Plug the holes and attach the battens to the walls securely, checking that they are level.

3 Fix the shutters
Functioning shutters are fixed to the battens with hinges. 'Decorative' shutters are fixed with brackets. Offer up the shutter and fix it to the battens by placing one screw only in each hinge or bracket and tightening. Check for alignment before you screw in the remaining fixings.

LISTED BUILDINGS

One of the anomalies of listed building regulations is that although a property may have had exterior shutters for much of its history, if they weren't there when the property was listed, you might not be allowed to replace them. If you are replacing rotten shutters, they must be in the same style as the originals.

SAFETY FIRST

If you are working at heights above ground level, make sure you follow the safety guidelines for working up ladders (see pages 40–1).

GLAZING

TYPES OF GLASS

Glass is made in a variety of thicknesses and choice depends on the size of the sheet required, the degree of exposure to the wind and the consequent suction loads on the surface. Prior to metrication, glass was sold by weight; now it is sold by thickness. Most domestic glazing uses glass at 4mm (about ⅛in) thick.

Sheet glass

Made in 3 grades: OQ (ordinary quality, used for general glazing purposes); SQ (selected quality); and SSQ (special selected quality). Sheet glass is a clear drawn glass: the opposite side is never completely flat and parallel so some degree of distortion occurs.

Float glass

Made by floating liquid glass over a surface of molten tin. This produces a similar glass to sheet glass, but is free of distortion. It is made in thicknesses from 3mm (⅛in) to 25mm (1in) to produce very strong glass suitable for glazing large picture windows and for glass items such as tabletops. Float glass is available in plain or tinted forms, as well as with decorative finishes produced by acid etching, electro-floating and sandblasting. Mirrors are also made from SQ grade float glass.

Patterned glass

Most often used for 'modesty' glazing in bathrooms or where both light and privacy is needed. A typical patterned glass is 'rough-cast': one side is smooth, the other textured. Available in plain and tinted

versions in thicknesses of 3mm (⅛in) and 5mm (¼in). The degree of transparency and light transfusion depends on the pattern used.

Wired glass

Manufactured with a metal mesh embedded in it, which helps to hold the glass together and reduces the risk of injury from falling glass. It is also accepted as a fire retardant. The mesh may be square (known as 'Georgian') or a diamond pattern. Difficult to cut if re-used, so it's best to buy it cut to size.

Toughened glass

Sheet, float and patterned glass can all be toughened by processes, which increase the strength of the glass by up to five times. Suitable for doors or where there are areas of possible sudden impact, since it shatters into granules rather than sharp shards.

Laminated glass

This safety glass is made by sandwiching a layer of tear-resistant plastic film between sheets of glass. It absorbs the impact of objects hitting it and stops it penetrating the pane. The plastic layer binds together any broken glass fragments, reducing the risk of flying glass injuries.

Solar control glass

Available in a range of colours in float, laminated and patterned forms, it is most used in commercial buildings such as offices because it reduces the transmission of heat, light, and glare from sunlight.

ORDERING GLASS

Measure the height and width of a window opening to the inside of the frame rebate. Take measurements from two points for each dimension and check that the diagonals are the same length. If the frame is out of true, make a template from stiff card. When you order figured glass, always give the height first then the width. This is vital since the pattern should run from top to bottom. If you give the width first, you'll end up with the pattern running horizontally. When you measure an irregular opening, such as an arched window, it's always better to make up a template in stiff cardboard. If the opening is to be glazed with figured glass, mark on the template the side that is to be on the outside of the house.

STORING GLASS

Store glass vertically at an angle of about 25 degrees, never flat on the floor. It should be kept in a dry place leaning on two wooden slats and propped against the wall, with a rag or newspaper underneath the top edge to stop it touching the wall.

HANDLING AND CARRYING

Sturdy gloves must always be worn when handling glass. They should not be too stiff – you need to be able to 'feel' the glass to handle it safely. Carry panes of glass vertically, using newspaper or bicycle inner tubes as 'laps'. Never grip glass tightly. If a pane is too large to be carried under one arm, get someone to help you. Avoid carrying glass up ladders unless it is absolutely necessary.

DOUBLE-GLAZING

FITTING DOUBLE-GLAZING

Most people fit double-glazing because of its insulation benefits, but it also reduces the amount of noise that enters a building. Glass is a good conductor of heat so a lot of internal heat can be lost to the outside. With double-glazing, air is enclosed between two panes of glass. Insulation is improved if the air is 'rarefied' – formed to a weak vacuum. In sealed-unit double-glazing, the two panes of glass are hermetically sealed during manufacture with a gap left between them. The double pane of glass lets the sun's heat enter a room, but stops it getting out. The disadvantage of sealed-unit double-glazing is the cost – particularly if your windows are not standard sizes. While the cost can be re-couped in reduced fuel bills, the 'pay-back time' can be reckoned in years, not months.

Secondary double-glazing is less costly and usually consists of a series of horizontal sliding sashes, which are installed inside the existing windows. While secondary double-glazing does block off draughts coming through gaps around sashes and between the wall and window frame, it also increases the number of windows you'll have to clean.

DIY DOUBLE-GLAZING

A cheaper – albeit temporary – alternative is to buy a DIY film glazing kit. This is simple to install. Double-sided tape is stuck all the way around the window frame and clear insulating film is fixed to the tape. The film is 'shrunk' to fit tightly across the window by heating it with a hair dryer. Although you won't be able to open the window without removing the film, this cheap method is ideal for the winter months – and works a lot better than cling-film.

DRAUGHT PROOFING

Most draughts come from badly fitting doors and windows. However, it is important to remember that insulation does not mean doing without ventilation: all solid fuel and gas appliances need a balanced flow of air. Stopping draughts around windows is easy to do yourself. If you are on a low income, receiving income support or are a pensioner, you may find that your local council will pay for and install draught exclusion for you so check with your local council. If you have a window that is never opened in winter, you can seal the gaps with a clear liquid draught seal. This can be peeled off again in summer without damaging the paintwork.

SELF-ADHESIVE FOAM STRIP

Normally about 6mm (¼in) thick, the strip is cut to length and stuck on the frames after they have been cleaned with warm soapy water. Make sure the strip ends fit snugly into the corners of the frame.

DRAUGHT-PROOFING STRIPS

Made of sprung nylon or metal, these are good for uneven gaps and last longer than foam strips. Most are pre-holed and come with fixing pins. Apply with the raised edge facing away from the window or door.

STAIRCASES

Staircases are subject to a great deal of wear and tear: the 'nosing' – the front edges of treads – can become worn; treads and risers come loose; balusters get damaged or broken and the balustrade starts to wobble dangerously. A staircase may have so many defects that the only solution is complete renewal. If a new staircase is to be fitted into an old house, any replacement will likely be made-to-measure and built on site. If a staircase in a modern house is damaged, you may be able to buy a factory-made replacement. In addition, kits are available to replace existing newel posts, centres and decorative knobs, base rail and spacer fillets, balusters and handrails. The photographs here show a close string balustrade with parallel long edges.

1 Preparation

Remove the old balustrade. Cut the base of the bottom newel post at a height 200mm (8in) above the pitch line, straight up from the nosing. Cut the top newel post 123mm (4⅞in) above the pitch line. Intermediate newels should be cut to 191mm (7½in) above the nosing.

2 Drilling the newels

Mark diagonal lines across the cut ends of the newel posts to find their centres. Drill out 50mm (2in) diameter holes in the centre to take the spigots of the new newels. Check the length of the spigots and mark the drill bit with a piece of tape so you drill to the required depth.

3 Finishing the cut ends

After the spigot holes have been drilled on all the newels, use a plane to finish the cut ends of the post to a convex contour. Set the new newel posts into position but do not glue them in.

4 Take the angle of the stair string

Using an adjustable bevel, take the angle of the stair string where it meets the base of the newel. Hold the balustrade base rail against the stair and mark on it where it meets the newels. Mark cutting lines at these points and cut the rail to length. Mark and cut the handrail.

5 Fix the base rail to the string

First, fix the balustrade base rail to the string with screws. Then fix the bolted handrail brackets into the posts and tighten them by hand with a spanner. Use a spirit level to check that all the posts are upright.

6 Glue the posts into place

Once the posts are upright and the rails fit properly, glue the posts into place using a gap-filling powder-resin glue or a PVA woodworking adhesive. Tighten up the bolts fully and when the adhesive is fully set, fit the cover buttons to conceal the nuts.

7 Fitting the balusters

Measure the vertical distance between the groove in the handrail and the groove in the base rail. Transfer this measurement to a baluster and mark it. Use the adjustable bevel to get the correct angle. Cut the baluster to size, check for fit, and then cut the others.

8 Spacing the balusters

Using pre-cut spacer fillets, space the balusters out equally along the entire run. Balusters must not be spaced more than 100mm (4in) apart in order to comply with current Building Regulations.

9 Fix the balusters and fillets

Using glue and pins, fix the balusters and the spacer fillets into position. Wipe off any excess adhesive immediately. When the glue has dried completely, the balustrade is ready for finishing. Lightly rub down the woodwork in the direction of the grain, varnish or prime and paint.

BUILDING REGULATIONS

- Staircases are subject to stringent Building Regulations:

- The minimum depth of stair treads – the bit you step on – is 220mm (8¾in).

- The height of a balustrade must not be less than 840mm (2ft 9in) or higher than 1m (3ft 3in). The height is calculated vertically from the pitch line – the 'invisible' line made by the stair nosings (the front edge of stair treads).

- The spaces between balusters must not exceed 100mm (4in).

- In private residential dwellings, a stair must have two handrails – one at each side – if the stair is more than 1m (3ft 3in) wide. On the wall side, the distance between it and the handrail should be no less than 50mm (2in).

- Modern staircases have fewer balusters than older ones; you should never alter the number because you risk weakening the whole structure.

- You will need the equivalent of two balusters per stair tread and one for the tread next to the newel. To calculate the number of spacer fillets needed, simply double the number of balusters and then add four.

FITTING STAIR CARPET

Stair carpet should be appropriate for heavy use (see pages 86–9). To prevent it wearing out too quickly, add an extra 460mm (1ft 6in) to the length and turn it under and onto the bottom step. Every nine months, shift the carpet up each stair tread by 75–100mm (3–4in) until the 460mm (1ft 6in) has been used up. After that, return the carpet to its original position, and continue to move it up as before. That way you'll avoid frayed edges on the 'nosings' of the treads for much longer. For maximum wear, lay stair carpet with the pile facing down the stairs.

MEASURING

To find the length, measure the depth of one tread – the bit you stand on – and the height of one riser – the flat bit at the back of the tread. Add the two together. Multiply by the number of stairs then add on the extra 460mm (1ft 6in). If your staircase bends, calculate the total carpet length as above, then measure each winding tread separately at the widest point.

FIXING

Strip carpets were traditionally held in position by wooden or metal stair rods. Gripper strips provide a 'tackless' system – it is the strips that are nailed to the treads and not the carpet. These are acceptable but can loosen and slip after a while. The most secure method of fixing on stairs is to tack the carpet down. You can use a staple gun to hold the carpet in position as you lay it, but then make it more secure by adding tacks spaced every 73mm (3in) across the treads.

1 Start at the bottom tread

Start at the bottom with the carpet lying face down on the first tread. Fix the back edge to the tread with a gripper strip or tacks. Stretch the carpet back towards you, over the nosing of the first tread and tack it to the bottom of the riser. Run the carpet up the stairs, pushing it firmly into each gripper strip with a bolster or adding tacks.

2 Carpeting a landing

At the top of the stairs there may be a landing that you wish to carpet as well. To avoid causing a trip hazard and to make the carpeting appear seamless, lay the carpet on the landing and bring the edge over the nosing of the tread, down the riser and a little way along the next tread down. Staple temporarily into position before tacking permanently.

3 Joining the carpet

Bring the stair carpet up to meet the riser of the landing. The two edges should be 'joined', with the stair carpet edge on top, and laid across the joint in the tread and riser.

4 Neaten the join

Use a bolster to press the carpet well onto the gripper strips at the base of the risers and to tuck in any of the folded-over carpet edges.

FIREPLACES

INSTALLING A FIREBACK

Years of intense heat damages firebacks, and cracks can let smoke and heat get behind the fireplace and weaken the brickwork of the chimney. Small cracks can be repaired: first let the fire back cool down for 48 hours before brushing away soot and dirt with a wire brush. Clean out the cracks with a sharp pointed tool, undercutting their sides to make an inverted 'V' shape. Brush out the debris and soak the area thoroughly with water. While the cracks are still wet, fill them with fire cement, available from builder's merchants or DIY stores. Use a small trowel and work the cement well into the cracks and trowel off any surplus. Smooth the filled surface with a paintbrush and clean water. Leave the cement to dry for several days before you light a fire.

If you have to replace the old fire back, do it in summer so the new one can dry out. Measure the width across its mouth and order a new one: standard sizes are 400mm (1ft 6in) and 450mm (1ft 8in). Cover the floor and hearth. Remove the grate: it may be resting on the back hearth or screwed down and sealed to the fire back with asbestos rope. Take out the screws, chip away the cement, and then, starting in one corner, attack the old fire back with a hammer and chisel. Take care not to damage the fire surround. Take out the fire back but leave the asbestos rope where it is. Clear out the rubble in the space behind to reveal the original brick lined opening. Clean up thoroughly.

New firebacks are supplied in one piece but these need to be separated into two for insertion. Using a bolster chisel and a hammer, tap very gently along the recessed line across it.

1 Placing the bottom piece
Mix up a mortar of four parts vermiculite to one part lime or cement. Trowel a layer of the mortar around the rear edge of the back hearth to make a bed for the lower portion of the fireback to sit on. Ease it into place, pulling it forwards so it compresses the asbestos rope packing at the edge of the surround. Cut two pieces of cardboard to the shape of the fireback bottom and place them immediately behind it.

2 Fill up the area behind the back
Fill up the whole area behind the fire back with mortar, using some rubble or bits of broken old fireback as in-fill. Use a piece of wood to tamp it well down as you go. Bring the mortar and rubble mix up level with the top edge of the fireback's bottom portion. Trowel a layer of mortar along the top edge of the fireback bottom portion.

3 Fitting the upper portion
Set the top portion of the fireback onto the layer of mortar on the top edge of the bottom portion. Fill up the space behind the fireback with more mortar and rubble. The slope from the top of the fireback to the rear of the chimney must run parallel to the slope of the rear edge of the load-bearing lintel that runs across the top of the fire opening. Trowel the flaunching smooth. Seal the fireback to the fire surround with fire cement.

FITTING A PERIOD-STYLE FIREPLACE

1 Strip off plaster

To install a period-style fireplace, you first have to strip off the plaster from round the fire opening. Strip off 50mm (2in) wider all round than the surround. Use a chisel to chip away the plaster and wear safety goggles to protect your eyes. Undercut the edge of the palster with the bloster, brush out the debris and dampen the area with a wet brush.

2 The hearth

The grate must stand on a level hearth. The existing back hearth will probably be fine, but if the previous hearth – often a ceramic tiled platform – has been removed, you'll have to install a new one (see box). If you have to build the hearth to the required size, check under adjacent floorboards first to make sure there are no pipes or cables.

3 Build up new hearth

The new hearth can be made of stone, brick, paving tiles or glazed ceramic tiles bedded onto concrete. Bed the hearth on dabs of mortar made of three parts sand to one part water. Even if you don't intend to burn solid fuel and the fire surround is purely decorative, it's a good idea to make the hearth fireproof so that the overall design is balanced.

HEARTHS

- Plaster fire surrounds can be fixed to walls with mortar or plaster. Apply to the wall and prop the surround up with battens while it dries.

- Building regulations require hearths to be at least 50mm (2in) thick and extend 300mm (1ft) in front of the grate and at least 225mm (9in) at each side of the fire opening – or the width of the fire surround, whichever is the greater.

4 The centrepiece

If the surround includes a cast-iron centrepiece, fit this first. Some just sit on the back hearth; others have lugs for screwing them to the wall (use metal wall plugs). Fit lengths of asbestos-substitute packing as expansion joints where the grate touches the fireback.

5 Install the surround

Offer up the fireplace surround and hold it level. Mark the wall for the screws and drill them. Fix the surround and check again for level. Where necessary, fit small wooden wedges behind the surround to level it. Make good any plaster on surrounding walls.

RENOVATING FIREPLACE SURROUNDS

MARBLE

1 Prepare the surface

Wash the marble down with warm, soapy water. Patch any small chips with putty made from kaolin powder – a fine white clay used in the manufacture of porcelain – and epoxy glue. Both of these are available from good DIY merchants.

2 Fill cracks

Fill the chips or cracks, allow to dry, and then rub down with a silicon carbide paper. Maintain the marble with regular gentle cleaning and polishing with a chamois leather. Keep it gleaming so it reflects the light cast by the flames of an open fire.

CAST IRON

Many cast-iron fireplaces have been painted white because they were considered too dark for modern interiors. A lot of Victorian and Edwardian homes just have one remaining fireplace – often a smaller bedroom fireplace called a 'Register'. Now the fashion in interiors has come full circle, the aim is to restore the cast iron to its former ornate glory. Stripped of paint and sealed with iron paste, cast iron becomes a silvery graphite colour.

It is possible to have cast iron professionally stripped, but this can be expensive and is a dirty job best done outside. For the DIY enthusiast there are blanket stripping kits, which include a chemical stripper attached to a 'blanket' of laminated paper and a neutralizer. Cast iron is quite soft and easily scratched, so scraping off paint is out of the question. Any chemicals used must be neutralized so they don't spoil the metal. Treat the stripped cast iron with a rust con-verter, which also acts as an inhibitor. Apply the iron paste with a brush and buff it to a bright sheen.

WOOD

Wooden fire surrounds are ideal for creating cosy, country-cottage interiors. Even when no fire is lit, the warm tones of natural wood make the hearth the focus of the room. Stripping wood is quite straight-forward (see pages 230–1) but remember that chemical strippers leach the natural oils from wood and dry them out. This is one of the drawbacks of acid stripping, where large wooden items such as doors, tables and fire surrounds are dipped into vats.

Exposed grains can be maintained and enhanced with a good wax polish, and any cracks or splits in the wood can be filled with a wood filler tinted with a little wood stain to match the surround. If a wooden fire surround is used with an open fire, you will need to maintain it regularly or the heat of the fire will dry it out. Wooden fireplace surrounds can also be treated to a variety of finishes to compliment your interior decor scheme. For more information on paint effects see pages 302–5.

Contents

2

PLUMBING

TOOLS & MATERIALS

In addition to the usual measuring and marking tools (rules, pencil, spirit level) and items like abrasive papers, a few more tools and items are required for undertaking routine plumbing work:

• A plunger is the first (and often the only) tool you'll need to clear a blocked sink or WC.

• You'll need a screwdriver to take out the screws that hold the sections of taps together.

• Two adjustable spanners are needed to tighten fittings. The most useful sizes are either 255mm (10¼in) or 350mm (14in) long.

• In situations where heavily corroded pipe fittings have to be removed, a pair of Stilson wrenches will let you clamp securely on one side of the pipe while you manipulate the other section of pipe with the other wrench.

• Pipes can be cut either with a rotary pipe cutter or a hacksaw. The standard hacksaw is either 255mm (10¼in) or 305mm (12¼in) long. Copper pipe is quite soft and easy to cut. You can use low-tungsten steel blades for this, but a stainless steel high-speed blade will be more durable, if more expensive. For pipes over 15mm (¾in), a blade with 32 teeth to each 25mm (1in) should be used. A junior hacksaw is useful for most pipe cutting as it can cut in awkward spaces more easily. Blades should be fitted with the teeth pointing *away* from the handle. Adjust the wing nut on the hacksaw to take up the slack in the blade and then give the wing nut *only three full turns;* don't over-tighten it.

• When you cut pipe, you need to secure it firmly. Use a pipe vice, or lightweight portable vice. Don't over-tighten the jaws or you may distort the pipe.

• If you have a large amount of cutting to do, consider investing in a rotary pipe cutter. These cut fast and accurately. There are two main types: one with two rollers and a cutter, and one with three cutters. Rotary cutters have three toughened wheels – one is the cutting wheel – mounted on a frame to form a triangle. These can be used on pipe of various diameters because the cutting wheel is fixed on an adjustable threaded spindle.

• Depending on whether or not you are using a hacksaw or a rotary pipe cutter, you will need a flat and a round file. If you are using a hacksaw, run the flat file across the face of the cut to remove any irregularities and then slightly chamfer the outer pipe ends; this will make it easier to connect fittings. Use the round file to remove the burrs from inside the mouth of the cut.

• Bending springs and bending machines (bought or hired) are the best at bending copper pipe. When you make bends, especially in small fittings such as 15mm (¾in) elbows, they should be used sparingly as water turbulence and pressure loss can result at such joints as water tries to negotiate its way through. Bending springs are pieces of tough coiled steel which stop the pipe from being flattened when it is bent. Insert them into the pipe, with the middle of the spring roughly where the point of the bend is to be. Next, bend the pipe: small bore copper pipe is easy to bend across your knee. Larger bore pipe may be harder to bend: drill a hole in a piece of stout wood that can be held securely in a vice. Thread the pipe through the hole and then bend it. If you over-bend the pipe the spring will get stuck: unbend the pipe a little or insert a screwdriver into the eye of the spring and turn in order to 'unscrew' it. If you have a lot of pipe bending to do it's best to hire a bending machine. Tighter, more precise bends are the result. Plastic pipe is not easy to bend so add elbow fittings.

• For capillary connections (see page 151) you'll need a Butane gas torch, plumbing lead, 'mole' tallow, solder, flux and fine wire wool.

• Thread connections will leak unless they are made watertight. Some plumbers use plumbers' hemp with jointing compound but PTFE tape is more usual. This is white plastic tape that is wound around the thread of fittings in an anti-clockwise direction to seal and lubricate the joint. If you are installing plastic pipes for water supply, these are joined by a solvent weld using a non-toxic cement.

TOOLBOX

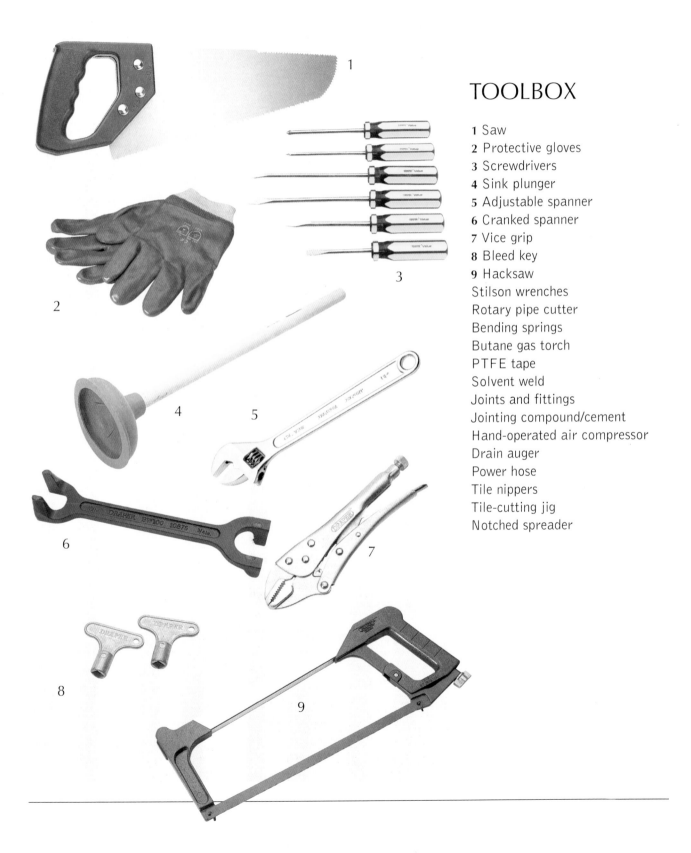

TOOLBOX

1 Saw
2 Protective gloves
3 Screwdrivers
4 Sink plunger
5 Adjustable spanner
6 Cranked spanner
7 Vice grip
8 Bleed key
9 Hacksaw
Stilson wrenches
Rotary pipe cutter
Bending springs
Butane gas torch
PTFE tape
Solvent weld
Joints and fittings
Jointing compound/cement
Hand-operated air compressor
Drain auger
Power hose
Tile nippers
Tile-cutting jig
Notched spreader

PLUMBING SYSTEMS IN THE HOUSE

THE RISING MAIN

The main 'artery' of any household's plumbing systems is the service pipe, more commonly known as the rising main. This connects the domestic plumbing system to the local water authority's mains which runs under the pavements. The householder's responsibility for the rising main begins at the water authority's stop-cock, usually found in a pit in the footpath outside the house, which can only be turned on or off with one of the authority's special shanked turn-keys. The rising main may be of lead in older buildings but most authorities have now replaced these with copper.

The rising main enters the house through the kitchen floor, generally under the sink. Just above the floor, at the base of the pipe, is the house-holder's stopcock. This is often combined with a drain cock that will allow you to drain the rising main if you need to. Stop cocks have arrows engraved on their bodies, pointing to the line of flow.

DIRECT AND INDIRECT SYSTEMS

In many older properties, mains water is supplied under mains pressure to all cold water taps and WCs, while hot water is fed indirectly from a storage cistern via the hot water cylinder. This is known as a direct system. It has the advantage that pure, clean drinking water can be drawn from any cold tap in the house and, because the storage tank in the direct system only has to provide water for the hot water system, it only needs to be a small one, holding 114 litres (25 gallons) and taking up very little space.

Most modern homes, however, are plumbed using the indirect system.

Water under mains pressure enters the house through a service pipe and goes via a rising main directly into a cold water storage cistern which is normally situated in the roof space. A branch pipe from the rising main supplies pure drinking and cooking water to the kitchen sink only. (Another pipe may be 'teed off' from the rising main to supply water to an outside tap or garage and, if this is the case in your home, this pipe should also have its own stopcock to enable you to turn off the external water supply and drain the pipe during frosty weather.) All the other cold taps are fed indirectly and under gravity pressure from the storage cistern.

The storage cistern also supplies cold water to the hot water storage cistern which is heated either indirectly by the central heating system or by electric immersion heaters. Hot water is drawn off from the top of the cylinder to hot water taps in the kitchen and bathroom. The indirect system needs a larger cistern of at least 227 litres (50 gallons) capacity. Older cisterns were made of galvanized steel, but today most are made of reinforced plastic or polythene, which are lighter and not subject to corrosion.

DRAINAGE

Drainage falls into two categories: that above and that below ground. The drainage system above ground consists of pipework from sinks, WCs, baths and gutters.

Below ground, the services are known collectively as 'drains'. Where a house is drained individually, the

entire system, up to where it joins the sewer, is the responsibility of the householder. Where a house is connected to a communal drainage system linking several houses, the arrangements for maintenance are not quite so clear cut. If the drains were constructed before 1937, the local authority is responsible for cleansing, but it can also reclaim the costs of repairs to the communal system from the householders. If the drains were constructed after 1937, the entire responsibility for repairs, cleansing and maintenance falls to the householders collectively.

Fitted to the pipes entering the drains are 'traps'. These act as water seals which prevent foul sewage air entering your home. The simplest form of trap is the familiar 'U'-bend in the pipe which is designed to contain water after the appliance has been used. Your lavatory also has a built-in trap. Baths, basin and sinks have traps fitted between them and their waste outlets. Because of their shapes, traps with horizontal outlets are called P-traps and those with vertical outlets are called 'S'-traps. The seal of the trap is the vertical distance between the normal water level in the trap and the upper part of the 'U'-bend. In a two-pipe drainage system traps normally have a 50mm (2in) seal while in the single-stack system the traps need deeper seals of 75mm (3in).

Depending on how old your house is, it will either have a two-pipe or a single-stack system. The two pipe-system is the older type and is more common, but similar methods are still used to maintain both systems.

GUTTERS AND DOWN PIPES

Rainwater is collected in the gutters along the line of your roof and is discharged into drainpipes. In some areas, householders are encouraged to collect rainwater in water butts for use in the garden, or they may be required to provide a soakaway to limit the amount of rainwater that collects on the surface of ground.

A soakaway is a pit not less than 3m (10ft) from the house, about 1.5m (5ft) or more deep and 1.5m sq. (5sq.ft) in plan. You can also buy perforated concrete rings from most builders' merchants with a cover to fit into your

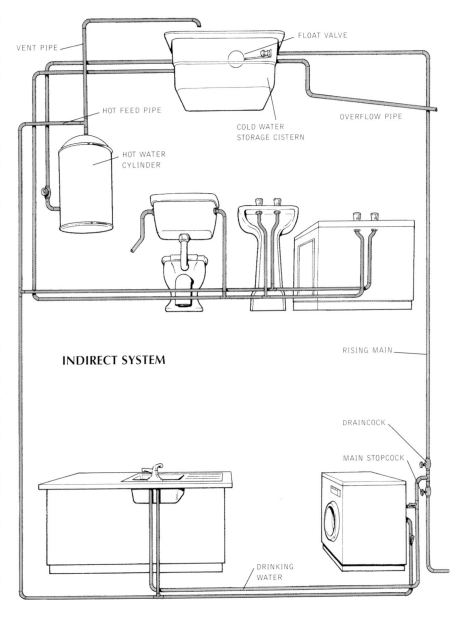

INDIRECT SYSTEM

pit. In either case, the pit is then filled to within about 300mm (12in) of the surface with hard-core and the surface soil is replaced. Under the gully there is a pipe which collects the rainwater and feeds it to the soakaway, which then allows it to slowly percolate into the soil.

CESSPOOLS AND SEPTIC TANKS

Not all country homes are connected to public sewers. Instead, waste is drained into a cesspool or septic tank. Current building regulations stipulate that cesspools should have a minimum capacity of 18cu.m (4000 gallons) but many older properties have much smaller ones that require pumping out every two weeks or so.

A septic tank is a complete waste disposal system in which the sewage is broken down very efficiently by bacterial action. A heavy sludge falls to the bottom of the tank while the relatively clear water with a thin layer of scum, floats on top. A dip-pipe discharges waste below the surface so that incoming water does not stir up the sewage.

The bacteria take around 24 hours to do their magic, so septic tanks are divided into chambers by baffles to slow down the movement of sewage through the tank. Partly treated waste passes through another dip-pile into a filtration system which allows more bacterial action to take place before the water is discharged into a local waterway or is distributed underground, through a network of drains which allow the water to filter through the soil.

DRAINING THE SYSTEM

Before you can work on any part of a plumbing system – even if you just want to change a washer on a tap – you will have to turn off and drain the water from it. A really useful DIY tip is to divide the system into relatively short runs of pipe by adding valves. See page 152 for advice.

DRAINING COLD WATER TAPS AND PIPES

Turn off the main stopcock to cut off the supply to the kitchen tap and every other cold tap on a direct system. Next, open the tap until the water stops flowing. To isolate bathroom taps, you'll need to close

the valve on the appropriate cold feed pipe from the storage cistern and turn on all the taps in that section. Don't panic if you can't find the valve: rest a length of wood across the top of the cistern and tie the arm of the float valve to it. This will shut off the supply to the cistern so you can empty it by running all the cold taps in the bathroom. If you can't get into the loft, turn off the main stopcock then turn on all the cold taps.

DRAINING HOT WATER TAPS AND PIPES

First of all, turn off all immersion heaters or boilers. Next, close the valve on the cold feed pipe to the cylinder and run the hot taps. Notice that even when the water stops flowing from the taps, the cylinder will still be full. Again, if you can't find the valve on the cold feed pipe, tie up the float valve arm, then turn on the cold bathroom taps to empty the storage cistern.

If you have a direct system, you have to drain the system by running the hot taps. But if you have an indirect system, if you run the hot taps first, the water that is stored in the cistern will flush out all your hot water from the cylinder.

When the cold taps run dry, open the hot taps. In an emergency, run the hot and cold taps together to clear the pipes as quickly as possible.

DRAINING A LAVATORY CISTERN

The simplest way to drain the cistern alone is to tie up the float valve arm and flush. If you need to empty the pipe supplying water to the cistern, either turn off the main stopcock in a direct system or, in an indirect system, close the valve on the cold feed from the storage cistern.

Alternatively, you could once again tie up the float valve arm on the storage cistern and empty all the water out through the cold taps. Keep flushing the lavatory until no more water enters its cistern.

DRAINING THE COLD WATER STORAGE CISTERN

First of all, you need to close the main stopcock on the rising main. Next, open up all the cold water taps in the bathroom. (If you have a direct system, then you need to open the hot taps.) At the bottom of the cistern will be the residue of water, which you will need to bail out.

DRAINING THE HOT WATER CYLINDER

If your hot water cylinder has sprung a leak, or you are intending to replace it, the first thing to do is to switch off any immersion heaters or boilers. Next, shut off the cistern's cold water supply, or drain the cold water cistern. Turn on all the hot taps and drain out the water.

If your hot water is heated by an immersion heater only, you should find the drain cock on the cold feed pipe just before it enters the cylinder. Attach a hose to this and drain the water still in the cylinder into the closest drain or sink situated at a lower level.

If your hot water is heated by a boiler that is not part of the central heating system, empty the cistern with a hose from the drain cock which is on the return pipe next to the boiler.

If your hot water is heated by a central heating system, you will need to empty the cylinder via the drain cock on the cold feed pipe from the storage cistern. The primary circuit, which heats both the central heating radiators and the heat exchanger in the cylinder, are still filled with water. (The primary circuit is drained from the drain cock next to the boiler.) If you don't need to empty the radiators, shut off both valves on them.

If after all this you discover that there aren't any drain cocks, don't panic. You can still drain the hot water cylinder by disconnecting the vent pipe. The vent pipe is the pipe that enters the top of the cylinder vertically. This pipe allows for the expansion of heated water and to vent air from the system. To drain the cylinder, disconnect the vent pipe and siphon the water out of the cylinder with a hose pipe.

PLUMBING REGULATIONS

Whenever you modify existing plumbing or install new plumbing, your local water authority requires that certain regulations are observed. These regulations have been designed to safeguard public health and reduce water wastage. If you are making straightforward replacements, you won't have any problems, but if you are planning on adding an extra bathroom or WC, you must seek advice from your water provider and your local council. You must also ensure that you do not contravene electrical regulations. All metal plumbing must be bonded to the Electricity Board's earth terminal near your meter. If you intend to replace a section of metal pipe with plastic you may in fact break the path to the earth, so you will need to make sure that you reinstate the link. Information on the earthing system is given on page 190, but if you are in any doubt whatsoever, you must consult a qualified electrician.

REPAIRS AND MAINTENANCE

PIPES – TYPES AND JOINTS

Many different materials have been used over the years for domestic pipework, so you may find various combinations of pipe materials in your home. While lead is no longer used for modern plumbing, many homes still have a lead rising main. This is fine, but any other lead plumbing should be replaced. Cast iron was most often used for soil pipes, and when these have rusted through they are generally replaced by plastic versions. Copper tubing is probably the most extensively used material: lightweight, easy to solder and bend,

it can be used for both hot and cold water supplies. Three sizes are used in domestic plumbing: 15mm (½in), 22mm (¾in) and 28mm (1in). Brass is used to make compression joints, taps, and stopcocks. Plastic pipes are a recent introduction and as yet, unstandardized, but they are cheap, lightweight, do not freeze or corrode, or affect other materials (copper joined to galvanized steel and brass to copper produce an electro-chemical action which causes corrosion), and depending on the types, can be used for both hot and cold water systems.

While copper pipes can be bent, with plastic pipes pre-shaped sections have to be inserted. It is necessary to use a 'fitting' in the following situations: when two lengths of pipe have to be joined in a straight line; to allow the introduction of a branch connection; to allow for a change of direction; to control the flow of water; and to release air and drain off water. There are three types of fitting: straight coupling; bent coupling or elbow; and branch fitting, and there are two types of pipe connectors: compression joints and capillary joints.

CAPILLARY JOINTS

These joints are soldered: the small space between the pipe and the 'sleeve' is filled with molten solder which solidifies and holds the joint together in a watertight seal. There are two types of capillary joints: in an end feed joint, solder is introduced into the mouth of the end feed joint and flows by capillary action into the fitting; the integral ring fitting already contains solder in a reservoir or 'ring'.

BENDS, OR ELBOWS

The direction of a copper pipe can be changed by bending it. Sometimes bends or elbows are used to join two pipes at 45 degrees or 90 degrees. At the lesser angle, the joint may be a capillary joint, but at 90 degrees, the joint will be a compression joint. A wrench is used to tighten a cap nut, and a ring of soft metal called an 'olive' is compressed to fill the joint between the fitting and pipe.

JOINTS

As well as bends or elbows, capillary and compression joints are used to connect pipes at various angles and in different combinations. Typical examples are straight connectors (for joining pipes in a straight line); tees (to join three pipes); and adaptors (to join pipes of different materials such as copper to galvanized steel, and to join new metric pipes to old imperial-sized ones).

SAFETY FIRST

- Never rest a lighted blowtorch on the floor or other surface. It may fall over. Always extinguish the flame and re-light as required.

- Hold a ceramic tile or a plumber's fibreglass mat behind the pipes to be soldered to deflect the heat away from flammable materials such as floorboards located behind or under pipes.

- Use long steady strokes when cutting pipe. Never start a new blade in an old cut or you could fracture the blade.

FITTINGS

Fittings are jointing systems used for connecting pipes, such as the bib tap pictured above. Other fittings in domestic plumbing include tank connectors (for joining pipes to cisterns); tap connectors (for joining a supply pipe to a tap or faucet); drain cocks (to empty pipes); and gate valves (a hand-operated on-off valve). See page 373 for advice on how metrication affects plumbing fittings.

SOLDERING CAPILLARY JOINTS

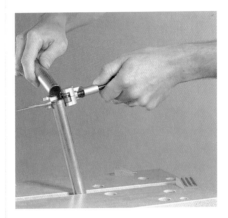

1 Measure and cut

Carefully measure the length of pipe needed, allowing extra for the entry into the fitting. With the pipe held securely – but don't apply so much pressure that it is distorted – cut the pipe squarely with a fine-toothed hacksaw, or rotate a pipe cutter around the tube.

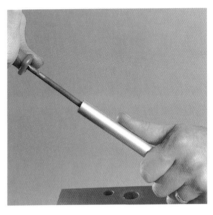

2 Remove burrs

Remove burrs on the cut end. Some makes of pipe cutter have a blade at the end to remove burrs, but if you've cut the pipe with a hacksaw, remove the burrs with a round file. Clean the outside with a file, making sure the ends are square. Clean the end of the fitting.

3 Adding flux

Copper must be clean and grease-free for a perfect soldered joint, so flux (a chemical cleaner) is applied to the metal to make a barrier against oxidization until solder is applied. Coat the ends of the pipe and fitting with flux then push the pipes into the fittings up to the stop.

4 Apply heat

For an integral ring joint, play the flame of the torch evenly around until a bright ring of solder appears at each end. For end-feed joints, heat the flux until it bubbles, then touch the end of the solder wire around the mouth of each sleeve until a bright ring appears all round.

JOINING PLASTIC PIPES

Plastic piping has several advantages over copper: it is less prone to 'furring up'; it won't burst if water freezes in it; and it offers good insulation – though it should still be lagged to improve it further. Its disadvantage is that it cannot withstand high temperatures. Do not use plastic pipe within 380mm (15in) of a boiler; link it to a copper pipe at that point (using special adaptors). Because it will melt, you cannot solder joints with a blowtorch. And because it is rigid, plastic pipe cannot be bent like copper tubing.

Instead, where a pipe needs a change of direction, bends and elbows will need to be inserted.

Although they are not as small as capillary joints, they have the advantage of being easy to fit. To make joints watertight, a variety of methods are used with plastic pipes. When using solvent welds, follow the manufacturer's instructions and use only the recommended solvents and lubricants. Straight runs of pipes can be joined with a socketed connector and then solvent welded, fusing the pipe and connector into a solid unit. There are also push-fit systems, some with a rubber seal in each socket that holds the pipe in place in the connector. These are for use with waste systems which are not under pressure. Other push-fit systems are designed for use with supply pipes, where water is under pressure. An 'O'-ring seals in the water as usual, but a metal grab ring behind the seal has barbed teeth pointing in one direction. The pipe can slide in, but can't be pulled out again.

1 Measure and cut

Measure the length of pipe needed and allow a little extra to fit into the sleeve of the connector. Cut the pipe with a fine-toothed hacksaw, making sure the cut is square. Revolve the pipe away from you as you cut. Smooth off any burrs with a file. Push the pipe into the sleeve to test for fit, then mark where the sleeve comes up to on it with a pencil (as the guide for applying solvent). Key the outside of the pipe with fine abrasive paper. Following the manufacturer's instructions, paint solvent onto the end of the pipe up to your drawn guideline.

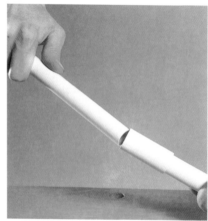

2 Push home the join

As soon as the solvent has been applied, push the pipe into the socket. Follow the manufacturer's instructions – some suggest that you twist the pipe a little to spread the solvent evenly. Align the joint correctly and leave for the recommended time. The solvent works by dissolving the surface of the 'mating' components. As it evaporates, the joint and pipe are 'welded' together into one piece of plastic to make the join completely watertight. However, you will have to wait some time before you can run water through these joins.

SINK, BATH AND BASIN TRAPS

In order to dismantle them easily, sink, bath and basin traps – the 'U'-shaped pipe that stops waste water returning back up into the sink or bath – are connected to the pipe work by compression joints that incorporate a rubber ring or washer to make the joint watertight. Like any other washer, these can degrade over time, and require replacing. Replacement washers are widely available, but make sure you buy the correct size.

FROZEN AND BURST PIPES

NAILING THROUGH A PIPE

Nailing a loose floorboard back into position can have serious consequences if you hadn't realized that there was a pipe run underneath. If you do nail through a pipe, leave the nail there. If you have already pulled it out, put it back. Water will still leak but only slowly, causing less immediate damage. Switch off the water supply feeding the pipe and make a repair.

SOLVENT WELD

If you are joining plastic pipes with solvent weld, be aware that is is highly flammable. Close the tin after use as it evaporates quickly. You'll need to work fast as solvent welds set firm in minutes – although it doesn't achieve its full strength for 24 hours, so avoid testing pipes with water for a least a day. Before joining water supply pipes, clean the inside of the fitting and outside the pipe with special cleaning fluid.

SEALING A LEAK

Leaks caused by splits or holes in copper pipes should be permanently repaired by inserting a new section of pipe. But until you can do this, make emergency repairs. Drain the pipe. Cut a length of garden hose to cover the leak. Slit the hose lengthways to cover the pipe – put the slit of the hose on the opposite side of the pipe to the hole, and bind it with two or three jubilee clips or wire loops twisted tight with pliers. Alternatively, use two-part epoxy putty. Clean the pipe on either side of the hole with wire wool, mix the putty and press it into the hole, building it up to a thickness of between 3–6mm (⅛–¼in). Let the putty 'cure' then bind the repair with self-adhesive tape. The only other reason for a leak is a mechanical failure at a joint. A 'weeping' compression joint can often be cured by tightening the nut that seems to be leaking by a quarter-turn. Use two spanners – one to hold the joint body firm, the other to turn the nut. Beware: over-tightening may crush the olive and the joint will have to be replaced with a new one.

LAGGING PIPES

One of the most common plumbing problems is caused by water freezing in pipes. Plastic pipes won't burst, but copper ones will. Cold water pipe runs in unheated areas of the house should be lagged. Foam-backed plastic tubing, available in different diameters, is sold pre-slit for fitting, and simply slips around the pipe. Successive lengths should be butted end to end and sealed with a PVC adhesive tape. In winter, don't forget to lag any runs of exterior pipes that feed outdoor taps.

SAFETY FIRST

- Water and electricity are a lethal combination. If you have a leak or burst, switch off and unplug any nearby electrical items.

- If you suspect that water has dripped into sockets or onto electrical cables, switch the electricity off at the mains immediately.

BLOCKAGES IN DRAINAGE

TOP: Hand-operated air compressors work in the same way as old-fashioned plungers: they clear any blocked waste with compressed air created by a pumping action, without blowing apart push-fit joints.

ABOVE: A drain auger is a flexible coiled wire that will pass through small diameter pipes to clear blockages. The corkscrew-like head is passed through the pipe until it reaches the blockage, the cranked handle is clamped on and then turned to rotate the corkscrew head to engage with the blockage. The auger is pushed and pulled until the pipe is clear.

SINKS

A choked wastepipe from a sink, basin or bath is indicated by slow or non-running waste water when the plug is removed. The first thing to do to try and clear the blockage is to use a plunger. The 'old fashioned' plunger is a simple – yet effective – hemisphere of thick rubber attached to a wooden handle. There are also modern variations including hand-operated air compressors, but essentially they all operate in the same way. Hold a damp cloth firmly against the overflow outlet with one hand and, with the other hand, place the rubber cup of the plunger or compressor over the waste outlet (plug hole) and plunge down sharply on the handle a few times.

If plunging doesn't clear the blockage, then it's likely that a solid object is lodged in the trap (the 'U'-shaped pipe under the sink). There are a number of ways to tackle this. Place a bucket under the basin or sink to catch the water. At the base of the trap, you will find a cleaning eye (use a wrench to release this) or a bottle trap on which the whole base unscrews. Let the contents of the drain fall into the bucket. Bend a hook on a length or wire – a coat hanger is ideal – and gently probe the section of pipe beyond the trap.

If the pipe is clear but the blockage is still intact, then it's in the branch of horizontal pipe running to the soil stack or outside to the vertical wastepipe. You may have an access plug in the joint to the horizontal pipe: if so, probe again with the wire. If you have no access plug, or the blockage seems very firm, then you can rent a drain auger to clear it.

WCs

When a WC pan fails to clear, it's not necessarily because it is blocked. First of all, check the level of the water in the cistern to ensure the pan is receiving a 'full flush' of water. Next, check that the flush pipe is connected squarely to the flushing horn of the pan and that there is no obstruction. In a very old WC, the joint between the flush pipe and pan was made of rags and putty: this is frequently the cause of obstructions on older WCs because putty squeezes through the WC inlet to obstruct the flow of water. Next, check the underside of the flushing rim: hard-water scale often builds up here unnoticed. Use a mirror and check with your fingers for possible build up. If all seems right then you need to 'plunge'. Don't use a sink plunger – it won't work. The cup of a WC plunger can either be a 'cone' shape, or look more like the sink version but with a metal plate behind the cup to stop it becoming inverted. If plunging fails, then hire a WC auger – the big brother of the sink auger. A WC pan that fills and empties slowly when flushed could also indicate a blocked drain; see opposite.

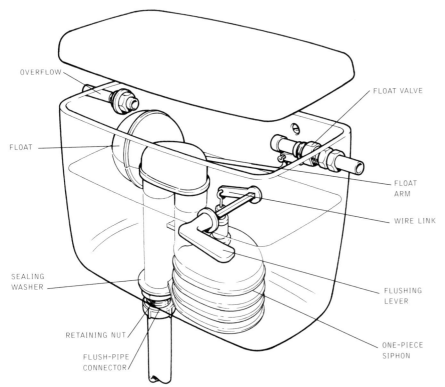

OVERFLOW

FLOAT VALVE

FLOAT

FLOAT ARM

WIRE LINK

SEALING WASHER

FLUSHING LEVER

RETAINING NUT

FLUSH-PIPE CONNECTOR

ONE-PIECE SIPHON

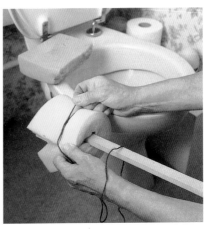

We never think to buy a toilet plunger until it's too late. In an emergency, improvise with pieces of foam or plastic carrier bags securely fastened to a mop head.

CLEARING DRAIN PIPES AND GULLEYS

Water overflowing from a manhole or gully is a sign of a blocked drain. Gullies can be cleared by hand or you can hire a power hose. If it still does not drain away smoothly, locate the blockage by raising the drain manhole covers. If you can see the blockage, remove it; otherwise, you'll need to hire a set of drain rods. Screw two or three together and insert the end into the flooded manhole. Feel for the half channel at the base and push the rod into the drain, turning it clockwise at the same time, in the direction of the blockage. Screw on more rods as required until the blockage is encountered and dislodged.

Gulleys can be cleared quickly with a high-powered water jet, which can be hired from any tool shops.

Wear strong rubber gloves to clear a gully by hand. Scoop out waste then rinse with a hose and disinfectant.

TAPS

The majority of kitchen sinks, bath tubs and bathroom basins are fitted with individual taps for hot and cold water. Wall-mounted taps are known as bib tabs, but those mounted directly onto the sink, basin or tub are called pillar taps. There are also mixer taps, which have a hot and cold valve linked to a common spout. Water regulations require that mains water and stored water cannot be mixed in a system, so a sink mixer has separate waterways to isolate mains-supplied cold drinking water from storage-cylinder-supplied hot water.

TAP DESIGN

In recent years there have been many changes to tap design, both in their appearance and in the mechanics of the tap itself. A traditional pillar tap comprises a capstan head – the cross-shaped handle – a metal shroud, which covers the gland nut, a spindle and headgear nut. This was attached to a jumper with a washer, which fitted into the tap body, which in turn fitted to the supply pipe. When you turn on this type of tap, the entire spindle, jumper and washer move up and down and turn along with the capstan head.

Now there are taps with non-rising heads: while outwardly they look like old spindle taps, inside, when they are turned on, a threaded spindle and washer unit rises up and down without turning. These have the advantage over old spindle taps because the washer is not twisted against the seat of the tap so it doesn't wear out as quickly. In other taps, the traditional rubber washer has been replaced with precision ground ceramic discs, which rotate on each other with little wear – and no build up of limescale deposits.

Reverse-pressure taps are a sort of upside-down version of standard taps. Here the head and spout hang from the water inlet and a check valve automatically shuts off the water if a washer needs to be changed. Where hygiene is of great concern – in hospitals, for example – electronic taps operated by photocells, which sense the presence of someone's hands, allow water to flow from the taps automatically.

PLUMBING PROBLEMS

A leaking tap is a common plumbing problem. Not only is the constant drip irritating but it is also a waste of a very valuable resource. And if the drip is from a hot tap, then you're wasting both the water and the fuel needed to heat it. The weak point in rising spindle taps and non-rising head taps remains the washer. When water is dripping from the spout, it's a sign of a worn washer. Washers for cold taps used to be made of leather, then black rubber, and hot tap washers first from a red fibre or rubber-asbestos before nylon ones were introduced. Hot and cold washers are still made, but it's a lot easier to buy a 'universal' washer as this can be used on either tap – but make sure you buy the right diameter.

If water leaks from the top of the tap head when you turn it on, then it's the gland packing or 'O' ring (on a mixer tap) that needs to be replaced. Both are very simple DIY repairs. Put the plug in the sink and then lay a towel in it – if a tap or tiny nut drops in, it won't get damaged or lost down the wastepipe.

LEAKING TAPS

REPLACING A WASHER ON A BIB OR PILLAR TAP

Before you unscrew the tap, drain the supply pipe, and then open the tap as far as possible. Where there is a metal shroud cover (like an inverted dome) unscrew it – by hand, if possible, or wrap the teeth of a wrench in protective tape. Lift the cover to reveal the head gear nut. Use a narrow spanner to unscrew this then lift out the entire assembly.

The washer is fixed to the jumper, which fits into the bottom of the headgear. With some taps, the jumper comes out with the head gear, while in others it lies inside the tap body. Prise off the washer. If it's held in place with a small nut, use a little penetrating oil to soften any corrosion, and then unscrew it. Fit a new washer, replace the retaining nut and reassemble the tap.

REPLACING A WASHER IN A REVERSE PRESSURE TAP

In this 'upside-down' tap, the washer is screwed upwards against the seat. You don't need to turn off the supply because these taps have an integral check valve which closes automatically. Loosen the retaining nut at the top of the tap body then unscrew the body itself – as if you were turning on the tap. Water will run out until the check valve kicks in, but keep on unscrewing until it comes off. Gently tap the nozzle then turn the body upside-down to tip the finned anti-splash device out. At the end of this device you'll find a combined washer and jumper. Prise this off and replace it, then put the tap back together in the reverse order, screwing the body back clockwise when you look down from above onto it.

CURING A LEAKING GLAND

When the spindle tap is opened or closed, the spindle passes through a gland (also called a 'stuffing box') which is on top of the headgear. To stop water leaking past the spindle when the tap is turned on, a nut forces watertight packing into the gland. If the spindle leaks, the packing has failed. In modern taps, however, the packing has been replaced with a rubber 'O' ring seal.

To replace the gland packing, turn the tap off fully; you don't need to shut off the supply. Remove the cross or capstan head: there may be a tiny screw at the side or it could be hidden under the decorative plug marked 'hot' or 'cold'. Lift off the head by rocking it gently from side to side. If it's very stiff, wrap a cloth around it and tap it from underneath with a hammer. Seal the leak by tightening the gland nut.

In most cases this won't stop the leak on its own: it's better to replace the packing. Use impregnated twine (available from plumbers' merchants) or twist a thread made from PTFE tape. Wind the new packing around the spindle and push it well into the gland with the point of a small screwdriver. Replace the cross or capstan head and secure it with the retaining screw at the side (or on top) and refit the decorative plug.

REPLACING 'O' RINGS ON MIXER TAPS

In most mixer taps, the gland packing has been replaced with an 'O' ring. Remove the shrouded head and the clip holding the spindle in place. Take out the spindle and take the old 'O' ring out of its groove and replace it with a new one then reassemble the tap. If water is leaking from the mixer taps swivel base, you'll have to find out the type of seal first before you can buy a replacement. Turn off both valves, unscrew the spout or remove the retaining screw. Note the type of seal and buy a new matching one.

REPLACING TAPS

Taps can be changed without altering the existing plumbing. If old or corroded fittings are difficult to remove, apply penetrating oil to the tap connectors and any nuts. Tap kits include full instructions on fitting replacement taps. Make sure that the taps you buy fit into the existing holes in your sink, basin or bathtub.

CISTERNS

Domestic cold water storage cisterns are normally located in the roof space, where the noise of them re-filling is less apparent and their high point creates a static head of pressure needed to ensure a strong flow at outlets. This cistern supplies all the cold taps in the house except for the one used for drinking water in the kitchen (which is supplied by the rising main) and water to the hot water cylinder. Cisterns provide a reservoir of water which equalizes the 'pull' on the mains, and provides against any reduction or shut down of the main supply. Old cisterns were made of galvanized steel. Electrolytic action – a chemical reaction in hard water conditions – and the build up of limescale means that the outlet pipes can become constricted and the cistern itself eventually corrodes.

New circular cisterns of lightweight polythene – much easier to lift into the roof space because they can be folded to pass through narrow access hatches – are standardized to a normal capacity of 227 litres (50 gallons). Make sure the cistern you buy has a lid to keep the water clean. You will need to drill holes in the new cistern to fit the inlet and outlet pipes. If you plan to take out an old steel cistern, it's a good idea to saw it into pieces using a metal-sheet saw.

INLET SUPPLY

The inlet supply to the cistern is controlled by a float valve which shuts off the water by means of an arm operated by a plastic or metal ball called a 'float'. This lies on the surface of the water and rises as the water flows in, raising a lever arm that closes the inlet valve at the determined level. The hole to fit the float valve assembly should be about 75mm (3in) below the top of the cistern.

One or two feed or distribution pipes can be taken from the cistern: one may feed the cold water supply to the hot water cylinder, while the other feeds bathroom washbasins and baths. The holes for these pipes should be drilled about 50mm (2in) above the bottom of the cistern. It's a good idea to fit gate valves on these pipes so you can cut off the water supply without having to drain the cistern.

OVERFLOW

The overflow pipe is a safety valve. If the float arm fails to shut off incoming water, the level in the cistern rises. To stop water flowing out of the cistern and into your home, the overflow pipe leads excess water out of the cistern and discharges it outside the building. The hole for the overflow pipe should be drilled 25mm (1in) below the level of the float valve inlet. The pipe must be a minimum of 22mm (¾in) diameter and should extend into the cistern with a bend taking its inlet about 50mm (2in) below level. This makes a water seal that stops any icy draughts blowing up the overflow pipe into the roof space.

VENT PIPE

The storage cistern also operates as a form of safety valve for the hot water cylinder. Heated water expands and it would be dangerous to contain it, so an expansion pipe must be fitted to the cylinder. The expansion or vent pipe is taken from the crown of the cylinder via an off-set fitting and curved just above the cold cistern. This vent pipe should not dip in the water or a siphonage circulation would start pumping hot water into nearly every tap in your home.

TROUBLESHOOTING

Cistern overflows: Check the float isn't leaking. Unscrew it from the arm and shake it. If you hear water inside it needs to be replaced. The water in it makes it too heavy to rise to the correct level to shut off the supply. If it's not leaking, the float may need to be adjusted (see opposite). If an overflow persists after adjustment, then the valve needs a new washer. Turn off the water supply, flush out the cistern and take out the spit pin under the valve holding the arm. Insert the tip of a screwdriver into the slot beneath the valve body and slide the piston out. Unscrew the end cap of the piston with pliers and pick out the old washer. Clean the piston with wire wool. Clean the inside of the valve body with fine abrasive paper wrapped around a pencil – take care not to damage the valve seat at the far end. Smear the surface of the valve with petroleum jelly. Fit the new washer, reassemble the valve and connect the float. Restore the water supply then adjust the arm to regulate the cistern's water level.

FLOATS AND VALVES

Apart from a leak caused by a split or hole in a cistern, the most common problems in cisterns are caused by faulty valves. The float valve in the storage cistern in the loft or roof space operates in the same way as the one in a WC cistern. Most modern WCs are washed down with a direct flushing cistern. Water is supplied to and fills the empty cistern through the action of the float or ball attached to the arm. As the water rises, the ball floats up and eventually closes the valve to shut off the supply.

In a direct action WC cistern, however, there is a second valve called the flap valve. This is hidden from view inside the siphon chamber. Take off the cistern lid and you'll see how the flush handle is connected by a wire link that goes into the siphon chamber. When you flush, the lever lifts a perforated metal plate at the bottom of the chamber. As the perforated plate rises, the holes in it are sealed by a plastic diaphragm called the flap valve so that the plate can push the water up over the 'U' in the chamber and down the flush pipe.

FAULTY FLAP VALVES

A sign of a faulty flap valve is when the WC won't flush first time – although you should check first that it isn't the lever that is the problem. Shut off the water supply, or tie the float arm to a batten laid across the cistern, and flush. Under the cistern you'll find a large nut holding the flush pipe to the cistern. Use a wrench and unscrew this. Remove the retaining nut clamping the siphon to the base of the cistern. A little water will run out. Inside the cistern, disconnect the flushing arm and ease the siphon out. Lift the plastic diaphragm off the metal plate and replace with a new one of the same size. Reassemble the flushing mechanism and then re-attach the flush pipe underneath the cistern and restore the water supply.

TROUBLESHOOTING

Corrosion in the cistern: If the cistern is showing signs of rust, drain the water and remove every trace of rust with a wire brush or abrasive paper. Fill any pit marks with epoxy resin. When the filler has set apply two or three coats of non-tainting bituminous paint. If a cistern is beyond repair, replace it immediately.

ADJUSTING FLOATS

The optimum level of water in a WC cistern is about 25mm (1in) below the outlet of the overflow pipe. In an old WC, the arm on the float valve may be made of metal: bend it downwards a little to reduce the water level, or straighten it to allow more water to flow in. In a modern WC, the float arm is probably made of rigid plastic: in this case it is likely that the valve is not fitted with a washer, but a sealing diaphragm with an adjustable screw to regulate the amount of water entering. Release the lock nut and turn the screw towards the valve to reduce the water level, and away from the valve to increase it.

INSULATION

If a loft or roof space has been properly insulated, it will be a lot colder than it was before because the warmth is staying down below where you need it. That leaves a problem: the roof space can now become cold enough for pipes and cisterns to freeze in winter, even if the rest of the house is cosy and warm. If the water in your supply pipe freezes you'll temporarily lose your supply, and since water expands when it freezes, it may burst the pipes.

As long as no insulation is placed directly under any cisterns in the roof, they will still get a small amount of warmth from below. Cisterns and pipes should be wrapped, and there are several ways to do this. Make a note of where the stopcocks are fitted: in an emergency, your quick action can save a great deal of time, money and trouble repairing water damage to coving and decorations below.

In addition to purpose-made cistern 'jackets' that are easy to install, thick slabs – at least 25mm (1in) – of expanded polystyrene make the ideal insulation for cisterns. The material is light and easy to cut to size and shape. The slabs – and the cut-out sections to accommodate fitting round pipes – are held together by taping round the sides of the cistern. Remember, don't cover the bottom of the cistern even if it is accessible. The slight amount of warm air rising from rooms below is needed to keep it freeze-free.

Circular cisterns or those with awkwardly placed pipes which make slab insulation difficult can be insulated with mineral wool or glass-fibre blankets sandwiched between two plastic covers. Before fitting, make sure the cistern is fitted with a water-resistant cover. Water will form on the underside of the cover and it should not be airtight. Specially moulded plastic lids are available, or you can make one from a sheet of expanded polystyrene.

INSULATING A COLD WATER CISTERN

1 The cistern
Traditionally, cold water cisterns were made of galvanized steel. When these corrode beyond repair they are replaced with plastic versions. These are lightweight and come in standard 227 litre (50 gallon) capacities – although larger ones are available. Some plastic cisterns are 'collapsible' and they can be wound with rope making it easier to get them through small access hatches into the roof space. Before you buy a new cistern, check the dimensions of the access and the amount of space in the roof so your new cistern can be installed easily. Because they are fairly flexible, plastic cisterns must be supported on a flat base.

2 Insulation
The simplest method of insulation is to buy a ready-made 'jacket' that fits around the cistern. Since tanks are standard capacity, so are the jackets. Remember that the 'lid' should also be insulated. The insulation jacket simply slips around the cistern and is held securely with plastic tape or one or two 'belts' of rope. Don't tie a fixed knot in the belt or you'll have to cut it off; instead tie a granny knot with draw loops, like the ones used to tie shoelaces. That way you'll be able to untie the belts easily to inspect the cistern and the float valve and carry out any repairs. Don't forget that the cold water pipes leading to and from the cistern also need insulating. If the pipes run between the joists you can lay blanket insulation over them. If not, then lay each of the pipe runs individually.

LAGGING

Insulation should be any home-owner's or tenants' priority. Where radiant heat is not contributing to keeping your home warm, the pipes and cylinders should be lagged.

A hot water cylinder without a jacket may keep your airing cupboard warm but it's wasting a great deal of energy. A lagged cylinder will keep a closed cupboard warm more efficiently. If you must have a warmer airing cupboard, don't remove the cylinder jacket; instead, remove a little of the lagging around a hot water pipe. If you ever need to replace a cylinder, buy a pre-insulated one.

If your cylinder is already fitted with a jacket, give it a squeeze or measure its thickness. It used to be thought that a mere 25mm (1in) thick insulation was enough, but with constant fuel price rises, this is no longer true. If your existing jacket is 'skinny', buy a thicker one. For extra insulation you could even put the second jacket over the first. The costs will be recovered in a few months in fuel savings.

LAGGING A CYLINDER

Cylinder jackets are 'tailored' to fit the size of cylinder and are fitted quickly and easily with retaining straps around the cylinder body. Measure the height and circumference of the cylinder to get the right size – it's better to have a jacket that is a little too big than one that is too small to cover the cylinder completely. Buy a good-quality jacket by looking for the British Standard kite mark (BS 5615). This will ensure that it is made from segments of 80–100mm

(3¼–4in) thick mineral-fibre insulation wrapped in plastic. Thread the tapered ends of the jacket segments onto a length of string and tie it around the pipe at the top of the cylinder. Arrange the segments evenly around the cylinder and wrap the straps or string around it to hold the segments securely in place. Make sure the edges of the segments butt together tightly and tuck the insulation around pipes and the thermostat.

LAGGING PIPES

Cold water pipes in the attic, loft or roof space should be lagged to stop the water in them freezing. Hot water pipes exiting from cylinders should be insulated against expensive heat loss. Mineral-wool bandage wrapped around the pipes and taped or tied at intervals is one of the cheapest ways to insulate pipes. This is fine for lofts and roof spaces where aesthetics are unimportant. A neater and quicker way – although a little more costly – is to cover pipe runs with flexible foam-plastic sections which can be taped together. Most tubes are pre-slit along their length so they can be sprung

over and around pipes. The joints between successive lengths are sealed with PVC adhesive tape. Where pipes bend, the tubes are 'nicked' along the slit edges so the tube can be bent without it bunching up and springing off the pipe. At elbows in pipes and at 'T'-joints, neatly fitting joints are made by mitring the ends of the tube or making wedge-shaped butt-joints. The tubing is made to fit different diameters of pipe and varies in thickness from 10–20mm (½–¾in). Some incorporate a metallic foil backing to reflect the heat back into hot water pipes. Check the diameter of the pipes first and measure the runs to calculate which size you require and how much insulation you need to buy.

SAFETY FIRST

When working in a loft, make sure you don't stand between the joists as the roof may not support your weight. Make a platform by slinging two or three planks across the joists to distribute your weight evenly.

KITCHEN SINKS

Alterations or improvements to kitchens invariably start at the sink. Fashions and styles have played their part here over the years. Fine 'Belfasts' – deep, white glazed stoneware sinks were once seen as old-fashioned and were replaced in many homes by shiny new stainless steel all-in-one sinks and drainers. Now many have decided these are outdated: stainless and enamelled steel and plastic sinks in a huge range of styles and colours make for more contemporary kitchens, while other people are busy reclaiming and re-installing Belfasts to complete a country-cottage or period-style kitchen.

One-piece sink tops are made to modular sizes that fit standard kitchen base units. Furthermore, they are available with single or double bowls and left or right hand drainers.

To complement the sink, a range of styles of taps is also available. These are much like the taps used in the bathroom except that they have extended pillars to enable you to fill a bucket from them. There is also one other important distinction for a kitchen mixer tap: because mains water for drinking must not be mixed with water from storage cylinders providing hot water within a fitting, a sink mixer has two separate water-ways to isolate one supply from the other. If you are buying a mixer tap for the kitchen sink, make sure it is the correct one, and, if you are installing a double bowl sink, get a mixer with a swivelling spout. See pages 156–7 for advice on fitting taps.

Fitting a like-for-like replacement sink into an existing kitchen unit is pretty straightforward, but if you decide on a different size, combination or layout of sink, then you may have to replace the base unit as well – or at least replace the worktop surround. To do this, you could either purchase ready-made surrounds or make your own – which requires only basic carpentry skills.

Follow the advice on pages 166–7 for boxing in a washbasin but adjust the design depending on what you want to use the storage space in your kitchen for.

1 Fit taps, overflow and waste
If you are making a straight like-for-like sink replacement, fit the taps, waste and overflow to the sink before you position it. Clamp the new sink in position with the fittings provided and then connect to the rising main cold supply, the nearest branch pipe of the same size from the hot supply and the pipes to the taps.

2 Making a new work top
Where a replacement sink will not fit into an existing kitchen unit worktop, a new one can be made easily. Laminated birch blockboard is available at DIY stores and timber merchants in a variety of decorative colours and patterns. Turn the new sink onto the laminate board and draw around the perimeter.

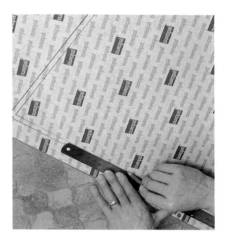

3 Measure and mark
If you cut the line you've marked, the sink would fall through it. The edge or lip of the sink should rest on the edge of the aperture. Measure and mark a line inside the first line to accommodate the lip of the sink. Mark also the position of the taps.

4 Start by drilling holes
To cut the inner line, start by drilling a hole in each corner. This will allow you to insert the blade of the saw to start cutting and will make it easier to saw around the corners.

5 Cut out the aperture
Using a power saw, cut slowly and carefully along the inner line to make the aperture for the sink. Cut out the holes for the taps.

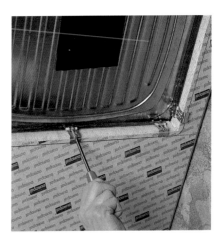

6 Fit the new sink
Fit the taps, overflow and waste to the new sink before you put it in position on the new worktop. Clamp the sink to the worktop using the fittings provided.

7 Connect the taps
Run a 15mm (½in) cold supply from the rising main and a branch pipe of the same size from the nearest hot water pipe. Connect the pipes to the taps with standard or flexible pipe and tap connectors. For more information on these, see page 151.

8 Fit the trap
It may be possible to fit the trap of the old sink to the new waste outlet. If not, fit a bottle trap with an adjustable inlet which gives the little bit of extra tolerance needed to connect with the old wastepipe. Run a 43mm (1½in) wastepipe through the wall behind the sink unit to the yard gully.

SAFETY FIRST

- The sink waste should be taken to an outside gully rather than connected with the main soil and waste stack. Current regulations require the wastepipe to pass through the grid covering the gully but stop before the pipe reaches the water in the gully trap to avoid siphoning up soiled water.

- When using a power saw, wear goggles to protect your eyes and a dust mask to stop you breathing in fine particles. If you are operating power tools for a long period, it is advisable to wear a pair of ear protectors as well.

WASHBASINS

Replacing an existing washbasin that is old, cracked or ugly is a simple procedure because you can utilize the existing plumbing and drainage. If you are installing a washbasin in a room that has never had one, then you'll need to think about running new pipes. How the wastepipe runs to the vertical stack must also be taken into account: it must have a minimum fall or slope of 6mm (¼in) for every 300m (1ft) of pipe and should not be longer than 3m (10ft). In a straightforward replacement, there's no need to worry, as you'll be using the wastepipe that already exists.

When connecting new washbasins to your existing pipes, be aware that the sizes and materials may not match. You could find pipes in a variety of materials, especially if it is an older house. Modern plastic pipes are not yet standardized so those supplied by one manufacturer might not be compatible with another's. Adaptors can be purchased for joining pipes of different materials, and also for joining new metric pipes to old imperial-sized ones.

When you choose a new washbasin, you'll need to decide on the type you want: wall-hung or pedestal are the most common types in domestic use. The hollow pedestal provides a little support for the basin, but mostly it just conceals the pipe-

work. Old-style wall-mounted wash-basins were often hung on large metal brackets, but modern ones generally have concealed wall mountings. You will need to make sure, however, that the wall is strong enough to support the weight of the vitreous china they are made from. Make sure that the basin has holes at the required spacing to take the taps – you'll probably want to replace these as well – or none at all if the taps are wall mounted. When you buy a new washbasin and taps, it's a good idea to 'dry test' them: bend over the basin and imagine you are washing your face. Make sure you can get both hands in the bowl.

REMOVING AND REPLACING A WALL-HUNG BASIN

1 Turn off the supply
Turn off the water supply to the basin. If you are using the existing plumbing, loosen the compression nuts on the tap tails and the trap.

2 Cut through supply pipes
If you are not using the existing plumbing but running new pipes to a re-positioned replacement, cut through the wastepipe and supply pipes at a point convenient for taking new connections.

3 Remove fixings
Remove any fixings attaching the basin to support brackets or pedestal and carefully lift it away from the wall. Remove the wall brackets by applying a little penetrating oil to avoid damaging the plaster. If this fails, lever them off.

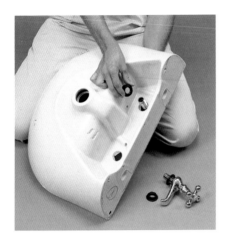

4 Fit the taps

Before you fix the new basin in place, fit the new taps. Manufacturers provide full instructions so follow them carefully. Make sure that the spouts face the right direction – into the basin – when you tighten them into place.

5 Fixing to the wall

Get a helper to hold the basin against the wall and check it is horizontal with a spirit level. Mark the position of the fixing holes for the wall bracket. Drill and plug the fixing holes, then secure the bracket to the wall and hold the basin to it with the supplied fixings.

6 Adding a wall batten

If, when you remove the old sink, you find that the wall behind the basin is damaged – perhaps from water splashes over the years – reinforce the wall with a stout wooden batten. Hack off the plaster, attach the batten securely, then mount the brackets.

7 Connect the plumbing

Fit the waste outlet using a washer or putty to make a watertight seal. Tighten the back nut. Connect the trap to the waste outlet and to the end of the pipe. Run flexible 15mm (½in) copper or plastic pipes to the taps and join with tap connectors. Make a compression or capillary joint to join to the supply pipes.

CRANKED SPANNERS

- Once a new washbasin is installed, test the plumbing for leaks. Turn on the water and check the taps, pipes and joints. Drain the system to repair any weeping joints.

- Professional plumbers use a special cranked spanner rather than a standard wrench to loosen the fixing nuts of tap connectors and the back-nuts clamping the taps to the basin. These spanners are designed so they fit into the cramped space under a bath or basin and can be hired.

BOXING IN A BASIN

1 Construct a framework

Unsightly plumbing can be hidden and storage space provided under the basin by boxing in. Access to the storage and plumbing is provided by doors hung on the front. Calculate the amount of timber required to make a framework. Note how it is strengthened at the base by a cross member. This also provides the support for the floor. On either side of the basin, but below the lip, there are timber members to support the top surface, which will be flush with the basin edge.

2 Clad the framework

Using fibreboard of the required thickness, the top and side panels of the box are clad and attached to the wooden framework with galvanized nails. You may have to cut the fibreboard into sections to fit, or draw a template of the sink and then cut. Note the curve of the basin at the corners and shape the pieces accordingly so there are no gaps between sections. When you cut, plane or sand fibreboard, you must wear a dust mask to avoid inhaling the sawdust.

3 Add the floor

Measure and cut the fibreboard needed for the floor and fix it with nails to the timber frame. Then, measure and cut two panels to fit at the front. In this picture, one panel is a simple rectangle, while the other is shaped to fit around the boxed-in pipes along the wall. Cut the door panels. Prime and paint the front, doors and floor as desired (see pages 234–5). Paints specially formulated for bathrooms – where condensation can be a problem – are available in a wide range of colours.

KITCHEN UNITS

• When installing units around a kitchen sink, leave space for any connections or additional plumbing you may wish to add in future.

• For advice on plumbing in washing machines and dishwashers, see page 178.

• For information on installing a waste disposal unit, see page 179.

• Make sure you are not boxing in any electric sockets. This could be extremely dangerous in the event of a leak from the pipes in the area.

SAFETY FIRST

• When you cut tiles with nippers, on a tile-cutting jig or with a hacksaw, wear protective goggles to protect your eyes from any flying shards of tile when they are snapped.

• A face mask must be worn when cutting fibreboard.

4 Apply adhesive

To make the top of the box waterproof and more attractive, it can be tiled. You will need to include the thickness of the tiles in your calculations so they are flush with the basin lip. Apply a proprietary waterproof tile adhesive, and lay whole tiles first.

6 Clean up tiles

When all the tiles are laid, apply a waterproof grout into the joins until they are well filled (see page 328). Wipe the grout from the surface of the tiles before it sets and smooth the joins – you can use a smooth piece of dowel for this. When dry, polish with a soft cloth.

5 Cut tiles to fit

Use round edge (RE) tiles at the front edge of the top to make a neat edge. Where a tile needs to be cut to fit, make a template out of card and mark the line on the face of the tile. Curves can be nibbled out with nippers a little at a time, or cut with a fine-toothed hacksaw.

Fibreboard doors are made more attractive when finished with paint and door furniture is added. The flush doors can be 'faux' panelled to match the main door. Ready-made stick-on panelling is available at DIY stores or you can mitre cut your own lengths of moulding (see pages 373–4 for advice on buying timber and blockboards, including lists of the standard sizes). If you use fibreboard, such as MDF, remember you must wear a face mask when you cut it to length, as breathing in the dust can be hazardous. MDF will require priming but once this is done, you can create a whole range of paint finishes, including 'special finishes' like faux marbling, graining and speckling. For more information on paint effects, see pages 302–5.

TILING

- Don't forget to seal the join between the tiles and the wall. This can be sealed with ceramic coving or quadrant tiles, or use a silicone rubber caulking compound to fill the gap which remains flexible to accommodate any movement.

- Sealants are available in a range of colours. You can also renovate grout with liquid colourant if you choose.

- See pages 320–3 for further advice on types of tiles and how to lay them.

ADDITIONAL TOOLS

A tile-cutting jig is a worthwhile investment if you are undertaking a lot of tiling. This handy device measures, scores and cuts tiles accurately and reduces the chances of breakage. Consequently the cost of the jig is repaid in fewer wasted tiles. The cutting edge is drawn along the channel of an adjustable guide and then the tile is snapped with the special pincer tool.

INSTALLING A WC

The location of a WC in your home is restricted by the need to use a 100mm (4in) soil pipe which has sufficient fall to discharge into the stack. However, it is possible to install a small-bore waste system, often called an electric WC. These have an electric pump and a shredder allowing waste to be discharged into a 22mm (¾in) pipe up to a distance of 50m (55yd) from the soil stack. This means that they can be installed in small spaces (under the stairs or in cellars) because they can pump vertically up to a maximum of 4m (4yd), so long as the space is adequately ventilated and the system has been approved by the local water authority. It must be wired to a fused connection unit – or via an approved flex outlet if fitted into a bathroom.

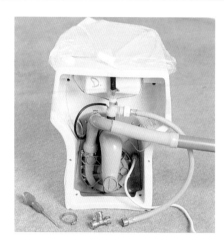

In an electric WC, the shredding unit fits neatly behind a conventional 'P'-trap lavatory pan. The system is activated automatically by flushing the cistern and switches off about 20 seconds later. For safety, the system should be wired to a fused connection unit.

The small-bore wastepipe from the WC must be connected to the soil stack at least 200mm (8in) above any other waste connections. It can be connected to the stack using a standard 36mm (1¼in) waste boss but it will require a 22–36mm (¾–1¼in) adaptor.

1 Construct framework
An unattractive cistern and ugly pipes can be concealed behind a 'box' with removable panels and a lid, providing additional storage and easy access in order to carry out plumbing repairs. Measure and cut timber for a framework and fix securely to the floor and walls. Use a spirit level to check alignments.

2 Make three panels
The front of the box is constructed of three separate and removable panels. You can use TGV, or sheets of hardboard or ply. Measure and cut the TGV, assemble using wood adhesive and attach a small supporting batten to the reverse. Use a nail punch or a hammer to drive home the nails.

3 Cut hole for wastepipe
The central panel needs a hole for the wastepipe. If you are using TGV, make the central panel in two sections and cut a matching semi-circle in each and assemble it around the wastepipe. If you are using boards, you may find it easier to use only two panels and cut the hole for the pipe where they butt together.

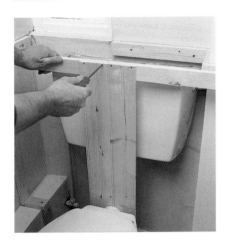

4 Fix the central panel

The central panel, which accommodates the wastepipe, is fitted first. Mark the position of the drill holes. Use quality screws so they will be easy to undo if you need to disassemble the box. Next fit the panel furthest from the flush lever.

5 Position final panel

Offer up the final panel. It will stand in front of the others until the flush lever is removed. Mark the position of the lever on the panel and drill a small hole to accommodate the arm of the flushing lever.

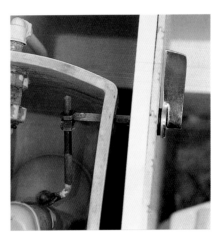

6 Replace flushing lever

Remove the flushing lever from the WC. Bring it forwards on its connecting arm and replace it through the panel. In most cases there is enough length on the arm, but you may find you have to replace it and the lever with a new one.

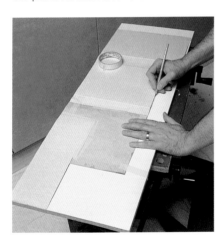

7 Make a template for the lid

If the 'lid' area is simply rectangular, measure the length and width, check the angles at the corners and cut a lid from a sheet of board. More complex shapes are easier to cut if you make a template out of stiff card. Do not fix the lid permanently – you'll need access to the cistern beneath.

8 Finishing

With the 'lid' in place, the box is ready for finishing. The front edge of the lid can be finished with a strip of quadrant moulding and the 'box' painted, stained or varnished to complement the surrounding decor.

PANELLING

- Place a rolled-up towel between the frame and the cistern to absorb vibrations when you screw the panels in position.

- Don't force the panels into position: if they fit too tightly, plane down the edge nearest to the wall. Any small gaps can be disguised later with a strip of moulding.

- Periodically take the lid off the box and check that all is well in the cistern. Remove a panel to check for any leaks from the seal on the overflow.

BATHS

ASSEMBLING AND INSTALLING

The majority of modern baths are made from enamelled pressed steel, acrylic or glass-reinforced plastic. One advantage of these baths over the cast-iron variety, popular in Victorian houses, is that it takes at least two people to lift a steel bath while one person can manage a plastic one alone. An added bonus is that you do not need to make sure that the floor is strong enough to support the total weight of a heavy cast-iron bath, the water and its occupant.

Modern baths generally possess levelling devices so they 'sit' correctly on the floor, while old cast-iron baths frequently require wedges under their feet to make them level if the floor is uneven. There are plenty of shapes, styles, sizes and colours available in modern baths: round, oval, corner-fitting, square and of course, the traditional rectangular shape – and you also choose where to position the taps. They don't need to be at the foot of the bath but can go anywhere you like. Avoid dark-coloured baths, as they tend to show dirt and limescale stains more easily so will require more frequent cleaning. If you want a whirlpool bath, it should be fitted by a qualified electrician.

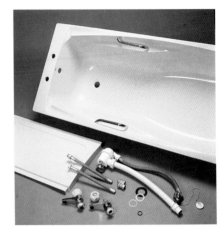

ABOVE: Many modern baths are available as 'kits' with all the necessary fittings. You will just have to provide any additional pipe needed to connect the taps to the supply and the waste outlet to the external hopper or soil stack.

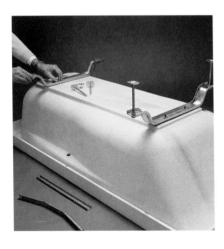

1 Fit the adjustable feet
Turn off the hot and cold water supply, drain the system and remove the old bath. Run new 22mm (¾in) supply pipes, or attach spurs to the existing ones. Turn the new bath on its rim and fit the adjustable feet (or the cradle for a plastic bath). Cut two boards to support the feet of the bath and spread the load evenly across the floor.

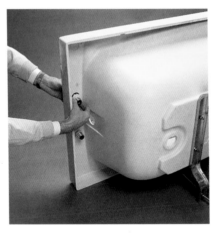

2 Fit the taps
Fit individual hot and cold taps by slipping the plastic washer supplied onto its tail and pass the tail through the hole in the bath. Slip a second washer on the tail and hand tighten the back nut to clamp it to the bath. Make sure that the spout faces in the right direction, then tighten with a cranked spanner.

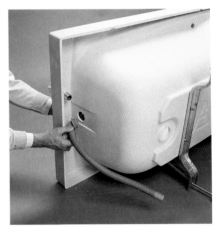

3 Fit overflow
A flexible plastic hose takes water from the overflow outlet in the end of the bath to the waste outlet or trap. Pass the threaded boss through the hole, slip a washer seal over the boss and screw the grille onto the overflow outlet. For a 'banjo unit', fit the overflow before the trap. The flexible pipe of a compression unit fits to the cleaning eye on the trap.

4 Fit copper pipes to taps

Fit a flexible 22mm (¾in) copper pipe onto each tap tail – or attach short lengths of standard 22mm (¾in) copper or plastic pipe with tap connectors ready for joining to the pipe runs of the hot and cold water supply pipes.

5 Fit waste outlet

Spread a layer of plumber's putty under the rim of the waste outlet, or fit a circular rubber seal. Before you insert the tail into the hole in the bottom of the bath, seal the thread with PTFE tape. Under the bath, add the plastic washer and tighten the large back nut bedding the outlet down onto the putty or seal.

BUYING BATHS

- Plastic baths are quite flexible so they are supplied in a metal frame to cradle them. Turn the bath on its rim to fit the cradle before fitting the taps.

- Make sure your new bath will fit into your bathroom: rectangular baths can vary in size from 1.5–1.8m long (5–6ft) and from 700–800mm (2ft 4in–2ft 8in) wide.

- While a corner bath will take up less wall space, it will take up more floor space than a rectangular bath of the same capacity.

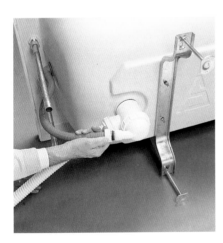

6 Connect the bath trap

Fit the trap and connect the cleaning eye of the trap to the hose of the overflow with the compression nut. If you are fitting a banjo unit, slip it over the tail of the waste outlet so it lies between it and the trap.

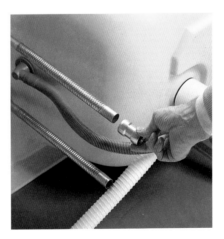

7 Connect to supply pipes

Push the new bath into position and check that it is level with a spirit level. Connect the pipes to the taps with the supply pipes with a compression joint. If space is tight, a soldered capillary joint may be preferable.

ADDITIONAL TOOLS

- PTFE tape (Polytetraflourethylene) Threaded connections leak unless they are made watertight. Traditionally, plumbers used strands of hemp but more often today PTFE tape is wrapped three times clockwise around threads instead.

- Adaptor couplings These may be necessary if you have to connect plastic pipes to copper plumbing (see pages 150–2 for advice on joining pipes).

- Cranked spanner See box on page 165.

BATHS

PANELLING

1 Make framework
New baths have optional moulded plastic panels but if you prefer a different finish, construct a simple timber framework to fit under the lip of the bath.

2 Panels
The sides and ends of the framework can be covered in your preferred panelling: TGV, laminated board or hardboard that you can finish as you wish. Remember to leave a removable section near the plumbing so you have easy access for inspection and repairs.

REMOVING LIMESCALE

Water is treated for harmful impurities to make it safe to drink, but the concentration of minerals is higher in some areas than others. 'Soft water' has a lower mineral content because it comes from rocky terrain, and runs overground. 'Hard water' is water that has run through the ground, accumulating a higher concentration of minerals. The minerals are deposited in the form of scale, which 'furs' up the inside of pipes, cisterns and hot water cylinders, as well as kettles. It is also responsible for stains in baths and basins.

There are several treatments available at DIY stores for removing limescale. Follow the instructions carefully regarding application since these treatments are usually acid based. To minimize limescale problems, make sure that taps aren't leaking and avoid buying dark-coloured bathroom suites. You could also consider fitting a water softener.

Leaky taps can cause rust stains in enamel baths and basins. These can often be removed simply by rubbing with half a lemon, but extremely stubborn stains or limescale deposits may require chemical cleaning, grinding and re-spraying by a professional bath renovation company. Smaller stains and flaws can often be treated with restorers and enamel paint.

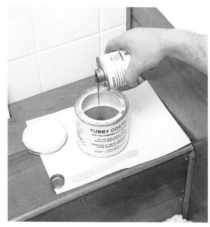

1 Renovating an enamel bath
Enamel baths are very fashionable and expensive to replace like-for-like. There are two-part paints specially designed to restore the surface of enamel baths and basins. The surface must be absolutely clean and dry: use white spirit to remove traces of grease.

2 Painting the bath
The renovating paints are self-levelling so they must not be brushed out too much. They are applied from the bottom of the bath upwards in a circular direction, often with a pad applicator. Follow the manufacturer's instructions regarding application and drying times.

SHOWERS

Showers use far less water than baths and many people consider them more hygienic as you are washing in a continuous flow of clean water. However, before you install a shower, make sure you consider the following.

A shower must comply with water authority requirements regarding water pressure. The hot and cold water supply must be under equal pressure: you cannot mix mains cold water with hot water from the cylinder. Since the hot water in the cylinder is under pressure from the main cold water cistern, the cold supply must also come from this cistern. It is illegal to connect the hot side of the shower to the cylinder and the cold side direct to the rising main. A second requirement for a shower is that the pressure is sufficient. This will depend on the height of the cold cistern above the shower sprinkler. The level of the cylinder is not important. For best results, the vertical distance (the head) between the shower sprinkler and the base of the cold water cistern should be at least 1.5m (5ft). Where a pipe run is short and with few bends, it may be possible to get a shower with a head of just 1m (3ft 3in), but this is the absolute minimum.

A third requirement is that the cold supply to the shower is taken by means of a separate supply pipe directly from the cold water cistern. If you were to take it from a branch that was supplying other fittings then there could be a loss of pressure on the cold side; in other words, if someone turned on a cold tap elsewhere, the cold water pressure to the shower would drop and scalding hot water would come out.

Don't be put off the idea of a shower even if you can't carry out the plumbing that this type of installation requires. Install an instantaneous electric shower instead, wherever the drainage is feasible. Cold water supply is taken to these in one 15mm (½in) pipe teed off the rising main and is heated within the unit.

FITTING AN INSTANTANEOUS ELECTRIC SHOWER

SAFETY FIRST

- Most instantaneous showers require their own 30 amp circuit from the consumer unit and a ceiling mounted 30 amp double pole switch must be connected to the circuit to turn the shower heater on and off.

- Shower units, metal pipes and fittings must be bonded to earth.

- If you have any doubts about the requirements, undertaking wiring or if you are inexperienced, hire a qualified electrician to carry out this work for you.

1 Hiding the pipework

If you want the pipework hidden, you will have to cut into the wall. In a stud partition wall the plumbing can run between the two skins. An alternative is to install a proprietary rigid plastic pillar in the corner to cover the plumbing and house the mixer and showerhead.

2 Mount the showerhead

In most instantaneous showers, the showerhead is connected to the control unit by a flexible hose and mounted on a sliding height-adjustable fixing. Decide on the height and position of the spray head mount, mark and drill fixing holes. Mount the shower unit and spray head.

3 Installing the plumbing

Turn off the water and drain the system. Run a single 15mm (½in) pipe from the rising main, through the stud partition to the hole made to house the shower unit. Join a threaded or compression connector to the supply pipe – whichever is specified by the manufacturer and appropriate to the water inlet in the shower unit.

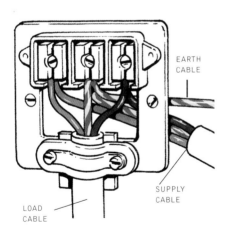

EARTH CABLE

LOAD CABLE

SUPPLY CABLE

4 Make the electrical connection

An electric shower needs a separate circuit: the circuit cable must be 6mm sq. (¼sq.in) two-core and earth protected by a 30-amp fuse in a spare

fuse way at the consumer unit or in a separate 30 amp switch fuse unit. The cable runs directly to the shower unit where it must be wired according to the manufacturer's instructions. If you are in any doubt, hire a qualified electrician.

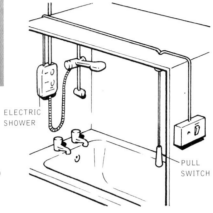

ELECTRIC SHOWER

PULL SWITCH

5 The isolating switch

The shower will have its own on-off switch but there must also be a separate isolating switch within the circuit. This must be out of reach to anyone using the shower – a ceiling-mounted 30 amp double pole pull cord switch with a 3mm (⅒in) contact gap and a neon 'on' indicator should be fitted. Fix the backplate of the switch to the ceiling, sleeve the earth connectors, and connect them to the E terminal on the switch. Connect the conductors from the consumer unit to the 'mains' terminal of the switch. Connect the conductors of the cable to the shower to the 'load' terminals. If you are in any doubt, you must hire a qualified electrician to carry this out.

6 Make good

Only after the plumbing has been checked for leaks and the wiring checked and approved by a qualified electrician can you make good the area around the shower unit. Remember also to make sure that the seal around the top of the bath or shower tray and the walls are watertight, and that grout between tiles is waterproof. Install a shower curtain to avoid soaking the floor.

FITTINGS

- It may be necessary to fit the shower tray on a raised plinth to get enough of a slope for the wastepipe to fall towards the drain.

- Clean your showerhead regularly, especially in hard-water areas. To remove limescale, soak the showerhead in a descalant, then rinse thoroughly. Reattach and turn on the shower to flush out any loose deposits.

INSTALLING A SHOWER CUBICLE

Shower cubicles are available as factory-assembled freestanding units or for fitting into corner sites. They usually come complete with shower tray, doors or curtain. Alternatively, you can construct your own from melamine-faced board or exterior grade plywood, panelled or plastered over on the exterior and tiled on the inside to make it waterproof.

1 Selecting the site

Decide on the position of the shower: for a freestanding cubicle, place the shower tray against a flat wall and either surround it with a manufactured cubicle or construct two stud partitions for each side. If you position a tray in a corner, two walls will be 'ready-made' so you can run a curtain around the other two sides of the tray, or install a manufactured corner entry with sliding doors, or construct one more mixed side wall and place a door or curtain across the cubicle opening.

2 The shower tray

Shower trays can be made of cast iron, steel ceramic or reinforced plastic. Plastic trays are inexpensive and lightweight, but they are a little flexible so the edges must be carefully sealed with flexible mastic instead of grout. Trays vary in size so measure the space first to make sure it will fit: they are generally between 750mm (2ft 6in) and 900mm (3ft) square and most stand on the floor with a surrounding apron edge of about 150mm (6in) high. To provide a fall for the wastepipe, some trays have a metal frame to raise it off the floor; others have adjustable feet to level the tray on an uneven floor. A plinth across the front of the tray hides the feet and the plumbing while still allowing access for repairs. A round outlet fits into the bottom of the tray and special shallow seal traps are connected to the outlet. Shallow seal traps are used for both showers and baths, where space is limited. They are fitted in the same way as an ordinary bath waste (see page 171) and, like bath wastes, they must discharge into a yard gully.

3 The partitions

Assemble the partition walls of a manufactured cubicle according to the maker's instructions. Some cubicles have 'lids': it is worthwhile fitting – or making – a lid as these contain steam within the cubicle so it condenses on the waterproof interior walls and not on the ceiling of the bathroom. If you have constructed your own cubicle partition, they should be of melamine-faced boards attached to the stud framework with metal angle brackets, or exterior-grade plywood over which ceramic tiles have been laid with waterproof grout on the inside of the shower cubicle.

SAFETY FIRST

- Make sure the shower tray surface is slip-proof or install a non-slip mat underfoot.

- If you are adding soap dishes or trays by drilling into the wall, make sure you avoid the electric cable.

- Always remember that water and electricity can be lethal.

OTHER SHOWERS

BATH/SHOWER MIXER

One of the simplest of all types of showers to install is a bath/shower mixer. They are available in a variety of styles from ultra-modern to retro chic – when they look a little like old-fashioned telephones. This type of shower is simply fitted like a standard bath mixer to the existing 22mm (¾in) cold and hot water pipes, while drainage is through the bath's waste outlet and pipe. You adjust the hot and cold taps to get the desired water temperature at the spout, and lift a button or lever on the spout to divert the water via the flexible hose to the showerhead. You can either hold the showerhead in your hand or attach it to the wall above the bath. The only restriction with this type of shower is that it must not be fitted if the cold water is supplied to the bath tap under mains pressure, which would make it impossible to guard against fluctuations in pressure: if someone turned on a cold tap elsewhere in the house, the shower would run only hot water, which could be dangerous.

THERMOSTATIC SHOWER MIXER

A thermostatic shower mixer eliminates all risks of danger or discomfort from the shower suddenly running hot or cold during use, since it delivers the water at a pre-determined temperature. If there is a drop of pressure on one side of the valve – either hot or cold – the pressure on the other side will be reduced to match it. A thermostatic shower mixer also removes the need to take a separate cold supply direct from the cold water cistern. However, the pipes should be joined as close as possible to the cold cistern and hot cylinder. This mixer cannot raise the pressure of the supply so it won't turn a trickle into a water cannon. If the shower performance is poor, you may have to fit an electric booster pump: hot and cold pipes are fed to the pump then back again under higher pressure to the shower mixer. You will need a two core and earth cable running from the pump to a switched fuse connection which must be out of reach of anyone using the shower.

SHOWER AND BATH PROBLEMS

• If there is insufficient water pressure in your shower, consider fitting a pump in the system. You can alter the flow and pressure by fitting a showerhead that adjusts to give different spray patterns. Note, it is not normally possible to install a pump shower if you have a combination boiler.

• If water is not draining from the shower tray, or is only draining slowly, follow the advice given on pages 154–5. It is worth fitting a compact trap under the shower tray. These have a lift-out tube making them easy to clean, and will catch hair and other debris that could form blockages.

• Grout at the edges of baths and showers can discolour and start to leak after a while. The only solution to this problem is to scrape it out and regrout. See page 328 for advice on grouting. Remember that if you have a plastic shower tray, grout will not be flexible enough and you should seal the edges with flexible mastic.

• Shower curtains will not be enough to stop water escaping onto the floor if you have a powerful shower. Fit a metal-framed or plastic-panelled unit with hinged, sliding or concertina doors that can be closed when you are inside and the water is turned on.

• Clean and descale your showerhead

KITCHEN APPLIANCES

WASHING MACHINES & DISHWASHERS

Washing machines and dishwashers are plumbed in the same way. The only difference is that a dishwasher uses cold water, while most washing machines are plumbed to both the hot and cold water pipes. Most washing machines and dishwashers will work with their inlet hoses temporarily attached to the hot and cold (or only the cold) taps and with an emptying hose hooked over the edge of a sink. However, they are much better to be permanently plumbed in as temporary tap fixings are more likely to leak and their use means that sink taps are 'out-of-action' until the laundry or washing-up has been done.

When you fix a machine permanently, the hoses still give enough length for the machine to be moved around 30cm (1ft), allowing you to clean around and behind it. The machine's vibrations would soon cause rigid pipes to break or joints to leak. The instructions supplied by the manufacturer with your machine should tell you what water pressure is required for it to operate efficiently and safely.

The storage cistern must be high enough to provide the right pressure. Where 15mm (½in) hot and cold water pipes run conveniently behind it next to the machine, you can use a valve, which bores a hole in the pipe without having to turn off the supply and drain the system. The valves are colour-coded for hot and cold and each has a threaded outlet to fit a standard machine hose.

If you have to run a branch pipe, turn off the water and drain the system. Take branch pipes from the hot and cold pipes (or cold only) supplying the kitchen taps. Run the pipes close to where the machine is to be located and fit a small appliance valve – either an in-line, right angle or tee-piece valve, whichever is the most practical to connect to the plumbing – with a standard compression joint for connecting to the pipework and a threaded outlet for the hose.

These small appliance valves are invaluable because you can turn off the water to service the washing machine or dishwasher without turning off the water supply to the rest of the house. Connect the blue machine hose to the cold supply and the red hose to the hot.

Washing machines and dishwashers are supplied with an outlet hose, which must be connected to a waste system to discharge dirty water into a yard gully or single waste stack. The standard method uses a vertical 43mm (1½in) plastic standpipe attached to a deep seal trap. The machine hose fits into the open-ended pipe to avoid siphoning back dirty water. Run the wastepipe through the wall into the yard gully or attach it to the drain stack with a strap boss and allow a fall of 6mm (¼in) for every 300mm (1ft) of pipe run.

TROUBLESHOOTING

You will only be able to repair minor faults to washing machines and dishwashers. Some of the most common problems are:

- **No power, or intermittent power:** Check the plug fuse and connections, or main fuse box. If these are intact, then the fault is most likely with the motor or there is a fault in the electrical system.

- **Water leaks:** Tighten the hose connector if it has come loose. A split hose or leak due to a fault within the machine can cause serious flooding, so fit an overflow safety valve onto the supply. This measures the amount of water passing through it. If a fault occurs and the volume of water exceeds the predetermined limit, the valve shuts off the water supply to the machine. Setting instructions are provided by the manufacturer to allow for the capacity of the machine. You may also need to clean or replace the filter in the supply pipes.

INSTALLING A WASTE DISPOSAL UNIT

Powerful steel teeth inside a waste disposal unit grind up food waste so that it can be mixed with cold water into a 'slurry' and washed down the drain. Despite these teeth, waste disposal units can only deal with soft waste such as vegetable peelings. They will not grind up hard items such as bones.

There are two types of unit: continuous feed units, which can have waste and water added while in operation, and batch feed units, which have to be loaded and covered before they can be switched on.

The unit is powered by an electric motor and installed permanently just below the sink plughole. The sink outlet needs to be 90mm (3½in): if your sink does not have this size outlet then you'll need a new sink or, if it's stainless steel or plastic, you can hire a special cutting machine to enlarge the outlet.

The unit must be permanently wired to the electricity supply via a fused connection unit fitted with a 13-amp fuse mounted above the kitchen work surfaces, where it cannot be accidentally switched on. If you are in doubt about undertaking electrical work, hire a qualified electrician.

BLOCKAGES

If the unit becomes blocked, loosen the sink trap to investigate, but make sure you place a bucket underneath.

1 Insert waste outlet and seal
Most units have a seal that fits over the tail of the plughole outlet. This usually comprises the outlet 'cover', a gasket and a back-up ring. Slot the outlet and seal onto the waste outlet.

2 Retaining collar
Under the sink, the waste outlet and seal are clamped, screwed or clipped by a collar to the waste disposal unit. A snap ring is attached that seals the unit and waste securely.

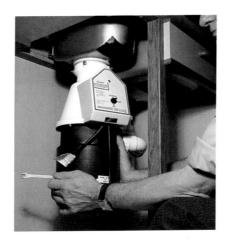

3 Attach the unit housing
Follow the manufacturer's instructions and bolt, clip or screw the unit housing the waste disposal to the collar under the sink.

4 Waste outlet
The waste outlet from the unit fits to a standard sink trap – but not a bottle trap. Make sure that if the wastepipe runs to a yard gully, it runs through the grille and just above the water in the trap. Wire the waste disposal unit to a fused connection unit.

CENTRAL HEATING SYSTEMS

DRY

Dry heating systems are normally electrical – though there are electric storage systems, which do heat hot water and circulate this around pipework. The most common form of 'dry' central heating is the storage unit. This runs off cheap rate electricity – usually at night when demand is at its lowest – and heats up refractory blocks with electric elements. These in effect are electric radiators: the heat stored in them at night is emitted throughout the day, but they can also be switched over to 'full-price' electricity if extra heat is required.

Some of these storage units are fan assisted, but they do not provide instantaneous heat. A ducted system – which can be operated by any kind of heating source – is where the heat exchange occurs by air circulation and fan assistance through electrically heated elements, out through grills with circulating hot water. Ducts or 'registers' of different sizes are placed in rooms to provide the heat. Ducted systems are normally installed as the house is constructed because of the ducting needed to circulate the warm air throughout the house.

SAFETY FIRST

Balanced flue boilers must have access to a ventilator fitted in an outside wall. It must be the correct size and should never be covered with wire mesh. Boilers that don't get enough air will create lethal carbon monoxide.

WET

The wet system derives heat from heated water circulated along pipes from a boiler to various heat exchangers – panel radiators, skirting or fan convectors or ducts. The water finally returns to the boiler along return pipework, to be re-heated and re-cycled. In modern small-bore and micro-bore systems – these terms refer to the size of pipes used – a pump is used to circulate and accelerate the water through the pipes and radiators.

Modern heating systems also provide domestic hot water – called the primary circuit. In some systems, the hot water is pumped for the primary, while in others gravity, or natural circulation, is set up by the expansion of hot water. Many early 'piped' heating systems relied on gravity circulation through large-bore pipes, which was neither economic nor efficient.

Open small and micro-bore systems make use of a feed-and-expansion cistern, usually situated in the loft, providing for the thermal expansion of hot water, which then discharges into this cistern to compensate for loss of water through evaporation. Because small- and micro-bore systems utilize separate flow and return circuits, an even temperature of flow water is thus maintained.

BOILERS

At the heart of any wet central heating system is the boiler, which can be gas, oil or solid fuel. Solid fuel boilers can provide very high levels of heat output. Where solid-fuel room heaters are used, however, an independent water heating system, such as an immersion heater, is necessary for the summer, when the room heater is not in use.

For both solid fuel – whether wood or coal – and for oil-fired boilers, the fuel must be stored in a large-capacity oil tank, bunker or shed. Some solid fuel boilers are 'hopper fed' a constant supply of fuel, which otherwise would have to be stoked by hand.

Gas can be mains supplied or, as in many rural areas, supplied in the form of bottled gas. Gas and oil-fired boilers can be either balanced flue or conventional flues. Conventional flues are free-standing and designed to be connected to an existing chimney – or a new prefabricated one.

Balanced flue boilers don't require a chimney. Instead their gases are passed through a horizontal duct in an outside wall. In the duct are two passages: one for incoming combustion air, the other for outgoing flue gases. Solid fuel boilers must be connected to a chimney.

RADIATORS

Radiators come in a range of sizes and styles. The larger the radiator, the greater its heat output and most radiators have fluted faces to increase their surface area even more.

An ordinary radiator is simply a double skin of metal through which hot water flows. At the top is a bleed valve to let out any air. There are also double and even triple panel radiators – panels mounted one behind the other and those with 'finned' rear faces to increase the amount of convected heat.

For each room in your home, there are 'ideal' temperatures. Central heating designers will calculate the heating requirements for each room and recommend radiators of appropriate outputs. All the heat outputs are then totalled, to give the boiler capacity.

THERMOSTATS

There are various control devices available for use with wet central heating systems that can save you a lot of money if used efficiently. Room thermostats should be placed in rooms where the temperature is fairly constant (i.e. not in a hall or kitchen). They can switch the boiler on or off to maintain the temperature they have been set for.

It is possible to divide your house into 'zones' so that you aren't heating the whole house during the day when only downstairs rooms are in use, or at night when just the bedrooms need to be heated. Zone valves (or heating-circuit controllers) linked to individual thermostats can provide a separate temperature for each zone, and can be linked to an automatic timer or programmer.

Simple timers have two 'on' and two 'off' settings, which are repeated each day, so you can set them to come on for a couple of hours in the morning before you leave for work, and during the evenings when you are at home. There is a manual override that can be used at weekends or other times when your routine changes.

CENTRAL HEATING BOILERS

- Boiler outputs are quoted in British thermal units per hour (Btu/h) or kilowatts (kW).
  10,000 Btu/h = 3 kW

- If you already have central heating and wish to replace an old boiler, the new one must have the same heat output as the old – unless you plan to extend the system in which case you should consult a qualified central heating engineer.

- When you buy a boiler make sure it is approved by the relevant body: the local Gas Board; Domestic Oil Burning Equipment Testing Association (DOBETA); the Solid Fuel Advisory Service or the Solid Smokeless Fuels Federation; the local Electricity Board; CORGI.

- Radiators and convector heaters should carry the approval sign of the Manufacturer's Association for Radiators and Convectors (MARC).

- Installation of boilers is strictly controlled and must be properly carried out. Certain aspects of boiler installation are covered by building regulations – namely the hearth, flue, chimney, proximity of combustible materials, and the supply of combustion air.

HANGING A RADIATOR

Conventional steel-panelled radiators are hung on brackets fixed securely to the wall. These generally consist of a piece of angled steel with hooks to match the slots in the brackets welded to the rear face of the radiator. Since they are fairly heavy when full of water, the fittings and fixtures must be strong. They must also be aligned accurately so that the radiator will be square and level. Some radiators may have more than two brackets, but this will depend on the size.

If a radiator is corroded or damaged it will have to be replaced. Where possible, try to obtain exactly the same model as the one you are replacing; that way you can simply drain and remove the old one, clean up the threads of the new adaptors and blanking plugs, wind PTFE tape round them, screw them into the new radiator, hang it on the wall and connect the valves to the adaptors. However, if your system is a little elderly, you may have to settle for a different pattern of radiator, and chances are you'll have to fit new wall brackets and alter the water pipes.

Each radiator will have four threaded tappings – one at each corner – used for the necessary fittings to suit the pipework runs. Generally one of the top tappings will not be used and will therefore be blanked off. The second top tapping is fitted with a bleed valve while the two bottom tappings are used for the manual or thermostatic control valve and a balancing lockshield valve.

Drain the system, remove the old radiator and take the old brackets off the wall. When you have re-connected the plumbing, allow the feed and expansion tank to re-fill and the system will fill automatically. Then, bleed all the radiators.

If you want to move a radiator to a different position in a room, perhaps because you are rearranging the furniture, you will have to take up the floorboards. Sever the vertical portions of the old feed and return pipes and either cap the T-joints or replace them with straight joints. Use capillary or connection fittings to connect new vertical pipes to the original pipework, making sure they align with the radiator valve. Re-hang the radiator as described below.

SERVICING

• When removing a radiator, remember that the water inside will be very dirty. Surround the area with old rags and bowls to catch drips.

• Gas suppliers offer a range of servicing schemes for boilers and entire heating systems. These can be worth the money, especially if you are trying to keep an old system on the go.

• To stop a leak from a radiator valve, try tightening the nut with a spanner. If this doesn't work, undo the nut and wind on a few turns of PTFE tape.

1 Measure the new radiator
Lay the new radiator face down on the floor and slide one of its brackets onto one of the hangers welded to the back. Measure from the top of the bracket to the bottom of the radiator and add 100–125mm (4–5in) for clearance under the radiator.

2 Mark the wall
Using the distance just calculated, mark a horizontal line on the wall where the radiator is to be hung. Use a spirit level to ensure a true horizontal. Next, measure the distance between the centres of the radiator hangers and make two further marks on the horizontal line at that distance apart.

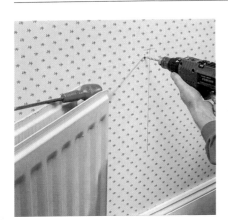

3 Fix the brackets

Line up the brackets, mark their fixing screw holes, then drill and plug the holes. Fix the brackets in place. Unscrew the valve adaptors from the bottom of the radiator with an adjustable spanner or hexagonal radiator spanner. Unscrew the bleed with its key, and the blanking plugs from the top of the radiator.

4 Fit the valves

Fit the valves so you can see where the pipes will come through the floor. With the protective plugs removed from the radiator, wrap at least five turns of PTFE tape around the threaded tails of the valve and screw them hand-tight into the radiator. Make sure the PTFE stays on the thread as you tighten.

5 Roughen the thread

If the PTFE tape starts to run over the thread, undo the valve and slightly roughen the thread with a hacksaw blade. Re-tape the thread more tightly, screw in to the radiator and then tighten first by hand, then with a spanner or Allen key. When the tails are tight, attach the body of the valves.

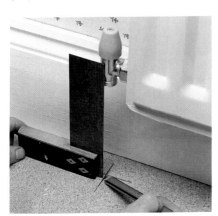

6 Marking holes for drilling

There are two ways you can run pipes: along the surface of a wall or under the floor. If the pipes are coming from beneath a wooden floor, hold a try square in line with the centre of the valve in two positions and mark the point on the floor. Where the two lines cross indicates the centreline of the valve.

7 Drill holes

Check there are no pipes or cables hidden beneath the floor. Use an 18mm (¾in) or larger wood bit to drill into the wooden floor. This will allow for clearance around the pipe. If the hole is too small, when they are full of hot water they will expand and creak against the floor.

8 Connecting pipework

If access is restricted, use push-fit joints. These are reliable but the pipe ends must be evenly cut so they don't damage the rubber seals. If you prefer, solder the joints and, if possible, make up lengths of pipes with elbows and solder them outside. You should be able to push them through the holes into the radiators.

BLEEDING A RADIATOR

A radiator that feels cool at the top and warm at the bottom has air in it, which must be 'bled' out. Each radiator has a bleed valve at one of its top corners, which is identifiable by the square-shaped shank in the centre. When you bought or had the radiators installed, you should have been given a bleed key. If this has been lost, then you can easily get a replacement from any DIY store or ironmonger's. Buy a plastic keyring for it, label it clearly and keep it in one place so you always know where to find it. Although it's not vital, switch off the circulating pump and the boiler. Place a jam jar or hold a cloth under the bleed screw and, using the key, turn the valve anti-clockwise about ¼ turn. At first you should hear air hissing out – if you place one hand on the radiator you will feel the heat rising to fill the gap. Keep the key in the valve because as soon as the hissing stops, water will start to dribble out. Close the valve tightly with the key. Don't, whatever you do, open the valve more than you need to – or remove it completely – as dirty water will come spewing out of the radiator.

Use a square-shaped bleed key to release the radiator bleed valve and allow trapped air to escape.

REPLACING A VALVE

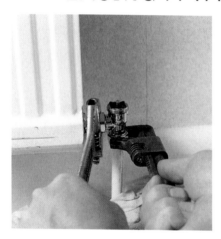

1 Remove the old valve
Drain the system and lay cloths under the valve to catch any remaining water. Hold the body of the valve with a wrench and use an adjustable spanner to unscrew the cap nuts that hold the valve to the water pipe and adaptor in the end of the radiator. Lift the valve from the end of the pipe and unscrew the adaptor from the radiator.

2 Preparing the new valve
The threads in the end of the radiator must be clean. Wrap PTFE five times around the threads of the new valve's adaptor then screw it into the end of the radiator by hand. Tighten 1½ turns with a spanner.

3 Fit valve to pipe
Slide the valve cap nut and new olive over the end of the water pipe and fit the valve to the end of the pipe. Align the valve body with the adaptor and tighten the cap nut that holds them together, holding the valve body firmly with a wrench. Next, tighten the cap nut that holds the valve to the pipe. Refill the system and check for leaks, tightening cap nuts as required.

TROUBLESHOOTING COMMON FAULTS

PROBLEM	POSSIBLE SOLUTIONS

BOILERS

Problem	Possible Solution
Boiler not working	Thermostat set too low – check setting is correct.
Timer/programmer not working	Check it is switched on and set correctly. Replace if faulty.
Pilot light goes out	Re-light following manufacturer's instructions. Replace unit if fault persists.
Circulating pump not working	Switch on pump and feel if there is slight vibration. If none, check wired connections to it. If still not working, shut it down, drain system, remove pump and clean or replace if necessary.

RADIATORS

Problem	Possible Solution
Cool at top, warm at bottom	Bleed radiator.
Cool in middle of radiator but top and ends warm	Corrosion in radiator. Remove, flush and re-fit or replace as necessary.
Do not heat up fully	Possibly due to poor circulation – air locks in pipes. Open vent plug on top of circulation pump. Close when water flows. Use small spanner and slacken nipple in flow pipe from pump. Close when water escapes.
Only some radiators warm up	Timer or thermostat controlling zone valve not set or faulty. Check timer/thermostat setting and re-set.
Single radiator does not warm up	Radiator switched off – turn on manual inlet valve. Thermostatic radiator valve incorrectly set or faulty. Lockshield valve incorrectly set – remove and adjust setting until radiator is as warm as others. Inlet/outlet blocked by corrosion – close valves, remove radiator, flush out or replace as necessary.

Contents

3

ELECTRICS

TOOLS & MATERIALS

For routine electrical repairs, such as wiring a plug or a fuse, just a few tools are needed. Most important is a torch. Keep one in a handy place and periodically check that the batteries are charged up.

• You should also always have handy a selection of fuse wire or cartridge fuses (depending on the type of fuse carriers you have).

• At least two screwdrivers with insulated handles will be needed. One should have a small blade, the other a larger one. You can buy a special electrician's screwdriver that deals with the screw connections in plugs. Also useful for larger jobs is a neon-test screwdriver: when the tip of the screwdriver touches a live wire, neon gas in the handle lights up.

• There are several types of pliers suited to electrical work: radio pliers are useful for bending the ends of bared flex around terminals. Alternatively, a pair of half round pliers is good for making loops in bare wire. Diagonal cutters come in a range of sizes and are good for cutting wire of all kinds: a small pair can also be used for stripping insulation if you don't have a pair of wire strippers.

• If your ambitions for your electrical improvements go beyond changing a plug, and include replacing socket outlets or ceiling roses, then you'll need drills and the appropriate bits, chisels, hammers and mallets. Extensive electrical jobs that require running cables through walls, under floors or in roof spaces, will mean that you will need to cut channels into walls in order to bury the cable (and then conceal it with plaster); to lift and cut floorboards; and to drill through joists and behind skirting boards. To prise up floorboards, you'll need a bolster and to cut them you'll need a tenon saw and if necessary a padsaw or jigsaw.

• You'll also need tools to help you 'make good' any surrounding areas: a float for plaster, plus decorating tools.

SAFETY FIRST

Electricity must be treated with respect: lack of knowledge and carelessness lead to danger. Most domestic electrical work can be carried out safely and correctly but always keep to the rules and put safety first.

• When electrical appliances are not in use during the day and at night, they should be switched off completely and the plug removed from the socket.

• Always turn off the electrical supply at the main switch before starting work. You don't have to deprive the whole house of power; turn off the main switch at the consumer unit, and remove the fuse controlling the circuit on which you are working, then restore the supply. Remember to put the fuse in a safe place.

• Pull out the plug of an electrical appliance before undertaking any adjustments or repairs, or when you have to change blades or bits on power tools.

• Turn off the light switch when you replace a blown-out light bulb.

• Electrical cables and flexes should never be knotted. Ideally they should be unwound and laid flat to their entire length.

• If you suspect that an appliance is damaged, take it out of service.

• Never attempt electrical work beyond your knowledge or capabilities. If you are in any doubt at all, hire a qualified electrician.

• Check you have really isolated any electrical equipment you are working on by testing with a neon test screwdriver.

• Periodically inspect the flexes on household appliances such as irons. Never patch up a length of worn flex: always replace it with the correct type and size.

• Never overload sockets with adapters and too many extra plugs and never 'hot wire' equipment by poking wires directly into the sockets.

• Always follow the correct codes when wiring circuits.
Flexible cables are colour coded
Brown – Live (L); Blue – Neutral (N); Green/Yellow – Earth (E).
Fixed cables are colour coded
Red – Live; Black – Neutral; Yellow and green – Earth.

• Wear rubber-soled shoes when you work on an electrical installation.

• *Any significant rewiring – especially new circuits – must be tested by a competent and qualified electrician. When 'new builds' and 'self build' houses apply for connection to the mains supply, they have to submit a certificate to the electricity board confirming that the wiring complies with the Wiring Regulations (see page 192). For a small fee, your local electricity board will test DIY wiring at the time of connection. Never attempt to make connections to the meter or Board's earth terminal yourself.*

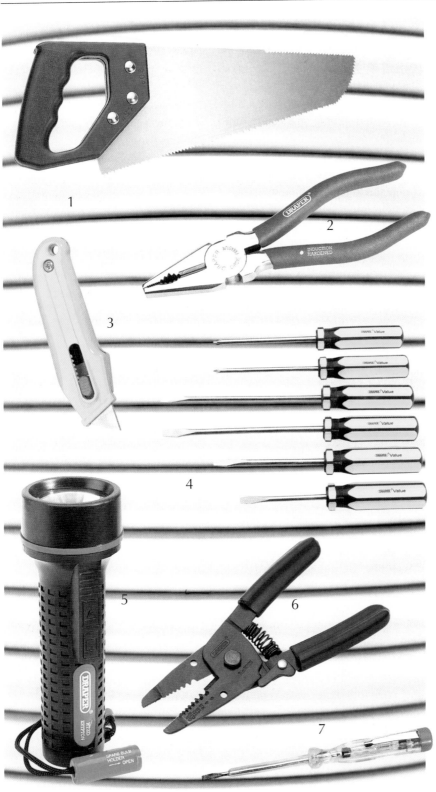

TOOLBOX

1 Tenon saw
2 Pliers: radio, half
round and diagonal cutters
3 Sharp knife
4 Screwdrivers with
insulated handles
5 Torch
6 Wire strippers
7 Neon-handled current tester
Fuse wire
Cartridge fuses
Wire strippers
Insulating tape
Sockets
Chisel
Hammer
Mallet
Bolster

HOW THE SYSTEM WORKS

Electricity is brought into your home from the main supply by a service cable, which ends at a terminal box called the service head or sealing chamber. This box contains a fuse that protects the whole installation and allows engineers to switch off the supply when they need to carry out maintenance work. Close to this box is the meter. From the main supply to your meter, the installation is the property and responsibility of your electricity supplier and at no time should you interfere with it. Beyond the meter, the electrical installation is the responsibility of the consumer.

The heart of the consumer's installation is the consumer unit, or fuse box. This box houses the main switch that governs the entire electrical supply to your home and the fuseways, which protect the individual circuits in the house. It also incorporates the main isolating switch with which you can turn off the supply of power to the whole house.

THE EARTHING SYSTEM

All of the individual earth conductors of the various circuits in your house are connected to one heavy cable in the consumer unit. This cable is sheathed in green, or in green and yellow, and it runs from your consumer unit to the consumer's earth terminal, which looks like a hexagonal bolt situated below the unit. In most houses in towns and cities, the earth cable continues from the earth terminal to a clamp on a metal sheath of the main service cable, just below the sealing chamber. Until recently, most electrical installations were earthed to the cold water supply. This meant that the earth leakage current passed along the metal water pipes into the ground in which they were buried. However, with more and more water systems being replaced by non-metallic, non-conductive pipes, this type of earthing is no longer reliable.

You will find that your pipework is connected to the earth terminal just in case one of the live conductors in the house touches a pipe at some point. The same earth cable is usually clamped to a nearby gas pipe on the householder's side of the meter before running to the consumer's earth terminal. This means that both the water and gas pipes are cross-bonded so that the earth leakage current passing through either of them will run without being hindered on to the clamp on the cable service sheath and so to the earth. These clamps should never, under any circumstances, be interfered with or removed.

PME

In country areas, electricity suppliers often use a different method of earthing the system known as PME (Protective Multiple Earth). In this method, the earth leakage current is fed back to the electricity board's sub-station along a neutral return wire, and then to earth.

Regulations regarding the PME method of earthing are very stringent and cross bondings to gas or water services usually need to be larger. If you are in doubt about the type of earthing method used in your area, always check with your local electricity supplier.

RCCB

Although the electricity companies go to great lengths to provide earthing, it is in fact your responsibility as a consumer. This is often done by installing an RCCB (Residual Current Circuit Breaker) into the house circuitry. Under normal conditions, the current that flows out through the neutral conductor is exactly the same as the one flowing in through the live conductor. If there is an imbalance between the two caused by an earth leakage, the RCCB will detect it and isolate the system. An RCCB can be installed as a separate unit or it can be incorporated into the consumer unit with the main isolating switch. See page 202 for more information on when RCCBs should be used.

MCB

In some consumer units you will find an MCB (Miniature Circuit Breaker), sometimes called a 'trip switch', instead of fuse carriers. There are two differences between MCBs and fuse carriers: current ratings for MCBs tend to be slightly different from fuse ratings, and the MCBs automatically switch to the 'off' position so a faulty circuit is clearly visible when you inspect the consumer unit.

If your MCB 'trips' to off, turn off the consumer unit's main supply switch and close the switch on the MCB to reset it – there is no fuse to replace. If the MCB switch or button won't stay in the 'on' position when you turn the main power supply back on, then there is still a fault on the circuit, which must be rectified. See page 202 for more information on MCBs.

RING CIRCUIT

The most common form of 'power' circuit used to supply the socket outlets into which portable appliances are plugged is known as the ring circuit or 'ring main'. This method of wiring consists of a loop of cable 2.5 sq. mm in cross section, that starts at the consumer unit and goes around your house, connecting socket to socket and returning back to the same terminals. This allows power to travel in both directions to the socket outlets or fused connection outlets and reduces the load on the cable.

The ring circuit runs from a 30 amp fuseway or a 32 amp MCB. It can supply appliances up to a rating of 3 kilowatts: table lamps, TVs, washing machines, portable room heaters, personal computers. Anything above that rating must have its own circuit.

The advantage of the ring circuit is that only one size and type of plug is used no matter what the appliance. There is, however, a cartridge fuse inside the plug and this should be changed according to the amount of power the appliance takes.

In theory, there is no limit to the number of socket outlets or fused connection units that can be fitted to one ring circuit provided that it does not serve a floor area of more than 100m sq. (120 sq. yd). This limit is based on the number of heaters, which would be required to heat the space. In practice, two-storey homes usually have one ring circuit for the upper floor and one for the lower floor. You can increase the number of sockets on the ring circuit by adding extensions known as 'spurs' (see page 202).

RADIAL CIRCUIT

The radial power circuit feeds a number of sockets or FCUs (Fused Connection Units) but, unlike the ring circuit, the cable on the radial circuit terminates at the last outlet. FCUs are sockets to which appliances are permanently wired and which have a fuse housed inside the unit. FCUs are useful for appliances that you don't

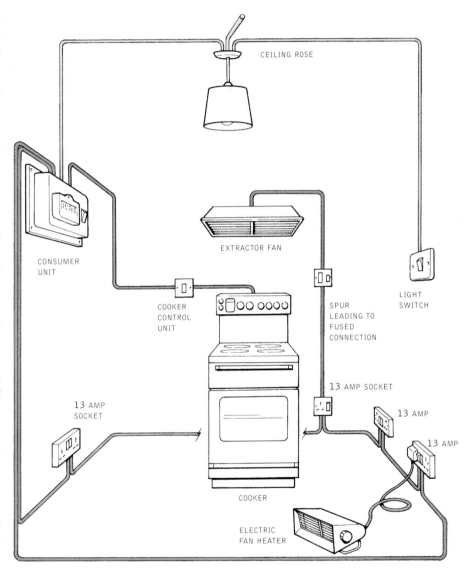

CEILING ROSE

EXTRACTOR FAN

CONSUMER UNIT

COOKER CONTROL UNIT

LIGHT SWITCH

SPUR LEADING TO FUSED CONNECTION

13 AMP SOCKET

13 AMP SOCKET

13 AMP

13 AMP

COOKER

ELECTRIC FAN HEATER

LIGHTING CIRCUIT

RING MAINS

SINGLE APPLIANCE CIRCUIT

SPUR ON A RING CIRCUIT

SOCKET OUTLET

want to keep unplugging – waste disposal units, freezers and fridges, or dishwashers – and have a switch and a neon light indicator to show when the current is flowing.

The size of the cable and the fuse rating depend on the size of the floor area to be supplied by the circuit: in an area of up to 20m sq. (24 sq. yd), the cable must be 2.5mm sq, protected by a 20 amp MCB or 20 amp fuse (which can be of any type). For areas up to 50m sq. m (60 sq. yd) you must use 4mm sq. cable with a 30-amp cartridge fuse or a 32-amp MCB (a re-wireable fuse is not permitted in this instance).

Any number of sockets or FCUs can be supplied from a radial circuit and spurs can be added if required. The circuits are called multi-outlet radial circuits. Powerful appliances such as electric cookers or showers must have their own radial circuit.

LIGHTING CIRCUIT

Domestic lighting circuits are also radial circuits, but there are two types currently in use: the 'loop-in' system and the 'junction box' system. In many instances, lighting systems in the home are in fact a combination of the two. The loop-in system has a single cable that runs from ceiling rose to ceiling rose and ends at the last rose on the circuit. From the ceiling roses, single cables also run to the various light switches.

In the older junction box system, each light has its own junction box situated on the single supply cable. A cable runs from each junction box to the ceiling rose while another runs from the box to the light switch. One

single circuit of 1mm sq. cable can serve the equivalent of twelve 100-watt light fittings – you can check the load by adding together all of the light bulbs on the circuit.

If you find that your load exceeds 1200 watts, then your circuit should be split to have two or more lighting circuits running from the consumer unit. If you have a very large house, needing long runs of cable, it is better to use 1.5mm sq. two-core-and-earth cable instead of 1mm sq. Lighting circuits also need to be protected by 5 amp fuses or 6 amp MCBs.

IEE WIRING REGULATIONS

In the UK the rules regarding electrical installation are governed by the Institution of Electrical Engineers (IEE) and laid down in a document known as 'IEE Wiring Regulations'. If you follow its recommendations, you can be confident that your work will satisfy your local electricity board. If

your work doesn't comply with the regulations, the board will refuse to connect you to the main supply. You can buy a copy of the IEE Wiring Regulations from the IEE itself or borrow one from your library. The methods in this book comply with IEE Wiring Regulations, but if you are planning on undertaking a job that is outside of the scope of these pages, you will need to consult an original copy of the regulations. *If you are unsure at any time about your competence, always ask for advice and help from a professional electrician. Always check that he or she is registered with the NICEIC (National Inspection Council for Electrical Installation Contracting). To be a member of this association, an electrician must be fully cognizant and must comply with the Regulations for Electrical Installations, the code of practice published by the Institute of Electrical Engineers.*

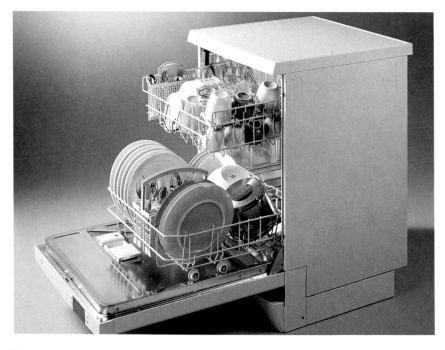

MAIN SWITCH

The main switch of the electrical system in your home switches off – and on – the supply of electricity to the entire house. Before any electrical inspection or work is carried out – such as checking and replacing a blown fuse – it is vital that the main switch is turned off. The main switch is located on the fuse box or the consumer unit. A problem with older-style systems, which have wall mounted re-wireable fuses with un-screwable safety covers, is that it is possible to get at a fuse without actually switching off the supply. The design of modern consumer units, on the other hand, means that the fuse covers can only be removed once the mains power has been turned off.

In some older houses, it is possible to find a mixture of 'fuse boxes' attached to the fuse board alongside the meter. These were often the result of additional installed circuits. This 'sprouting' of sub-boxes can often mean that the wiring is poorly labelled, so you won't know for certain whether a circuit is isolated safely or if a particular fuse is correctly rated unless you know what type of circuit it is protecting.

Furthermore, old cabling was usually covered in rubber and cotton, which perishes after about 25 years. Such wires are dangerous because they may become exposed in a metal conduit, which may be earthed to pipes, and serious, if not fatal, electric shocks are very possible.

OLD FUSE BOX

If you have, or suspect you have, an old-style fuse box, get it inspected and tested by a fully qualified electrician. This must be done before you carry out work on any part of the electrical system in your home. A qualified electrician will be able to advise you whether to replace the old fuse box with a modern consumer unit. If your fuse box is found to be in good working order, ask your electrician to label the various circuits for you.

MODERN CONSUMER UNIT

Examine your consumer unit and become familiar with it. Remember that even when the unit is switched off, the cable that connects the main switch to your meter is still live. On some units, the main switch is in the form of an RCCB – a residual current circuit breaker. This can trip automatically, switching off the main supply of power to the entire house in case of a serious fault, or can be operated manually.

Not all main switches operate in the same way. Before using it, make sure you know whether yours should go up or down to switch it off.

FUSES

Switch off the main switch and pull out an individual fuse carrier. The carrier contains a fuse that will be one of two types: either a single or double-bladed re-wireable contact, or a cartridge fuse. The re-wireable carrier will have a thin wire running from one contact to the other and will be secured at each end with a screw.

Fuse wire comes in a variety of different thicknesses, which have been calculated to melt or 'blow' at a particular temperature. If you over-load a circuit, the temperature rises, and the fuse blows and 'shuts down' the circuit. Cartridge fuses look a little like the 13 amp fuses you find in

plugs, only bigger. Like fuse wire, cartridges vary in size depending on their 'rating'.

SAFETY FIRST

In an emergency, and before undertaking any inspection of fuses at the consumer unit, always switch off the supply of electricity to the entire house by operating the main switch on the consumer unit. You can then remove the individual circuit fuse or MCB for the part of the circuit you need to work on.

TABLE FOR FUSE RATINGS

Circuit	Fuse	Colour coding	Wire diameter
Doorbell, lighting	5 amp	White	0.20mm
Immersion heater	15 or 20 amp	Blue or yellow	0.50mm/0.60mm
Storage heater	20 amp	Yellow	0.60mm
20m sq. radial circuit	20 amp	Yellow	0.60mm
50m sq. radial circuit	30 amp	Red	0.85mm
Ring circuits	30 amp	Red	0.85mm
Electric shower	30 amp	Red	0.85mm
Cooker – up to 12 kW	30 amp	Red	0.85mm
– over 12 kW	45 amp	Green	1.25mm

• Fuse wire is supplied wrapped around a card with the ratings clearly labelled (see right). Never use fuse wire that is heavier than the one intended for the circuit. Never insert any other metal into a fuse carrier, as this can be hazardous.

• Cartridge fuses are marked with the amp rating and are colour coded (see table above and picture above right). The fuse carrier should also be marked and colour-coded correspondingly.

WIRING A CONSUMER UNIT

It was once common to have separate main switches and fuse boxes for each circuit – lighting, the cooker, the immersion heater and, perhaps, a number for power outlets. When extra circuits were added, it was likely that an ill-assorted jumble of fittings and circuitry would result, making it unclear which circuit was which and what electrical load was being borne.

In modern practice, the compact consumer unit means that the fuse holders of correct amperage for the appliance or circuit are easily identifiable. The unit should be placed as close to the electricity meter as possible, and it is best mounted on a board to protect it from damp.

Cables are fed through the consumer unit usually through convenient 'knock-outs' – easily pushed out sections. The wires should be insulated by rubber grommets located in these holes to prevent the sheath covering the inner wire core from chaffing. One entry hole is used for the circuit wiring, and another for the meter 'tails', which are connected to your electricity board's meter.

Unless you are extremely confident about doing electrical work, this job should be left for a qualified electrician. In any case, you will have to have your unit inspected by the Electricity Board before it is connected to the mains.

SAFETY FIRST

Wiring a consumer unit is a professional job which should only be undertaken by experts and is not recommended for you to try for yourself. However, if you do decide that you do have the expertise to carry this work out yourself, after installing the new consumer unit, you MUST arrange for the Electricity Board to test the circuits and to connect the unit to the meter and the earth. Connection of the consumer unit to the meter and earth may only be done by your Electricity Board. Do not make these connections yourself under any circumstances.

NEW CONSUMER UNITS

- If you buy a new consumer unit, get one with MCBs (miniature circuit breakers) or cartridge fuses. Install a 20-amp fuse carrier or MCB for each heater circuit and a 15-amp fuse carrier or MCB for an immersion heater circuit.

- Do not mount the new consumer unit on the Electricity Boards' meter board even if there appears to be space for it. The new unit should be mounted on a separate board, close to the meter. Paint or varnish the mounting board on both sides to protect the unit from any dampness on the wall.

1 Mount the unit
The new consumer unit should be mounted on 18mm (¾in) plywood board. Cut the board to size, push through the 'knock-outs' in the back of the unit, lay the unit on the board and mark the position of the holes for the fuse ways, meter leads and earth wire. Drill 18mm (¾in) holes in the board for the cables. Screw the board to the wall using plastic insulators to space it and then fix the unit to the board.

2 Run the circuit cables to the unit
One at a time, run each circuit cable into the consumer unit and prepare the wires ready for connection. The circuits are wired in the same way to separate fuse ways with the red wire connected to the terminal on the fuse way. The black wire is connected to the neutral terminal block and the earth wire, which must be sheathed green/yellow, is connected to the earth block.

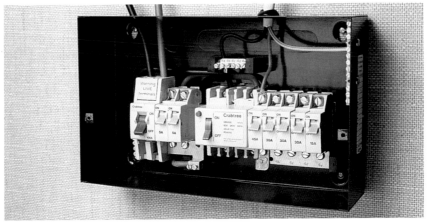

3 Cut back the sheath

To connect the cables to the consumer unit, cut back the sheath on the wires and connect the red cables to the terminal on the fuse carrier. Firmly twist the wires with a pair of pliers and tighten them securely in place so that no dangerous stray wires, which could cause short circuiting, are sticking out. Strip, twist and attach the black and yellow/green wires to their correct terminal points in the same way.

4 Meter leads

The meter leads use 16mm sq. single-core cable. The live conductor is insulated in red; the neutral is insulated in black. Both live and neutral single-core cables are also often sheathed in grey. Feed the meter leads into the consumer unit. Connect the red, live conductor to the live (L) terminal on the main isolating switch, and the black lead to the neutral (N) terminal on the main isolating switch. Connect 6mm sq.

single-core cable to the earth block in the consumer unit. The other end must only be connected to the earth terminal by the Electricity Board. Do not under any circumstances attempt to make these connections yourself. Secure the cover onto the consumer unit and call your local Electricity Board, who will arrange to visit, test and connect the unit to your meter and to the Earth.

RIGHT: A typical modern consumer unit combining the main switch (far right) and fuse boxes, which usually contain around 6 fuses: 30 or 45 amp fuse (red) for a cooker; 30 amp fuses (red) for socket outlet ring circuits; a 15 amp fuse (blue) for an immersion heater; and 5 amp fuses (white) for lighting circuits. Instead of cartridge fuses, some modern consumer units may contain MCBs (miniature circuit breakers).

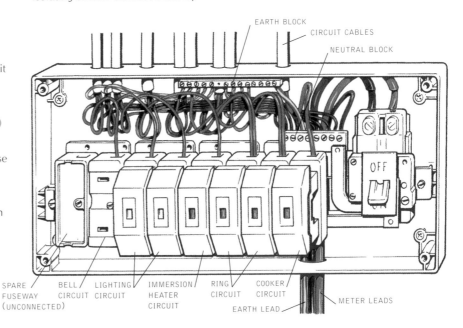

CABLES AND FLEXES

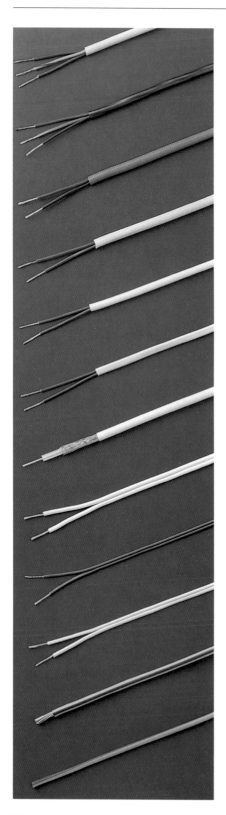

LEFT: Each conductor inside a flex is made up of many fine wires twisted together. The most common flex in domestic use is three-core circular sheathed flex, where each bundle of wires is insulated from the next by a colour-coded sheath: brown (live); blue (neutral) and green/yellow (earth). This may have an outer sheath of white PVC, or where the flex must be more 'flexible' – such as for an iron – the inner cores are often sheathed in unkinkable braid.

Not all flexes are three-core, however. Parallel twin flex, with its two conductors insulated by PVC, running side-by-side, is often used for small, low-powered appliances such as shavers. Flat twin-sheathed flex has brown (live) and blue (neutral) colour-coded conductors housed in a flat PVC sheathing. This is used for double-insulated light fittings and small appliances. Two-core circular sheathed flex again has insulated and colour-coded live and neutral conductors. It is mostly used for wiring pendant lights.

While we tend to use the generic term 'wiring' to mean any electrical 'conduits', professional electricians make a distinction between the fixed, permanent wiring of electrical circuits, which use cables to carry the current, and portable electrical appliances such as table lamps, which are connected to the fixed wiring by conductors of flexible cord, commonly called flex.

SINGLE-CORE CABLE

Single-core 6mm sq. cable is used to connect the consumer unit to the earth, and 16mm sq. single-core cable is used to connect the unit to the electricity meter.

TWO-CORE AND EARTH CABLE

This is the type of cable that runs unseen in your house – under the floors and behind walls. It is used for the fixed wiring of the electrical system in your home. It normally has three conductors: insulated live (red) and insulated neutral (black) plus an earth conductor lying between them. The earth conductor is not usually sheathed – except for the grey or white outer sheath that covers all three – except where it is exposed, such as at a socket outlet in a wall. Here it should be covered with a green and yellow sleeve, which you can buy. Some two-core and earth cables are sheathed in heat-resistant sleeving to safeguard them where extra heat may be generated – such as in enclosed light fittings.

THREE-CORE AND EARTH CABLE

This type of cable is used in two-way lighting systems – where lights can be switched on and off at different switches. This cable has three insulated conductors – red, blue and yellow – and a bare earth.

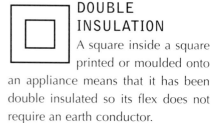

DOUBLE INSULATION

A square inside a square printed or moulded onto an appliance means that it has been double insulated so its flex does not require an earth conductor.

RUNNING A CABLE

1 Cutting the channel
Electrical cables must be fixed to the structure of the house. This can be in hollow voids between floors where it cannot be seen or, where they would otherwise be on 'display', cables are buried inside walls. In stud partition walls this is quite straightforward, but in solid walls, you should mark the cable runs on the plaster. Turn off the power to the circuit. Allow a channel of about 25mm (1in) wide and cut both sides with a bolster and hammer then hack out the plaster with a cold chisel.

2 Coping with obstacles
Ideally, cables should run vertical to switches or sockets. Electrical cables should never be run diagonally across walls: once covered and finished, it's impossible to tell where the cable is located and you may inadvertently nail or screw into the live cable. Where cable has to run horizontally, it must be within 150mm (6in) of the ceiling and 300mm (1ft) of the floor. Where you meet an obstacle – such as a dado rail – use a power drill to cut the cable channel behind the rail.

3 Burying the cable
Sheathed cable can be safely buried, although many prefer to bury it within a further plastic channel. The cable is secured in the channel with plastic clips nailed over the cable. Restore power to the circuit to check that the installation is working.

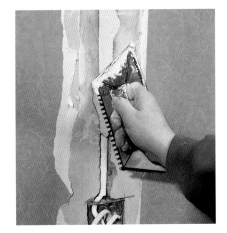

4 Making good
Turn off the power to the circuit. Apply plaster to the cut channel in the wall. Finish and make good the wall decoration and connect the switch/socket. For advice on Plastering, see page 54.

CIRCUIT CABLE SIZES (IN MM SQ.)

Size	Type	Circuit
1mm sq.	2-core & earth	Lighting, doorbell or chime transformer
2.5mm sq.	2-core & earth	Ring circuit; Spurs; 20 amp Radial; Immersion heater; Storage heater
4mm sq.	2-core & earth	30 amp Radial
6mm sq.	2-core & earth	Shower unit: Cooker (up to 12 kW)
10mm sq.	2-core & earth	Cooker (over 12 kW)
6mm sq.	Single core	Consumer earth cable
16mm sq.	Single core	Meter leads

PLUGS

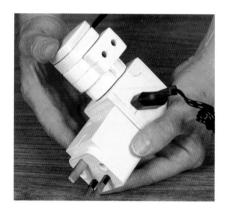

If you use socket adaptors, you can risk overloading the socket.

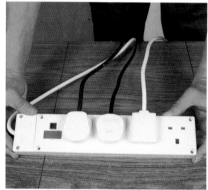

A multi-way trailing socket is safer, especially with built-in surge control.

Look for the British Standards kite mark on all plugs.

Until recently, when a new electrical appliance was purchased, you had to buy a plug to fit on it. Today, most new portable electrical appliances are fitted with a plug that conforms to British Standards BS 1363. If you need to replace a plug at any time, make sure it conforms to this standard.

Square-pin plugs have a small cartridge fuse in them to protect the appliance: the most common in domestic use are 3 amp (red) for appliances up to 720W or 13 amp (brown) for those from 720–3000W.

While the plug fitted to the appliance is approved for safety, good practice often stops when consumers plug the appliance into a socket. Always remember to turn off the appliance before plugging or unplugging into a socket. A socket, which itself can be switched on and off – these are preferable to unswitched ones – should be turned off when plugging in or unplugging an appliance. Socket adaptors – where two or three appliances can be plugged into a single socket – can be dangerous as it is difficult to know which plug belongs to which appliance. A multi-way trailing socket is ideal for hi-fi equipment and computer systems: buy one with a neon light indicator, and preferably with a surge control. If you have to use adaptors, flex connectors (which extend the length of flex on an appliance) or extension leads, then the problem really is that you don't have enough sockets or the ones you have are in the wrong place.

DO'S AND DON'TS

- Never over-extend a flex to a socket: these can cause trip hazards and damage your appliance.

- Never extend a flex by twisting the wires together to join two pieces – even if you use insulating tape.

- Make sure that the correct rating of fuse is used in the plug to suit the appliance.

- Over-long flexes or trailing extensions are dangerous. The best type of extension lead is the type wound on a drum that can be wound up when not in use. This comes in 5 amp and 13 amp versions – buy the

latter so that you can run a wider range of appliances and tools without overloading it. However, this type of lead must be unwound from the drum before use. Keeping the lead coiled tightly inside can cause it to overheat.

WIRING A PLUG

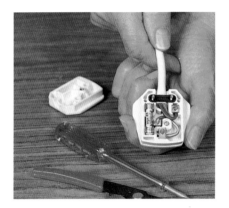

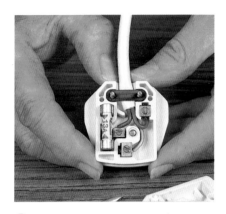

1 Trim the sheath

Remove the plug cover by loosening the large screw. Position the flex on the open plug to determine how much of the outer sheath needs to be removed: the cord clamp must clamp sheathed flex, not the individual conductors. Slit the sheath lengthwise, peel it back, fold it over the knife blade and cut it off.

2 Trim the conductors

Position the flex again so you can trim the conductors to the correct length. They must take the most direct route to their terminals and lie snugly in the channels. Cut them to length and strip off about 12mm (½in) of the insulation from each then twist together the filaments to make them neat.

3 Secure the conductors

Connect each conductor to its terminal. Post-terminal plugs have a barrel with a hole in the side and a screw on top: fold over the bared wire ends in these. Clamp terminals have a post and screw: wrap the bared ends clockwise around the post and screw the clamp nut down. Tighten the cord clamp and replace the cover.

REPLACING A BLOWN FUSE

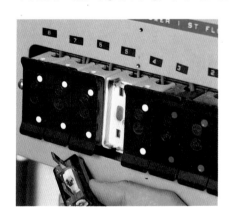

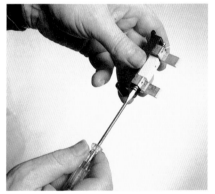

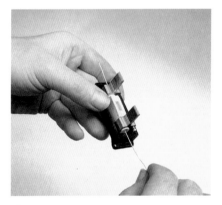

1 Look for the blown fuse

Turn off the power at the main switch. Remove the cover from the consumer unit and look for the failed fuse. A close look at a blown rewireable fuse will normally show up a broken or even vaporized wire and possible scorch marks on the fuse carrier.

2 Rewireable fuses

Pull gently on the end of the wire with a screwdriver. If the wire is broken, loosen the two terminals holding the fuse. Extract all the broken fuse wire then wrap a length of the correct rating fuse wire for the circuit clockwise around one terminal and tighten the screw on it.

3 Replacing fuse wire

Run the wire across to the other terminal. Leave a little slack in the wire, so you can attach it to the other terminal in the same way. If the wire passes through a tube in the fuse carrier, the wire has to be inserted first before either terminal screw can be tightened.

MCBS AND RCCBS

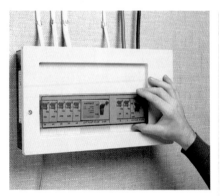

MCBs

In some consumer units there are MCBs (miniature circuit breakers) in place of the usual fuse holders. These don't have fuses in them: when a fault occurs, the MCB automatically switches off and the MCB switch will be in the off position on the board. Turn the main switch off, press the button or turn the switch on the MCB to on, and turn the main switch back on. If the MCB will not stay on, it means there is a fault on the circuit.

RCCBs

Poor practice with electricity can be fatal. A common fault is to plug a garden appliance into a nearby indoor socket. A long trailing lead from the kitchen to a lawnmower in the garden is dangerous and contravenes IEE Wiring Regulations. A socket supplying mains power to garden tools or outdoor equipment must be protected by an RCCB (Residual Current Circuit Breaker) with a trip rating of 30 milliamps. As

soon as a fault occurs, the RCCB switches off the power before anyone using the appliance gets an electric shock. You can protect yourself with an RCCB by installing a socket with a built-in RCCB (above left), by plugging an adaptor-type RCCB into a standard 13-amp socket (above right), or by fitting special plugs with RCCBs built-in to attach to the leads of all the power tools used outdoors, or by fitting an RCCB near the consumer unit to protect the entire ring circuit.

ADDING SOCKETS TO A RING CIRCUIT

One of the easiest ways to install extra sockets is to convert singles into doubles (see opposite). However, if the spur already has two sockets, you cannot convert either of them to a double socket.

To find out whether a socket is on the ring or if it is the only one on a spur, switch off at the mains and remove the faceplate. If there are two sets of wires, the socket is either on the ring or it is the first socket of two on the spur. Attach the two tester leads of a continuity tester to the two red socket wires. The tester bulb will light

if the cable is part of the ring but not if it's on a spur. Where a socket has only one set of wires, it's on a spur – but it could also be the last of two sockets. Call the first socket 'A'. Look for another socket nearby that could be on the same spur. Call the second socket 'B'. Remove B's faceplate and twist together the black and red cores of the cables going towards A. Remove A's faceplate and connect the leads of the continuity tester to the red and black wires. If the tester lights, A and B are on the same cable and you must not double either.

If you want a new socket in a new position it can be installed by means of a spur. You can have only one socket on this spur, but it can be a double. There are a couple of places where you can make the supply connection: to an existing socket outlet to which no spur is already connected; and at a joint box inserted in the ring circuit. If the ring runs close by and under the floor you'll have to 'guesstimate' its route, then lift a floorboard or two to confirm it. Use 2.5mm sq. cable for the spur. Switch off power at the consumer unit.

SINGLE SOCKET TO DOUBLE SOCKET

If you have to unplug one appliance in order to plug in another one because you only have a single socket, or if you have to use an adaptor plug so that you can have both appliances plugged in at the same time, you can easily change a single socket to a double. Multiple sockets are excellent: not only do they look tidier but they are also safer. Examine your sockets carefully: if you find any cracked or broken faceplates – often caused by vacuum cleaners running into them or furniture knocking them in a house move – they should be replaced. Replacing a damaged socket with a new similar one is very straightforward.

While any style will fit a flush-mounted box on a surface-mounted socket – the ones most likely to be damaged – check the replacement carefully because the faceplate may have squared corners, which won't fit exactly onto a round cornered pattress, and vice versa. In such a case it's a good idea to buy a new one, with a matching pattress as well.

You should also think about replacing unswitched sockets for switched ones: this can be done without having to alter any wiring or fixing. Switched sockets have an On/Off switch – and sometimes a neon indicator light – which give added protection as appliances such as TVs, radios and table lamps can be switched off 'at the wall' at night or when not in use.

In a straightforward replacement of 'like-for-like' single sockets, first switch off the power at the consumer unit and isolate the supply to the circuit by removing the appropriate fuse. Unscrew the fixing screws on the faceplate and pull it gently out of the box. Loosen the terminals and free the conductors. Make sure everything is in order inside the pattress, and then connect the conductors to the terminals of the new socket. Refit the faceplate, using the original screws if the new ones supplied don't match the thread in the pattress.

1 Remove the old socket

Switch off the power at the consumer unit and remove the appropriate fuse to isolate the circuit you are working on. Remove the old socket: if the old single socket was flush mounted into the wall, release it from the metal box and disconnect the wires from all the terminals. Coil the wires inside the box. Mark the size of the new double box on the wall, over the old single box.

2 Fit the new box

To take the new double box, you will need to enlarge the recess in the wall. Prepare the new double metal box by removing the knockouts in the required entry positions and insert a rubber grommet into each to stop the sheathing from chaffing. Pass the cables through the knockouts, ensuring that the outer insulation is within the box, and screw the box into the recess.

3 Wire the new socket

For both flush mounted (left and far left) and surface mounted (above) sockets, coil the wires inside the box and make good any repairs to the wall, allowing any filler or plaster to dry completely before proceeding. Enclose the earth wire in green/yellow sleeving, wire up the new double socket, and secure the faceplate. Restore power and test both socket outlets.

FIXING A FLUSH-MOUNTED SOCKET TO MASONRY

1 Mark the position of the new socket

Hold the metal box of the socket against the wall and draw around it in pencil. Next, mark the chase or channel running up to the socket from the skirting board to the drawn outline. Use a masonry drill and bore a series of holes just inside the lines to the required depth of the recess.

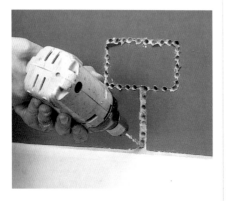

2 Cut away the masonry

Using a bolster and cold chisel, hack away the plaster down to the brickwork. Cut away the brickwork to the depth of the drill holes so that the socket box lies flat with the plaster. Fit the box in the recess. Mark the wall through the fixing holes and drill the wall for screw plugs.

WIRING THE SOCKET

To accommodate the cable, you'll need to knock through one or more of the blanked out holes in the socket box where it lies over the chase of the channel dug in the wall. Fit a grommet into each knockout hole to stop the sheath from chaffing. Feed the cable into the box and screw the box to the wall.

Where a single cable is involved, strip off the outer sheathing of the cable, separate the conductors and connect them to their correct terminals. Black to neutral – N; red to live – L; and earth – which you must insulate with a length of green/yellow sheathing – to earth – E.

If necessary, fold over the bare ends of the wires so that they don't protrude from the terminals. Bend each conductor so it fits into the box. Attach the faceplate and tighten the fixing screws gently until the plate fits firmly against the wall or pattress of the socket.

CONNECTING TO AN EXISTING SOCKET

Having fitted the new socket and wired it, you will need to run a cable – the spur cable – from this new socket to an existing one. Switch off the power and remove the existing socket. You may have to enlarge the pattress of this socket, or knock out another hole to accommodate the spur cable. Feed the spur cable into the pattress, strip away the outer sheath of the cable and separate the individual conductors. Twist the bare ends of the each conductor in the spur cable with the matching conductor ends on the ring circuit. Then insert the 'doubled' conductors into their appropriate terminals: red – Live (L); Black – neutral (N), and Green/yellow – Earth (E). Replace the socket, turn on the power and test the new spur socket.

CONNECTING TO A JUNCTION BOX

To connect a spur socket to the ring circuit you will need a 30-amp junction box with three terminals. This will have knockout entry holes for the cable or a rotating cover that blanks off unused hole. The cover must be screw fitted.

Turn off the power to the circuit. Lift a floorboard close to the new socket and in a position where you can connect to the ring without stretching the ring circuit cable. Make a platform for the box by nailing two battens near the bottoms of two joists and then screwing a strip of wood between them. Loop the ring circuit cable over the platform. Remove the cover of the junction box and screw the base to the platform. Break out two entry holes. Rest the ring circuit cable across the box and mark the amount of sheathing you need to remove. Slit the sheathing and peel it away from the individual conductors. Don't cut the live (red) and neutral (black) conductors; just slice enough of their insulation away to expose a small section of bare wire that will fit in the terminal.

Cut the earth wire – this will be the bare wires, which now need sleeves of yellow/green on the two cut ends. Take out the screws from the terminals

and lay the wires across them – the earth wire in the middle terminal, and the live and neutral wires on the ends. Push the wires in securely with the tip of a small screwdriver. Now run the cable of the newly installed socket to the junction box. Cut and prepare the ends of the wires and break another entry hole in the junction box to accommodate them.

Make sure now that the wires are matched up according to their colour, so that the live, neutral and earth wires share the same terminals. Replace the fixing screws and check that the wires are secure in their

terminals and the cables are snug in their entry holes to the junction box and that their sheathing runs right into the junction box.

Fit the screw cover on the box and then, to take the strain off the terminals, clip each of the cables to a nearby joist. Switch the power back on and test the new socket. Replace the floorboards. It is a good idea to mark clearly on the floorboards the location of the junction box and cables underneath.

BELOW: A consumer unit.

LIGHTING

LIGHTING CIRCUITS

The lighting system in your home is supplied with power from a feed cable to all the lighting points and to the light switches. Lighting circuit wiring follows two general patterns: the loop-in system and junction-box system.

In the loop-in system, cable goes from the consumer unit to each of the roses of the lighting system in turn and is connected to them (or 'looped-in'). Separate cables connect the rose to the lamp holder, and a third cable connected inside the rose leads to the switch – the 'switch drop'. There may also be a branch line leading to another lighting point, but the number of terminals available restricts such branches to only one per rose.

In the junction box system, cable passed from the consumer unit travels via a series of 5-amp junction boxes to which each ceiling rose and wall switch is individually connected.

Your home may well have a combination of the two systems, particularly if lights have been added after the circuit was first installed. Both are, in fact, multi-outlet radial circuits. Unlike the cable of a ring circuit, the cable in the lighting system does not return to the consumer unit. Instead, after looping in and out of ceiling roses or junction boxes, the cable ends at the last rose.

Lighting circuits require 1mm sq. PVC-insulated and sheathed two-core and earth cable. Each circuit is protected by a 5-amp fuse, so it can carry a load of up to 1200 watts – that means twelve 100-watt bulbs or their equivalent. That's why you'll often find that each floor of your home has a separate lighting circuit.

If you want to add an extra light to a circuit, you must first determine the current loading, and find out which lights are on which circuit. Switch on all the lights in the house, then switch off the mains power at the consumer unit. Remove one of the lighting fuses from the consumer unit and restore the power. Check which lights did not come on: these are all on one circuit. Repeat with the second lighting fuse, then the third, until you have plotted all the lighting circuits in your home.

Add up the total wattage on the circuit you wish to add to: lightbulbs of 100 watts and over should be taken at their face value; those bulbs with less than 100 watts, should also be counted as 100 watts. As long as the extra light does not take the load on the circuit above 1200 watts, you can add an extra light.

LOOP-IN CEILING ROSE

A modern loop-in ceiling rose will have three terminal blocks to accommodate the two cut ends of the circuit cable plus the switch cable. The red (live) conductors of the circuit feed cable run to the central live terminal block and the neutral (black) conductors run to the neutral block on one side, while all the earth conductors run to a common earth terminal. The red (live) conductor of the switch cable is connected to the remaining live terminal in the central block. Power runs through this conductor to the switch and back to the ceiling rose through the black (neutral) conductor on the switch cable. This 'switch-and-return' wire is in fact live when the light is switched

on, and should therefore be clearly labelled by having a piece of red insulating tape wrapped around it to distinguish it from the other black conductors (which are neutral).

The black 'switch-and-return' conductor is connected to the third terminal block in the rose. The earth conductor from the switch cable is attached to the earth terminal that is shared by all the other earth conductors, including the one belonging to the actual pendant light flex if it is a three-core flex. The brown (live) conductor from the light pendant is attached to the terminal on the switch block while the blue (neutral) conductor from the light pendant is attached to the neutral block. You can identify the last ceiling rose on a loop-in system by the fact that, because the circuit feed cable does not have to exit out of the rose to carry on to the next rose on a circuit, only one set of cable conductors is connected, with the switch cable and lamp flex attached.

JUNCTION BOX SYSTEM

A ceiling rose in a junction-box system will have the live (red) conductor connected to one of the outer terminal blocks, the neutral (black) to the other, and the earth conductor to the earth terminal. The flex conductors of the lamp are wired to match: brown (live) to the live terminal block holding the red conductor and blue (neutral) to the neutral block holding the black conductor. If the flex is three-core (with an earth conductor in green/yellow), this is connected to the earth terminal along with the cable earth.

MOVING A CEILING ROSE

Pendant ceiling lights in a room aren't always positioned where you want them. Often they are placed in the centre of the ceiling, which can create quite harsh illumination. A softer effect can be achieved by moving the rose further to one side of the room. Ceiling roses can easily be moved, especially if your house has recently been built or has been re-wired to bring it up to modern standards. If you have, or suspect you have, old wiring then check it first before you start work. If the cable is contained in old rubber sheathing or if existing pendant lights have a twisted fabric covered flex, then don't touch it. Get a professional, qualified electrician to inspect your electrical system and update it as necessary.

Moving a ceiling rose will require you to lift the floorboards in the room above. For advice on how to do this see page 74.

It is not enough just to switch off the power at the light switch on the wall; you will also need to switch off the power at the consumer unit and remove the fuse of the lighting circuit you are working on.

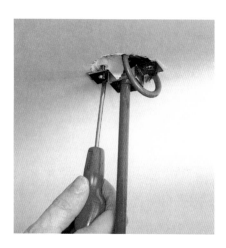

1 Remove the ceiling rose

Only after you have switched off the power and removed the circuit fuse can you unscrew the cover of the ceiling rose you want to relocate. Let the cover slide down the pendant flex. Remove the wood screws that fix it. Inspect the connections so you can re-wire it in the same way – make a quick sketch diagram if it helps. Identify the switch-return wire – if it has not already been labelled. If there is only one red and one black conductor, then the rose is on a junction box system and won't have a switch cable. There will be two or three cables running into the rose. Label them carefully as the switch and circuit cables. Disconnect the conductors from the cable terminals and separate any that are twisted together. Unscrew the backplate from the ceiling. Remove the rose, flex and lamp holder complete.

2 Install in new position

Measure carefully to locate the old and the intended new position of the rose and mark it on the floor above the ceiling you are working on. Lift the floorboards over both positions. Pass enough 1mm sq. two-core and earth cable from the old rose position to the new position, leaving at least 150mm (6in) spare at each end. If the cable has to cross joists, drill 12mm (½in) in them about 50mm (2in) down for safety, or notch the tops of the joist to take the cable and protect it with a length of protective channel (available at electrical stores). If the room above the rose is a loft area, space cable clips to the joists to secure the cable. Downstairs push a screwdriver through the ceiling at the new light position: if it hits a joist, make a new hole to one side. The cable can still pass through to one side but will be concealed by the rose screwed to the joist. If the screwdriver falls between two joists, fix a 'noggin' to the joists on each side. Never fix a ceiling rose to the plaster ceiling alone – it won't be able to support the weight of the lamp. At the new position, feed the cable through the hole in the ceiling. Strip back the sheath to expose about 75mm (3in) of the red (live), black (neutral) and bare wire (earth) conductors. Strip off about 12mm (½in) of the insulation and sleeve the bare earth wire in green/yellow sleeve, leaving 12mm (½in) bare at the end.

3 Connect to the terminals

Feed the cable through the hole in the ceiling. Push the cable through the hole in the back of the ceiling rose. Re-connect the conductors to their terminals, then gently pull the surplus cable back up through the ceiling. Screw the rose into position on the joist or noggin, and replace the rose cover. On the floor above, pull the old cable back

through the old hole in the ceiling. The 'old' supply cable will be joined to the new length of cable via a 30-amp junction box, secured on a platform between the joists made from a strip of wood that sits on the battens. Make sure that all the bare earth wires are insulated in green/yellow sleeves in the ends of both cables. Remove the screws from the terminals and lay the conductors across them: the colour matched wires from both cables will share a terminal: the earth (green/yellow) conductors in the middle terminal; the red (live) and the black (neutral) conductors on the end terminals. Replace the fixing screws and tighten with a screwdriver making sure that the conductors are secure and the cables fit in their entry holes with their sheathing running into the box. Fit the cover on the junction box and fix each length of cable to a nearby joist with cable clips to take the strain off the

terminals. Switch on the power and test the light. Replace the floorboards and fill up and make good the old rose hole in the ceiling (see pages 54 for advice on patching plaster).

BESA BOX

Some ceiling lights dispense with ceiling roses: these are known as 'close-mounted' ceiling lights because they are mounted close to the ceiling and not hung from a flex as a pendant light.

A close-mounted ceiling light is screwed directly to the ceiling by means of a backplate that houses the lamp holder. Sometimes, close-mounted lights are supplied without a back-plate, but wiring regulations require all unsheathed conductors and terminals to be enclosed in

a non-combustible housing. If you are using a light fitting with no backplate, you must fit a BESA box in order to comply with the safety regulations.

A BESA box is a plastic or metal box that is fixed into the ceiling void so it lies flush with the ceiling. There are screw fixing lugs on the box that should line up with the fixing holes on the light fitting's cover plate – but check that they do before you buy. The light is attached to the BESA box by two machine screws.

TRACK SPOTLIGHT

Track lighting systems can transform a dull room into a new environment. Ceiling fixings are supplied by the manufacturers of track systems. Remember, though, that the number of lights on the track must not overload the lighting circuit: all the lights on the circuit must not exceed 1200 watts – that's only twelve 100-watt light bulbs on the whole circuit. Make sure that your circuit can carry the load.

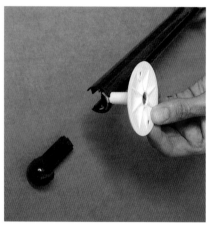

SAFETY FIRST

Don't simply switch off the light at the wall switch. Always turn off the main power at the consumer unit and remove the lighting circuit fuse before you start working on the wiring.

1 Switch off the mains power

Identify the lighting circuit you will be working on, switch off the main power at the consumer unit and remove the fuse for the circuit. Unscrew the ceiling rose cover and let it slide down the flex of the pendant light. Disconnect the light flex from the rose to free the lamp.

2 Track lighting system

Track manufacturers supply the appropriate fixings to attach the track to the ceiling. At one end of the track will be a terminal block housing into which the cables from the ceiling rose are wired. There will also be an 'end stop' for the track, which must be fitted.

3 Mount the track

Position the track on the ceiling: the terminal housing block should be situated where the old ceiling rose was located. Mark the position of the track fixings on the ceiling and then fix the track securely to the ceiling.

4 Connect the cables

Pass the current cables from the ceiling rose into the fitting of the track lighting system and wire it to the cable connector inside the housing. If the circuit you are working on is a loop-in system, mount a junction box in the ceiling void to connect the cables.

5 Attach the lights

Slide or clip the individual lights to the track. It should have an 'end stop' to prevent the lights coming off the track and to contain the current within the track. Follow the manufacturer's instructions. Replace the circuit fuse and return the power to test the lights.

FITTING A DIMMER SWITCH

1 Switch off mains power
Isolate the power to the lighting circuit you are working on. You will need to examine the existing switch in order to find out the type of wiring that feeds it so you can buy the correct dimmer switch to accommodate it.

2 Mount the wall box
The dimmer switch must be mounted into a flush-mounted metal wall box. If you are replacing a surface-mounted switch, you will have to cut out a recess in the wall that is deep enough to hold the box so it is flush with the wall surface.

3 Make good the surrounding area
Make sure that the flush metal box is free from dust, plaster debris and projecting screws in the central area of the box. Make good the wall area around the box as required (see pages 54–7 for advice on plastering).

4 Install the dimmer switch
Make sure that no wires are trapped between the plate and the box. In the case of brass or chrome plates, a PVC shield must be fitted between the plate and the wall, and the earth lead on the plate must be connected to the earth terminal in the box.

5 Fix the faceplate
Using the screws provided, attach the faceplate. Don't over tighten the screws. Replace the circuit fuse and test the dimmer. Don't worry if you hear a faint buzzing sound from the dimmer switch – this is from the radio interference suppression coil fitted in it.

SAFETY FIRST

The metal plates of brass (and chrome) accessories MUST be correctly earthed. Connect the fixed earth wire to the earth terminal provided on the accessory/metal plate and then connect a short length of wire from this terminal to the terminal in the wall box. Bare earth wires must be sheathed in green/yellow sleeving.

Do NOT:
• connect a brass fitting to a cable that has only two wires.
• connect a brass fitting to a plastic surface-mounted box.
• underload or overload a dimmer switch.

INSTALLING SECURITY LIGHTS

Dark porches and passageways beside homes are uninviting – except to unwelcome intruders like burglars. A simple light that illuminates the back or front door will welcome visitors and help them to find your home more easily. This type of light also allows you to check on the identity of any callers before you open the door to them at night.

In all cases where lights are for outdoor use, only those designed specifically for the purpose must be used. All fittings must be weatherproof and the lamp or bulb itself secured in a moisture-proof rubber gasket or cup that surrounds the electrical connection. Use only recommended cables in order to comply with IEE Wiring Regulations.

A straightforward porch light, operated by a switch located inside your home, is installed by a procedure very much like that of adding a new interior light. You can take the power

MCBs

If you buy a new consumer unit, get one with MCBs (miniature circuit breakers) or cartridge fuses. Install a 20-amp fuse carrier or MCB for each circuit.

from a ceiling rose – in the hallway perhaps – and run it to a 20-amp four-terminal junction box screwed to a board positioned between two ceiling joists. For added security, the supply cable should be run through a short length of protective conduit with a plastic grommet in each end, where the cable runs from the interior wall to the exterior wall and light.

A range of exterior lights is available, including automatically activated lights, which have sensors that detect a caller's presence.

INSTALLING GARDEN LIGHTS

Garden lights situated on paths and steps are not only functional and provide safe access in the darkness, but they can also provide an attractive backdrop for summer evening barbecues and parties.

Low-voltage garden lights can be powered directly from the mains electricity of your house, but you should always hire a professional, qualified electrician to install these for you – don't try to DIY. You can, however, install lighting that connects to a low-voltage transformer. There is

a wide range of attractive lights and lanterns connected by low-voltage flex that can run along the surface of the ground. The flex can be a trip hazard, so it is advised that these lights are considered 'temporary installations' and removed and stored after use.

Ecologically friendly solar lights are now available for use in gardens. These don't require any wiring as they are powered directly by sunlight, so there is no further cost after the initial expenditure on the lights.

SAFETY FIRST

- Outdoors, use only proper outdoor light fittings.
- Protect all outside installations with residual current circuit breakers (RCCBs) to ensure instantaneous response to earth-leakage faults.
- Low-voltage garden lights powered by mains electricity should only be installed outdoors by a qualified professional electrician.

DOMESTIC APPLIANCES

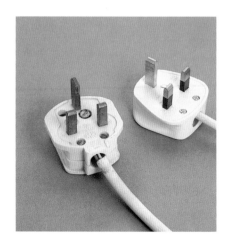

Note that the older plug on the left has dangerously protruding wires.

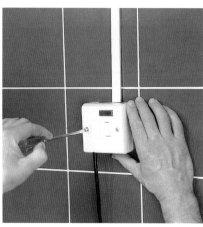

A fused connection unit with on/off switch and neon indicator light.

New cartridge fuses are easily fitted by removing the retaining screw.

Small, portable appliances such as radios, portable hi-fi systems, televisions, and table lamps as well as small kitchen 'gadgets' such as food processors and electric kettles, are designed to run from power supplied to 13 amp wall sockets. In the past, there were a variety of plugs including round, two- and three-pin plugs. Today, there are standard 13 amp square pin plugs fitted to all lights and portable appliances.

New safety developments include rigid plastic or unbreakable casings, neon indicators to show when they are 'live' and partially insulated pins to stop you getting a shock from a plug that has only been part way pulled from the socket.

13-AMP SOCKET

All sockets function in the same way, but there is a range to choose from, including coloured faceplates to match your interior decor, and ones

with a neon indicator lights. There are single- and double-switched and unswitched sockets. Triple sockets are available, but these can only be wall mounted and not recessed to fit flush with the wall. If you have low wattage equipment such as hi-fi's or computers and their peripherals, it may be more convenient to plug the components into a 4-point trailing socket.

FUSED CONNECTION UNIT

While 13-amp sockets and plugs are designed so that appliances can be moved from one room for use in another, some other appliances are permanently fixed in one position. A fused connection unit is a way of joining the 'hard' circuit cabling in your house to the flex of an appliance. The junction has the added protection of a cartridge fuse similar to the one found in an ordinary 13-amp plug. Electric cookers, waste disposal units, wall-mounted heaters, extractor fans,

and electric showers are all types of appliances connected to the power supply via a fused connection unit. Because these appliances are wired to fused connection units, there is no danger of damaging or accidentally removing a plug. A fused connection unit is the only power point – apart from a shaver socket (see page 220) – that you can install in a bathroom.

A fused connection unit can replace a socket on the ring circuit, or you can lead an extra spur of cable from an existing socket to supply the fused connection unit. Fused connection units are single – never double – although you can have a single fused connection unit and a regular socket in a dual box. Choose a fused connection unit with a switch for added safety, and a neon indicator light to remind you the appliance is switched on. As with all electrical appliances, when not in use, switch off at the controls, then at the 'socket'.

COOKERS

Some appliances, such as electric cookers, have a power load greater than 3000W (3kW). These cannot be wired into the ring main because they would overload it. Cookers are generally about 8kW, but there are bigger ones with loadings up to 12kW, which need to be installed on their own 30-amp circuits run in 6mm sq. two-core and earth cable protected by 30-amp circuit fuse.

A cooker with a loading of more than 12kW will need a 45-amp circuit run in 10mm sq. cable and a 45-amp fuse. Each separate radial circuit needs its own fuseway: often in new consumer units there are one or two spares for this purpose, or you can fit an individual switch fuse unit. This will do exactly the same job as your consumer unit, but it will only be 'looking after' one appliance. If you choose the individual switch fuse, choose one with an MCB.

COOKER CONTROL UNIT

The cable that supplies power from your consumer unit to the cooker runs to a cooker control unit, fitted within 2m (6ft 6in) of the appliance. This control is a double pole-isolating switch. It must be in easy reach of the cooker, and easily accessible.

One single control unit will serve both parts of a split-level cooker, with cables running to both hob and oven, as long as the control unit is within 2m (6ft 6in) of both. If this isn't possible, then you'll have to install two separate control units. The connecting cables must be the same size as the cables used in the radial circuits and should be sheathed in heat-resistant insulation.

TERMINAL OUTLET BOX

Free-standing cookers need to be wired with enough cable to allow them to be moved away from the wall so that you can clean behind. The cable is connected to a terminal outlet box, screwed to the wall about 600mm (2ft) above the floor, while the cable from the terminal outlet box to the cooker control unit is 'fixed'.

SAFETY FIRST

If you are wiring a cooker to a switch fuse unit, you must not connect your meter leads to the electricity company's meter yourself. Contact your electricity supplier who will arrange to test your installation and connect you to the mains if your work is approved. If you are in any doubt about installing powerful or large 'non portable' appliances, consult an electrician.

HEATERS

Electric room heaters – fans, bar fires, oil-filled electric radiators and storage heaters – are often considered to be 'expensive' to run. One unit of electricity – a kilowatt hour or kWh – is the amount used by a 1000W piece of equipment, such as a single electric bar fire, in one hour. A 2kW electric fire will use the same amount of energy in half an hour.

Look at your electrical 'gadgets': you will find their power usage in watts marked on them. On average a 2kW heater on full heat will use 2 units per hour. But heaters such as these should not be banished merely for the sake of economy. If you need to heat a room quickly, it is cheaper to switch on an instant electric heater for a few minutes than to turn on your central heating system and heat the whole house.

FAN HEATERS

There are numerous fan-assisted heaters on the market. These contain a fan inside the housing, which helps to circulate the heat throughout the room. Some models have speed controls to vary the fan. To save energy – and money – choose a fan heater that has a thermostat: when the room reaches the optimum set temperature, the thermostat will make sure that it is maintained by switching the heater off or on as required.

CONVECTOR HEATERS

Convector heaters can be used in wet central heating systems in place of conventional panel radiators. Unlike these, convectors don't give off heat in the form of direct 'radiation'; instead, hot water from the boiler passes through a finned pipe inside the heater, which absorbs the heat and transfers it to the surrounding air. There is an opening at the top of the convector through which the warm air escapes while, at the same time, cool air is drawn in through an opening in the bottom of the heater to be warmed and emitted in turn. Some convectors also incorporate a fan to speed up the circulation of warm air.

BAR HEATERS

In many ways, the two-bar electric radiator with its curved reflective back plate remains the favourite instant room heater. Over the years there have been many attempts to make these functional devices more attractive – including making their housing look like a sailing boat.

Bar heaters heat up quickly, you can have one or two bars on, and there is something psychologically 'warming' about seeing the red glow of the elements. For efficiency, make sure the reflective back is kept clean of dust – and never make toast on them.

SAFETY FIRST

- Follow the manufacturer's instructions on the positioning and use of all electrical heaters.

- Do not cover electric heaters and never place them near any flammable materials.

- Don't over-extend the flex to a socket, as this could damage the heater and cause a trip hazard. Don't try to patch up frayed flex; replace it instead.

- Make sure you use the correct rating of fuse in the plug.

For optimum efficiency, choose a fan heater with a built-in thermostat, which will keep the temperature in the room constant.

TELEPHONE EXTENSIONS

If you already have a telephone line you can install extensions, provided your line is connected to a master socket – a square white box with a shuttered socket aperture. A master socket can only be fitted by an authorized engineer from your telephone company. There must no more than 50m (54yd) of cable between the master socket and the furthest telephone extension. Make sure you have a socket converter: this plugs into the master socket and has a length of cable attached and as many extension sockets as you need plus enough cable cleats to fix the cable at 300mm (12in) intervals. You will also need an insertion tool. If you buy an approved telephone extension 'kit', this will normally be included.

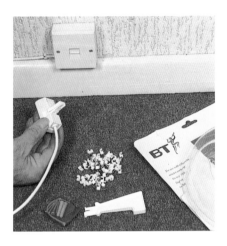

1 Start at the master socket

Decide where you want to fit the extension and plan the shortest possible route for the cable. This can be fitted along walls or skirting boards, above ceilings and below floors, but must be kept at least 50mm (2in) away from mains electric cabling.

2 Fix the cable

Working from the master socket, fit the cable in place with cleats. The socket converter should reach the socket easily, but don't plug it in until the extensions have been fitted and connected. When the cable reaches the extension, cut the cable leaving about 75mm (3in) spare.

WIRING

- Push the green wire with white rings into the connection marked '1'; the blue wire with white rings into '2'; the orange wire with white rings into '3'. On the other side of the socket fit the white wire with orange rings into connection '4'; the white with blue rings into '5', and the white with green rings into '6'.

- To add more telephone extensions – the maximum number of extension sockets is normally five – wire them from the first extension, connecting the wires in the order stated above and push them into the connection on top of the existing wires.

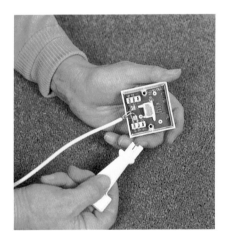

3 Wire the extension

Use a sharp knife to cut away the cable entrance hole at the bottom of the plate. Strip off about 32mm (1¼in) of the outer sheath of the cable with a trimming knife. Use the insertion tool to connect the six wires as explained in the box (left).

4 Fix extension socket to wall

At the position marked for the extension, drill and plug a hole in the wall. Unscrew the front plate of the extension socket. Screw the socket into the drilled and plugged hole in the wall or screw it to the skirting board. Fit the front plate using the two screws provided.

TV AERIALS

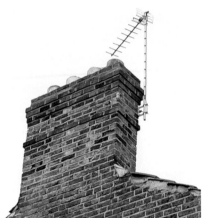

A TV aerial on a chimney stack, a satellite dish and a set-top aerial.

Television broadcasts are made on different wavebands or groups of channels and your receiving aerial is matched to the appropriate band or group. There are five aerial groups: A, B, C/D, E and W. A television dealer or rental company will advise on which group will serve you best. The size and type of aerial will also affect the quality of signal you receive: if you live close to a main transmitter or relay station, then an aerial with 6–8 elements should work well. If you live at the edge of a transmission coverage area, you may need an aerial with 18 elements in order to pick up a strong signal. Where signal coverage in an area is strong, a low-gain aerial is used, but where it's weaker, a multi-element high-gain aerial strengthens the signal. For people who move home periodically, and take their TV aerial with them, a log-periodic aerial picks up moderate signals if it can be directed at a transmitter.

POSITIONING

The position of the aerial is crucial for receiving strong signals: it must be as high as possible and with a clear view to the horizon. This is because VHF television signals travel by line of sight. To judge the direction an aerial should point, look at your neighbours' aerials. In areas where reception is poor – in narrow valleys, where there are lots of tall trees or even in inner cities where there are tower blocks close by – the aerial may have to be mounted on a tall mast or fitted with a booster to improve the signal strength.

INTERNAL AERIALS

If you live near a high-power transmitter, you may receive strong enough signals to give you good reception via an indoor aerial, but you may find that passing cars, movement in the room, and, on windy days, trees blowing in the garden or street, will cause interference. You can improve picture quality by moving an indoor aerial as high as possible – to an upstairs bedroom or even to the loft.

AERIAL LEADS

The lead connecting the aerial to your television set should be a low-loss 75-ohm co-axial cable. Because there is some loss of signal between the aerial and the set, the lead should be kept as short as possible and avoid sharp bends. The connection of the plug at the end of the aerial should be sound.

Repair any damaged connections by stripping the end of the cable and reconnecting it to the plug. Use a sharp knife to split the outer sheath 32mm (1¼in) lengthways. Fold or push back the copper wire mesh to clear about 20mm (¾in) of the hard plastic inner insulation. Using wire strippers, remove 13mm (½in) of the inner insulation to reveal the single copper wire at the core. Slide the cap down the cable (note that some cables don't have a cap; instead there is a cable clamp, which screws over the cable). Open the jaws of the cable grip and fit it over the exposed mesh and outer sheath. Make sure there are no 'whiskers' sticking out and the mesh does not touch the inner wire. Squeeze the cable grip with pliers to close the jaws tight onto the sheath. Feed the inner wire into the pin moulding and insert the moulding into the plug body. Then slide the cap up the cable sheath (or replace the cable clamp) and screw it to the plug body.

DOORBELLS

Doorbells, buzzers and chimes are essential, particularly if you live in a flat. Without some way of attracting your attention, visitors, post and other deliveries can end up standing for hours on the doorstep. Whether you choose a simple 'one note' buzzer or a set of chimes that plays a medley of your favourite tunes, installation is very straightforward.

The 'bell' can be positioned anywhere convenient as long as it is not over a source of heat. For the most part, the bell is usually in the entrance hall so it can be heard throughout the house. Doorbells are generally the 'trembler' type: when power is supplied to the bell it activates an electro-magnet that causes the striker to hit the bell. This can be battery or mains-transformer operated.

Buzzers work in the same way, except that a striker hits the magnet instead of a bell. Chimes have two tubes or bars tuned to different notes and between them is a wound coil known as a solenoid, which acts like a magnet. When the bell push is depressed, a spring-loaded plunger in the solenoid strikes against one tube

FITTING

To fit your doorbell, you will have to drill a small hole in the doorframe and pass the bell wire through to the outside. Buy a kit that includes full manufacturer's instructions.

to release a note. When the bell push is released, the spring throws the plunger against the other tube to make the second note. There are also chimes with microprocessors built in, which will provide you with a whole range of different tunes.

BELL PUSHES

Bell pushes are switches that are only 'On' when someone presses them. Inside the push are two contacts to which the circuit wires are connected. One contact is spring-loaded so that when the bell push is depressed it completes the circuit. When the bell push is released, it springs back to its 'rest' position, breaking the circuit. The little light that you often see on bell pushes is 'On' continuously, and has to be supplied by mains power because, even though it's just a tiny bulb and a trickle of charge, it would soon drain a battery. You can also get luminous 'glow in the dark' bell pushes that don't require power.

BATTERIES AND TRANSFORMERS

As well as a choice of sounds, you can install a doorbell that is battery or transformer operated. Some bells and chimes have a battery or batteries housed inside their casing, while others are operated by a built-in transformer, which reduces the 240-volt mains power to a lesser voltage needed for the equipment.

The battery, bell and bell push are connected by fine insulated 'bell wire'. Because it is generally two-core wire and very fine, it is most often surface run – along the top of skirting

The components of a simple doorbell: the bell push, bell wire and box.

boards or in the angle between the wall and ceiling. Bell wire also connects a transformer to a bell and bell push. The transformer is connected to a junction box or ceiling rose in a lighting circuit with 1mm sq. two-core and earth cable. On a ring circuit, a spur is run in 2.5mm sq. two-core and earth cable to an unswitched fused connection unit fitted with a 3-amp fuse, then with 1mm sq. two-core and earth cable from the unit to the transformer 'mains' terminals. If, on the other hand, you have a spare 5 amp fuse way in your consumer unit, you could run 1mm sq. two-core and earth cable from this to the transformer 'Mains' terminals.

If you are uncertain about undertaking any electrical work, there are also 'wireless' doorbell systems, which are operated by batteries inside the bell push and in a receiving sounder unit. The two components generally have to be placed in a straight line with each other and within an optimum receiving distance.

ELECTRIC SHOWERS

An electric shower is plumbed into the mains water supply and it is the mains water pressure that causes a switch inside the unit to start a heater, which heats up the water as it flows to the shower heat. Because there is little time to heat the flowing water instantaneously, electric showers

REGULATIONS

- See pages 174–7 for advice on the different types of shower available, along with the plumbing regulations regarding showers and the construction of shower cabinets.

- If you want to install a shower in a bedroom, it must be more than 3m (9ft 11in) away from any socket outlets, and they must be protected by a 30 milliamp RCD.

require a heavy load – from 6kW to 8kW of power – that's 6000–8000 watts, using 2 units of electricity every 15 minutes.

Because they have this heavy load, like electric cookers, electric showers must have there own separate radial circuit. The circuit cable must be 6mm sq. two-core and earth cable and be protected by a 30-amp fuse in a spare fuse way in the consumer unit or in its own separate switch fuse unit. The cable runs directly to the shower unit and must be wired exactly according to manufacturer's instructions.

Electric showers must also have their own on-off switch – just like an electric cooker. But because the combination of water and electricity is lethal, the shower unit, metal pipes and the fittings must be bonded to the earth. If these came into contact with live electrical conductors they would become extremely dangerous. IEE Wiring Regulations require all metal components in bathrooms, including central heating pipework, to be

connected to each other by an earth conductor, which itself is connected to the terminal on the earthing block in the consumer unit. This is known as 'supplementary bonding' and it is now required for all new bathrooms – even if there is no electrical equipment installed in the room and even though the water and gas pipes are already bonded to the consumer's earth terminal near the consumer unit. This bonding should be tested by a qualified electrician.

With electric showers there must also be an isolating switch in the circuit that is out of reach of anyone in the shower. These isolating switches are ceiling mounted 30 amp double-pole switches operated by a pull cord. Inside the switch are the two cables: one is the radial circuit cable, the other the shower cable.

If you are uncertain about undertaking any electrical installation, always hire a professional qualified electrician to carry out the work for you. Don't take risks.

SHAVER SOCKETS

At about 1000 shaves per penny, an electric shaver is actually cheaper than heating up water for a soap-and-blade shave. Shaver sockets – familiar to us from hotel bathrooms – are the only sockets you are allowed to have in bathrooms. Inside them are transformers, which isolate the 'user side' of the units from the 'mains' so they cannot cause an electric shock. A shaver socket for installation in a

bathroom must conform to British standards BS 3535. Other shaver sockets are available for use in bedrooms but must never be installed in a bathroom, so check first before you buy one. Shaver units can be wired to a spur on a ring circuit or to a junction box on an earthed lighting circuit. If your lighting circuit is not earthed, seek professional advice regarding up-dating your wiring.

SECURITY ALARMS

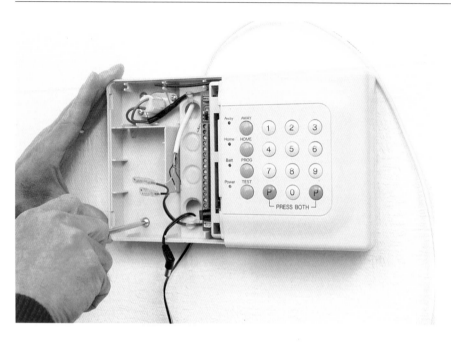

The home security market offers a huge range of burglar alarm systems; some are suitable for DIY installation, but others require fitting by professional installers. There are two basic types: one sounds an alarm if someone tries to break into your home, while the other detects any intruders inside.

When you buy an alarm system, make sure that the alarm is audible over a fair distance. Anything with a sound level below 95 decibels won't be heard, especially if there is heavy traffic noise. Tell your neighbours you are installing an alarm and make sure you choose one with a bell that stops after about 20 minutes so you don't keep them awake all night.

Before you invest in an alarm system, make a thorough check of the security of the doors, windows and other possible access points to your home. Add lights to dark corners at the front and back door (see page 212); fit window locks and good-quality door locks (see page 122) and make sure french windows and patio doors are also secure. Take advice from your local Crime Prevention Officer, and join (or even form) a Neighbourhood Watch Scheme.

BREAK-IN ALARMS

The basic elements of the 'break-in' type of alarm are the sensors, the control unit, and the alarm bell, siren or buzzer. The alarm bell itself is fitted onto an outside wall – in a very prominent position so it acts as a deterrent to burglars. In areas of high crime, it's best to fit an alarm that is also set off if a burglar tries to remove the cover or cut the wiring circuit.

The control box is the 'brains of the unit: when a signal is received from one of the sensors, it sets off the audible alarm. Sensors can be magnetic window and door switches: movement of the magnet operates a switch, which sends an electrical signal to the control box, which in turn activates the alarm. The power supply can be either mains or battery – and some mains-operated systems have a battery-powered back-up, so that if power is cut off accidentally or deliberately, the battery takes over.

In most cases the alarm system is set with a key or a code number, which is input on a push button panel. If you live in a small flat or have a room in which precious items are located, there are also small, single-box devices available, which will set off an audible alarm by the movement of a door, window or by the sound of a break-in. There are also battery-operated door alarms with delay switches: these give legitimate occupants time to enter and leave a room without triggering it.

A burglar alarm control unit.

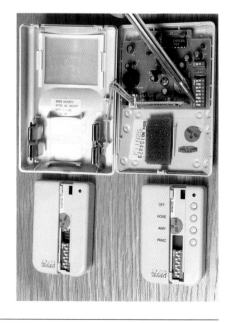

SCANNING DEVICES

Infra-red scanning devices should be positioned high up in the corner of the room where they can scan a wide area. If you have pets, adjust the height of the beam so they won't trigger the alarm.

MAGNETIC CONTACTS

Magnetic contacts can be fitted on doors and windows to trigger the alarm when they are opened. Some can pick up the vibrations caused by attempted entry.

POSITIONING ALARM CASINGS

The bell casing should be placed prominently on an exterior wall, and may be the only burglar-deterrent you need.

INTERNAL ALARMS

The simplest DIY form of internal alarm is a string of empty tin cans left in a strategic position. Though not guaranteed to work, they are about as effective as some sensors, such as pressure pads placed under a mat or carpet. Not only do sensor pads get worn with · age and become unreliable, but professional intruders will simply avoid walking where they suspect they might be located. A further disadvantage of a sensor-pad system is that the alarm can easily be set off by household pets.

Ultrasonic and infrared systems are far more sophisticated types of internal alarms. Ultrasonic alarms send out sound waves that are bounced back to them: anything inter-rupting the signal – a door opening, or a person moving in the room – will automatically trigger the alarm. An infrared alarm is triggered by an intruder's body heat, yet this type of alarm system is not affected by slow-warming heating systems.

Panic buttons can also be fitted at bedsides: these are particularly useful for the elderly and infirm. These operate an alarm even if the system is not switched on, so they are useful during the daytime as well.

It can be useful to choose a system that lets you separate your house into 'zones' so that, for example, you can have the alarm switched on for the ground-floor at night, but it won't be triggered by upstairs occupants making trips to the bathroom.

SAFETY FIRST

- Professionally installed systems should comply with British Standards BS 4737 (wired systems) and BS 6799 (wireless systems). Alarms suitable for DIY installation should comply with BS 6707.

- Inform the police if you are having an alarm installed and supply them details of two key holders who can give them access in your absence.

- It is possible to have your alarm system monitored by a company who will inform the police as soon as it goes off. Otherwise, they will not respond unless they are alerted by a neighbour.

Contents

WOOD WORKING

4

TOOLS & MATERIALS

One of the best investments any do-it-yourselfer can make is a portable workbench: they fold up for easy storage, and they have a vice for holding wood and other materials securely when you saw, drill or plane.

• Measurements can vary from one rule to another so use the same one throughout the entire project.

• The familiar try square is used for marking lines that run at right angles to edges and faces. Professional woodworkers generally use a carpenter's steel square. This is basically a single piece of 'L'-shaped heavy gauge steel that is engraved with various measurements: metric on one side, imperial on the other.

• The line of cut is best marked out with a marking knife. The scored line not only gives a much more positive position for the cut but it also severs fibres in the wood providing an ideal starting point for the saw or chisel, and reduces the potential for chipping the end of the wood.

• A tenon saw is the best all-purpose saw for cutting straight lines. It is usually 30cm (12in) long and has 13 to 15 teeth per 25mm (1in).

• Chisels used in woodworking are of three types: mortise, firmer and bevel-edged. The first type is for making deep slots for mortises and ranges in size from 6mm to 12mm (¼in to ½in). Bevel-edged chisels are lightweight. They should never be used with a mallet. Firmer chisels come in a range of sizes: 25mm (1in), 13mm (½in), and 6mm (¼in) should meet most or all requirements. Chisels and smoothing planes need regular sharpening if they are to be used efficiently and safely.

• To keep cutting tools in first-class order, use a combination oilstone. This has coarse/medium or medium/ fine grade surfaces. It is lubricated with oil and used to sharpen blades. Alternatively, a diamond stone, which has a grid of durable diamond particles set in plastic can be used.

• Striking tools – hammers and mallets – are needed for a number of purposes. Mallets are used to drive chisels into wooden joints, while hammers are used to drive joints together or to nail joints. Mallets have a 'springier' striking action than hammers, which are used for sharper blows. Useful hammers to have in your tool box are a claw hammer (the claw is for removing nails) and a lighter pin hammer. A nail punch is also a handy tool to have.

• Hand screwdrivers are available in a wide range of styles and prices, from flat tip to star head, it is important to remember to use the right tip width for each task.

• When you need an extra pair of hands to hold your work, a 'G'-clamp is ideal. These range in size from 25mm (1in) to 300mm (12in).

• A hand drill is still an essential item and there are a number to choose from. The Archimedean drill, also known as a fret drill, is used for boring small-diameter holes in thin-section wood. Braces are available with sweeps of 150–300mm (6–12in) with or without a ratchet. You'll also need an assortment of drill bits. A power drill should ideally have a reverse action – for taking out screws – and variable speeds for coping with all types of bits and materials.

• For smoothing wood, a medium-sized smoothing plane about 225mm (9in) long will enable you to tackle a range of jobs.

• Final smoothing of wood before applying a finish such as a varnish or wax, involves wearing away wood fibres with abrasive materials such as glasspaper. The particle sizes are graded as 'grit' and these are numbered. In general, work through the grades, starting with the coarser grit up to the finer ones until the wood is smooth and there are no visible sanding marks left. Abrasive papers are graded from Very Coarse, Coarse, Medium, Fine, to Very Fine. You can buy rubber sanding blocks with a detachable foot and hidden spikes, which hold the abrasive paper firmly at both ends. These are less hard on your hands than a piece of abrasive paper wrapped around a cork sanding block as the paper does not curl up around the sides.

• The glue you use will depend on what you want to achieve. See page 235 for information on the different types of adhesives.

TOOLBOX

1 Chisel and punch set
2 Bradawl
3 Power drill
4 Measuring tape
5 Tenon saw
6 Try square
7 Sander
8 Rubber-headed mallet
9 Wood saw
10 Wood drill bits
11 Adjustable workbench
12 'G'-clamp
Marking knife
Combination oilstone
Hammers
Screwdrivers
Braces
Plane
Abrasive papers

TYPES OF WOOD

Mahogany: This reddish-brown timber with a straight grain is a very important timber for furniture, cabinet making and high-quality joinery. It is most often used for staircases, banisters, handrails and panelling, as well as for floors. Mahogany is an easy wood to work with and it nails, screws and glues well. While care is needed if you want to stain mahogany, it will varnish and polish well.

Beech: This timber is pale cream to pinkish-brown but is often 'weathered' to a deep reddish-bronze colour after steaming. It is the most popular general purpose timber, used for furniture, flooring, interior and, when treated, exterior joinery. When rotary cut, beech is also used as utility plywood and it can be sliced to provide decorative veneers.

Douglas Fir: This is a softwood with a high bending, medium resistance to shock loads and a very poor steam bending rating. Douglas Fir can be worked with ease using hand or power tools, but it does tend to blunt cutters. This light reddish-brown timber is the world's most important source of plywood, while the large solid baulks are used in heavy construction work.

European Whitewood (Spruce): The colour of spruce varies from almost white to a pale 'straw' yellow and it has a natural lustre. It is used as plywood, for interior building work and domestic flooring. It's quite an easy wood to work with hand tools, and it also holds nails and screws, and glues easily. Paint, stains and varnishes all work well on spruce and terrific finishes can be produced.

Western Red Cedar: The sapwood is white, while the heartwood ranges from a dark, chocolate brown in the centre, to a salmon pink outer zone, which matures to a uniform, reddish-brown. Once dry and exposed, the timber weathers to a beautiful silver grey, which makes it the ideal choice for shingles, weatherboarding and timber buildings such as sheds. It is not a strong wood but it's easy to work with hand tools and doesn't blunt blades. Copper or galvanized nails should be used, because the wood's acidic properties can cause corrosion of metals and black stains in the wood in damp conditions. It's a wood that is easily glued, and takes stains of the finest tints without fading, although you may find that the grain tends to 'lift' after a while.

Teak: Teak is a wood that has a reputation for strength, durability, and for its decorative appearance. Widely used in furniture and cabinet making, decking, staircases, panelling, flooring and garden furniture. It does have a severe blunting effect on cutting edges,

SAFETY FIRST

When working with wood, it is important to protect yourself from dust, debris and noise pollution.

- Always wear goggles or a visor. Eye injuries are among the most commonly reported DIY injuries.

- Wear a dust mask that fits snugly around the contour of your nose: the dust from some woods and man-made boards can be toxic, as are the fumes from some chemicals and adhesives. If you are working in an enclosed space, always make sure there is adequate ventilation.

- Always keep hand tools sharp. Sharp chisels, blades, planes and saws are easier to control and therefore safer to work with. The rule is: always make cuts away from your body.

- Whenever you use power tools you should wear ear protectors. Never operate power tools wearing loose clothing, and tie back long hair. Beware trailing cables when you use hand-held power tools.

- Make sure your power tools are correctly wired and remember to switch off the power at the mains when you make any adjustments to the machines.

- Get a first-aid kit: make sure it includes bandages, gauze, scissors, a pair of tweezers, some antiseptic swabs, cream or lotion to rub on any cuts or grazes. If you have a workshop, display a basic first-aid chart on the wall and familiarize yourself with the recommended first-aid practices.

and you'll need to pre-bore holes for nails. Wear a face mask, as teak dust can be a severe irritant. Iroko, from the tropical forests of Africa, is sometimes used instead of teak, but it lacks teak's 'oily' feel. It's most common use is for parquet flooring when under-floor heating is present.

Parana Pine: This is Brazil's major timber export. It has almost no visible growth rings, and its honey-colouring makes it a very attractive wood, although it is not very durable. Its grain makes it widely used as drawer sides and because it has few knots, it is often used for staircases.

Light/Dark Red Meranti/ Seraya: The light red timbers are used extensively in interior joinery, for light construction work and domestic flooring. The dark red timbers are also used for exterior joinery, cladding, and shop fitting. Generally easy to work with, both timber types nail, screw, glue, stain and polish well.

Oak: The world's most popular timber, the genus Quercus produces the true oaks, of which there are more than 200 species. English oak is used for high-class interior and exterior joinery, furniture and cabinet making, flooring, fine art sculpture and the finest whisky, sherry and brandy casks. It stains, polishes, varnishes and glues beautifully, but oak is corrosive to metals and prone to blue stains in damp conditions.

Plywood: This is made by glueing together odd numbers of veneers with the grain of each sheet at right angles to its neighbour, and is available in sheets of 1.2m x 2.4m (4ft x 8ft).
3-ply: This is commonly used for the bottom of drawers and the backs of cabinets. It varies in thickness from 3mm (⅛in) to 6mm (¼in).
Multi-ply: This board is available in a range of thicknesses and is used to construct furniture.
Birch ply: This is a whitish board that is used for superior performance and quality. It looks good 'on its own' but it also stains and polishes well.

Blockboards: These are similar to plywood, except the inner 'core' is made of strips of wood. There are three grades, which refer to the width of the core boards: battenboard has the widest strips, in excess of 25mm (1in), while other blockboards are available with strips of 6mm (¼in) to 25mm (1in) wide. Both plywood and blockboard are also available with special decorative surface veneers such as oak or teak.

Particle boards: In particle board, timber is reduced to fibres then glued back into sheets with synthetic resins. The most common type of particle board is chipboard, which is available in several different qualities.

Fibreboards: The most well-known fibreboard is MDF (Medium Density Fibreboard). Some people love it because it is inexpensive and very versatile; others loathe it as 'ersatz' wood. MDF needs to have its edges treated by applying a solid or veneer lipping. Face masks and goggles must be worn when working on MDF.

See page 373–4 for advice on buying wood from timber yards.

STRIPPING WOOD

Most woodwork in and around your home will have been painted or varnished. If it is relatively new and in good condition, then it will generally provide a sound surface for new paint. In most cases, however, so many coats of paint have been added on top of each other that woodwork looks sticky, has visible drips or brush marks, has blistered or flaked, or it is impossible to tell exactly how sound the underlying wooden structure is. In these cases, it is far better to strip off the old finish and start afresh.

Removing paint by hand with just a scraper is very hard work and should really be restricted to small areas. There is a variety of scrapers: some have serrated edges for scoring through the paintwork and a flat blade for scraping off; others are triangular in shape – called shave hooks – and can be used on flat and moulded areas. Cabinet scrapers have a rolled steel blade and these remove paint and polish on wooden surfaces but are hard on the hands as constant pressure is needed. Faster methods of stripping include both chemical and mechanical methods. Each has its advantages and drawbacks.

STRIPPING WOOD CHART

METHOD	FINISH						
	OIL-BASED PAINT ON WOOD	WATER-BASED PAINT	VARNISH	WOODSTAIN	WAX	OIL	SHELLAC/FRENCH POLISH
SANDING	✓	✓	✓	✓	✗	✗	✓
LIQUID STRIPPER	✓	✓	✓	✗	✗	✗	✗
CABINET SCRAPER	✓	✗	✓	✗	✗	✗	✗
'BLANKET' PASTE STRIPPER	✓	✓	✓	✗	✗	✗	✗
WHITE SPIRIT	✗	✗	✗	✗	✓	✓	✗
METHYLATED SPIRIT	✗	✗	✗	✗	✗	✗	✓
HOT-AIR GUN	✓	✗	✗	✗	✗	✗	✗
CAUSTIC DIPPING for large items	✓	✓	✓	✗	✗	✗	✗

BLOW TORCHES

Blow torches burn off paint and varnish and, although they are now available in handy refillable liquid gas containers, they carry a risk of fire. The blow torch technique is to heat the paint or varnish just enough to make it soft so it can be scraped away. Never put a lighted blow torch down and leave it unattended; don't burn the paint or varnish; and don't let the hot scrapings fall onto combustible materials, such as the newspaper you put down to protect the floor. Scrapings should be deposited immediately into a metal bucket. You must also take extra care when using a blow torch next to glass or plastic laminates.

While stripping with a flame is fast and efficient, the potential to scorch wood is always there. Paint will easily cover scorch marks, but the appearance of wood that is to be varnished will be spoiled by them. Electric hot-air strippers are ideal for stripping oil-based paints and

Hot air guns strip paint quickly but can scorch the underlying wood.

Electric sanders remove the top layer of wood as well as the paint.

Always wear protective gloves when using chemical strippers.

varnishes from wood and metal. They work almost as quickly as blow torches with less risk of scorching or fire, but the same precautions apply.

SANDING

Electric sanders are good for preparing painted and varnished surfaces that are to be repainted. Multi-functional and detail sanders are particularly useful as they combine different-shaped bases and profiles that allow you to sand right into corners or around detailed mouldings such as balusters. While it is efficient, electric sanding also removes the top surface of the wood as well as the finish and produces a great deal of dust. Wear a face mask and make sure the room in which you are working is well ventilated.

LIQUID STRIPPERS

White spirit is suitable for removing wax and oil finishes on wood but will not remove paint or varnish. Though gentle and effective, it removes the nourishing waxes and oils, thus drying the wood, and can leave it

looking dull. Methylated spirit can only be used to remove shellac-based finishes such as French polish and is used by professional furniture restorers because of its 'gentleness'.

When it comes to stripping large or 'fiddly' areas of woodwork, the most convenient methods – although not the cheapest – are gel, liquid, or paste strippers. Because of their fluidity, liquid strippers are only suitable for use on wood that is, or can be laid, horizontal, otherwise it just slips off. Gels are thicker and will 'grip' most vertical household joinery. Many proprietary strippers will remove all types of paint, varnish and lacquer but you'll need to reapply if there are several layers or finish to be removed.

Neutralize the stripper by washing down the wood with white spirit or water; follow the manufacturer's guidelines. While water is cheaper, it will raise the grain on wood and may cause joints to swell. Despite their claims to 'low odour' you must still work in a well- ventilated room and avoid naked flames. Watch out too if you wear spectacles with plastic

lenses, and remove watches since the caustic strippers will 'melt' plastic.

PASTE STRIPPERS

Paste strippers have a thick, creamy consistency, which makes them ideal for stripping vertical and even overhead surfaces, and they can be pressed well into mouldings and intricate shapes. Again they need to be neutralized. They have a tendency to leave the stripped wood somewhat dark. Paste strippers are also available in 'blanket' forms: these are expensive but don't need neutralizing and remove the paint cleanly, requiring very little scraping. This makes them ideal for delicate objects or easily scratched surfaces. Once applied you wait – sometimes for hours – for the paint to solidify onto the blanket, which is then peeled away.

Whatever method you use, work safely and follow manufacturer's instructions. After wood is stripped, it should be treated as if it is 'new' timber: filled and sanded, knots sealed, then primed, and finished.

FILLING HOLES

Where plaster is used for filling dents and cracks in plasterwork (see page 54), fillers are used for filling larger indentations in wood. The main difference is that fillers have to match the colour of the piece of wood and require an elastic nature to cope with the movement of wood. It is also important that the right type of filler is used. Bear in mind the type of finish you want to achieve and the way the wood will be used, from a tough durable repair to exterior woodwork (such as doors and window frames) where the repair will be painted over; a repair to a floorboard; or a repair to a piece of fine wooden furniture. The most common fillers are cellulose, wood stopping, plastic wood, epoxy resin-based filler, and shellac and wax sticks.

Cellulose fillers come in powder form for mixing with water, or ready mixed in tubs or tubes. These are ideal for repairing holes in particle board because an exact match can be difficult, even with a stain or pigment. Wood stopping is a traditional filler with very good adhesion, which can be smoothed and shaped when hard.

Wood stopping is available in both interior and exterior grades.

Plastic wood is available in two-part or one-part form. It is formulated to resemble wood when dry and comes in several wood shades to provide a close colour match. Plastic wood dries out very quickly, so always replace the lid immediately. To get a good strong adhesion, the wood must be clean and dust free. Plastic wood is solvent-based, so you'll need to work in a well-ventilated area or wear a mask. Once set, it shrinks a little, so leave it a little thick to dry, then shape it and smooth it just like wood.

Epoxy resin-based fillers also come in wood colours and provide a very strong adhesion. The wood needs to be treated first with a hardening agent in order to 'toughen up' any soft wood fibres. These fillers set by chemical action, which, once started, cannot be stopped. The filler and hardening agent are mixed together according to manufacturers' instructions; only mix enough at a time to work for a few minutes to avoid waste.

Shellac and wax sticks are generally used for repairs to fine furniture and under traditional finishes. Shellac sticks are sold in a variety of colours and are a concentrated form of the shellac used in French polishing. The manufacturers of wax finishes also make wax sticks for small repairs. These coloured sticks are designed for use on surfaces, which will be waxed, or on pieces that are already polished. Wax and shellac sticks need to be warmed with a soldering iron and the molten wax or shellac pushed into the chip or hole in the wood with a small filling knife and any excess scraped off carefully when dry.

SANDING AND LEVELLING

A power drill with disk sander.

The general term for smoothing wood prior to applying a finish is 'abrading'. This is simply the wearing away of wood fibres by the sharp teeth of abrasive material.

Abrasive papers have abrasive particles bonded to their surface: glass paper (or sandpaper) is the

WOODWORKING

- A very quick – and cheap – filler, ideal for filling large holes in wood, can be made simply by mixing PVA adhesive with some sawdust to match the wood you are repairing. Add the sawdust to the glue, and mix thoroughly until a thick yet workable consistency is achieved.

- Be extra careful when power sanding: it is easy to take off too much material. Use coarse abrasives for shaping and rounding, and finer ones for a smooth finish.

cheapest abrasive paper; garnet paper is harder and better quality and used for fine finishing of furniture; silicon-carbide paper is often called wet-and-dry paper, because it can be used either way. Use it wet for removing the glaze from paint before repainting: the water acts as a lubricant and also keeps down paint dust, which may contain lead. The particles are called 'grit' and these are numbered. Generally, you work through the grades, starting with the coarsest and working through to the finer ones until the wood is smooth and there are no sanding marks.

Other methods of abrading wood include rasps and files (bars of variously shaped steel with patterns of teeth cut onto their surface), or surform tools (a combination of files and planes). Steel wool, graded by '0's – the more '0's, the finer the wool – is used with white spirit for taking the gloss off sealers and varnishes before recoating.

Belt sanders abrade faster than other power sanders but must be held firmly to prevent them snatching at wood.

POWER SANDING

Power sanding is done with an attachment to a power drill or with a specially designed sanding tool. The most popular sanding attachment for a power drill is the disc sander. This has a flexible backing pad that holds a removable abrasive with a screw and washer. Because the disc always cuts across the grain of the wood, leaving marks that are difficult to remove, you should reserve this tool for 'rough' work.

ORBITAL SANDER

Orbital sanders use ½ or ⅓ size abrasive sheets, which are cramped to a padded baseplate. These are available as attachments for power drills or as separate power tools. The sanding action is elliptical and is ideal for sanding large panels flat. Let the weight of the tool itself do the work, but keep it moving up and down and across the work piece in a gentle sweeping action.

BELT SANDER

A belt sander is a semi-professional power tool that has a continuous 75mm or 100mm (3in or 4in) wide belt, which passes over a flat bed via two rollers. It can also be inverted for flat and curved sanding once the tool has been securely cramped to a workbench. A belt sander is ideal for final smoothing after planing, for levelling floorboards and for getting into corners where a large, hired floor-sanding machine cannot reach. Hold onto it firmly as you work so that it doesn't snatch at the wood or take off across the surface.

Bench planes smooth long pieces of wood.

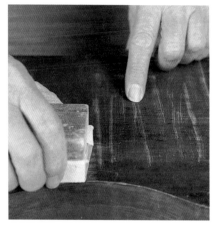

Sanding against the grain produces visible scratch marks.

Use progressively finer abrasive papers for sanding.

PLANING

Planing prepares wood for accurate marking and cutting of joints (see pages 236–7), and also smooths the wood ready for the finishing steps. Plane blades should be razor-sharp and carefully adjusted to shave off just the right amount of wood required. Planing is a skill that takes practice, so be prepared to spend some time getting used to the tool and the techniques needed to sharpen, adjust and use it accurately.

There is a wide range of wood-working planes to cope with all kinds of work, but a long bench plane gives an accurate result. While a small plane follows the contours of the surface of the wood, a long plane rides over high spots in the wood, gradually removing them until the wood is even and a single, long shaving can be removed.

Bench planes are 350–380mm (14–15in) long and are used for levelling and smoothing long lengths of timber. A block plane is useful for small work and for end-grain

trimming: these are available in sizes from 90–200mm (3½–8in) long.

You will need to make sure the wood you are smoothing is held completely flat and that you are working with the grain. Set the plane's cutter and blade depth for the merest skimming cut and test that the shavings are paper thin. Working with a skewed, drifting stroke, start planing at the furthest end of the wood, skimming off any high spots, and back up along the length of the wood.

If this sounds too complicated, a power planer is a great way to achieve a quick finish. The blades, however, soon become nicked and can result in thin ridges on the wood running in the direction of the grain, which you have to remove with a smoothing plane in the end.

A good alternative is a surform, a sort of combination tool of file and plane. The open-toothed structure of the surform allows you to cut and shape wood like a hot knife through butter and work without the teeth becoming clogged up.

SANDING

Always sand in the direction of the grain of the wood. Before the final sanding, dampen the wood with water to raise the grain. When it has dried, sand with very fine abrasive paper for a perfect, smooth finish.

SANDING

- Beeswax or candle grease applied to the face of a plane will make planing easier when the entire face of the plane is in contact with the wood.

- To sand end-grain, rub the grain of the wood with your finger. When rubbing in one direction feels less rough than rubbing in the others, sand the grain in that direction only – not to and fro.

- Sanding in curved areas is best done by wrapping abrasive paper around a short length of dowel.

TREATING AND SEALING

KNOTS

Wood knots are dark rings in planed timber. They are caused by the small branches, which grew from the main trunk of the tree and they need to be treated before the wood is finished. Loose knots in wood are a sign of poor-quality timber and, if the knot has fallen out completely leaving a hole, this will have to be filled with wood filler before finishing.

Most knots are resinous: they continue to seep sap even after finishing. This can cause bleeding through paintwork and a dark yellow stain will appear. If you are applying clear varnish, there is no need for knotting solution, as the varnish will seal the knot. But if you want to apply a paint finish, treatment with a knotting solution is necessary.

USING KNOTTING SOLUTION
On new wood that has not dried out , knotting solution is used to treat knots so they don't seep and spoil a finished paint effect. A treated area will not accept a colour wash as well as bare wood, so apply the solution to the knot alone. A fine artist's paintbrush is ideal for this.

TREATING PALE WOODS
White knotting solution, which is transparent when dry, is ideal for use on pale woods. Dab a little of the knotting solution onto a clean dry rag then rub it well into the knot. The solution will dry very quickly, leaving little or no visible marks underneath any subsequent finish.

GLUES

Modern glues are fast, reliable, easy to use and strong. Some are 'user friendly': they take time to set and dry, allowing you to make adjustments during assembly and even to disassemble pieces in the future. Others fix forever, making a bond that is stronger than the wood itself.

Adhesives for wood and man-made boards include PVA woodworking glue; synthetic resin; rubber-based contact adhesives; cyanoacrylates (the 'super-glues') and acrylic adhesive. Yellow glue is a 'fast-tack' glue, almost transparent and non-toxic. It's good for sanding and can be used indoors and out. For joints that

need to be waterproof, two-part epoxy resins are needed; note that in powder form they can be toxic. Always follow the manufacturers' guidelines on application and storage. Some glues contain solvents that can give off dangerous fumes, so work in a well-ventilated area. Check what solvent is needed to remove the glue: some simply need water; others require methylated spirits, acetone or even (for superglues) a special solvent. Whichever glue you use, apply it sparingly and immediately wipe off any excess.

PVA, or white glue, made from petrochemicals, is one of the most

common and is non-toxic. Squeezed straight from the tube, it becomes transparent. When you sand it, however, it goes a little rubbery.

MEASURING

MARKING AND CUTTING GAUGES

A marking gauge is used to score a line parallel to the edge of a piece of wood. A small metal spike is set on the wooden shaft with an adjustable stock, which slides up and down it. The stock is set at the required distance from the spike. The face of the stock is then pressed firmly against the edge of the timber and the tool is pushed away from you to scribe the line.

A similar gauge, a cutting gauge, is used to cut across the grain of wood. If you tried to scribe a line with a marking gauge here, the spike would tear the wood's surface. In place of the spike, a sharp blade is held in the shaft with a removable wedge.

A third type of gauge is known as the mortise gauge. This has two pins, one fixed and one moveable for marking the parallel sides of mortise and tenon joints.

Remember, when you measure and mark wood, always do so on the face side or face edge – the best looking side or edge of a piece of timber. Professional carpenters use a looped letter 'l' for the best side, and a small 'x' for the best edge.

USING A MARKING GAUGE
Tilt the gauge at a slight angle so that the spike is touching the wood's surface.

TRY SQUARES AND BEVELS

Try squares are used for marking lines that run at right angles; avoid dropping them as they can be knocked out of true. The carpenter's square is designed primarily for large jobs such as tabletops, cupboard frames and doors. The short arm (the 'tongue') is 40.65cm (16in) long and the long arm (the 'blade') is 60.95cm (24in) long. Because it is made out of a single piece of steel, it's strong, precise and pretty much 'idiot proof'. The long arms of the square mean that they are in contact with the workpiece for longer, which gives greater accuracy. You don't have to keep measuring and marking a series of short lines.

Sometimes known as a 'T' bevel, or a bevel gauge, the sliding bevel is another tool used for marking and laying out angles. It is used like a standard try square, but the blade can be adjusted to take and mark out any angle. Bevels either have a blade pivoted in the middle of a wooden stock (handle), or a blade slotted so that it slides along the pivot.

To draw an angle, the wing nut or screw is loosened, the blade set to the required angle against a protractor – or set against an existing angle – the nut is tightened, and the angle then transferred to the work piece. Hold the stock of the bevel hard against the edge of the work piece.

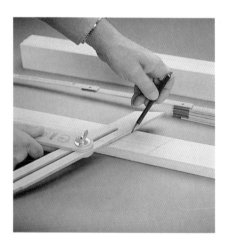

USING A SLIDING BEVEL
Transferring an angle with a sliding bevel. The wing nut is loosened to set the blade to the required angle.

CUTTING

TENON SAW

The tenon saw (below), also known as a back saw, has a blade stiffened with a heavy metal strip folded over its top edge. It is a good, all-purpose woodworking saw, and has fine teeth filed at an angle, which allow it to cut across the grain of timber without tearing the fibres.

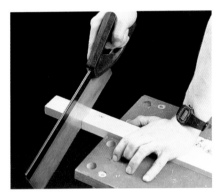

FRAME SAW

The frame saw is fitted with very fine blades for cutting curves. To stop the blade from bending it is held secure in a frame. A coping saw blade is held between two pins that swivel so you can turn in the direction of the cut while the frame is held clear. It is one of the most useful frame saws because its teeth are coarse enough to cut thick timber as well as thin boards.

PAD SAW

This is also known as the compass or keyhole saw because it is used for cutting holes in panels. It has quite a wide blade, so a pad saw is good for straight cuts in thick timber.

POWER SAWS

Circular saws are available as attachments to electric drills, but a purpose-made one is more powerful. It is used for straight cuts in timber and board, but is normally limited to a maximum depth cut of 40mm (1⅝in). More versatile is the jigsaw, which will take a range of blades and has variable speeds. A power jigsaw can cut both straight and curves and is easy to operate – once you learn to keep the pressure constantly against the surface of the wood.

USING A RIP SAW

A rip saw cuts wood along its length. Set the work at an angle and height so you can look directly down the line to be cut. When you start to cut, place the blade well to the waste side of the marked cutting line. Hold the blade at a low angle with your index finger pointing along the blade. Make a few initial dragging strokes to establish the cut, and then make gradually increasing strokes until you are using the full length of the blade.

CROSS CUTTING

When you come to about 5cm (2in) of finishing a cut across the grain of wood, quickly hook your free hand around the waste piece to support it and make your sawing strokes increasingly lighter until the wood is sawn through.

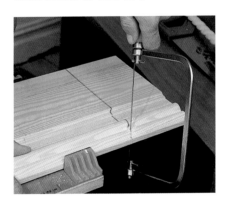

DRILLING

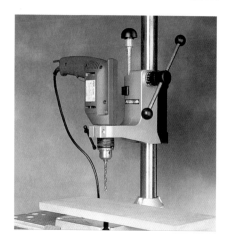

HAND DRILL

Also known as a wheel brace, the hand drill is good for drilling small diameter holes, and can be used in confined spaces. It is operated by turning a small drive wheel at the side and although it is much slower than a power drill, it is easier to control. To get a hand drill moving, move the handle to and fro until the drill bit bites into the wood, then turn the handle to drive the bit clockwise.

BRACE

A brace is used for drilling larger diameter holes and is invaluable in situations where it is not possible to run an extension lead for a power tool. A brace is operated by pushing the middle of the tool round in a circular sweep. Braces are available with sweeps of 150–300mm (6–12in), but good braces will have a ratchet mechanism, which allows you to make 'part sweeps' in spaces where a full sweep is impossible.

ELECTRIC DRILL

There is a wide range of power drills available. Most have 2–4 fixed speeds with a switch to select the one appropriate to the job: slow speed for drilling masonry, high speed for clean drilling in wood. A reverse action is useful if you want to use a screwdriver bit with a power drill: this lets you drive in screws as well as take them out again. Use a drill stand and pre-set the depth stop and fix to the stand before starting work.

SAFETY FIRST

- Unplug power tools before attaching accessories or changing a drill bit.
- Never lift a power tool by its flex.
- Always use the appropriate safety devices for the tools.
- Tie back long hair, make sure sleeve cuffs are secure and out of the way. Wear appropriate eye protection and a dust mask.
- Keep tools, bits and blades sharp and clean and stored safely out of reach of children.

DEPTH MARKING

Professional woodworkers make their own depth stop blocks – small blocks of wood cut to the appropriate size, which slide on the drill bit. The 'working end' of the bit protrudes out at the correct length from the end of the block. A quick method is to wrap some masking tape around the bit at the correct depth. When the drill bit has bored to the line of the masking tape, the hole will be the correct depth.

JOINING

SCREWS

Screws are made of a variety of materials, including mild steel, brass, copper and aluminium. They can be black japanned, galvanized or plated with nickel, tin, zinc or chromium. Standard screws have what is known as a single start thread, but some have a twin start head, which reduces the number of turns need to drive it home. These types of screws are also hardened, making them suitable for use with power tools.

Screws are measured by their length: the distance between the tip and the part of the head that will lie flush with the surface of the wood. A second measurement is the gauge – the diameter of the screw's shank. Screw gauges are numbered from 1 to 20 – the thicker the screw the higher the gauge number (see page 375).

Screws for woodworking come with a range of head shapes. Those with countersunk heads are used where the screw head is to be recessed flush with the work surface or just below it. Round-headed screws are used with sheet materials that are too thin to take countersunk

screws. Often these are used for metal fittings and can have decorative heads, which remain on view; bathroom mirrors are often attached to walls with domed-head screws, which have a threaded hole in the centre of the head into which a decorative dome can be screwed.

There are also special 'tamper-proof' screws known as clutch heads. These can be tightened but don't offer any grip if you try to unscrew them. All screws – apart from clutch-head and domed-head ones – are available as cross-slot or as single-slot screws. Where heavy sections of timber are being joined, coach screws are often used. These are heavy-duty screws with nut heads, which are screwed into a start hole with a spanner. Chipboard screws, on the other hand, are specially designed with a double spiral thread and taper only at the end to give them a strong hold in this relatively weak material.

CABINET FIXINGS

Special connectors called 'knock-down' fittings are strong and easy to fit. These are useful for joining chip-

board sections to construct cabinets. The plastic joins pull the boards together when screws are fitted through the joints. The plastic join is fitted to one board with two screws, then screwed through again to join the second board. This system avoids having screw or nail heads on view and means that the piece can be disassembled in future (see left).

DOWELS

Dowel joints use small wooden pegs or dowels in place of hand-cut timber joints. The joint can be any configuration: 'L'-shaped, 'T' shaped, or 'X'-shaped. Two pieces are butted or mitered together with a series of carefully aligned drill holes to accommodate the dowel. Normally these pegs are made of stout wood and manufactured in short lengths in three main diameters: 6mm, 8mm, and 10mm ($\frac{1}{4}$in, $\frac{5}{16}$in and $\frac{3}{8}$in) with flutings or grooves along their lengths. The grooves allow glue to disperse evenly; without them, the dowel would compress the glue in the bottom of the drill hole.

ADHESIVE JOINS

Choose the right glue for the job in hand (see page 235) and make sure you know all there is to know about mixing, setting times, and any necessary precautions. Do a dry run before you actually glue up any joint. Work in a clean, dust-free environment – and choose somewhere you won't be interrupted.

The mating faces – the two faces of wood to be joined – must be clean and dust-free. Assemble the joints together, clamping them if necessary – keep some small offcuts of wood handy to protect the piece from the jaws of the clamp.

Once you've done a trial assembly so you know which piece goes where, use a low-tack masking tape to cover the areas outside the joint that you want to keep free of glue. You can use a fine artists' paintbrush

PVA glue is good for interior woodwork. Joints set within 24 hours.

For outdoor use, you can get waterproof PVA, or use two-part epoxy-resin.

to apply glue to small areas. Assemble the joint, checking for alignment and squareness and then clamp it. Wipe off any excess glue that may have oozed from the joint immediately – when dry, some glues will repel paint finishes or remain visible underneath it. Wait until the glue is set (check the manufactuers' instructions), then peel away the masking tape and scrape or sand the surfaces to a fine finish.

Because of their difficult shape, some repairs to joints – particularly on chairs – are difficult to keep clamped until the adhesive dries completely. One of the best ways to clamp a chair – or any other odd-shaped structure – is to use a length of rope or webbing about 50mm (2in) wide and a stout stick clamp – a bit like a tourniquet. This is great for pulling chair legs onto stretchers but be careful that you do not over-wind and break the other joints in the chair. And beware when the stick is unwound – once loosened, they have

a habit of spinning suddenly so watch you don't get hit in the face.

Glue guns are useful for accurate spot-glueing. The gun is fitted with a rod of solid glue – various types are available – that is heated until it melts then discharged as a liquid, or with a cartridge of cold glue that is forced out when you pull the trigger. Both types tend to be fast-setting.

GLUEING

• To remove a dribble of glue from a joint, wait until the glue has become rubbery, then cut off the dribble with a sharp chisel.

• Candle wax will stop glue sticking where it is not required.

• Make sure you have the manufacturers' recommended solvent handy: it is inevitable that you'll get some glue where you don't want it – normally on your own hands or clothes.

SAFETY FIRST

• Remember, some glues contain solvents that can give off dangerous fumes, so make sure that the area you are working in is sufficiently ventilated at all times.

• Super-glues can bond human skin, so take care when handling them and wear gloves if possible.

REPAIRING OLD FURNITURE

CHAIR

TWO-PART ADHESIVES

Some straight adhesives are 'two-part' preparations. The two parts are supplied in separate containers and must be mixed in the recommended quantities. Use a clean, dry ceramic tile as a mixing palette.

1 Scrape off old glue

Remove all the old glue, scraping it back to the wood, and apply a PVA-based glue to the tenon parts of each piece then tap it gently back into place. Wipe away any surplus adhesive immediately before it sets.

2 Make a 'tourniquet'

To keep the seat frame and legs of a chair rigid when glueing, use a length or rope or webbing as a tourniquet. Put some soft padding at the four corners to stop the rope/webbing making any marks. Turn a stick to tighten the rope/webbing.

3 Breaks across rails

If a broken rail is made of dowel rod, take the broken piece to a DIY supplier and get a new piece of a similar diameter and colour. Cut and shape the new dowel using a rasp and sandpaper.

4 Repairs using dowel

Where a break is across the grain of a large rail, it can often be repaired by inserting sturdy dowel to link the two broken pieces together. The hardest part of this is aligning the holes.

CHAIR REPAIRS

- Another way to deal with a badly fitting or loose joint is to use a special glue, which expands as it dries, thereby acting as a filler. This is available at most good DIY stores.

- Where a shape makes it awkward to clamp pieces together, wind a length of cord tightly around the break until the adhesive sets.

- See pages 254–5 for advice on recaning chair seats.

DRAWERS

Drawers suffer wear and damage over time simply because they are constantly being opened and closed. Loose joints can easily be repaired by taking the drawer apart, cleaning out the old adhesive, and re-glueing the pieces. When you repair any pieces of furniture, only repair the weak or damaged joints, leaving any sound joints alone.

In old drawers the bottoms are generally made out of thin boards, glued together edge to edge. Sometimes these boards split – either because too much weight has been placed on them, or because they have shrunk. Replacing these boards will mean you have to dismantle the drawer, because they are usually set into grooves in the sides. A temporary repair to a split drawer bottom can be made by glueing a wide strip of stiff canvas along the underside of the split using PVA adhesive.

If a drawer flies out of its hole when you open it, the drawer stop has become dislodged. This happens when the runners have slipped or have become distorted. A sticking drawer is often caused by damp or high levels of humidity, which causes wooden drawers to swell. The drawer needs to dry out slowly and once thoroughly dry, it should be rubbed lightly with sandpaper before being lubricated with a candle stub or a bit of soap. Drawer knobs are also often pulled off. Don't wrap scrolls of paper or string around the shaft of the knob, as this will most likely make the hole bigger in the long run. A better solution is to re-fix the shaft in place with a gap-filling adhesive. If the hole is still too big, try adding some sawdust to the adhesive.

1 Dismantle the drawer

If the side of a drawer has become loose or damaged, you will need to fix or fit a replacement. First dismantle the drawer and clean up the joints. Ease apart the joints – the steam from a boiling kettle often helps. When clean and dry, apply PVA adhesive to the joints.

2 Reassemble the drawer

Fit the loose or replacement panel. Gently ease the joints together. If the joint is a rebated joint, it can be secured further with pins. Make sure that the drawer is still square. If you need to, make a tourniquet to hold the joint while the adhesive dries.

3 Remove excess adhesive

Carefully wipe away any excess adhesive that may have oozed from the joint as the drawer was being reassembled. Follow the manufacturer's guidelines regarding setting times and allow the adhesive to dry out thoroughly before replacing the repaired drawer into its aperture.

INFESTATION, ROT AND WOODWORM

Woodworm and rot are the bane of many households. Although woodworm can be found in nearly every home, it is easily treated and the tell-tale holes can be covered up. Dry rot, however, is not so easily dealt with, and drastic measures are called for.

WOODWORM

The chances of seeing a living woodworm are almost nil: dull brown in colour and only about 3mm (⅛in) long, they spend most of their life eating away wood underneath the surface. Each beetle can lay as many as 60 eggs in cracks and crevices of wood and these hatch into grubs, which bore down into the wood forming small but extensive tunnels.

The grubs stay in the wood for up to three years, eventually coming close to the surface of the wood when they become adult beetles. They then bite their way out of the wood to lay new eggs, and the whole cycle begins all over again.

Woodworm will attack rough timbers in a loft and any untreated wood such as floorboards and furniture. Look for signs of attack in late spring: small holes about 2mm (⅟₁₆in) in diameter and little piles of wood dust. For limited attacks you can brush or spray on woodworm killer fluid and allow it to soak into the holes. But where there is a large infestation, call in the professionals. Beetles landing on treated timber will die, as will emerging beetles, breaking the lifecycle.

Furniture can be protected from attack by using an insectidal furniture polish. Check before you buy antique or second-hand furniture: a few holes do not mean there are grubs inside, but as a precaution it is best to treat them by injecting killer fluid into each hole and use an insectidal polish. Don't forget that woodworm can also be present in the timbers of upholstered furniture and you may have to remove upholstery before you treat the wood.

BATS

If you have bats in your roof space you must inform the Nature Conservancy Council if you plan to spray the space with wood preservative, in case it harms this protected species. If bats have nested in your loft, be happy – they feed on woodworm beetles.

MOULD GROWTH

White furry deposits or black spots on timber, plaster or wallpaper are mould growths and are usually the result of condensation. When they are wiped from the surface they cause little damage other than staining. First sort out the cause of the dampness or condensation. The affected spots can be treated with a mild solution of household bleach.

WET ROT

This occurs in timbers where there is a high moisture content and as soon as the cause it treated, the wet rot is halted in its tracks. Wet rot is most often found around doors and windows that have been neglected, allowing rainwater to penetrate joints.

The first sign is often peeling paintwork, which, when removed, reveals timber that is spongy when wet and crumbly when dry.

DRY ROT

This is a fungus, which, in time, can reduce solid timber to a flaking mass which crumbles when touched. It is less common than wet rot, but is a much more serious form of decay, which can spread through doors, windows, floorboards, skirtings and joist – in short, throughout the entire structure of a house. It can even travel through brick walls and attack your next-door neighbour's house. And, it can also be found in furniture that has been stored or moved very infrequently.

The first sign of dry rot is a musty, mushroom-like smell. Despite its name, dry rot actually thrives in damp, warm, still conditions. A tiny leak in the plumbing or a faulty damp-proof course can be the initial cause, providing the moisture on which the fungus grows.

Strands spread from initial spores into cotton wool like growths. When established, they turn into wrinkled 'pancakes' which produce rust-red spores that soon infect the surrounding timbers.

If you find any signs of dry rot it is vital to deal with it immediately and eliminate all traces. This means dealing first with the cause of the dampness, then cutting out and burning all the infected timber and masonry and treating the entire area with dry rot fluid (available from good DIY stores).

FINISHES

Although paint is the usual finish for woodwork around the house because it gives a good protective and decorative coating, there is a wide range of surface finishes and colours available for the DIY market. These include stains, varnishes and polishes that allow you to add colour to woodwork without completely covering its natural beauty, while transparent finishes provide a durable protective finish without altering the natural colour of the wood.

No finish is better, however, than its preparation: a smooth, clean surface is essential because any blemish will be exaggerated by the finish. The most important tools are brushes and a wide range is available for different specialist applications. Most are made from hairs or bristles – either synthetic or natural – and it is worth buying good-quality brushes to achieve a fine finish.

SAFETY FIRST

- Remember, work in a well-ventilated area when applying wood finishes.

- Always follow specific manufacturer's guidelines on measures for personal protection, such as particular types of protective masks for working with different paints, removers and lacquers.

- Never allow naked flames anywhere near solvents.

FINISHES FOR WOOD

FINISHES	OIL PAINT	GLOSS/EMULSION	WOOD STAIN	PROTECTIVE WOOD STAIN	VARNISH	COLOURED VARNISH	OIL	WAX POLISH	FRENCH POLISH	COLD CURE LACQUER
SUITABLE FOR:										
SOFTWOODS	✓	✓	✓	✓	✓	✓	✓	✓	✗	✓
HARDWOODS	✓	✓	✓	✓	✓	✓	✓	✓	✓	✓
OILY HARDWOODS	✓	✓	✓	✗	✓	✓	✓	✓	✓	✓
PLANED WOOD	✓	✓	✓	✓	✓	✓	✓	✓	✓	✓
SAWN WOOD	✗	✗	✗	✓	✗	✗	✗	✗	✗	✗
INTERIOR USE	✓	✓	✓	✓	✓	✓	✓	✓	✓	✓
EXTERIOR USE	✓	✓	✗	✓	✓	✓	✓	✗	✗	✗
DRYING TIME: HOURS										
TOUCH DRY	4	1	½	4	4	4	1	–	½	1
RECOATABLE	14	3	6	6–8	14	14	6	1	24	2
SOLVENTS/THINNERS										
WATER		✓	✓							
WHITE SPIRIT	✓	✓	✓	✓	✓	✓	✓	✓		
METHYLATED SPIRITS									✓	
SPECIAL THINNERS										✓
NUMBER OF COATS										
INTERIOR	1–2	1–2	2–3	2	2–3	2–3	3	2	10–15	2–3
EXTERIOR	2–3	2–3	–	2	3–4	3–4	3	–	–	–
METHOD OF APPLICATION										
BRUSH	✓	✓	✓	✓	✓	✓	✓	✓	✓	✓
PAINT PAD	✓	✓	✓	✓	✓	✓	✗	✗	✗	✗
CLOTH PAD (RUBBER)	✗	✗	✗	✗	✓	✓	✓	✓	✓	✓
SPRAY GUN	✓	✓	✓	✓	✓	✓	✗	✗	✗	✓

Varnish tends to darken the colour of the wood.

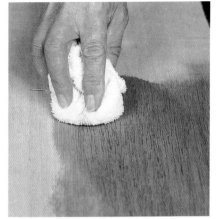

Dampen your wood with a little water to see the effect staining will have.

Undiluted paints cover up the grain and patterns on wood.

VARNISH

Varnish is a protective finish favoured by carpenters and joiners because it is suitable for wooden pieces that will be exposed to continuous wear and tear, such as furniture, staircases, windows and doors. Varnishes come in a variety of forms with different properties and range of applications. Some have good waterproofing qualities; others are fast drying. They are known by their resin ingredients – polyurethane being the most widespread.

Varnishes are applied with a brush and are available in gloss, satin and matt finishes: matt and satin finishes contain a flatting agent to make an irregular surface that does not reflect light with the same directness as gloss. A matt finish will also show the nature of the wood better than a gloss varnish on which reflections tend to hide the wood's figuring – the pattern of the grain.

STAINING

Stains consist of dyes dissolved in a medium and are used for colouring wood. Stains soak into the grain of the wood, giving a tint – unlike the pigments used for colouring paint, which lie on the top of the wood's surface as a solid layer. The medium, which carries the dye is what determines the characteristics of the stain, such as drying time and spread. There are water or oil-based stains available ready to use, but powdered pigments can also be bought for mixing with methylated spirits.

A stain should enhance the grain and improve the appearance of the wood. It needs to be easy to apply and maintain its colour without fading. Wood stains will not protect the wood, however, so you will have to seal them with a clear varnish or wax polish to prolong its life.

COLOUR WASH

Woodwork is often painted with a thick layer of opaque paint that completely covers the true nature of the wood beneath it. While this is ideal for covering 'cheaper' wood or fibre boards, on more valuable and attractive wood, such as floorboards or TGV panelling, colour-washing allows these qualities to show through. There are ready-made colour washes on the market but creating your own colour washing is easy: select the colour of emulsion paint you want – from the thousands on offer – and dilute it with water until it is a thin, milky consistency. The more water you add, the more transparent the wash. Dilute emulsion dries very quickly, so you can build up more 'intense' colours by adding more 'layers'. Colour-washed floors – or any other items that need to be hardwearing – will require varnishing afterwards. See also page 302.

DECORATIVE EFFECTS

LIMING WAX

Although they don't offer much protection to bare wood, as dirt can easily penetrate unless the surface is sealed, waxes do provide a traditional, soft finish. One of the most popular is a limed-wax finish, which is used on open-grained woods to highlight the grain. Kitchen cupboards and bare floorboards can be revitalized using this simple method. A limed finish was traditionally achieved by using quick-lime and was applied to deter wood-worm and other parasites. Today, much more user-friendly – and less toxic – methods are available. New wood that has been limed gives the appearance of years of wear, while old wood is enhanced. After opening up the grain of the wood with a wire brush, the rich paste of clear wax and white pigment used to make the 'pickled lime' effect is applied. Ready-made liming waxes are available but because of the price they are not really for use on floors. However, you can make your own 'replica' paste with white emulsion paint and white plaster of Paris. Add water if the mixture is too thick.

1 Strip back to bare wood

To achieve a good limed finish, strip back to bare wood before applying the liming wax. With a porous hardwood, such as oak, the grain of the wood is raised so that the paste is absorbed into the pores of the wood. Brush the wood vigorously with a stiff brush in the direction of the grain. In less grainy softwoods, such as pine, the grain can't be raised so there is no need to brush it. The final effect will be formed by the pale wax sitting in carved surfaces and mouldings. You can, if you wish, stain the wood at this stage and then seal it.

2 Clean the surface

To remove the fine dust created by the rubbing, use a tack cloth. These are small, versatile, long-lasting oily cloths that are ideal for cleaning wood, metal, plaster and any other surface except for glass. They pick up the dirt and dust from the surface and from the tiny grooves in the grain, and hold the particles tightly, leaving a completely clean surface. Work the tack cloth over the wood, moving in the direction of the grain and paying attention to the corners and angles of grooves and moulded areas and details.

SAFETY FIRST

- Follow the advice given on pages 230–1 when stripping wood. Wear protective gloves, goggles and face masks, as appropriate.

- It's a good idea to wear protective gloves when liming as the wax can cause an allergic reaction on sensitive skins.

3 Apply the paste

Remember that wood will mark easily once it has been stripped, so take care not to damage it. Liming paste is a combination of wax and white pigments and is supplied ready mixed. Apply the paste with a soft cloth before rubbing it into the pores, working across the grain. A piece of old, clean hessian is ideal for this, or you could use a large piece of wire wool. At this stage, the wood will look very white, but don't worry. Leave the wax to dry for the time recommended by the manufacturer.

4 Remove excess

Before the paste is fully dry, the excess needs to be wiped off. This can be done with a piece of clean hessian or, depending on the type of finish you want, use a clean cloth dampened with a finishing oil to remove excess. Make sure that the grain is filled evenly and that you don't wipe off too much of the wax. You will soon see where the pores and the grain have picked up the liming paste. If your cloth becomes overloaded with paste, replace it with a new piece. For an ultra-smooth effect, rub with fine-grade sandpaper and then wipe with a damp cloth to remove any dust.

5 Allow to dry

Leave the liming paste to dry – preferably overnight – then burnish the surface and buff it to a high sheen. The surface now needs to be sealed: apply several coats of neutral wax polish and buff each successive layer to a sheen with a soft cloth. To maintain the finish simply add coats of neutral wax polish when required. If you need a waterproof finish – on kitchen or bathroom cabinet doors perhaps – use a finishing oil to remove the excess liming wax.

FINISHING OILS

An oiled finish penetrates the grain and nourishes the wood and also produces a subtle sheen. It is naturally water repellent and seals the pores, protecting against dirt. Danish oil is suitable for most interior surfaces because it has a relatively short drying time. Oiled finishes are not hard finishes so scratches and knocks will show – but you can simply wipe the surface over with a little more oil on a cloth.

WAX POLISHES

Good wax polishes contain a mixture of beeswax and a hard polishing wax like carnauba. They do not provide a durable finish, so are only suitable for indoor use.

STAINING

WOODSTAIN

Applying a finish to wood not only changes its colour but also provides protection from dirt, heat and spilt liquids. Wood stains and dyes allow the wood to 'breathe' but still provide a resistant finish that won't flake or peel. Different types of timber can be treated with the same colour woodstain, but, on each, the effects will be different. Commercial stains range from the lightest wood colours such as Golden and Light Oak, through to the darkest, such as Rosewood and Blue-Black stains.

Dyes are the colouring agents of stains, and can be dissolved in alcohol, water or oil. These dyes become part of the wood and their translucence allows the natural beauty of the grain to show through. The idea of woodstaining is to enhance the inherent colours of the wood, but bright colours can also look extremely effective: experiment with some undiluted fabric dyes. For more subtle effects, pulped rhubarb leaves left on the surface of timber impart a very slight colour change. Remember that rhubarb leaves are toxic if eaten so don't store the pulp in food containers and discard both pulp and container carefully after use.

Standard wood dyes are not suitable for exterior use. They may fade in sunlight and some could be toxic for wildlife in the garden. Choose an exterior-grade woodstain or a coloured wood preserver instead. Before applying it, treat the wood with a clear wood preserver to prevent insect or fungal damage.

French polishing is one of the most traditional methods of finishing wood, especially fine furniture. When polished, the wood is buffed to a high sheen, which is, unfortunately, very easily scratched and marked by water and heat. French polishing requires a great deal of skill and patience, but there are also much simpler shellac polishes, which can be applied with a brush, and these are available in a variety of colours. They are applied with a soft pad known as a 'rubber', first of all in overlapping circles, then figures of eight, and finally in straight strokes that run parallel to the grain.

Whatever finish you select for your woodwork, it's a good idea to have a test run first on a piece of waste wood – both to enable you to practise your technique and to give you the opportunity to check if the final result really is the one you want.

STAINS

- Although stains dry lighter, they will end up darker when the final finish, such as a varnish, is applied. Dampen a small area of stained wood with a little water – this will give you an idea of how dark a stain will look when varnished.

- Always keep a wet edge when applying stains – this will help avoid patches of colour.

- Stains are a good way of making new timber look old: you can 'distress'; new wood further by hitting it with a bag of bolts, then staining it. You can even add a few ring marks – just place a tin on the wet stain.

1 Prepare the wood

Any finish is only as good as the preparation. Where necessary, apply wood stopping (on stripped floorboards) or knotting solution(on new wood); see page 235. Wet the wood and lightly sand. This will prevent the grain swelling and raising if a water-based stain is applied. Make sure you cover the entire area of the wood, and follow the grain. Use a tack cloth to remove any remaining dust before applying the stain. Take your time to do a thorough dust as short cuts at this stage will affect the finished appearance.

2 Apply the wood stain

Water stains are supplied in both powder form, which you make up with water in different proportions depending on the colour required, or as 'ready-to-use' stains. Stains can be applied with a rag used in a circular motion (this is good for small areas of wood, such as table tops where an 'even' stain is vital). On larger areas of wood, such as floor-boards, wood stains can be applied with a sponge applicator or a brush. Remember that different woods have different absorbencies, so make a test run on a piece of waste wood to see how many applications of wood stain you need to create the desired effect.

3 Wipe with a lint-free cloth

After each application of wood stain, wipe the surface of the wood with a lint-free cloth. Apply second or subsequent coats of stain until you have achieved the depth of colour you want, wiping down after each application. To finish the stain and enhance the grain of the wood, there are a number of options, but your choice will depend on the degree of durability you require: a varnish, a floor sealer (which is a tough matt finish and not as slippery as wax or varnish), or a wax finish. After the finish has been applied, leave for a few minutes, then wipe off the excess with a clean, lint-free cloth. Allow to dry thoroughly – check the recommended drying times – then add a second coat if required.

AFTERCARE

Some manufacturers produce a wood stain with a clear finish for redecorating stained woodwork without darkening its appearance. It can be cleaned with a damp cloth or mop, but don't use proprietary floor cleaners.

SAFETY FIRST

It can be a good idea to wear protective rubber gloves when handling woodstain, as the chemicals may irritate your skin. Keep the room well-ventilated while you work.

RENOVATING OLD FURNITURE

HALL TABLE

Often old furniture – whether reclaimed or inherited – is too dark and heavy-looking for modern interiors. Old items of furniture can be given a new lease of life by stripping the wood back to its original state and applying a lighter finish. Natural wood finishes are ideal for cottage-style furniture, but you can rejuvenate any item with a range of different finishes such as liming (see page 246), crackle-glazing (see page 305), staining (see page 248) and varnishing (see page 245). Stripping, especially with chemical strippers, can remove a lot of the natural oils in the wood, but applying a wood restorer will help to nourish the grain.

1 Apply the stripper

Wearing rubber gloves and working in a well ventilated space, apply the stripper with a paintbrush, following the manufacturer's instructions. Some types of stripper are 'one-coat applications', while others require a first coat and a topcoat. Leave for the time stated.

2 Remove the stripper

Remove the stripper using fine-grade wire wool. As the wire wool becomes clogged with old finish and stripper, replace it with a new piece. When all the old finish is removed, sand the table in the direction of the grain, with a fine-grade abrasive paper.

SAFETY FIRST

- Wear strong rubber gloves when you use chemical strippers. Avoid splashing the fluid onto your skin and onto plastic surfaces: spectacles with plastic lenses and plastic watch faces will 'melt'.

- Dispose of waste and chemical stripper carefully: read the manufacturers' instructions on storage, use, and disposal.

- See pages 230–1 for more advice on stripping wood.

3 Apply wood restorer

Use a tack cloth moistened with a little white spirit to remove any sawdust and neutralize any remnants of stripper. Apply a wood stain, if you like. Use a clean soft cloth to apply some wood restorer, rubbing it in circular movements to penetrate the grain

4 Apply Danish oil

Applying Danish oil gives furniture a natural-looking sheen. Apply the oil with a soft cloth, using small circular movements. Leave to dry and repeat a number of times. Once the oil has penetrated the wood, polish it to a bright sheen with a dry cloth.

SCHOOL DESK

Old school desks make attractive pieces of furniture and are ideal for storing household stationery, phone books and pens. They can also be reconditioned for youngsters to do their homework on. The 'all-in-one' desk and seat of this school desk is supported by metal legs. All ferrous metals, which contain iron and steel, are prone to rust – especially metal, which has previously been painted. See pages 284 and 300 for more detailed advice on stripping and restoring old metals, and see page 230 for methods of stripping wood. Follow all the safety advice: wear protective gloves when using chemical strippers, and wear goggles and a dust mask when using electric sanders.

1 Cleaning the metal

Before painting any metal items, clean them and rub them down to give a keyed surface for the paint to adhere to. Electric detail sanders make sanding quick and easy – but, for a perfect finish, give any item one last sand by hand with a fine wet-and-dry paper.

2 Apply rust inhibitor and primer

If your sanding has revealed patches of rust, sand the areas again and apply a rust inhibitor or converter to protect it from more rust forming. Where metal is to be painted, a red oxide primer or proprietary metal primers should be applied to protect the surface.

PREPARATION

Make sure all metal is covered with rust inhibitor or converter: where necessary disassemble the components and treat each piece separately. Check also that the fixing screws, or nuts and bolts are in good order.

Sand all the wood carefully in case there are any splinters. See page 224 for advice on the different kinds of finishes that would be suitable for you desk.

3 Finishing the wood

Depending on the condition of the desk, you may need to strip with a chemical, or simply sand it down. Choose your finish: a tinted varnish will colour and protect the wood, but a clear varnish will offer greater protection. Lightly sand between coats to remove brushstrokes.

TRANSLUCENT FINISHES

Translucent finishes on wood enhance their appearance. Hardwoods such as oak often need only a clear protective finish, while softwoods can benefit from tinted finishes, which give them a richer, darker colour.

PINE CHEST OF DRAWERS

Good-quality pine furniture is easy to obtain and if you shop around you can usually pick up a bargain. In the past, much pine furniture was sold already treated and finished – usually with a yellow-orange polyurethane varnish. While this gave a good deal of protection, tastes and fashions in interiors have gradually changed and furniture manufacturers responded to the increasing DIY market by providing pine furniture that was untreated, ready to accept a huge range of decorative finishes. Untreated pine should cost less, and it requires little in the way of preparation. The instructions given here for treating a chest of drawers could be adapted for any other items of furniture.

1 Remove feet

Don't forget to unscrew the feet from the chest of drawers before you start. Thread them through the bottom of an old shoe box so you can paint or stain them without holding onto them. Put the fixing screws in a safe place.

2 Drawer knobs

Before painting or staining the drawers, remove the knobs. You can update an old piece with new drawer knobs, which are available in different styles. If you don't want pine knobs, there are brass and white porcelain ones available.

3 Applying the stain

Any knots in untreated pine will need to be sealed with knotting solution or shellac to stop sap from oozing out and turning yellow. Cover each knot, extending beyond them by about 50mm (2in). Apply your chosen stain with a brush or sponge applicator. 'Build up' the colour by adding further layers of stain.

4 Finishing

Water-based stains and dyes, which are easy to use can be finished with any type of varnish or wax polish. Choose the finish and apply it according to the instructions supplied. Wax polishes give furniture a soft-looking finish: clear wax is a good neutral finishing polish while tinted waxes add depth and lustre.

5 Reassemble

Whatever finish you have chosen, leave it to dry for the time recommended by the manufacturer. Screw on the feet and drawer knobs and reassemble the chest of drawers. If you are reconditioning an old chest with damaged drawers, see page 242 for advice on fixing them.

REFINISHING A WOODEN CHEST

1 Stripping

A huge range of strippers are available, from 'strong' caustic versions for heavy-duty stripping, to softer strippers, which remove the surface finish without eating down into the original wood. Always follow the manufacturers' instructions.

2 Filling cracks and splits

Small cracks can be filled with a wood stopper but long splits are best filled with thin strips of wood. Apply wood glue to the strips and gently tap them into the splits with a wooden or rubber mallet. Wipe away any excess glue.

3 Clean up metal

Locks, hinges, brackets and any other metal fixings deserve a little care and attention. Use a proprietary metal cleaner suitable for the fixings and follow the manufacturer's instructions.

4 Oil finishing

Most proprietary wood-finishing oils are based on tung oil, a natural oil that penetrates the wood. They also contain resins and driers to give heat- and water-resistance so the surface will not chip or scratch. Two or three coats are usually needed to build up a soft sheen that doesn't obscure the wood's beauty.

OIL FINISHES

Using an oiled finish on this wooden chest has brought out the natural, rich patina of the wood.

SAFETY FIRST

- Work in a well-ventilated space when using strippers and oils and don't allow naked flames or cigarettes nearby.

- Always wear protective gloves when using stripper or applying finishes.

- Oils heat up as they dry – by oxidation – and this can be a fire hazard if applicator rags are left wadded up in a bunch in a bin. Dispose of used oil rags by dousing them first in a bucket of water. If left overnight, the rag will be safe to throw away.

RECANING A CHAIR

Chair seating in rattan cane from the Malay Peninsula became popular in Holland and France in the 17th century, when it was used to create furniture of great elegance and style. It was one of the fashions brought to Britain by Charles II at the time of the Restoration of the Monarchy, but the techniques used in cane seating are several thousand years old. Perhaps the earliest example is a magnificent caned day bed found in the tomb of Tutankhamun. In and out of fashion many times since its introduction to Britain, much of the cane-seated furniture that can be found today in antique shops or junk stores was produced between 1840 and 1930. Time, dirt, dryness and wear and tear mean that in most cases, these seats need repairing.

It is seldom possible to patch up a damaged cane seat or back, so it is always better to renew the cane completely. The 'six-way standard' pattern is the one most commonly found on antique furniture and comprises two vertical 'settings', two horizontal 'weavings' and two diagonal 'crossings'. This is actually quite simple to do and it makes a very strong and attractive seat or back.

Chair seating can be bought from craft shops in small quantities – enough for a single seat – or from wholesalers, if you have a large number of chairs to restore. You will need seating cane in three sizes: No. 2 split cane for vertical settings and horizontal weavings, No. 3 for diagonal crossings and No. 6 beading cane to finish the final surround on the seat. You'll also need a short length of thicker basket cane (No. 12) for plugging the holes, and about 20 golf tees for use as temporary pegs to hold the cane in place while you pull it tight from hole to hole.

CANING

- Cane can be worked dry, but it's easier if it's supple: rub it with beeswax or soak it in cold water for five minutes and store it in sealed plastic bags.

- When a length of cane runs out, peg the short end leaving a 75mm (3in) tail under the rail. Start the new cane in the adjacent hole leaving a similar tail and pegging it firmly.

- Pre-1850 chairs are usually finished with a short peg of No. 12 cane tapped into each hole to secure the cane seat, while those made after 1850 are usually finished with a beading of No. 6 cane laced down over the holes with No 2 cane.

1 Locate the centre hole

Cut away the old damaged cane seat, remove any beading and, working from the underneath, knock out the old pegs. Clean/strip the frame of the chair as desired (see page 230) but be careful not to block up any holes. Begin by finding the centre holes at the front and back: count along the holes to the last in the back row (not the corner hole) and then count the same number in the front. Mark the holes with golf tees or pegs.

2 The first setting

Push a prepared cane down through the marked front hole so that about 75mm (3in) hangs below the seat. Put a golf tee in the hole to secure the cane. Pass the cane down through the marked back hole; pull it taut and secure with a golf tee. As you thread the cane, make sure you keep the smooth side up so that there is no roughness on the seat. As you are working, you should keep all back-to-front settings parallel to this, pegging them carefully.

3 The first layer

Thread a length of No. 2 cane through the next hole on the left, move the tee to that hole and secure it. Keep threading between front and back until the left side is filled. At the end of the back row, use side holes until the front row of holes is full, but keep the four corner holes clear. Complete the right side in the same way.

4 Crosswise weaving

Begin the first crosswise 'weaving' with No. 2 cane, starting at the second hole from the back on the left. Work from side to side on top of the first setting and fill in each hole except for the corners, keeping the tension quite firm.

5 Second layers

Fit a second set of front-to-back settings on top and to the left of the first, starting at the front. Peg carefully so that the settings lie parallel as they come up and down through the same holes. Then do a second side-to-side weaving, going from right to left so the canes are alternate to the first weaving.

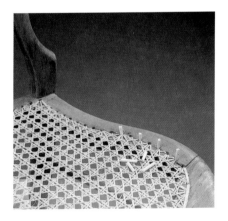

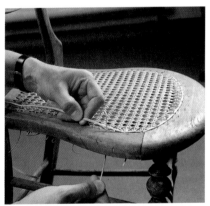

6 Diagonal crossings

Starting at the back corner, weave under the side-to-side canes and over the front-to-back canes. Take the cane down to the front corner hole and up the next hole in the front row. Weave to the corner, then work the other half of the seat. Do the second set of diagonal crossings in the same way from the other back corner.

7 Securing the ends

Secure all the ends in alternate holes with pegs. Cut a short length of No. 12 cane and make a point at one end. With a hammer, tap the pointed end into a hole and cut it with secateurs just above the chair rail. Tap the peg until it is just below the surface. Leave the corner holes and those to either side empty.

8 Beading

Push a piece of No. 6 cane through a corner hole and bring up one end of No. 2 cane. Bring the long end of No. 2 cane through the second hole, over the No. 6 cane, and then down through the same hole. 'Lace' all the unplugged holes. Drive in cane pegs at corners then cut off all the ends neatly under the chair.

SHELVING

FIXING AN ANGLE BRACKET SHELF

There are lots of different forms of shelving available, but before you buy, think about what you want to use the shelves for. Do you want them to be attractive or purely functional?

Shelves not only have to stay up, but not sag under the weight of the objects placed on them. A load that is cantilevered on brackets from a back wall imposes great stress on the fixing screws – especially the top ones. If the screws are too short or too small a gauge, or if the wall plugs are inadequate, the weight may pull the brackets off the wall. The wider the shelf, the greater the danger of this happening.

Shelves will sag if the span between brackets supporting them is too long in relation to the thickness of the shelf board or the weight placed upon it – or both. Solid timber or blockboard with its core running lengthways are the most sturdy types of wood to use for shelving. Veneered chipboard, very popular because of its 'clean' appearance will actually sag under quite light loads so it will need more supports or supports placed at shorter spans. See page 258 for advice on the maximum spans for shelves using different materials.

The type of wall on which you fix a shelf determines the type of wall fixings you need. On a solid masonry wall, a shelf can be fixed anywhere, but on a stud partition wall, it must be fixed to the hidden timber studs (find them by tapping along the wall). If the studs are in the wrong position, you'll need to use special fixings (see tools box). For most ordinary shelving, brackets fixed to a masonry wall with 50mm (2in) screws and proper wall plugs will be strong enough.

1 Mark the height of the shelf

Decide on the position and height of the shelf on the wall. Temporarily nail a straight batten of timber at the position marked. Using a spirit level, check that the batten is horizontal.

2 Mark the position of the brackets

Offer up the shelf brackets to the batten, butting them well up against the edge. Use a pencil and mark through the bracket fixing holes onto the walls. Do this at each end of the shelf and for each intermediate bracket if needed (see tip box, and the chart on page 258).

3 Drill the fixing holes

Drill into a masonry wall with a masonry bit and insert the plastic wall plugs. Use a slow speed on a power drill and make a 'clean' horizontal drill hole. If you need to, mark the depth of the hole on the drill bit with a piece of masking tape.

4 Screw brackets to the wall

Offer up the first bracket to the batten and screw it to the wall using the appropriate length and gauge screw. Too short or too small a gauge will make the fixing insecure and the shelf could collapse under the load. If you are using a power drill, select a low speed and withdraw the drill every 5 seconds to let the tip cool down. If the wall is very hard, use a drill with a hammer action. Only apply light pressure if you are drilling into plasterboard to avoid damaging the surface.

5 Check verticals

Mark the positions for the screw holes of the other brackets. Drill one hole for the furthest bracket and secure it to the wall with just one screw, then drill one hole for each of any other brackets. When each bracket is attached to the wall, check that it is vertical with a spirit level. The action of driving in the screws can push the brackets out of true and this needs to be corrected or the finished shelf will not be level. When all the brackets are fixed and level, the guide batten can be removed.

6 Attaching the shelf

The timber, blockboard or veneered shelf should be securely attached to the brackets with screws from underneath. Use a spirit level to keep the shelf true: this will stop you putting undue upwards pressure on the bracket as you screw. When you are fixing a bank of shelves, fit all the brackets first, place the shelves on top of them then use a plumb line to align the ends before you fix them to the brackets.

SHELVES

- A 25mm (1in) thick timber or blockboard shelf for a heavy load like books will need to be supported at every 900mm (3ft) along its length. Veneered chipboard of the same width needs to be supported every 750mm (2ft 6in).

- If screws are difficult to insert, lubricate them with a little oil.

- Even short shelves should have their brackets placed well in from the shelf ends to avoid sagging.

- For extra support, a hardwood batten can be glued to the underside of a shelf.

- Brackets must be big enough to support almost the entire width of the shelf.

ADDITIONAL TOOLS

Fixings for hollow walls of plasterboard on studs or lath and plaster are available: special wall plugs, plastic toggles and collapsible anchors all have segments, which open out or fold up behind panels and grip them in some way.

DISPLAY SHELVING

Display shelving is not really suitable to carry heavy loads, but it is an ideal way to display small, lightweight items – and keep them safely out of harm's reach. Display shelving is a great way to utilize 'dead space' – the areas of a wall that aren't used – such as small alcoves or corners. This type of shelving is fitted quite simply by fixing battens to the side and back walls. The shelves can be rested on the supports – but this does mean that they are loose and can be pulled forwards and off the battens. For extra security, lost-head nails can be driven through the shelves into the battens and the nail holes filled with wood filler. No other support is necessary, providing the weight the shelf carries is not excessive, and the span is no more than 800mm (2ft 8in) long. If it is longer, then it's a good idea to glue and screw a batten to the front edge of the shelf to strengthen it. This can then be decorated to match the shelf.

1 Mark the positions

Make use of a small alcove space by adding some shelves. Decide on the exact location and measure the length and depth. Calculate the amount of timber needed to make a shelf of the desired proportions. Measure and mark the position of the shelf on the walls in pencil and carefully drill holes of the required size and then insert the plugs.

2 Fix the first batten

Attach the short side supports to the wall. Use a spirit level to make sure they are completely horizontal – otherwise the shelf will end up tilting forwards or backwards. Fix the second side batten in the same way. It's a good idea to measure the height of the batten from the floor once more so the two battens are absolutely opposite.

RECOMMENDED SHELF SPANS

MATERIAL	THICKNESS	LIGHT LOAD	MEDIUM LOAD	HEAVY LOAD
SOLID WOOD	18mm (¾in)	800mm (2ft 8in)	750mm (2ft 6in)	700mm (2ft 4in)
MDF	18mm (¾in)	800mm (2ft 8in)	750mm (2ft 6in)	700mm (2ft 4in)
BLOCKBOARD	18mm (¾in)	800mm (2ft 8in)	750mm (2ft 6in)	700mm (2ft 4in)
CHIPBOARD	16mm (⅝in)	750mm (2ft 6in)	600mm (2ft)	450mm (1ft 6in)
GLASS	6mm (¼in)	700mm (2ft 4in)	n/a	n/a

3 Fix the batten to the rear wall

In an alcove space, fix the long supporting batten to the rear wall, lining it up with the two side supporting battens. Use a spirit level to ensure accuracy. Use a good number of screws spaced equally along the length of the batten to provide a secure fixing.

4 Construct the shelf

A neat appearance is achieved when the supporting battens are hidden from view by a batten attached to the front edge of the shelf. This can be a simple straight piece of timber, or you could shape it into a double ogee, or you might even choose to cut a fretwork pattern into it.

5 Attach the shelf

The shelf should fit quite snugly against the walls on top of the battens. Don't force the shelf down – if it's too big, sand or plane one edge a little. Test the shelf for fit, then remove and finish it with paint, stain, or varnish. It's easier to do this when the shelf is removed.

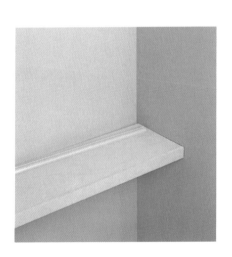

SHELVES

- When constructing your shelf, a straight batten is best if the span of the shelf is around 800mm (2ft 8in): this will add extra support to the shelf and stop it from sagging.

- Don't forget to treat all new timber before you finish it. Use knotting solution to stop sap from oozing and turning yellow.

- Wipe off any wood glue that oozes from joints immediately. If left, it will repel some finishes or show up lighter under others.

SAFETY FIRST

- If you use MDF (medium density fibreboard) for shelves or other structures, you must wear a face mask when you cut or drill it.

- Watch out for hidden electrical cables that may be buried behind walls when you drill into them.

- Don't overload shelves: they will sag and pressure is placed on the wall fixing, which can be torn out.

- To avoid accidentally knocking into them, don't place shelves on walls where there is 'through traffic'.

6 Fix the shelf

For extra security, you can drive lost-head nails through the shelf and into the timber battens. This will stop the shelf slipping forwards or the back lifting if a weight is placed at the front edge.

CORNER SHELVING

While there never seems to be enough storage space in our homes, ironically each room has a fair amount of 'dead space' – areas where nothing happens. Most often this is in corners. In kitchens, wall-mounted cupboards that extend into corners are often difficult to reach all the way into, so tend not to be used to their full extent. Straight ends of runs of cupboards also tend to stick out at 90 degrees, and seem designed for shoulders to hit them!

One way of making use of dead corner space is to design shelves that fit into the angle. It is after all just a 90-degree angle – or thereabouts! A corner cupboard is a square cupboard cut across the front at 45 degrees. These attractive corner cupboards can sometimes be found in antique shops but they are quite expensive. Modern versions in pine can also be bought – but since very few homes have absolutely straight walls set at perfect right angles, they often don't

fit snugly. The best solution is to make your own. Only basic woodworking skills are needed and the finished result will be a completely unique design because you have made it and finished it to your own specifications.

The corner shelving can be made of wood, blockboard or a fibreboard such as MDF, and can be painted, stained, varnished, or given any finish you desire (see pages 244–9) to complement the interior decor scheme of the room.

1 Measure and cut materials

Having decided on the location of the corner shelf unit, the most important part of the job is to measure accurately the height, width and depth of the unit you wish to construct. Make a quick sketch of your proposed design, and then draw out each piece, marking the dimensions. Try to cut the pieces you need from the wood or board without too much waste.

2 Assemble the two panels

The largest pieces of the unit are the two side panels. These are joined together to make an angle in order to fit into the corner of the room. Check the angle of the corner of the room, transfer this measurement to the piece and fix the panels. If your woodworking skills are advanced, make a self-squaring join by mitring along the length of the panels. Alternatively, glue and pin the two panels – but remember to allow for the slight overlap on the join when you measure and cut one panel. Wipe off excess glue and allow to dry fully.

3 Cutting the shelves

The unit can have as few or as many shelves as you wish, but the two most important elements, which will give strength and support to the unit, are the base and top boards. Measure and cut the triangular-shaped boards. In the example shown, these have been cut so they project slightly from the front and are also shaped at the front corners to give a more professional look. Fit the base board: this will keep the two side panels secure in their angle.

4 Position the shelves

Measure and mark the position of the shelves on both sides of the inside face of the unit. Fit the shelf: you can attach supporting battens to rest it on or use small brackets or other patent shelf fixing systems.

5 Fix the top

With the shelf or shelves inserted and fixed, fix the top triangular board. Glue and pin it into position, wiping off any excess glue immediately. Allow to dry thoroughly. The shelf unit is now ready to be painted, or extra details added.

6 Adding details

If you have any spare wood or board, you can add some extra interest to the unit by cutting some shaped panels to attach to the front. Cut the shaped piece from the wood or board with a jigsaw and sand to remove rough edges.

TEMPLATES

- Make a full-size paper pattern out of thin card of all the pieces you need to cut and place them onto the board. Arrange the 'templates' so that you can cut them out from the board in the most economical way without wasting too much material. If you are using wood, arrange the templates so that they follow the line of the grain.

- The double ogee is an attractive pattern: you can make a cardboard template by drawing out half a curved shape on a piece of tracing paper, and transferring it to the cardboard. To get the mirror image, simply turn the tracing paper over.

7 Front edges

The cut ends of timber or board can look 'raw' or unfinished, and they won't accept a paint or stain finish to the same degree as the rest of the material. To finish the front edges, cut two strips – either straight or shaped (they can even extend above or below the unit) – to fit over them. Glue and pin them into place.

8 The finished unit

The corner unit is secured to the wall: it can be hung on brackets or fixed directly to masonry walls with screws and wall plugs. The choice of finish, whether paint, stain, varnish or any other decorative effect, is up to you.

FIXING A PLATE RAIL

Additional storage space is always welcome and two simple but effective solutions maximize the overlooked space high up on walls and on the backs of doors. Shelves on the back of cupboards are particularly good for storing small or difficult-to-store tall items, making them immediately accessible. Wall space can be utilized more completely by adding a plate rail. Not only do these optically lower the height of a high ceiling, but they also provide a safe, out-of-the-way yet still visible place to display small items such as antique china. They are easy to fix and there are a range of stylish wall brackets to choose from to complement your decor.

There are several kit forms available, or you could make your own. It's a good idea to attach a small strip of batten along the top of the rail so that plates won't slip off. Be careful when you drill into any wall because there may be unseen electric cables or water pipes hidden behind them. Solid masonry or brick walls need to be drilled with a masonry bit and the holes plugged. If the wall you are working on is a stud partition, you can fix the rail to the studs: locate them by tapping the walls. Otherwise, there is a range of fixings specially designed for hollow walls, which open out and grip behind the panel. Make sure that there are sufficient brackets to support the length of the rail so that it doesn't sag or put undue stress on the fixings (see page 258).

1 Mark the position

Decide on the position and height of the rail. You will probably need to work on a ladder so make sure it is secure and level so you can work safely. Mark the position of the rails and the brackets and then drill and plug the holes.

2 Attach the first bracket

Start at one end and attach the first bracket to the wall. Offer up the rail to the wall and fix it in position – pre-drill holes in the rail for ease. Use screws at least 50mm (2in) long and suitable plugs to fix the rail to the wall. Continue to add brackets at intervals.

3 Fix the shelf

Drive screws through the shelf into the tops of the brackets to fix the shelf to the brackets and stop the shelf working loose and sliding forwards. If necessary add a strip of beading or batten to the top of the shelf to support the bottom lip of plates so they are displayed upright.

4 Finishing

Many kit-form plate rails come in natural wood. If you prefer, you can paint, stain or add any finished effect you wish to complement your decor. It's a good idea to apply any finish before fixing to avoid marking the surrounding walls with paint or varnish.

FIXING SHELVES TO THE BACK OF A DOOR

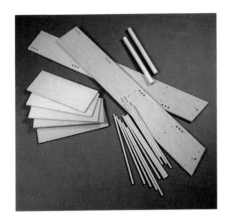

1 Materials
The 'storage system' is basically a 'ladder'. You will need two long lengths of timber or board for the sides, two shorter lengths for the top and bottom and a number of lengths for shelves. Three lengths of dowel per shelf look attractive and stop items slipping out.

2 Assemble the 'ladder'
Measure and mark the position of the shelves on the outer 'legs' and fix them with screws. The shelves on this unit have been angled slightly so that items placed in them lean backwards slightly. This stops things falling out when you open the door.

3 Adding laminated surfaces
Inexpensive wood or fibreboard can be enhanced with a laminated surface. You can stick laminate to any flat, dry surface – plywood, blockboard and chipboard are ideal. Use a proprietary contact adhesive and follow the manufacturer's instructions.

4 Finished unit
Finish the shelves with any finish you choose before you fix the unit to the door. The shelves will be quite heavy so make sure you use appropriate fixings. Flush door cavity fixings come in a range of lengths so make sure they are right for your door.

LAMINATES

Plastic laminates are available in a range of colours, patterns and textures, normally in sheets of 2400 x 1220mm (8ft x 4ft) and 1.5mm ($\frac{1}{16}$in) thick, but most stores offer a cutting service, so take accurated measurements with you.

You will need contact adhesive to fix the laminate down. The coated surfaces must be allowed to become touch-dry because solvent that has not evaporated will be trapped between the two surfaces creating a permanent bulge.

Edging strips are also available for making neat edges for shelves and worktops. Some have a self-adhesive backing and are secured in place by using a hot iron over brown paper.

ADDITIONAL TOOLS

Off-cuts of laminates are often available, but they will need to be cut to shape. Some craft knives can be fitted with special laminate scoring blades, which are drawn across the surface of the laminate before it is snapped. Lay the laminate face side up. Use a straight edge along the cutting line and draw the scoring blade over a few times. Lay a piece of wood alongside the scored line and bend the free side of the laminate upwards until it snaps. Rough edges should be cleaned up with glasspaper.

CUPBOARDS

FITTING NEW FRONTS TO KITCHEN CUPBOARDS

Fashions and tastes in kitchens are constantly changing. Fortunately it is possible to update tired, old-fashioned or battered and worn cupboards without going to the significant expense of replacing them completely. There is a wide range of primers and paints, including metallic versions, designed especially for melamine, which means that you can re-paint and restyle them as you wish (see pages 278 to 306 for painting advice). An old cupboard can be instantly enlivened simply by changing the knobs and drawer pulls.

A more drastic way to update old or tatty cupboards is to add new fronts. Many DIY stores stock a huge range of replacement doors and drawer fronts that fit standard-size kitchen units. Some are unfinished so that you can paint or stain them as you wish; others are already finished and ready for installation. If you are feeling particularly enthusiastic, you could even design and make your own replacement fronts.

It can look attractive if you fit fluorescent lighting underneath your cupboards to illuminate the work surfaces. You'll need a switched connection unit fitted with a 3 amp cartridge fuse to supply the power.

CUPBOARD DOORS

Cupboard doors come in for a great deal of wear and tear: they get grimy, chipped and worn at the edges and often the edging strips work loose on laminated surfaces. Before you buy replacement doors, you will need to measure each one accurately. Make a note of how many you need and the exact number and type of hinges used. If the existing hinges are in good condition, these can probably be re-used – as long as the new doors are not too heavy for them. If not, you will need to buy replacements.

1 Old-style kitchens
Melamine units, which were popular in the 1970s, were extremely durable. While perfectly functional, these old kitchen cabinets can be a little dull and unexciting. Don't despair, however, and don't reject the underlying 'carcasses' – the framework. This basic structure will probably be solidly built and ready for you to improve on. See the picture on page 266 showing how this kitchen unit was thoroughly updated.

2 Remove the door
Carefully remove the existing doors, taking care not to 'rip' the hinges from the units and thus make the fixing holes bigger. It may be possible to put the new doors back in exactly the same position. If this is not possible, fill the old holes with filler and sand down when dry. Reposition the hinges to avoid drilling into the old filled holes. New hinges – either flush-fitting or 'lift-off' – are available in a range of sizes.

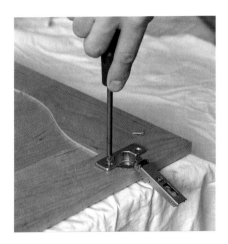

3 Attach hinges to new doors

You can re-use the old hinges, but if the replacement doors are solid wood or heavier than the old ones, buy new, stronger hinges. Two hinges are sufficient for 'short' doors – one near the top and one near the bottom.

4 Mark the hinge positions

Measure and mark the position of the door hinges on the inside of the cupboard. Make existing holes more secure by using an expanding filler. Make sure that the measurements inside the cupboard correspond exactly with the position of the hinges on the new doors.

5 Attach the hinges

Most cupboards will be made of plywood or fibreboard. Because they are 'soft' they won't hold screws very well and need special hinges fitted to the frame. Make sure the fixing screw length is less than the thickness of the cupboard; otherwise they will come out through the other side.

6 Attach the door

Offer up the new door to the cupboard and fix the concealed hinge. If it is a lay-on door it will be possible to adjust the hinges after the door has been hung.

KITCHEN CUPBOARDS

• When you measure for new doors remember that if the doors are inset – that is, they close into the cupboard frame – they will need a clearance of about 2mm (⅟₁₆in) to swing easily. A lay-on door – one that closes to overlap the carcass – needs an overlap of about 16mm (⅝in).

• If you have to 're-locate' hinges because the existing holes are too big, remember to fill the old ones with filler to make them look neat.

• If you are hanging new kitchen cupboards on a stud partition wall and there are no studs in the places where you need them, you can use cavity fixings instead. You insert the fixing into the wall and secure it with a screw or bolt. As the screw is tightened, some of them expand to grip the lining, while others have a toggle that springs out behind the lining.

• Make sure you paint or apply any finishes to your kitchen cupboard doors before you hang them.

DRAWER FRONTS

1 False drawer fronts
False drawer fronts, with boards that overlap part of the cabinet front and conceal the gap between the cabinet and sides of the drawer, can be removed and replaced with new stylish ones.

2 Unscrew the handles
Take off the handles from the old drawer fronts; keep the fixing screws for future use. The false front of the drawer will be fixed to a shallow backing board. Working from inside the drawer, unscrew the false front.

3 Fix the handles
Using a steel tape or rule, locate the centre of the drawer front for a single drawer knob, or equidistant positions for two knobs. If there is a tier of drawers, make sure all the knobs line up. Fix the handle or handles.

4 Attach the new false front
Using 4 x 31mm (No. 8) countersunk screws, attach the new drawer front to the backing board. Make sure the drawer front is level and the overlap at each side is even. Attach the front firmly, but don't over-tighten the screws.

UNIT SIDES

1 Using laminates
The sides of units – where a row of cabinets ends, or at the side of a built-in cooker – are often left on view. Sheet laminate, available in a range of colours, patterns and textures, can be used to disguise old units, adding the finishing touch to your reworked kitchen units.

2 Using decorative mouldings
The top and bottom edges of units can also be treated to a makeover. Architectural moulding, available in a range of wood and in various profiles, can be cut to length. Where corners turn, a simple mitre cut at the joining lengths makes a professional finish.

3 The finished units
This is the same kitchen as on page 264. There was nothing wrong with the layout of the units; they were just a little old-fashioned. A new-look kitchen need not mean ripping the whole thing out! With imagination, time, care and patience, any room can be completely transformed.

MAKING FITTED WARDROBES

For many people, bedrooms have to double as work and living spaces, and storage – whether for documents, clothes, or things that you just don't want to throw away – can be a problem. The actual construction of fitted furniture is quite straight-forward. The key to success – as with all DIY projects – is in the planning and taking care over the design and details for a professional finish.

Carry out a survey of the place where the wardrobe is to be fitted and make a sketch with accurate measurements. This can be used at the design stage to produce a more accurate plan and materials list.

When measuring, bear in mind that it's a rare house that has walls that are completely straight or upright! Be sure to measure the width of the space and the ceiling height at several points. At the design stage, it is the narrowest width or shortest length that will determine the dimensions of the fitted unit. To check if the building is out of square, use a spirit level in conjunction with a straight edge.

Decide whether the work should be carried out completely 'on site' or whether sections can be 'pre-fabricated' ready for assembly. The 'pre-fab' way means less mess in the bedroom – but don't forget you have

to get the components through the door! After measuring up, draw a sketch of the fittings, making a note of dimensions and other details; for example, don't forget that clothes hanging space needs to be at least as deep as a coat hanger. Bear in mind the standard sizes of sheet materials and doors: it's easier to tailor the framework to accept a ready-made door than it is to tailor the door to fit a framework. Prepare a detailed drawing, to scale on graph paper, showing the layout and design. Make a list of the materials – including paint and hardware – so you have everything you need.

1 Using dead space

Design your fitted wardrobes so that they utilize previously unused spaces, for example between the old wardrobe and the adjacent ceiling or wall. Take all the measurements carefully and transfer them to a scale drawing. Select your timber, using the descriptions on pages 222–3 and the guide to buying timber on pages 373–4, and decide on the fittings and finishes you want.

2 Cut the main components

Using your measurements and scale drawings, measure and cut the timber for the main components. Take extra care when using power tools and always wear a face mask when cutting or drilling fibreboard. Each time you cut a member for the framework, label it clearly so you know what it is and where it needs to go.

3 Construct the framework

The underlying structure for this fitted wardrobe is made of a 'carcass' of wood. This forms a framework onto which the doors will be hung and into which rails and drawers will be fitted. The framework is constructed in the same way as you would construct a framework for a stud partition wall (see pages 52–3 for instructions).

4 Screw battens to walls

Inside the framework the space is divided by shelves. To support them, wooden battens are screwed to the side and back walls of the wardrobe space. Use a masonry drill at slow speed to drill the plug the holes and then fix the battens.

5 Add top shelf

A useful 'above the head' storage space is made by adding a shelf along the top of the wardrobe. The rear and side edges rest on supporting battens attached to the walls; the front edge rests on the inside of the framework.

6 Add base fascia board

A professional look is achieved by paying attention to the details. The gap between the wardrobe door and the floor should be hidden behind a fascia board. Doors and drawers can either be made to close flush, or close against the frame with a little overlap.

FITTINGS

- To hang a wardrobe door you could use flush-fitting Hurlinge, which is fitted directly to the door and frame without the need for recessing.

- Add strips of 30 x 15mm (1 x ½in) door stop beading to the inner face of the frame after any door catches have been fitted.

- Long shelves will sag in the middle and therefore need further support with additional cross members in the framework.

7 Fit trimmed strips

In 'non-opening' areas – such as the small strips at each side of the wardrobe near the side walls, or the wardrobe and the ceiling – fixed panels are made to close the gaps. These need to be measured and cut accurately if they are to fit perfectly, so take your time.

8 Hanging doors

Doors can be bought ready-made for wardrobes, or you could fashion your own. Avoid doors that are too heavy – they place unnecessary strain on the hinges and framework. Lightweight doors can be attached with decorative brass cabinet hinges, or butt hinges – which come as left-hand or right-hand opening. For door hanging tips, see page 116.

9 Drawers

If you have an existing chest of drawers, you could incorporate it as a module within the wardrobe. Alternatively, you could strip down an existing chest of drawers – remove the false fronts and handles and replace with flush panel fronts with a cut-out hand hole.

10 Shelf battens

There is a wide range of patent shelving systems available, such as these metal 'slots' into which shelves slide. To make your own, construct a simple ladder framework with the shelves supported underneath by wooden battens. Don't make them too wide, or they could sag.

SAFETY FIRST

- Remember that access is needed to existing plumbing and electricity services. Check for 'traps' – short pieces of floorboard left by builders to give access to electrical junction boxes, plumbing and so on – and take care that you don't block them.

- Note any runs of electrical cables and water pipes to avoid damaging them during the work. A socket outlet nearby will have cables running under the floor or up through the wall: establish the run of the cable and mark it lightly on the adjacent wall or floor.

11 Hanging rail

No wardrobe is complete – or any use – without a full-length hanging rail for clothes. A sturdy metal rod held securely in brackets at each side is all you need. Make sure the rod is rigid and not overlong, otherwise it will sag under the weight of clothes. Remember to check the position against a coat hanger before you fix it.

MAKING A TABLE

This type of table can have a whole host of uses – a workstation, a dining table, or an extra preparation surface in the kitchen. By making a table yourself, you can customize it to suit your needs: not only can you make it the ideal height, but you can also finish it to suit your decor. The construction uses mortise and tenon joints, which are secured further with dowels. Because the table legs have been purchased ready-turned and with the mortise 'slots' ready-cut to accept the table rails, you will need to cut the tenons. Decide on the dimensions, then draw up a cutting list of wood: if you buy wood as sawn board you must allow for waste when you convert it from its sawn state to planed size (see pages 373–4).

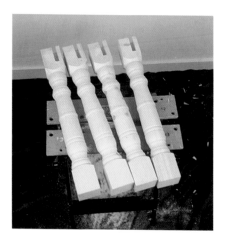

1 Table legs
Attractively turned table legs can be bought 'ready-made' with the mortises pre-cut. There are various styles to choose from, or you could salvage existing legs from a broken table, strip them of their original finish and treat them as new.

2 Mark position of dowel holes
Visible screw and nail heads look unattractive. Instead, the mortise and tenon joints between the legs and the frame are secured with glued dowels. Measure and mark the position of the dowel holes on the faces of the legs.

3 Drill dowel holes
Commercial dowels are made to match standard drill sizes: 10, 8 and 6mm diameters (⅜, ⁵⁄₁₆ and ¼in). A table this size should use 10mm (⅜in) dowels: select the appropriate drill bit and mark the depth on the bit with some masking tape, then drill the holes for the dowels.

4 Side rails
The side rails will need to be cut to the desired length: two matching short and two matching long rails for a rectangular table, or four matching lengths for a square table. Set the mortise gauge a little over the mortise width then score the position and shape of the tenon in the ends of each rail.

5 Cutting the tenons
Score the lines deeper and then use a sharp chisel to pare a bevel along the waste of the face shoulders to guide the saw. Cramp the tenon and saw along the scored lines. Turn the rail over and remove the other side's waste from the shoulder. Pare with a chisel or plane the tenon until it slides into the mortise.

6 Drill dowel holes

The tenons will be further stabilized in the mortises by the dowels. Slot the tenon into the mortise and hold it square. Push a pencil through the drill holes made in the leg to mark the position of the drill holes through the tenon. Cramp the rail and drill through the tenon cheek, using the correct-sized bit, taking care not to split the wood.

7 Assemble the legs and rail

When all the tenons have been cut, assemble the table frame and legs by slotting the tenons into the mortises. Apply some wood glue to the dowels and insert them into the drilled holes. Insert all the dowels and then gently tap them home with a wooden or rubber mallet and saw off any excess length.

8 Prepare the tabletop

Measure the perimeter of the table frame once again. Decide how far the tabletop is to extend out from the frame and add this to your measurements. Measure, cut and prepare the wood or board for the tabletop. A power sander is an ideal tool for smoothing uneven surfaces. After sanding, use a tack cloth to remove surface dust.

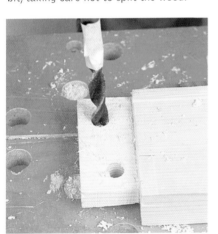

9 Secure the tabletop

To stop the tabletop sliding loose from the frame, secure it with a couple of plastic corner joints at each edge on the underside of the tabletop. Finish the table to match your decor.

FITTING A KITCHEN WORKTOP

Whether you are building new kitchen units or renewing old ones, easy-to-clean laminated worktops are ideal surfaces. Standard lengths are available from DIY stores in a range of colours, patterns and textures. The beauty of these is that the front edges are finished – often bull-nosed (slightly rounded).

It is also possible to buy matching laminate strips for finishing cut edges. You will need to cut the apertures for drop-in sinks and hob plates. Remember that manufacturers use different methods of attachment – some supply a template as a guide for cutting around. If not, then turn the sink or hob plate upside down and trace around it. You will also need to apply a proprietary sealer between sink bowl rims and the laminate to prevent water seepage. Instructions supplied with hob units will probably specify an asbestos lining to the underside hosing, which should be carefully fitted for safety.

Plan your work in an organized fashion so that the main work surface can be cut from one single length of laminated board. Where there is a join, the butted edges of the two pieces of laminated board are sealed with a proprietary sealer. This is available in a co-ordinating range of colours. Make sure you wear the appropriate safety face and eye wear when cutting laminated boards and remember to work from the face side to avoid chips and splits at cut edges.

1 Use the template

Where the manufacturer of a drop-in sink or hob plate has provided a template, follow their instructions on using this as your cutting guide. If no template is supplied, turn the drop-in unit upside down and trace around it. Note that this is not the cutting line.

2 Mark the cutting line

If you were to cut along the first line you traced, the drop-in unit would fall through the hole. A second line needs to be scribed inside the first to support the lip of the unit. Measure and mark the cutting line carefully – especially at the curved corners.

3 Drilling the corners

Start by boring holes at the corners. To stop the drill bit from slipping on the laminated surface, place an 'X' of masking tape on the marked position. Keep the drill bit vertical and make the drill hole large enough to accept the blade of the jig or pad saw.

4 Swing the aperture

Insert the jig or pad saw into the drilled hole and cut along the cutting line. Place a stool built up to the required height underneath the work surface: this will support the piece of laminate being cut and reduce the risk of splitting or cracking the edges of the cut laminate.

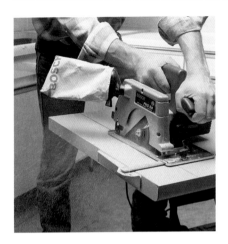

5 Cutting to length

In long runs of units, you may have to use additional lengths of laminated boards. Working with the laminated side face up, cut the boards to length. Where runs of board end at corners, measure the angles of the walls carefully – don't assume that they run at right angles.

6 Face visible edges

Where any cut edges are visible, they should be faced with laminate strips. Some are self-adhesive; others will require proprietary adhesive. Use a block of waste timber to press the laminate into position. Trim off waste, and sand using fine-grade glasspaper.

LAMINATE ADHESIVES

- The adhesives used to glue laminates bonds to itself immediately. This can be a problem when you are trying to line up edging strips onto the cut edges. The solution is to slide a sheet of brown paper between the laminated strip and the surface, line up the laminate, then slide out the paper and press the two adhesive-coated surfaces together.

- Once a laminate is in place, make sure it makes good contact. Press it down firmly with a spare block of wood. Allow the adhesive to set firmly before you trim away any waste laminate. Use a fine, flat-cut file or a small block plane to trim and file downwards. Filing upwards could chip the laminate surface.

7 Sealant

Where two lengths of cut board meet, the butt edges are sealed tight with a proprietary sealer (available in a range of colours). Where necessary, use a water-resistant version. The sealant is applied by a gun mechanism, which forces it through a nozzle into the join.

8 Sealing against walls

Worktop edges that butt against walls can be sealed and finished with angled strips. Cut these to length but allow for any mitre joins in corners to make a professional finish. The angle strips are fixed using a proprietary adhesive.

SAFETY FIRST

- Follow the manufacturer's operating instructions when using power tools. Do not remove any safety guards from the tools.

- Keep electrical flexes well away from the cutting blade or drill bit.

- Wear appropriate eye and face protection when cutting and drilling laminated boards.

PAINTING & DECORATING

Contents

TOOLS AND MATERIALS

To produce a professional result in home decorating, it is essential to use the right tools for the job.

• A stripping knife – one with a blade around 75mm wide (3in) – is used to strip off paint from flat surfaces. For awkward corners and around decorative mouldings, triangular or shaped shavehooks are useful. Hot-air strippers can save time but don't use them near glass or plastic.

• You'll need abrasive paper to rub down the surface and a filling knife to repair cracks.

• Professional decorators use paint kettles but any container with a handle will do. Tie an old nylon stocking over the top and pour the paint through it to strain out bits of dust and paint skin that might spoil the finish.

• Most indoor decorating jobs can be done with 50mm (2in), 25mm (1in) and 12mm (½in) brushes, but for walls and ceilings you'll need a larger 100mm (4in) or 150mm (6in) brush, or you could use a roller. There are 'cutting-in' brushes with angled tips for painting difficult places like window frames. A crevice brush has a long wire handle, which can be bent to different angles.

• Paint is quicker to apply with a roller, and often gives a more even finish. You can buy rollers with diamond or diagonal grooves cut into the surface, which allow you to create textured finishes. Corner rollers and

pipe and radiator rollers are also available. You'll need a tray for your paint and a stepladder with a platform at the top on which to place the tray.

• Paint pads come with disposable foam pads and you can buy sets of different shapes and sizes. These sets normally include a paint tray, which should have a built-in scraper. Other pads have paint wheels, which govern the amount of paint that can be loaded. Paint pads can also be used to apply glue size when wallpapering or for soaking wallpaper prior to stripping from walls.

• Wallpaper requires just a few basic tools. While a purpose-made paste brush is preferable, an ordinary large paintbrush can be used. Professional decorators use a collapsible papering table but you can improvize by using any wipe-clean table or a flush door laid over a kitchen table. A bucket to hold the paste will also be needed: tie a piece of string across the top on which you can rest the brush and wipe off any excess paste. For smoothing the paper, a paper-hangers' brush made of soft bristles is essential.

• You'll need measuring and marking tools, a pair of scissors (there are specialized wallpaper scissors available, but a pair with rounded ends to the blades will do just as well) and a plumb line so that you can achieve the true vertical. You'll need a trimming knife with a sharp blade for cutting away excess paper and a seam roller for gently rolling the seams where the sheets of wallpaper meet.

• When tiling, a spirit level and a plumb line are essential, as is a gauge stick, which you can make yourself from a length of wood (see page 322). A metal or plastic tile adhesive spreader is useful for working on small areas, but if you are tiling a large area, such as a wall, a notched trowel is best.

• Tiles will often have to be cut to shape and for this you'll need a tile cutter, along with a straight edge. The simplest form is a tungsten carbide-tipped scriber, but now there are lots of 'complete kits' available, which include radius cutters (for cutting circles out of the middle of tiles). There are also tile pincers and nippers, which are used to 'nibble' away at the corners of tiles so they fit around taps and switches. A carborundum stone is useful for smoothing off any rough edges. To drill through a tile, you'll need a drill and a masonry bit.

• When it comes to applying grout, nothing works better than a sponge, while a neat finish is best achieved with a small wooden stick with a rounded end – the sort of stick you find on an ice lolly is perfect. Use the right adhesive for the job in hand: thin bed adhesives on smooth, level surfaces and waterproof, flexible and heat resistant where required. Where tiles are exposed to running water, the grout must also be waterproof.

• You will need protective clothing, and dust sheets to cover the floor and any furniture or other items that can't be moved.

TOOLBOX

1 Wallpaper brush
2 Cutting-in brush
3 Paint tray and roller
4 Measuring tape
5 Filling knife
6 Spirit level
7 Sandpaper
8 Paintpads
Stripping knife
Hot-air strippers
Paint kettle
Paintbrushes
Stepladder
Paper-hangers' brush
Tile cutters, pincers and nippers
Carborundum stone
Dust sheets

TYPES OF PAINT

The type of paint you select depends on both the finish you want and the material you are decorating. Various additives adapt the qualities of paint for different uses.

Emulsion paint is the most popular and practical finish for walls and ceilings. It has a binder made from synthetic resins, which are dispersed in a solution of water. Exterior-grade emulsions, specially formulated to be weatherproof, are also available.

Solvent-based (oil) paints are a mix of oils and resins. Paints made from natural resins are very slow to dry so most modern paints contain synthetic versions to make them fast drying.

During manufacture, along with the pigments that give the wide range of colours, certain additives are included to give paint qualities such as high gloss, or non-drip.

Thixotropic paints are sold as non-drip paints. These are almost jelly-like in the tins, letting you load the brush quicker without drips. In other instances, manufacturers add extenders to fill and strengthen the paint. Cheap, budget paint contains lots of filler. While you get more paint for your money, it often means the paint doesn't cover as well and so you need extra coats. Reinforced emulsion has powdered mica or similar fine aggregate added to it to make a water-thinnable exterior grade emulsion paint that dries with a textured finish.

Paint that is too thick cannot be properly applied and needs to be thinned down before use. Some finishes require special thinners supplied by manufacturers, but most domestic solvent-based (oil) paints can be thinned with white spirit, while emulsions can be thinned with water. Turpentine will thin oil paints but it costs more than white spirit.

The proportion of pigment to resin affects the way in which paint sets. A shiny, gloss paint has approximately equal amounts of resin and pigment. A higher proportion of pigment produces a matt (dull) paint. By adjusting the proportions, it makes it possible to produce eggshell or satin finishes. Matt paints cover well because of their high pigment content, while the resins in gloss paints give them their strength.

Solvent-based (oil) paints are suitable for painting metal. There is a wide range of specialized finishes available: metallic finishes (which contain aluminium, copper, bronze or even gold powders); non-setting security paints used for rainwater and down pipes (the paint remains slippery to prevent intruders scaling walls via external pipes); non-slip paints (ideal for metal spiral staircases and external fire escapes); and radiator enamels (a heat stoving acrylic paint, which can also be used to repaint central heating boiler cabinets, refrigerators, washing machines, and cookers).

PREPARING PAINT

Whether you are using freshly purchased tins of paint, or making use of some 'left-overs' from a previous job, always remember to wipe the paint can to remove dust and dirt. Then prise the lid off with the side of an old, sturdy knife blade. Don't use a screwdriver, as this could make the lid buckle up and stop it from forming an airtight seal so it will be difficult to open next time.

Gently stir liquid paints with a clean, broad wooden stick to blend the pigment with the medium. There's no need to stir thixotropic paints but if the medium has separated, stir it and leave it to gel again before use.

Where a skin has formed on paint, cut around the edge with a knife and lift the skin out in one piece with a clean stick. Next time you put away a tin of paint, store it upside down. Then if a skin does form, it will be at the bottom of the tin.

Old paint needs to be strained through a nylon stocking or a piece of muslin into the paint kettle, so that any loose bristles, flakes of dust and dirt or bits of paint skin are removed.

Before you dip a brush into your paint, you'll need to prepare it to make sure it's clean and not shedding any hairs or fibres. Even new brushes will shed hairs so it's a good idea to rub the bristles in the palm of your hand to dislodge dust and loose bristles. Professional decorators never use a new brush for finishing paintwork. Instead they always 'run in' new brushes by painting on primers and undercoats.

Prepare new rollers by soaking them in warm, soapy water for a few hours before use. This will release any loose fibres that might spoil the finish. Rinse in clean water and dry the roller thoroughly before use.

BRUSHES AND ROLLERS, CARE AND CLEANING

Suspend brushes in water so the level covers the bristles to stop them drying.

Drill a hole in the handle of your brush and insert a wire to suspend it with.

During short breaks, wrap brushes in kitchen foil to exclude the air.

TAKING A BREAK

During short breaks in work, professional decorators wrap their brushes in plastic bags, clingfilm or tin foil, so the paint doesn't dry on the bristles. You can also use a rag moistened with the appropriate solvent to keep out the air and stop the paint from drying out.

During longer breaks, to save the process of cleaning oil-based paints from brushes, decorators suspend their brushes in a jar filled with water so the level covers the bristles. The brush has a hole drilled through it, just above the metal ferrule, through which you can insert a nail or wire which lays across the mouth of the jar. This stops the bristles from becoming bent out of true.

CLEANING UP AND STORING TOOLS

At the end of each job, brushes should be thoroughly cleaned. When stripper is used to remove excess paint from bristles, decorators always wrap the handles of their brushes in plastic bags secured with rubber bands so the stripper doesn't remove the varnish from the brush handle. Afterwards, brushes are hung up to dry and then, to help maintain their shape during storage, a rubber band is placed around the bristles.

WATER-BASED PAINTS

Brushes, rollers, pads and other tools used with water-based paints should be cleaned using soap and water. First, wipe off any excess paint onto old newspaper, then fill a container – a large-necked jar is ideal – with mild household detergent and suspend the tools in it for a few minutes. Don't let the water cover wooden handles as this causes the wood to swell and eventually to split. 'Swizzle' the brushes around in the water and then work the bristles of the brush into a bar of household soap, right down to the ferrule, to dislodge the paint. Any paint that is really dried in can be removed with a nail brush. If this fails, try restoring it by suspending it in a proprietary brush cleaner overnight.

Rinse brushes well in clean water and then stand them in a container of warm water with a dollop of hair conditioner for around 20 minutes. The conditioner will stop the bristles from becoming brittle and breaking off onto your next paint job. Squeeze out the excess water, shake the brush and leave it to dry, ideally suspended by the handle.

SOLVENT-BASED PAINTS

As with water-based paint, wipe the excess onto old newspaper before suspending your brush in a jar of white spirit or proprietary brush cleaner. Stir the brush vigorously and press it against the side of the jar to dislodge paint. When you take the brush out of the solvent, draw the bristles across the edge of the jar top to 'squeeze' out excess solvent. Use a stiff brush or nail brush to 'comb out' any dried-in paint. Keep repeating the process in clean solvent until the brush is clean and then wash it in soapy water and rinse it well. Again, it's worth conditioning brushes, especially after harsh solvents have been used.

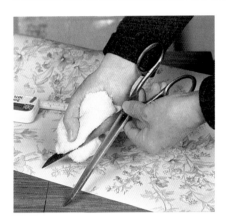

Clean paste from the blades of wallpaper shears so they cut cleanly.

Dipping and wiping brushes on the edge of paint tins makes a mess.

A string tied across a paste bucket can be used to scrape off excess adhesive.

Sponges, combs and rollers should be cleaned and stored in the same manner as brushes, but don't soak plastic decorators' combs in white spirit or they'll dissolve. Just wipe them over with a rag lightly dampened with solvent to remove oil-based paints.

STORING PAINT

Odd bits of paint left over at the end of a job are often kept in the original can in the vain hope that one day it will come in useful for touching up. Most of the time, when you take the lid off these leftovers, the paint has set hard because the seal on the lid no longer fits tightly. Left-over solvent-based paints will leach out fumes from ill-fitting lids and can be a serious fire hazard. Any left-over paint is better stored in a glass screw-top jar of the right size. Label the jar with the make, type (emulsion or gloss) and colour. This way it will keep for years. If the manufacturer has ceased making the same colour, you will be able to have it copied using the colour-mixing systems now available in paint and DIY stores. In the short term, to stop a skin of paint forming on the top, a circle of kitchen foil, cut to the approximate diameter and placed on top of the paint before the lid is replaced, will solve this particular problem.

USING PAINT KETTLES

You'll never see a professional painter and decorator dipping his brush directly into a can of paint. Instead a small amount of paint is poured from the tin into a kettle so that the rest remains completely clean and uncontaminated by grit and dust.

To avoid cleaning the kettle each time a new paint is used, professionals will line their kettles with kitchen foil. When one paint is finished with, the foil is removed and thrown away, and the kettle re-lined for the next paint.

WALLPAPER PASTE

Clean brushes and rollers by washing them thoroughly in warm water. Once again, it can be useful to condition brushes before storage.

Leaving brushes to stand in jars of solvent will distort the bristles. They are best suspended from a nail or wire across the mouth of the jar.

PREPARING WALLS

The best-painted walls are only as good as their preparation. Time spent cleaning and making good walls and ceilings prior to receiving their finish is time well spent. As a general rule, although some paint finishes will disguise an uneven wall, the aim of careful preparation is to ensure that walls and other surfaces are as flat and smooth as possible. Paint and wallpaper are not just decorations; they also protect the surfaces from wear and tear. But these finishes may crack, flake, tear or fall off the wall if the surface is not prepared carefully. For a perfect finish, make sure the surfaces are clean, dry and free from crumbling plaster and flaking paint.

The first task is to clear the room of furniture and furnishings: take down curtains and, where possible, roll up carpets. This will give you a clear space in which to work, and will avoid damage should there be an accidental spill. Don't forget to remove light fittings and shelves, and if there is anything left in the room, move it to the centre and cover it with a dustsheet. Cover the floor with newspaper – but not in areas where you will be heat-stripping paint.

Painting over wallpaper is a quick-fix solution, but the results aren't always very good, because paint can soften the existing adhesive and cause it to start 'bubbling'. Stripping away old wallpaper can seem a daunting task, but some modern wallpapers, including most vinyls, are called 'easy strip', which means you can simply pull away the wallpaper leaving the backing paper in place.

Try lifting a strip of wallpaper in one corner to see if it will pull away. If it does and the under paper is in good condition, leave the under paper on the walls to serve as your lining paper. If the under paper is damaged or creased, then you'll have to strip this off as well.

STRIPPING BY HAND

There are two main methods of removing existing wallpaper and the layers of lining paper underneath. The first is by hand: if the wallpaper will not pull away, or the backing vapour is damaged, give it a good soaking with warm water with a little washing-up liquid and a handful of cellulose paste mixed well together. The washing-up liquid acts as a wetting agent and the paste holds the

WASHING

- If a wall is washable, start at the bottom of the wall and work upwards: dirty trickles are absorbed less by an already wet surface. However, leave the skirting boards to last, as they are often the dirtiest area on a wall.

- Strip off wallpaper using a broad-bladed stripping knife but take care not to dig into the plaster or you'll have to fill the blemish.

- Before you start on the next stage of decoration, allow the walls to dry thoroughly, and then rub smooth any rough projections with glasspaper.

warm moisture in place while it softens the existing adhesive. Apply the solution to the wall with a wide brush or a roller and give it plenty of time to soak in.

Use a scraper and start peeling off the wallpaper. If it had a wipe-clean surface, or has been painted over, then you'll need to break up the surface by scoring it with a serrated scraper and then wetting it.

Don't be tempted to use a wire brush – you'll end up with tiny rolls of wet paper that will dry like concrete on the wall plaster and you might also get rust posts on the surface of the new wallpaper.

SAFETY FIRST

- Be extra careful when working up ladders – especially if you are steam stripping.

- Take great care stripping around light fixtures, electrical sockets and switches: switch the power off at the consumer unit for extra safety.

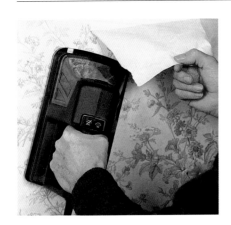

STEAM STRIPPING

The second method of stripping wallpaper is steam stripping. This is best where layers of paper have been added on top of each other. Don't try using a boiling kettle and an old steam iron; not only is this dangerous, but it also doesn't work. Steam strippers can be hired easily and cheaply from tool-hire stores and are simple to use. Steam stripping is best done on a dry day when you can open the windows – otherwise you'll end up with a sauna in your house. Remember that the steam is hot, so wear gloves at all times. While steam stripping is quicker than doing it by hand, you'll still need to work slowly and carefully, especially if there is any loose plaster around, as even the lightest of steamers can gouge into the wall. The technique is to hold the plate close to the wall and allow the combination of heat and steam to soften the paste. This way – in theory – you should be able to scrape away several layers in one go. In practice, however, be prepared to steam over the walls again – particularly where strips of paper have been overlapped.

CARE WITH ELECTRICAL FITTINGS

Don't forget that steam condenses into water so pay extra care and attention when you strip wallpaper from around electrical sockets and light switches with a steam stripper. For safety's sake, identify and isolate the power and lights in the room in which you are working. Don't just switch them off at the wall, turn off at the consumer unit too to avoid the risk of water coming into contact with live wires. Let the walls dry out thoroughly before you return the power to the room. A room that has been professionally wallpapered will have had the light switches taken off so there are no visible edges of the cut wallpaper – these are masked by the faceplate. You will have to remove the faceplate to strip the paper off cleanly. Where the wallpaper has been cut around to fit the perimeter of the faceplate, a very light steam should be enough to lift the paper so you can pull it away.

WASHING DOWN SURFACES

Always wash your surface after stripping and before applying paint or wallpaper. Start with the ceiling, if it's in good condition. Wash it thoroughly with sugar soap, or a weak solution of warm water and washing-up liquid, and then rinse it well. Washing is particularly important in rooms such as kitchens where grease will have been deposited. Open fires and cigarette smoke will also leave their mark. Walls should always be washed if they are to be repainted. If you're not sure if an existing wallpaper is washable, do a test on a small patch where it won't show. If the paper absorbs the water or the pattern is affected, the wall is not washable. Wash by sponging and rinsing overlapping sections – and don't stop until you've finished, otherwise you'll end up with 'tidemarks'. Skirting boards are the dirtiest part of the walls, so always clean them last.

STRIPPING AND PRIMING METAL

APPLYING PRIMER
Take your time and work the primer into all the nooks and crannies of your metalwork.

APPLYING RUST INHIBITOR
Proprietary rust inhibitor should be painted onto the cleaned metal surface with a paintbrush.

A surprising amount of metal is used in and around our homes – for central heating radiators, gates and railings, drainpipes and guttering and window frames. It seems odd, however, that metal, which is strong and hard-wearing, should be used in areas where it comes into contact with the one thing that causes it to corrode: water. Paint on its own won't protect metal from rust, although it will slow down the rusting process. Inhibitors and primers are required to completely protect it from being affected by rust.

Where metal has been used in and around your home, check it routinely for rust. Look for telltale signs: blistering or flaking paint means water has penetrated. If you find any, set to work immediately. Scrape off the paint to expose every spot of rust. Light deposits can be removed using wire wool or wet-and-dry paper dipped in white spirit. Where the rust is heavy – i.e. where the surface of the metal has become 'pitted' – use a wire brush or wire wheel or cup brush attachment to a power tool. Next, paint a proprietary rust inhibitor onto the cleaned metal surface: always follow the manufacturer's instructions as some inhibitors remain on the surface to protect the metal while others must be washed off after a few minutes. Wash grease off with white spirit and wire wool.

As soon as the metal is clean and dry, apply a primer. For general interior metalwork, use a red oxide primer. For exterior metalwork, use a red lead, zinc phosphate or calcium plumbate primer. Take extra care to work the primer into all the 'nooks and crannies' and pay particular attention to sharp edges and corners, which often get chipped and where corrosion can start.

STRIPPING PREVIOUSLY PAINTED METALS

Most metal surfaces are painted or finished with an oil-based paint, which slows the process of corrosion. If existing paint on metal is sound,

SAFETY FIRST

- Whether you remove the rust by hand or with the help of a high-speed tool, goggles must be worn to protect your eyes from fragments of flying rusted metal.

- Wear heavy-duty rubber gloves when using chemical strippers and take care if you wear spectacles with plastic lenses as they can be damaged if stripper is splashed onto them.

- Beware old paint: it may contain lead. Bear in mind when you strip down paint from older items and homes that there may be lead in the dust that's created. Wear safety glasses and a dust mask and work in a well-ventilated space. If you suspect lead in the paint, don't scrape it down; use a chemical stripper instead. Where you must rub down, use dampened wet and dry paper to stop the dust from forming.

then a wash, rinse and dry is often all that's needed to make it shine again. Sometimes, however, it's better to strip away all the paint on metal and begin again from scratch, particularly on intricately moulded pieces where additional layers of paint will gradually clog up and obscure details.

If the metal piece is portable, you could get it professionally stripped by sandblasting or caustic dipping. The best DIY method to strip metal is with a chemical stripper. A hot-air stripper is of little use on metal – the metal simply gets hot before the paint itself actually gets soft. A gas blowtorch might work but you could easily end up cracking a piece of cast iron.

Once stripped, again apply a rust converter or inhibitor to remove or neutralize rust. Clean the stripped metal with a wire brush then wash with white spirit and prime the surface of the metalwork with a zinc phosphate or red oxide primer, working it well into moulded areas and corners. See pages 300–1 for advice on painting metalwork.

METALWORK

- Before you chemically strip metal, make sure it really is metal. Some intricately moulded fireplace surrounds, for instance, may in fact be made of soft plasterwork on a wooden support. Tap the surround and listen carefully to the sound it makes, or scratch away a small area of paint to reveal the ground.

- Enamelled finishes on metals (such as enamelled bathtubs or solid fuel stoves) are made using a process which bonds the finish chemically to the metal. The only effective way of removing the enamelled surface is to have it sandblasted.

- Radiator paint is specially formulated to stay white. Other types of paint may be affected by heat and turn slightly yellow. It is possible nowadays to buy heat-resistant paints in a range of colours to match or complement your interior schemes.

- Corrosion on brass – especially on door furniture – occurs when the clear protective lacquer washes away. Corrosion can usually be removed with a patent metal polish, but heavy deposits are easier to remove with washes of a mix of 1 level teaspoon of salt and the same of vinegar mixed in 300ml (½pt) of hot water applied with fine wire wool.

FINISHES FOR METALWORK

FINISHES	OIL PAINT	EMULSION PAINT	METALLIC PAINT	SECURITY PAINT	RADIATOR ENAMEL	NON-SLIP PAINT
SOLVENTS/THINNERS						
WATER		✓				
WHITE SPIRIT	✓		✓	✓		✓
SPECIAL/PROPRIETARY					✓	
METHOD OF APPLICATION						
BRUSH	✓	✓	✓	✓	✓	✓
ROLLER	✓	✓	✗	✗	✗	✗
SPRAY GUN	✓	✓	✗	✗	✗	✗
CLOTH PAD (RUBBER)	✗	✗	✗	✗	✗	✗

PREPARING TILES AND PAINTED WALLS

PLASTER WALL

After you have stripped your walls back to plaster rendering, you are ready to apply paint or wallpaper. Paint can be applied directly onto plaster; emulsion paint is the preferred medium because it acts as a sealer and is not soaked in too much. New plaster, however, must be perfectly dry before painting, or patches of discolouration may occur. If oil-based paints are used, the paintwork may blister and peel off. Furthermore, efflorescence – white, crystalline deposits of salt – can appear on newly painted walls as the salts rise to the surface of the plaster as it dries.

Wallpaper also provides a good base surface for painting over, provided it is clean, dry, not torn and has no loose areas. If wallpaper is damaged, then painting over it will just make it worse. Always make a test patch first: a dark patterned wallpaper may require two or more coats of emulsion paint to cover it. You might find that dark patterns show up through your paint several days after painting.

FILL CRACKS

If a wall is in good condition, all the preparation required is to wash it down, scrape off any loose material and make good any cracks or holes with filler. Rake out any loose plaster from cracks and holes with a scraper or filling knife and fill using an interior-grade cellulose filler mixed to a creamy consistency – or, if you prefer, use a ready-prepared filler. Dampen the plaster around and inside the crack with a wet paintbrush and press the filler well in. Leave the filler standing a little proud of the wall; some fillers shrink when they dry and any that dries proud can easily be smoothed flush with abrasive paper.

Small holes are best filled with a dab of filler applied with a clean fingertip. Where a crack or hole is deep, it's best to fill it by building up in layers, allowing each to dry thoroughly. For more advice on repairing plaster, see pages 54–7.

PREPARING TILES

When you are preparing a wall for tiling, it must be clean, dry, grease-free and flat. Screws, nails and any other projections must be removed and cracks filled and smoothed down. A previously painted wall is a good basis for tiling, but if the paint is flaking, blistering or damaged, it's best to strip it off. Gloss paint should be scored to provide a keyed surface to ensure proper adhesion. If a surface is already tiled, but you want to change it, you can strip off the old tiles. This is a long and dirty job, and once started there's no going back. You'll need to chop out one or two tiles with a chisel and then prise off the rest. Wear protective goggles to protect your eyes from flying shards of tiles. Hack away any old adhesive that remains. Alternatively, to give a new look to old tiles, you can paint them (using special tile primer and paint) or tile over them as long as the old tiled surface is completely flat. Check for flatness with a spirit level. In either case, the surface needs to be sound, clean, level and grease-free, so clean it carefully with white spirit.

BASECOATS

BASECOATS

Primers seal surfaces prior to painting. They make a non-porous base and reduce the amount of paint needed to create a perfect finish. There are several types of primer but they generally fall into two categories: oil-based and acrylic primers. Oil-based primers are available in different formulations for wood, plaster and metal and are used before an undercoat is applied. Acrylic primers, on the other hand, not only dry faster but can also be used as a primer and undercoat on bare wood and plaster. Because they are water-based, acrylic primers will, however, raise the grain of wood, which will then need to be sanded down.

A good sealer for porous or dusty surfaces can be made by mixing PVA with water – follow the manufacturer's recommendations with regard to quantities. Damp stains can be covered with a proprietary stain block available in both brush-on and aerosol formulations. While these effectively obliterate damp stains, they will not cure damp, so always make sure that the cause of the damp is treated first.

LINING PAPER

The most common wallpaper defects are caused because the walls have not been lined. Lining paper makes the wall surface smooth and even and provides the correct amount of porosity to ensure maximum adhesion when the wallpaper is hung over it. Lining paper comes in different qualities and weights, so select the one that is right for your wallpaper. Hanging lining paper horizontally ensures that no joins will align with the joins in the wallpaper, which is hung vertically. If your walls are very uneven or have fine, hairline cracks, then hanging a double lining – the first vertically and the second horizontally – will smooth out the walls. You can also line a wall prior to painting it – a good idea if the previous paint was a dark colour. The lining will obliterate it so that the old colour does not adversely affect the

new colour or bleed through. Hang the lining paper vertically in this case, as you would hang wallpaper; that way the joins will be fewer and less visible when painted.

PAINTING

EXTERIOR WALLS

On average, the outside of our homes will need redecorating every five years or so. This can be a big job and one that requires a great deal of care, planning and preparation. If the exterior surfaces are not properly prepared, paint can peel and crack, and water can penetrate down to the underlying structure causing more than just cosmetic damage. Damp, heat and frost all affect exterior paintwork: damp will cause paint to peel; heat will cause it to blister; and frost will leave gloss paintwork looking flat.

Choose a warm, dry day with little wind following a spell of dry fine weather to redecorate the exterior of your home – late summer or early autumn is the best time. This way, exposed timber will have had a chance to dry out. Start work as soon as the morning dew has dried and finish work in time for the paint to dry before the evening dew arrives. Begin at the top of the house and work downwards, cleaning, repairing and repainting as you go.

Divide the job into manageable sections: work on one side of the house at a time and remember that long spells on ladders can be extremely tiring, making accidents more likely. Exterior decoration will almost invariably require ladders or scaffold towers. Before you start work, inspect your ladders or hire the necessary equipment so you can work safely and efficiently at heights. Never improvise with equipment and avoid the temptation to over-reach. It may be time-consuming, but it's safer to come down from a ladder and reposition it so you can reach areas safely without over-reaching.

1 Working with a brush
Choose a 100–150mm (4–6in) brush, which will hold plenty of paint, for working on exterior walls. Use an old brush, if you have one, as the roughness of exterior surfaces will soon wear down the bristles. On wood and metal, use the same brushes as you would for interior work (see page 280) and clean and care for them in the same way.

2 Using a roller
If you use a roller for exterior painting, use an old one or buy an exterior grade, shaggy nylon roller, which will last longer on rough exterior surfaces than the softer types used for interior decoration. Paint in small sections so that the edges don't dry out before you have painted the adjoining section.

3 Painting pipes
If they have not been previously painted with bituminous paint, the interiors of gutters and the outsides of gutters and drainpipes can be painted with two coats of exterior-grade gloss. If bituminous paint has been used already, apply a coat of aluminium sealer to the old surface before you apply gloss paint. Otherwise, the bituminous paint will bleed through the gloss, spoiling the finish.

4 Treating exterior woodwork
Make repairs to doors and window frames, rub down and sand surfaces or strip back finishes to bare wood. Prime wooden surfaces before undercoating, working the primer well into nail holes, and into the end grain of wood.

5 Finishing exterior woodwork
When the primer has dried, sand it over gently and fill any holes with exterior-grade wood filler and sand smooth. Next, add two coats of exterior-grade gloss for extra protection, lightly rubbing down the surfaces between applications. Gloss paint should be applied as soon as the undercoat has dried.

FINISHES FOR MASONRY

FINISHES	CEMENT PAINT*	EXTERIOR EMULSION	REINFORCED EMULSION	SPIRIT-THINNED MASONRY PAINT	TEXTURED COATING	FLOOR PAINT
SUITABLE FOR:						
BRICK	✓	✓	✓	✓	✓	✓
STONE	✓	✓	✓	✓	✓	✓
CEMENT RENDER	✓	✓	✓	✓	✓	✓
CONCRETE	✓	✓	✓	✓	✓	✓
PEBBLE DASH	✓	✓	✓	✓	✓	✓
DRYING TIME: HOURS						
TOUCH DRY	1–2	1–2	2–3	1–2	6	2–3
RECOATABLE	24	4	24	24	24–48	12–24
SOLVENTS/THINNERS						
WATER	✓	✓	✓		✓	
WHITE SPIRIT				✓		✓
NUMBER OF COATS (NORMAL CONDITIONS)	2	2	1–2	2	1	1–2
METHOD OF APPLICATION						
BRUSH	✓	✓	✓	✓	✓	✓
ROLLER	✓	✓	✓	✓	✓	✓
SPRAY GUN	✓	✓	✓	✓	✗	✓

* Cement paint will not cover surfaces already painted with emulsion or oil-based paint

INTERIOR WALLS

However tempting it may seem, trying to save money by buying cheap brands of paint can actually work out more expensive in time, money and effort than buying a quality brand and making sure the surfaces are sealed and primed. Poorer quality paints tend not to cover as well so you'll need more – that's why they are often in such large cans – and you may have to paint two or three coats to get an even finish.

Make sure you have enough paint in the same colour and finish to complete the job. Paints are made in batches and there may be slight variations in colour between batches. It's better to have an unopened can of paint left over than to run out of paint halfway through and, in any case, most DIY stores will exchange unopened paint for other useful materials. When you have decided on your paint 'family' – water- or oil-based – and the finish – matt, silk or gloss – make sure you stick to it.

Start decorating at the ceiling and work your way downwards through the room, finishing with the wood-work. Clean up any drips as they happen and remove any loose bristles as they fall out of the paintbrush. Always follow the manufacturer's instructions as some paints – except non-drip gloss and solid emulsions – may need stirring with a clean, flat stick before you apply them. Make sure your stirrer is clean so that old paint doesn't bleed into the new. Remember the professional painters' methods: decant paint into a paint kettle, and, if you are using old paint, pour it into the kettle through a piece of muslin or a clean, old nylon tight leg stretched over the neck of the can.

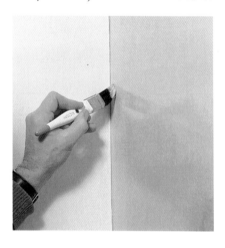

1 Small brushes
Rub the bristles of new brushes in the palm of your hand to dislodge any dust and loose bristles. Start at the top of a wall in the corner and 'cut in' the edge using a small brush. A wide brush won't fit easily into the angle and it's harder to keep a straight edge. If you are right-handed, work from right to left, if left-handed, work from left to right, and apply the paint in vertical strokes overlapped with horizontal ones. Work in an area approximately 1m sq. (1sq.yd), keeping a wet edge at all times.

2 Using a brush
You can hold the brush in any way that is comfortable, but professionals use the 'pen grip'. Hold the handle like a pen between your thumb and forefinger, your other fingers gripping the side of the metal ferrule while your thumb rests on the other side. Apply emulsion paint in vertical strokes, then spread it at right angles to even out the coverage. Emulsion dries without visible brush strokes, but oil-based paints don't, so finish off each section with light, vertical strokes.

3 Using a paint pad
Paint pads need to be loaded with paint from their own special tray so that you always pick up an even amount of paint. To apply the paint in a continuous cover, keep the pad flat against the wall and sweep it gently across using even strokes in any direction: criss-crossing strokes are good for emulsion paints while for oil paints, end the sweep with an upwards stroke to prevent streaks.

4 Using a roller

Rollers apply paint to walls and ceilings much faster than a brush and are ideal for covering large areas. Choose your roller carefully as there are different 'sleeves' to suit different types of paint. Shaggy, long-haired and sheepskin rollers are best for textured walls while fine, foam rollers produce smooth, even finishes. Dip the roller into the reservoir in the tray and roll it gently on the ridged section to ensure an even 'pick up'. Use zigzag strokes in all directions to cover the surface and watch that you don't let the roller spin away from the wall at the end of a stroke otherwise you'll end up splattering paint on the floor and adjacent walls. Cover walls by working in small, manageable sections and keeping wet edges. You'll still need to 'cut in' corners with a small brush, however, as a roller will not reach right into the angle.

FINISHES FOR INTERIOR WALLS & CEILINGS

FINISHES	EMULSION PAINT	REINFORCED EMULSION PAINT	OIL-BASED PAINT	UNDERCOAT	PRIMER/UNDERCOAT	CEMENT PAINT	TEXTURED COATING
SUITABLE FOR:							
PLASTER	✓	✓	✓	✓	✓	✓	✓
WALLPAPER	✓	✗	✓	✓	✓	✗	✗
PAINTED SURFACES	✓	✓	✓	✓	✓	✗	✓
BRICK	✓	✓	✓	✓	✓	✓	✓
STONE	✓	✓	✓	✓	✓	✓	✓
CEMENT	✓	✓	✓	✓	✓	✓	✓
DRYING TIME: HOURS							
TOUCH DRY	1–2	2–3	4	4	½	1–2	6
RECOATABLE	4	24	16	16	2	24	24–48
SOLVENTS/THINNERS							
WATER	✓	✓				✓	✓
WHITE SPIRIT			✓	✓	✓		
NUMBER OF COATS (NORMAL CONDITIONS)	2	1–2	1–2	1–2	1–2	2	1
METHOD OF APPLICATION							
BRUSH	✓	✓	✓	✓	✓	✓	✓
ROLLER	✓	✓	✓	✓	✓	✓	✓
PAINT PAD	✓	✗	✓	✓	✓	✓	✗
SPRAY GUN	✓	✓	✓	✓	✓	✓	✗

PAINTING AWKWARD AREAS

Redecorating can be made simpler, quicker and less frustrating if many of the 'obstacles' that impede progress are removed first. Painting around fixtures and fittings such as ceiling roses, wall switches and sockets, door furniture and pipework, can be time-consuming and this is often where drips and dribbles occur, which mar the finished room.

Where possible any obstacles should be removed: switch off power to electrical fittings before exposing connections; wedge open doors so you don't get locked in or out after door knobs have been removed; and, where possible, remove radiators so you can clean and paint behind them. If this all sounds too complicated, there are solutions: mask off sockets and switches with low-tack tape – but still turn off the power to them at the consumer unit; wrap door knobs in kitchen foil and pendant light fittings in polythene. Remember that awkward areas are also those that collect dirt, dust and grease. Before you apply a new finish, make sure they have been thoroughly cleaned.

BEHIND RADIATORS

If you don't want to take a radiator off the wall, let it cool down completely and get a long, thin feather duster and sweep behind it thoroughly to remove dust and cobwebs. Use a radiator or crevice brush to paint the wall behind. These have either a long wire or angled plastic handle, which allows you to reach behind panel radiators quite easily. Take care not to paint over any valves or fittings as you may end up sealing them tightly open or shut and you won't be able to operate them in the future.

MASKING OFF

Even professional decorators with years of skill and experience know that paint will find its way onto surfaces where it was never intended. Professionals don't take unnecessary risks and completely mask off areas to keep them safe. Low tack masking tape is ideal because it can easily be peeled off without removing the painted or papered surface below. For this reason, don't use ordinary clear PVC sticky tape. To protect exposed copper central heating pipes from drips and dribbles of paint, tape newspaper around them right along their length.

But masking tape can also be used to create interesting decorative effects – stripes around a room, the neat edge of a 'trompe l'oeil' dado, or areas painted in two or more different colours. There is even a three-sectioned striping tape – used for painting 'go-faster' stripes on cars. You apply it to the surface, peel away the middle strip, apply paint inside the masked area and, when touch dry, peel off the mask.

CEILINGS

- When you paint a ceiling, unscrew ceiling roses so you can paint right up to the back plate with a small brush. You must switch off the power at the main switch, identify and remove the fuse supplying power to the fitting before you expose any electrical connections.

- If you have sensitive skin, wear gloves or apply a barrier cream when painting. Wash off paint splashes with warm soapy water rather than paint thinners. Wear old clothes that you don't mind getting paint on. It's bound to happen at some stage.

CEILINGS

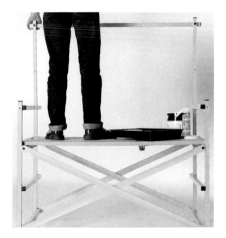

USE SCAFFOLD TOWERS

Painting or wallpapering a ceiling will be easier, quicker and much safer if you use the correct equipment to enable you to reach and work safely at heights. Where possible, avoid using a stepladder – the temptation to over-reach and overbalance can lead to avoidable accidents. Redecorating ceilings can be tiring, especially as it is a job that is best done in one go. You can make a scaffold tower by slinging a sturdy scaffold plank between two pairs of stepladders, but it is far better to use a scaffold tower. These have a stable rectangular base and can be adjusted for height. Scaffold towers can be hired at tool-hire shops and the small added expense is more than compensated for by a job safely and well done.

If your tower has castors at the base, allowing you to move it easily, make sure the wheels are lockable. Scaffold towers are available in a range of heights and sizes. Your tool hire shop will be able to advise you on the best size to suit your purposes.

ROLLERS

Because even the best decorators find that paint drips, ceilings are painted first in the order of decoration. Rollers are the ideal tool to use to paint ceilings, but you'll still have to cut in the edges with a small brush because a roller won't reach right into the angle. Start painting by working away from the main source of light and paint in 600mm (2ft) wide bands. Apply a fresh load of paint from the roller just clear of the previous application and blend in the edges for an even coverage. Take care when you work around ceiling roses and other electrical fittings: where possible remove them by switching off the power at the consumer unit and isolating the fuse before exposing electrical connections. Where large pendant lamps are difficult to move, switch off the power as before and wrap the lamps in polythene bags to keep them free of paint spots.

If you are using a roller to paint a ceiling, you will need a stepladder with a platform on which the paint tray can be placed while you work.

PAINT PADS WITH EXTENDED ARMS

Paint pads work in a similar way to rollers: they are ideal for painting large areas such as walls and ceilings evenly and smoothly. As with rollers, it is possible to extend the reach of pads with arms that will enable you to reach heights more easily. Loading the pad from its special tray with its extended arm can be a little tricky, however. You don't need to apply pressure to the pad, just sweep it gently across the ceiling in criss-crossing strokes for even coverage. You will also need a smaller pad or brush to cut in the edges of the ceiling where it meets the walls and where two walls meet.

TEXTURE

On textured ceilings it is better to apply two thin coats of paint than one thick one so that the texture does not become obliterated.

CORNICES AND MOULDINGS

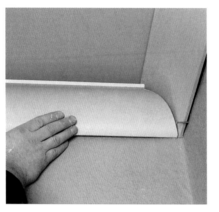

Elaborate ceiling cornices and moulded details are all too often caked in layers of distemper and old paint that have built up over years, obscuring the fine details. Once a very popular finish, distemper is powdered chalk or whiting mixed with a glue size. The problem occurs when you try to paint over it, as when it is wet it re-dissolves and comes away with the newly painted surface. If cornices and mouldings have been treated with distemper you will need to apply a stabilizing primer to bind the surface. Alternatively, because it is water-based, distemper can be removed – if you have the time, energy and a cornice worthy of display. Wet an area thoroughly and scrub it with an old toothbrush until the moulded detail becomes clear, then, using a pointed stick – a wooden barbecue skewer is ideal – scrape away the distemper from the details. Once removed, stabilize the cornice with primer. Other paint covers can be removed by scrubbing gently with a stiff bristled brush and wiping the surface with white spirit. Thick build-up of paint is best removed using a paste stripper.

NEW COVING

There are several types of coving: builders' merchants sell one made of gypsum plaster and they also supply the special adhesive required to fix it. Other covings are made of polyurethane, polystyrene and fibrous plaster. Polyurethane and polystyrene coving is best cut with a sharp blade, while fibrous plaster is cut with a fine-toothed saw. Always cut from the face side. Cut ends of fibrous plaster should be lightly sanded with fine glasspaper, but polystyrene and polyurethane coving cannot be sanded, so make sure your cuts are clean and accurate. You can buy specially prepared corner pieces if you don't want to cut your own mitred corners. Plaster coving can be painted, while polystyrene and polyurethane can be left unpainted. If you do decide to paint these, use emulsion paint as gloss paints will create a serious fire hazard. Before fitting coving, wall and ceiling paper and paint should be stripped off to reveal bare plaster. Adhesive is applied to the back of coving; with plaster coving, the wall and ceiling must also be dampened with water.

STRIPPING DETAILS

Stripping moulded details can be done 'dry' using a scraper or sharp blade, but take care not to scratch or damage the surface beneath. Chemical strippers in gel or paste form are ideal for removing layers of paint that are obscuring details. Follow the manufacturer's instructions regarding application carefully.

SCRAPE OFF WITH FINE WIRE WOOL

Fine grade wire wool is the best tool for removing the strippers and old paint without damaging the surface. When the ball of wire wool becomes clogged with debris, replace it with a new piece.

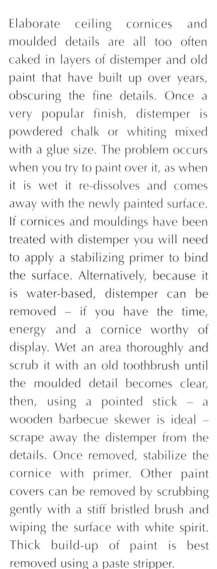

PAINTING WOODWORK

DOORS

The different sections of a panelled door are painted in sequence starting with the mouldings. Work in strokes parallel to the grain of the wood to avoid streaking the paint. Once the mouldings are complete, paint the centre panels. Finish each stroke with an upwards stroke so that there are no visible brush marks. Don't press the brush into the panel too hard or the paint will become tacky and streaky. Next paint the muntin – the central vertical panel – and the cross rails – the horizontal panels at the top, foot and middle. Paint each of these following the direction of the grain, and finish the vertical panel with upward strokes. The last sections of the door to be painted are the stiles – the outer vertical panels at each side of the door. When these are complete, paint the edge of the door – brush from the edge, not onto it. While the paint is drying on the face and edges of the door, wedge it open at the bottom so that it does not come into contact with the doorframe and mar the paintwork.

FLUSH DOORS
Flush doors are easier to paint if you take them off their hinges and lay them over trestles. Start at the top and work downwards in sections blending each section into the other. Finish each part with light parallel strokes in the direction of the grain.

Doors aren't just functional room dividers; they also add character to a home. They come in for a great deal of wear and tear, however, and deserve to be well-maintained. Paint panelled doors in the sequence described. If you remove the door handle, it is a good idea to keep it in the room with you, just in case. Alternatively, wrap the handle tightly in kitchen foil to protect it from splashes.

WINDOW FRAMES

1 Strip off old paint

Window frames are generally narrow pieces of wood and will only take a limited number of layers of paint before their details are obscured. Strip off the old finish carefully, taking care not to break the glass windowpane.

2 Fill and rub down

With the old paint removed, check the frames for damage or rot. Fill any cracks, treat the timber with an appropriate timber preservative where required and lightly sand the wood. Clean off dust with a damp cloth.

WINDOWS

- Remove masking tape as soon as the paint is touch dry. Don't leave masking tape on for too long or it will be difficult to remove.
- Painting the glazing bars of window frames is easier if you use a cutting-in brush, which has bristles cut at an angle to let you work right up to the glass with a thin line of paint.
- Keep casement windows open while they dry: if you have removed the catch and stay, keep the window open by wrapping a short piece of coat hanger wire around a nail in the underside of the frame.

3 Mask off

To ensure that no paint gets on the windowpanes, use low-tack masking tape and mask off. Leave a very slight gap – 1.5–2mm ($\frac{1}{16}$–$\frac{1}{8}$in) is enough – between the edge of the glass and the frame so that the edge of the paint seals the join between them.

4 Painting sash windows

Pull down the top sash and paint the meeting rail of the top sash and the accessible parts of the vertical members; reverse the position of the sashes and complete the top sash. Paint the bottom sash and then the frame – not the runners. Paint the runners only when the frame is dry.

USING A PAINT SHIELD

You can buy specially designed plastic and metal shields to help you paint straight edges without getting paint onto windowpanes. They can be a little tricky to hold in place, but are good if you are 'touching up' paint.

STAIRCASES

Staircases have to be used on a regular basis, so you will need to plan ahead when painting them so that they can remain functional while new paint dries. The simplest way to tackle painting a staircase is to paint the balustrade (handrail) first. Make sure that you avoid drips and dribbles of paint as you work, especially where your brush touches the edges or mouldings. Then move to the top of

the stairs and paint the treads (the part you step on) and risers (the upright back of the tread). If you cannot take your staircase out of commission for long enough for the paint to dry, then on one day paint all the risers but only every other tread. Cut some pieces of paper or stick 'post-it' notes onto the unpainted treads so that users know which treads they can walk on. The next day, paint the remaining treads, clearly marking where feet can be placed. Next paint the balusters, the newel posts and string. Make sure you have enough light and that you can reach the upper, exterior parts of the balusters safely. Intricately moulded balusters and newel posts can be tricky to paint, so to avoid touching and smearing new paint, paint every alternate baluster and let them dry.

SKIRTING BOARDS

Skirting boards are the last pieces of fixed joinery to be painted in a room sequence. Treat skirting boards in the same way as any other woodwork: at some stage they will be so overloaded with coats of paint that you'll need to strip it off and start at the bare wood. You could use a hot-air stripper but take great care that hot-stripped paint does not land on flammable material. Chemical stripper is a lot safer – use a gel or paste so it adheres to the vertical skirting without dripping onto the floor and use a stripping knife to remove the 'waste'. Follow the

manufacturer's instructions regarding application and neutralizing afterwards. Much of the problem in painting skirting boards occurs when paintbrushes pick up bits of dirt and fluff from the floor, which is then deposited on the new paint. The best way to solve this problem is to sweep the floor thoroughly and then slide wide strips of cardboard under the skirting, which will also protect the floor from paint marks. Don't use newspaper – it inevitably gets bunched up, torn and bits get stuck to the paint.

PAINTING METAL

CAST-IRON FIREPLACE

Over time many original period features, such as cast-iron fireplaces, have been painted over. This was often because they were no longer in use and their black colour was considered too dark for modern, light interiors. Rather than decorate to match their ornate style, many people preferred just to 'blank them out' with a heavy layer of paint.

A restored and working fireplace is very attractive and nowadays can add substantially to the value of your home. Many homes still have small cast-iron fireplaces in the bedroom – called 'registers' – which were moulded from a single piece of cast iron. When cast-iron fireplaces are stripped of layers of paint, and then sealed with iron paste, they are a silvery graphite colour, which catches the light beautifully.

We tend to think of cast iron as a very hard material: in fact it's quite soft, porous and very easily scratched, so any stripper applied to the surface must be neutralized with water as soon as it has been removed. See page 284 for more advice on methods of stripping metal safely. Whenever possible, dismantle the item and work on it outdoors.

SAFETY FIRST

- Always wear heavy-duty gloves when you strip cast iron: the stripper is extremely caustic and can cause skin irritation.
- If you have to strip and paint metal indoors, good ventilation is essential. When using a spray gun, goggles and a respirator should be used.
- Note that spray paint is highly flammable. Don't leave spray guns unattended if there are children and animals in the house.

FIREPLACES

- It's much easier to strip large items, such as fireplaces, outdoors, laid flat on the ground. If a fireplace is still fitted, take care to protect the surrounding areas by covering walls and floors with dustsheets and newspapers.

- Black lead makes an attractive finish on cast iron. Use a soft cloth to spread it across the surface then work it into patterned areas with a toothbrush. When you have finished, buff to a shine with a soft, clean cloth – an old 'T'-shirt is ideal.

1 Ready for restoration

An old cast-iron fireplace can be restored to its former glory by stripping away the layers of paint to reveal the intricate decorative details. Use an appropriate chemical stripper: because cast iron scratches easily, a blanket stripper is a good way to remove the old paint (see page 284).

2 Finishing

Once all the old layers of paint have been removed, it's a good idea to treat the cast iron with a rust converter, which also acts as a rust inhibitor, stopping new rust forming. The iron paste or polish is simply applied with a brush or soft cloth and then buffed to a brilliant sheen to catch and reflect the light.

GARDEN BENCH

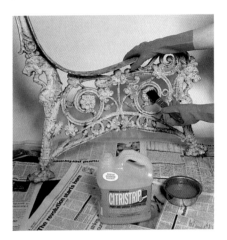

1 Strip off the finish

The highly decorative ends of iron garden benches have often suffered from neglect: the visible parts may have been painted while the 'inside' edges have been forgotten. Dismantle the bench before you work on it to help you reach the less accessible areas. Strip off the paint using a chemical stripper.

2 Neutralize

When all the stripper and old paint has been removed, the metal surface should be neutralized with clean water. Use a household brush to scrub the metal, making sure you get into all the nooks and crannies.

3 Apply rust inhibitor

Carefully check the bare metal for spots of rust and apply a rust converter or inhibitor and leave it to penetrate the surface for at least half an hour before removing with fine-grade wire wool.

4 Finish

Intricate shapes and surfaces are best repainted using a spray or aerosol applicator. Choose an appropriate metal paint – they are available in finishes such as 'shiny' or a 'hammered' finish. When dry, reassemble the bench seat.

SPRAY PAINTING

- Applying paint with a spray gun or aerosol is the quickest and most efficient way to paint large areas and 3-dimensional objects. Keep the aerosol or spray gun about 225mm (9in) from the object and pull or depress the trigger.

- Keep the gun or can moving using even parallel movements and overlap each line of spray by about 100mm (4in).

- Clean the nozzle of the spray gun or aerosol between coats otherwise it will clog up as the paint dries.

- Spray paint will go everywhere, so, where possible, work outdoors or carefully mask off surrounding areas.

- Always follow the paint manufacturer's instructions and safety guidelines regarding storage, use breathing masks and dispose of empty aerosols carefully: never puncture the cans and don't attempt to incinerate them.

- Contact your local authority for advice on the disposal of low-grade chemical waste, such as paints and solvents. Don't ever discharge them into the water course.

DECORATIVE PAINT EFFECTS

Decorative paint effects have been used since ancient times: trompe l'oeil scenes of gardens, colonnades and views over bays were used by the Romans to decorate the walls of their villas. Since then, numerous paint effects have been popular, including antiquing – the art of making objects look older than they really are by 'distressing' them with a cracquelure finish, which replicates the fine network of cracks that can be seen on 'old master' paintings and antique porcelain and cabinets.

For many years, however, the materials and techniques of decorative paint effects remained the carefully guarded 'trade secrets' of master craftsmen – and forgers, of course. Today, an enormous range of products is easily available that allows the enthusiastic do-it-yourselfer to exercise their own creative imaginations and transform plain surfaces using such techniques as liming, marbling, crackleglazing, stencilling, rag rolling and a whole host of other exciting effects.

See page 246 for advice on how to lime your woodwork.

COLOURWASH

The natural beauty of wood is all too often hidden under a thick layer of paint. Colourwashing, on the other hand, allows these qualities to show while still adding colour to a room. It's a very simple technique to use on bare wood and you can vary the density of colour as you wish simply by adding more, or less, water to the paint mix. Bare wooden floors can be transformed by colourwashing them in thin transparent layers of diluted emulsion paint, which is absorbed into the wood. While there are ready-made colourwashes available, there are numerous advantages to using diluted emulsion: it dries quickly, there are thousands of colours, tones and shades to choose from, and emulsions are cheaper. You can also use any number of colours to create patterns simply by masking off areas and colourwashing them in different tones. The diluted emulsion, once soaked into the wood, will look less intense in colour, so it's a good idea to experiment first so you can see how many layers you'll need to build up the colour to the level you want. Because diluted emulsion dries very quickly, this won't take as long as you might think. If colourwashed objects have to be tough and durable, you will need to finish them with a long-wearing, protective topcoat of acrylic varnish.

STIPPLING

Many decorative paint effects begin with a simple, flat basecoat of paint in a colour of your choice over which other colours are added. Stippling is an ideal way to create a two-tone textured appearance. The main thing to remember with a stippled effect is that the basecoat colour will still

remain the dominant colour in the scheme. The stippled effect is easily created using a sponge or a 'ball' of cotton rags. Each will give a slightly different finished look: a sponge will give a fine stipple while rags will give a bolder, more 'dappled' effect. Experiment with both to find the look you want: in either case, dampen the rags or sponge with water, squeeze out the excess, dip into the stippling colour and 'dab' it gently onto the base colour. If you add too much stipple colour, don't worry. You can always 'blot' it out by stippling over it with the original base colour – or even add a third, different, colour.

RAG ROLLING

Rag rolling – and its 'sister' effect of bag graining – also involve a stippling action. But, unlike stippling, these techniques are used to remove paint from a surface rather than add it. Most often it is a darker colour laid over a lighter base colour, and here the rolled or bagged colour will be the dominant colour in the scheme. While the topcoat of colour is still wet, a piece of cloth, folded into quarters and rolled into a 'sausage', is rolled upwards from the base of the wall. As it picks up paint, the rolled cloth leaves behind a pattern in the wet paint producing a delicately textured effect.

A similar but more 'random' and irregular effect can be achieved by using a plastic carrier bag half-filled with loose rags dabbed onto the wet paint. While rag rolling is a simple technique, it can get a little messy, and you will need plenty of cloths and carrier bags as they will soon become over-loaded with wet paint picked up from the surface.

SPECKLING

This is one of the simplest ways to introduce colour, texture and interest to a surface. Once again, it is the background or base colour that remains dominant in the scheme, but it will be modified by random 'speckles' of one or more colours. The only drawback to speckling is that it can be a messy process, so cover any surfaces and adjoining areas you want to be kept 'speckle free' and cover electrical fittings with masking tape. Oil paint reduced with just a little white spirits is the preferred medium for speckling – you can even use metallic paints to add a sparkle. The tip of a stiff bristled brush is dipped into the speckle colour and then held about 100mm (4in) from the surface. A small stick – an old wooden school ruler is ideal – is dragged across the bristles towards you, launching flecks of colour onto the surface. Once this colour is dry, you can add a second speckle colour, if you choose.

DECORATIVE EFFECTS

- Be prepared to experiment on a small area first to see the effect of different textures, colours and effects. Remember that any colours and effects will look different under different types of lighting – natural daylight, candlelight or electric lights. Don't worry if in the end you don't like what you have achieved: it's only paint so you can always strip it off again or paint over it.

- If you make a mistake while speckling and get too much paint in one area, use a sponge to dab on base colour, wait for it to dry then start again.

- To 'distress' paint on woodwork, let the topcoat dry then use a medium-grade abrasive paper to rub through to previous layers, giving an impression of wear and tear.

- Natural sea sponges give a better effect when stippling than synthetic ones. Blot the sponge first on a piece of paper to remove excess paint.

- You can buy special 'stippling-off' brushes that remove some of the top-coat colour and give the effect of a reverse pattern.

GILDING

Gilding is an ancient technique that traditionally involved applying a very fine layer of gold to the surface of an object; today a whole range of metallic finishes such as silver, copper and bronze are available. Because of its value, real gold is often substituted in decorative schemes with 'Dutch metal', which is gold coloured and comes as transfer sheets. This is available from artists' materials suppliers but it can be a little tricky to apply. Fortunately, gilt effects also come in a range of easy to use alternatives: gilding powder, in a range of metallic finishes, can be brushed onto a 'tacky' surface or mixed with a medium to create a metallic paint. By far the easiest way to add a touch of richness is with a gilt cream. This can be used to add highlights. Try it on stair balusters, moulded cornices, picture and mirror frames and door panelling – or, it can be used to 'touch up' existing gilt that has lost some of its sparkle. The gilt cream is simply applied using either a clean finger or a brush and, when dry, buffed up to a sheen with a soft cloth.

MARBLING

Simulated marble is not an easy technique to master so be prepared to practise. Take a look at some 'real' examples of marble: black, white and grey are not the only colours. There is a huge range of marble – Sienna, Carrara, Serpentine, Egyptian green, to name just a few. When you create a 'faux marble' effect, you will be working with a limited colour range – perhaps just three different colours – but you can create an infinite range of subtle tones and shades. Artists' oil paints create the best marbling effect: they take a while to dry so allow time to work on the whole effect while still wet. These can be expensive, so use them for smaller objects; for larger surfaces, you could use oil-based interior paints in a satin finish.

2 Veining

The veins in marble are the most outstanding feature. With a fine artists' paintbrush, draw the veins using colour mixed from your three pigments. Paint veins in varying thicknesses and directions. Use a piece or photograph of real marble as a guide.

1 Mottling

Over a light basecoat colour, start with the darkest of your three colours and gently stipple it onto the surface. Then move to the mid-tone colour, blending the two colours where they meet by dabbing the brush gently while the two are still wet. Repeat with the lightest tone of the three colours.

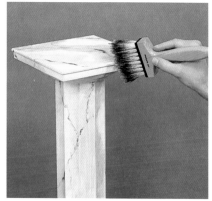

3 Blotting and blending

Any thick lines of paint can be blotted with a tissue or clean rag to reduce them. 'Feather' the veins by brushing gently backwards and forwards over the surface with a soft paintbrush. Let the paint dry and then seal the surface with a semi-gloss polyurethane varnish and buff to a sheen with a soft cloth.

CRACKLEGLAZE

1 Coating with glaze

Crackleglazes are water-soluble glazes that are applied as a 'sandwich', either between two layers of paint or between wood and a layer of paint. Apply an even coat of the glaze to the surface, painting in one direction.

2 Adding top colour

Now add a 'top' colour. Stir the colour well and brush it onto the surface in the opposite direction to the direction you applied the crackleglaze. Don't over-brush, or you'll stop the cracking process

3 Second coat of glaze

Adding the second part of a two-part crackleglaze to the surface will open it up and create a fine, criss-cross network of cracks. You can speed up the cracking process by gently heating the surface with a hairdryer, but this will create slightly deeper cracks.

4 The finished product

Although it dries clear, the glaze causes the paint on top to crack, thereby revealing the underlying wood or painted colour. The beauty of crackleglazing is that it gives tired, old and worn items a rejuvenating facelift, while new items treated in the same manner will be 'aged' in soft, mellow way.

STENCILLING

Stencilling patterns or motifs is a great way to introduce accents of colour into a room. Stencils can be simple or 'naive' in style – ideal for children's rooms – or they can be intricate and grand, making them perfect for more formal rooms. Cut the designs from stiff stencil card and apply the paint using a stiff, round bristle brush in a dabbing motion through the cuts in the card. Stencil paints are water-based, but acrylic or oil-based stencil paints can be bought in small pots, while the sticks are wrapped in sealed film. Small 'tester' pots, available at DIY stores, make ideal stencil paints.

You can buy ready-cut stencils and pattern books for you to cut your own. You'll need a sharp scalpel to cut the card. If you can't find a motif or pattern you like ready-made, leaf through some books, look at some antique ceramics or visit your local museum for inspiration and draw your own. If you make a stencil out of stiff acetate, you will be able to transfer the design onto it using a photocopier.

PAINT PROBLEMS & SOLUTIONS

TROUBLESHOOTING COMMON FAULTS

PROBLEM	POSSIBLE CAUSE	SOLUTIONS
Sagging i.e. streaks in paint	Overloading the paintbrush; not spreading the paint enough; incorrect 'laying off' of gloss paint.	While paint is still wet, brush out and lay off to remove streaks. If paint is tacky, leave to dry, then rub with fine wet and dry paper.
Cissing i.e. 'see through' effect in paint	Poor paint coverage: paint insufficiently stirred, over thinned or over brushed when laid off.	When paint is dry, sand down thoroughly and apply another coat.
Cracking or flaking	Water-based paints: underlying surface is dusty. Oil-based paints: underlying surface is damp.	Strip off paint, prepare surface, seal and prime appropriately.
Drips	Overloaded brush; not laying off evenly.	When dry, rub away drip with wet-and-dry paper then repaint.
Visible brushstrokes	Paint too thick; poor quality bristles on brush; paint not laid off correctly.	Sand back area when dry, and re-apply paint.
Blisters	Moisture or air trapped under surface of paint.	Strip off paint, fill any holes, treat damp, prime and repaint.
Wrinkles	Oil-based paint applied over a previous coat that has not completely dried: gloss paint applied too thickly.	Sand back completely and repaint, allowing sufficient drying time between coats.

Television makeovers and lifestyle magazines rarely show decorating 'disasters' and consequently most of us simply go to paint stores, choose a colour, go home and start painting – without any thought for preparation or understanding of the materials we are using. You should always take your time not only to select colours, but also to choose the right type of paint finish. Always read the labels and ask for advice. Your paint finish – the topcoat – must be compatible with the primer, so double check to make sure. While most people can easily handle painting a wall, the novice decorator may experience one or two common paint problems such as cissing, sagging, drips and visible brush marks. Some of these are caused by the painting technique and with practice these faults will disappear. Other common problems are due to inadequate preparation. If you want a truly professional finish, then you have to start in a professional manner. Cutting corners at the preparation stage will show up and affect the finish.

CISSING

This is a common problem: it's the 'see through' effect where newly applied paint has not completely covered the underlying surface. This often happens if you try to paint over gloss with an emulsion without keying the gloss surface correctly beforehand. Surprisingly, though, the most common cause of cissing is simply that the paint has not been stirred sufficiently. Don't stir paint with the paint brush – you'll get paint all over it – and you. Use a long, flat stick and make sure you get right to the bottom of the can and mix it well. Cissing will also be likely if you dilute paint too much: paint that is too thin won't cover evenly and while you may have saved some money by extending the paint, you'll make up for it in the time needed to add subsequent coats.

DRIPS AND SAGS

Even professional decorators make the occasional drip, but their skill lies in knowing how to rectify errors. Drips are most common in oil-based paints, which can be a little difficult to handle. The most common causes are simply an overloaded brush, or not laying off evenly. Dip the brush into the paint so that only one third of the length of the bristles are covered. More paint on the brush will dribble into the ferrule and down the handle. Make sure you spread out the paint evenly as you brush to avoid sags or streaks in the paint.

CRACKS, FLAKES, BLISTERS AND WRINKLES

While drips, cissing and sagging are the result of a faulty painting technique, most other common paint defects are caused by inadequate preparation of the surface to be painted. Most often it is dirt, fluff, or animal – even human – hairs that get stuck to the paint and spoil it. Dirt and grit mixed into the paint will get covered and create little 'pimples', which spoil a smooth surface finish. Dust and thoroughly clean the surfaces and all the surrounding areas

immediately prior to painting. Cracking or flaking of newly applied emulsion paint is an indication that the surface was dusty and this has stopped the paint from adhering properly. The same effect but on new oil-based paints, however, is a sign of underlying moisture – either damp or rotten wood, or the previous coat was not completely dry. Painting on top of a still-wet surface can also cause wrinkles and blisters in paint: you must allow each coat to dry completely before you add a subsequent coat.

WALLPAPERING

HOW MANY ROLLS OF WALLPAPER DO YOU NEED?

Measure the height and the perimeter of the room. Next, draw a simple plan showing doors, windows and other features such as a fireplace. Use the chart below to work out how many rolls of paper you'll need. Follow the measurements down the left hand side of the table: these are for the distance around the room. Then follow the numbers across the top, which show the ceiling height. Where the two numbers converge, this gives the number of rolls needed. Add an extra roll for wastage. Normally, four pieces of paper are cut from one roll for a standard ceiling height, but if you are using a large-patterned wallpaper that needs matching up, you may only get three or even two pieces from a roll.

		WALLS (height from skirting)						
	metric	2.15–2.3m	2.3–2.45m	2.45–2.6m	2.6–2.75m	2.75–2.9m	2.9–3.05m	3.05–3.2m
	imperial	7'–7'6"	7'6"–8'	8'–8'6"	8'6"–9'	9'–9'6"	9'6"–10'	10'–10'6"
	9m/30'	4	5	5	5	6	6	6
	10m/33'	5	5	5	5	6	6	7
	12m/39'	5	6	6	6	7	7	8
	13m/43'	6	6	7	7	7	8	8
	14m/46'	6	7	7	7	8	8	9
	15m/50'	7	7	8	8	9	9	10
	16m/52'	7	8	9	9	9	10	10
	17m/56'	8	8	9	9	10	10	11
	18m/60'	8	9	10	10	10	11	12
	19m/62'	9	9	10	10	11	12	13
	21m/69'	9	10	11	11	12	12	13
	22m/72'	10	10	12	12	12	13	14
	23m/75'	10	11	12	12	13	14	15
	24m/79'	11	11	13	13	14	14	16
	26m/85'	12	12	14	14	14	15	16
	27m/89'	12	13	14	14	15	16	17
	28m/92'	13	13	15	15	15	16	18
	30m/98'	13	14	15	15	16	17	19
	32m/105'	14	15	15	16	17	18	19

DISTANCE AROUND THE ROOM (doors and windows included)

PREPARING PASTE

There are various pastes available: cold and hot water for use on all types of papers except vinyls; fungicidal for use on vinyls; cellulose paste for lighter, thinner wallpapers; and overlap adhesive for securing 'peeling' wallpaper. Select the correct paste for your paper's weight and, if you mix your own, follow the quantities specified on the packet. Mix fresh paste each day. Measure the water into a bucket then sprinkle in the paste, stirring to ensure it is evenly distributed. Let it stand for the recommended time, then stir again.

PASTING

1 The first strip
Place a length of paper design-side downwards on the table, so that it slightly overhangs the nearest edge of the table and one end. This will stop paste getting on the face of the paper. Apply adhesive with a pasting brush, spreading it evenly all over but not on the area 300mm (12in) away from the far edge of the table. Move the paper to slightly overhang the other edge of the table and paste the uncovered area.

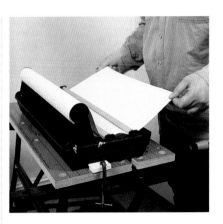

2 First fold

Fold the pasted paper onto itself about two-thirds of the way down and move the remaining paper along the table. Cover the remaining paper with adhesive as before, until the entire length is covered evenly with paste.

3 Second fold

Fold the newly pasted bottom length of the paper onto itself as before, so that its edge is almost touching the top fold. Gently lift and 'pleat' the bulk of the top part of the paper in soft folds so that you can lift it easily and transfer it to the wall without tearing it.

READY-PASTED

A number of wallpapers are available ready-pasted, including vinyl coated. These are supplied with a water-activated adhesive already applied to the back of the paper. Measure and cut the wallpaper to the required length, half fill the special tray with water and place near the wall where the paper will be hung. The strip of wallpaper is then loosely rolled with the design facing inwards, and placed into the tray of water and immersed for the recommended period. Always follow the wallpaper manufacturer's instructions, as different weights of wallpaper will require different 'soaking' times. Fold and hang the paper as normal. Sometimes ready-pasted wallpapers have too much paste, which shows at the edges. After hanging, wipe away excess paste with a damp sponge.

LINING WALLS

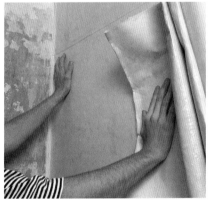

1 Crosslining a wall

Using a spirit level and straight edge, draw horizontal pencil lines the width of the roll of paper apart around the room. Start in a corner and work from ceiling to skirting board. Cut, paste and fold the lining paper and smooth the paper onto the wall with a paperhanger's brush.

2 Continue lining around the room

Keep cutting, pasting, folding and hanging lining paper until you reach the final 'length' at the skirting board. Push the lining paper into the angle between the wall and the board with the paperhanger's brush and trim off excess with a craft knife.

SAFETY FIRST

If you use a fungicidal paste, don't let children touch or taste it and always wash your hands after use.

HANGING ON WALLS

Don't try to take a short cut by omitting lining paper, even if your walls look smooth and flat without it. If you hang your lining paper vertically instead of cross-lining it, make sure the edges don't lie in the same place as the edges of your wallpaper. Let the lining paper dry thoroughly before you start hanging your wallpaper.

Once the room has been measured and lined, make sure you have all your tools and equipment ready and in place. Inspect each roll of wallpaper carefully, making sure the design and colours are as required and that there is a sufficient quantity to complete the job. Check that all the rolls of paper are the same shade not only by batch numbers, but also by unwrapping them and visually comparing them, one against the other. Check and then double check your measurements before you cut any wallpaper. Unroll the first roll, design side upwards. Measure and cut the first length remembering to allow extra for trimming purposes.

If the paper has a pattern, place the second length on top of the first when you unroll it and take care to match up the design. Use a pencil and mark 'T' (for top) and 'B' (for bottom) in pencil on the back of each length of patterned paper. Paste and fold the first length, let the adhesive soak a while, and in the meantime measure cut, paste and fold the second length.

Draw a vertical line where the first length of paper is to be hung (see box opposite) and work in a clockwise direction round the room.

SAFETY FIRST

- You will inevitably have to use ladders to paper the tops of your walls. Make sure you follow all the advice about safety on ladders on pages 40–1. Consider using a scaffold tower if your room has particularly high ceilings, or form a bridge with a sturdy plank of wood between two stepladders.

- Never lean sideways off a stepladder. Only work on the area straight in front of you, then get down and move the stepladder to hang the next strip.

- Wear shoes that grip the steps of the ladder firmly and make sure shoelaces are firmly tied.

- Carry paperhanger's scissors in your hand, so that you can throw them clear if you slip while on the ladder.

1 Hanging the first length
Take the first length of pasted paper and, with one hand, hold the top section against the wall and line up the left edge with the vertical drawn line. Hold the folds of the paper with the other hand. The top edge of the paper should be placed at the junction of the wall and ceiling or cornice with a 50mm (2in) overlap for trimming. Press the paper well into the angle.

2 Smoothing the paper
Using a paperhanger's brush, gently but firmly smooth the wallpaper into position. Work downwards, brushing the paper from top to bottom to remove any bubbles or creases. Leave the bottom edge loose, just resting on the skirting board, and return to the top edge.

3 Creasing the fold

At the top edge, where the paper overlaps the wall and the ceiling or cornice, run the blunt edge of a pair of paperhanger's scissors gently across the line on the paper between the wall and ceiling. This will emphasize the crease and create a clear cutting line for the final trim.

4 Cut the excess

Gently pull away the top edge of the wallpaper from the wall and cut along the creased mark with the scissors. Push the cut edge of the wallpaper back into place with the paperhanger's brush. Return to the bottom of the wall and trim off the overlap. Wipe off any paste left on the ceiling, cornice or skirting.

Subsequent lengths of wallpaper are hung loosely from the top and, where necessary, the pattern matched before it is smoothed into position. The two edges of the wallpaper should butt tightly together but should not be allowed to overlap. Overlapped edges may not stick.

Where a final drop of wallpaper is not the full width of the roll, measure and cut to width and length but leave a 50mm (2in) overlap at one long edge. Butt the length up against the adjoining length to form a tight join and crease and trim the edges as before.

WALLPAPER

- Clamp wallpaper lengths to the pasting table with four large bulldog clips. This stops the paper re-rolling.

- Start the hanging sequence with a straight drop from ceiling to floor, starting at one side of a window. You will work away from the window in both directions towards the darkest corner of the room. Patterned papers should be centred on the chimneybreast.

- Never assume that the walls in your home are straight. To ensure that wallpaper is hung absolutely on the vertical, plumb and then draw a vertical line from the ceiling or cornice to the skirting board. The first continuous drop of wallpaper should be hung alongside this line for accuracy.

- When trimming excess wallpaper, you can use a sharp craft knife, if you prefer, instead of scissors: leave the paper in place in the angle and run the knife along the crease.

- Remember to allow for waste during pattern matching. Some random pattern drops have to be hung with each length the opposite way up, so make sure you read the labels carefully.

AWKWARD AREAS

Rooms are full of obstacles: doors, radiators, windows, chimneybreasts and corners. When you approach an external corner – an edge that sticks outwards into the room – simply hang the nearest drop, then paste, fold and hang the corner piece so that an overlap of paper wraps smoothly around the corner by about 50mm (2in). To avoid bubbles and creases, nip diagonal cuts in the edge and smooth them flat with a paperhanger's brush. The next drop of wallpaper is hung overlapping and covering the 'snips'. If you are using a vinyl wallpaper, you will need to use an overlap adhesive so that the paper sticks to itself on the overlap.

WORKING AROUND A CORNER
Don't attempt to work around a corner using a single length of wallpaper – it will just crease, bubble and even tear, and, because corner edges are seldom straight and true, any pattern will be thrown out of line. Take one length around a corner so that it overlaps by about 50mm (2in) and make a series of diagonal snips at the edge so they stick smoothly to the wall. Hang the next length covering the snipped edge and lined up with the wall edge.

DOORS

1 Hang the last full drop
When you come to a door, hang the last full drop of paper up to but not over the door, smoothing it down from top to bottom with a paperhangers' brush to remove air bubbles.

2 Hang the second length
Paste the next length of paper – but do not apply paste to the area of paper that will be cut away to allow for the door. Hang this length of paper and allow the unpasted area to fall loosely over the door. Cut the paper leaving a 50mm (2in) overlap at the top.

3 Trim at the side
Press down on the top corner of the doorframe to make an indentation in the paper. Cut diagonally from the edge of the paper at 45 degrees to this indentation. Brush the wallpaper into the angle between the wall and the doorframe and then trim excess paper.

4 Over the door
Using the unpasted piece of wallpaper, which hung over the door in step 2, cut, paste and hang the short drop from the ceiling or cornice down to the top of the door frame. Repeat steps 2 and 3 on the other side of the door frame.

WINDOWS

If a window is wide enough, hang one drop centrally over the top. If it is not, drop a plumb line to one side of the window, about 120mm (5in) less than the width of the wallpaper, so that the first drop of wallpaper overhangs the window frame. Paste and hang the paper so that it lies loosely over one edge of the window frame. Using the paperhanger's brush, gently brush the paper into the angle between the wall and the window frame to crease it. Carefully peel the paper back and then cut along the creased line and brush the wallpaper back into position. Alternatively, you can leave the creased paper in place and trim it using a craft knife, leaving the paper in place in the angle and running the knife along the crease. Use a seam roller to press it down, if necessary.

STAIRS

Wallpapering a staircase is not as difficult as you might think because the paper is measured, cut, pasted, folded and hung as for any other surface. The difficulty lies in gaining access to considerable heights, so the main thing with this job is that you can reach safely. Never lean over the balustrade to reach walls: hire adjustable ladders specially designed for staircases. A safe, sturdy working base will have its rewards in smoothly hung paper with closely butted edges and accurately trimmed top edges.

1 Identify the longest drop
The first drop of wallpaper you make on a staircase should be the longest. Drop a plumb line and then mark an accurate vertical line on the wall. This will act as the guideline for hanging this and subsequent lengths of wallpaper. Mark the wall with a pencil at intervals down the plumb line then join up the marks with a straight edge to make the vertical guideline. To ensure it is accurate, make a plumb line long enought to hang the entire length of the stairwell.

2 Position the first length
Take your time when you position this first length to make sure that it is vertically true as it will be difficult to correct mistakes later on. Never use the wall as your guide – even in modern homes, they are rarely straight. Instead, always refer to the plumbed line. Paste and hang the first drop to the left of the drawn line, smooth out any air bubbles with a paperhanger's brush and trim off excess. Hang the second drop, butting the edges tightly together.

LIGHT FITTINGS

Whenever you paint or wallpaper around a light switch or electrical socket, you must always switch off the power at the mains, and identify and remove the fuse for that circuit.

Wallpapering around obstacles such as these requires a steady hand and a great deal of patience: don't rush, otherwise you will spoil the effect. After all, it's these little details that make the difference to a professional finish. There are two ways of making wallpaper 'fit around' switches: you can either remove the faceplate of the switch – but only after the power is switched off – which makes working easier, or, if you prefer, you can very carefully cut around the switch or socket. Use decorator's scissors and make sure the blades are kept free of paste.

1 Loosely hang the drop of paper
When you arrive at a switch or socket, loosely hang the drop of wallpaper on the wall. Using a paperhangers' brush gently press the wallpaper against the switch or socket to make an impression – but not a hole – in the wallpaper. Carefully cut a 'star' by making four small diagonal cuts from the centre to the corners.

2 Trim away excess
Fold back the four pointed triangles pressing their edges into the angle between the wall and the switch. If you take the faceplate off the switch or socket, you can smooth the cut edges and replace the faceplate to hide them. Alternatively, carefully trim away the excess with scissors or a craft knife and brush the paper's edges into the angle.

RADIATORS

The best way to wallpaper behind a central heating radiator is to remove it from the wall completely (see page 182) but, if this is not possible, switch off the radiator and let it cool down. Measure and hang a full drop of paper, but brush down the top half of the paper on the wall only, allowing the bottom end to fall loosely. Next, carefully pull the lower part of the paper away from the wall and trim it to fit behind the radiator. Make two creases or marks in the paper indicating the location of the radiator wall brackets. Cut upwards through the paper to these marks. Lower the pasted paper behind the radiator so that it passes on either side of the bracket. To smooth the wallpaper into place, use a long stick with a well padded end – several old clean 'T'-shirts tied to the end work well – or a clean, dry crevice or radiator roller with an angled handle.

If you can't manage to get behind the radiator, you will have to trim off the drop – leave about 150–225mm (6–9in) extra length that you can tuck behind the accessible top part of the radiator. At the bottom, where the wall is visible, 'patch' with paper that matches the pattern at the base of complete drops on the walls to the sides of the radiators.

WORKING AROUND RADIATORS
If you can't remove your radiator from the wall, trim the wallpaper so that you can tuck a length behind it.

SEAM ROLLERS

Go over all the butted edges of wallpaper joins with a seam roller when the paste is nearly dry to ensure adhesion at the edges – don't use a roller on embossed paper or you'll 'squash' the raised pattern.

FITTINGS

If you take down any wall fittings before you cover a wall, you'll probably still want to know exactly where the screw holes are. Push a clean matchstick into each hole or wall plug and leave it sticking out slightly. When you paper, you can ease the matchstick through the paper as you smooth it. For other types of wall coverings, you'll need to make a small cut with a sharp trimming knife.

WALLPAPER BORDERS

Wallpaper borders are an attractive way to divide up walls so that the height of ceilings appears 'optically' lower. Look for accent colours in your existing furnishing fabrics for your border colour ideas. There are hundreds of attractive styles of paper borders for you to choose from – some are even designed specifically to look like dado rails. Borders are hung horizontally around the room so you'll need to make sure they are absolutely level. If you are hanging a border up at the ceiling angle, you'll need to have easy and safe access for working at heights. Hanging the border is quite straightforward as most run in one continuous 'strip'. Don't work around or into corners in one piece, however: follow the guidelines for papering around the corners in a room. Most borders are pasted like other wallpaper, but ordinary paste won't adhere very well over vinyl or washable papers so you should choose a self-adhesive paper for use over these.

1 Measure and mark

The first step in border hanging is to measure and mark down from the ceiling or cornice to where the bottom of the border will be. For a dado effect, measure from the skirting board upwards. Use a spirit level and a straight edge to guide you and mark a pencil line all around the room at this height.

2 Hanging the border

Measure the length of each wall and cut your border strips allowing a 50mm (2in) overlap on each one. Try to cover each wall in one continuous strip and form neat seams in the corners. If you have to use two strips, overlap their ends and match up the pattern precisely. Then use a sharp knife to cut through both layers, peel away the off-cuts and press the seam flat.

USING WALLPAPER BORDERS

Be creative with wallpaper and borders: use a border to create a dado rail and paper the walls in two different patterns or colours, or use a different paper above a picture rail for added interest. You could also use 'left over' wallpaper to paper the panels of a door: this all-over look in which walls, ceilings and door panels were papered uniformly was popularized in France, and is often associated with 'toile de Jouey', the charming textile patterns in rural themes. Using border papers is limited only by your imagination: add small cut-out sections of border patterns to the corners of doors or kitchen cabinets, or even a number of them 'tumbling' down the walls. Use borders to create 'faux' frames for serving hatches, pin boards and bathroom mirrors.

OTHER TYPES OF WALLCOVERING

There are many other types of wall coverings available apart from wallpaper. The only difference between hanging wallpaper and hanging a wall covering perhaps made of cotton, hessian or any other material, is that instead of pasting the paper, it is the wall that is pasted, so that there is less chance of spoiling the delicate (and more costly) faces of wall coverings. Apply a band of paste to the wall that is a little wider than the width of the covering – that way you won't have to apply paste right up to the edge of the first drop.

FABRIC WALL COVERINGS

Fabric wall coverings such as hessian (which is made from jute), linen, silk and satin, provide a range of coloured or neutral textured wall effects, and, furthermore, hessian can be painted with either gloss or emulsion. Fabric wall coverings should not be hung on newly plastered walls. Allow the walls to dry out for at least six months then rub them with a medium abrasive paper and apply an alkali- resistant primer. Unbacked fabric coverings should be hung on walls that have been lined first and it's a good idea to use lining paper that's the same colour as the top cover so if the joins do pull apart or shrinkage occurs, the gaps will be less noticeable. Paper-backed fabrics are available, but while these are more expensive, they are easier to hang and the paper backing prevents creases and wrinkling. Paste can be applied to paper-backed fabrics rather than to the wall, but it's important that the fabric does not become too wet. Use a felt-covered roller to smooth out each fabric length taking care not to press too hard or you can stretch the fabric and may cause the paste to seep from the joins.

GRASS CLOTH

This is a textured wall covering consisting of barks and grasses held together with thread and glued to a paper backing. While very attractive, these coverings are also very fragile and are not suitable for locations where there is heavy use or through traffic. Because they are made of natural materials, you should expect considerable irregularities in texture and in colour. Cutting and trimming can be a problem: you'll need a sharp curved blade to stop it from fraying. The lighter types of grass cloth are easier to hang than heavier ones, but these are also the most delicate.

CORK AND FELT

Cork wall covering consists of very thin sheets of cork or cork shavings bonded to a paper backing and makes a warm, textured, honey-coloured room scheme. You'll need to hang cork covering with a recommended PVA glue to ensure adhesion, and the walls will need to be smooth. While cork is flexible, it will snap if forced over large bumps in walls. Felt is an interesting wall covering: it is available in a huge range of colours and in widths of up to 700mm (2ft 4in) that can be a little unwieldy, so it's easier to roll a length of felt on a wooden batten suspended between two step ladders and position the felt from the skirting board upwards. To butt the joins, the edges of the felt need to be very slightly teased out to create less of a harsh line so the two adjoining lengths blend together.

FOAMED POLYETHYLENE

This is a lightweight wall covering made completely of foamed plastic with no backing paper, but the surface has the feel of fabric and springs back into place if you press it gently. You'll find it in DIY and decorating stores and it comes in a range of colours, styles and patterns. Although it's made of plastic, it is still quite delicate so save it for use on walls where there isn't much wear and tear.

LINCRUSTA & ANAGLYPTA

Lincrusta is a heavily moulded wall covering made of linseed oil and fillers fused onto a backing paper or fabric before the raised pattern is added by an engraved steel roller. It was often used to simulate wood panelling as well as stonework, tiles, wrought iron and even fabrics. Some Lincrustas are sold ready-coloured, while others are plain, ready for hanging and finishing. Anaglypta is made by bonding wood pulp (or high quality cotton fibres in Supaglypta) in a sort of *papier-mâché*, which is then passed between embossing rollers. It is very durable – highly resistant to cracking – and looks a little like decorative plasterwork. It is available in low- or high-relief patterns, but the very deep reliefs are made from vinyl (Vinaglypta) either as solid forms or heated in ovens, which 'blows' or expands the plastic and embosses it.

WALLPAPER PROBLEMS

TROUBLESHOOTING COMMON FAULTS

PROBLEM	POSSIBLE CAUSE	SOLUTIONS
Paper tears easily	Too much paste used; paste too thin; blunt tools.	Check consistency of paste; apply less paste to paper; sharpen scissors and blades.
White seams showing	Paper not butted together properly; no lining paper has been used; paper has shrunk.	Butt seams correctly and roll with seam roller. Line walls prior to hanging paper. Allow sufficient time for paper to soak after pasting.
Bubbles	Too much paste used; paste coverage uneven; paper not given adequate soaking time before hanging.	Pierce bubble with point of craft knife to allow excess paste to escape and wipe with damp sponge. If bubble full of air, pierce and apply a little paste with artists' brush and then sponge down.
Creases	Generally occur when paper is hung around or into a corner.	Make series of cuts in edge of paper so it lies flat around corner. Small creases, treat as bubbles (above).
Lifting seams	Walls not lined.	Lift back problem seam, use artists' brush to apply paste, roll seam back into place with seam roller and wipe with a sponge.
Unstuck paper	Walls not lined; residue of distemper.	Remove wallpaper from affected area, wash walls thoroughly, line wall and re-hang paper.

Even professionals will from time to time experience one or more of the most common problems that occur when you work with wallpaper. Don't panic. Even when things seem to be going badly wrong, there is usually a very simple cure.

UNSIGHTLY MARKS

Wallpaper can discolour if it is hung on walls that have not been properly sealed or if you happen to get some paste on the designed face of the paper. Remember that colours will fade if they are subjected to strong sunlight. Occasionally, you may find small patches of mould growing on wallpaper. This could be due to damp walls or heavy condensation, or old patches of size or paste left on the walls at the preparation stage. While wallpapers will cover minor defects in walls, the cause of any damp must be checked before you cover it up. Rust spots can show up if you hang paper over steel pins that have not been sealed. When preparing a wall for papering, check it carefully and mask or seal any old nails or pin marks before you line it.

PASTE PROBLEMS

Where you have difficulty matching up the pattern on two drops of paper it is likely that your pasting technique is at fault. Under- or over- soaking the wallpaper reduces its ability to adhere to the wall and makes the paper difficult to handle. Follow the paste manufacturer's instructions regarding proportions, mixing and setting times: too thick a paste will cause bumps and lumps, too thin and

the water will over-soak the paper, which can cause it to tear. Blunt scissors won't cut a true line, and the edges of the paper will become frayed; keep wallpaper scissors clean by wiping off the blades after each cut. If your wallpaper starts to fall off the wall in complete strips it's because you didn't line your walls first and there are patches of distemper that have made the paste lose its stickiness. The only solution is to take the wallpaper off the walls, clean the walls and, where necessary, apply a stabilizing solution. Then line the walls and re-hang the wallpaper.

SEAM TROUBLE

When two drops of paper have not been butted together closely enough, you may find a narrow white seam showing. Make sure you soak the paper for the correct time or it could shrink as the paste dries. Sometimes heavier and darker wallpapers are manufactured with a white edge, and the makers provide special colour-matched pens for you to obliterate the white. Seams that don't stick are nearly always caused by not lining the walls before hanging paper. Carefully lift back the seam and apply a little strong adhesive with an artists' brush then roll the paper back into place with a seam roller and wipe the seams to remove excess adhesive. If the paper has a raised pattern, don't press too hard on to it or you'll squash the pattern. Seams should butt up against each other, not overlap. If they do, you might find the seams don't stick, so treat these as you would for lifting seams.

Smooth your paper downwards and outwards with a paperhanger's brush.

BUBBLES

Bubbles in wallpaper are probably the most common problem experienced by the home decorator. Sometimes bubbles will disappear when the paste has dried out, so it's worth waiting a while before tackling them. If a bubble seems to be full of paste it could be because you applied a little too much, or when you were smoothing down the paper on the wall you overlooked smoothing downwards and outwards towards the edge. Simply pierce the bubble with the sharp tip of a craft knife or scalpel and allow the excess paste to escape, carefully sponging down the 'empty' bubble afterwards to clean any paste from the face of the paper. Sometimes bubbles are full of air – perhaps this bit of paper did not receive any or sufficient paste – again, pierce the bubble and use a fine artists' brush to apply a very little paste and smooth the bubble down with a sponge.

TILING

TYPES OF TILING MATERIALS

Tiled wall and floor surfaces are durable, attractive and easy to clean and maintain. Available in a range of sizes, shapes and colours, tiles can be used to create an infinite range of decorative effects.

HARD-GLAZED CERAMIC TILES

When we think of tiles most of us immediately think of square, glazed ceramic tiles. These hard-glazed and fired tiles are made for both floors and walls – but don't use wall tiles on floors as they won't take the weight of furniture and heavy traffic. Mostly they are indeed square, but they vary in dimensions according to their use and from manufacturer to manufacturer – so make sure you buy enough of the same type because you may find additional tiles from different sources are slightly larger or smaller. Rectangular and irregular-shaped ones are also available and the typical shapes include hexagons, octagons and diamonds, as well as 'interlocking' tiles with more elaborate shapes or curved edges.

You can create plain fields of tiles in a single colour, or be adventurous and create walls of patterns and colours.

MOSAIC TILES

Mosaic tiles are small versions of standard ceramic tiles. Laying them one at a time would be too much like hard labour, and getting accurate spacing between them a nightmare, so manufacturers have thoughtfully joined lots of little squares of tiles into bigger squares by bonding them to a paper or mesh ground. You can pop out individual tiles and replace them with different-coloured ones to create a decorative effect. Because they are small and the backing is flexible, they are great for covering curved surfaces and it's a lot easier to fit them into fiddly or irregular areas. Square mosaic tiles are the most common, but you can also get hexagonal and even round ones. If you are planning on completely covering a bathroom – walls, floor, bath panels and shower trays, then compare prices and styles available from swimming pool suppliers.

STONE AND BRICK

Masonry facing tiles are often used to simulate stone or brick as a feature on chimneybreasts. These 'tiles' are actually made of reconstituted stone in imitation of the real thing and can look unconvincing if handled poorly. Brick tiles are more 'authentic' looking because the best ones are actually 'slips' – slivers of kiln-produced bricks – and they come in a whole range of traditional and modern brick colours and textures. Thick unglazed quarry tiles, available in brown, red, black or white, are suitable for flooring.

MIRROR AND METAL

Mirror tiles can be attached to walls with self-adhesive pads in each corner. Often, mirror tiles are used as

'Hand-made' glazed tiles will each have a unique surface and you should expect slight variations in colour. Although they will generally be the same dimensions, you should buy tiles from the same batch.

inserts in larger fields of ceramic tiles and are available in a range of finishes – silver, smoky grey and bronze are just a few of those available. Don't expect to get a perfect reflection unless your walls are absolutely flat.

Lightweight pressed metal tiles can be fixed in the same way as mirror tiles. These are available in aluminium, bronze or gold colours with satin or bright finishes. Because metal tiles are not grouted, they are not suitable for use in bathrooms or kitchens where food can get caught, or mould can grow in the crevices.

GLAZE

Most ceramic tiles are coated in a thick layer of glaze that makes them hard-wearing, waterproof and easy to clean. Unglazed tiles have more subtle colours but they may need to be sealed in some way to prevent them absorbing grease and dirt, particularly if they are going to be used in the kitchen.

MEASURING

MAKING A GAUGE STICK

Most ceramic wall tiles are 108mm sq. x 4mm thick (4½sq.in x ⅛in) or 152mm sq. x 6.4mm thick (6sq.in x ¼in). The most popular are the smaller tiles as these are easier to work with. There are self-spacing tiles available, but most often you'll need 3mm (⅛in) plastic lugs, which are placed between the tiles to space them out at exactly the same distance.

Setting out the prepared surface and the tiles accurately is vital if you want to hang the tiles properly. You can make a gauge stick, which will plot the position of the tiles on the wall. Lay several tiles along a length of 50 x 12mm (2 x ½in) softwood. Butt the tiles together with spacing lugs or add spacers for square-edged tiles unless these are intended for close butting. Next, mark the position of each tile on the gauge stick. Starting at skirting level, hold the stick firmly against the wall and mark the positions of the tiles on the wall. If you are left with a very narrow strip at the top of the wall, move the rows up by half a tile width to make a wider margin. Mark the centre of the wall and use the gauge stick to set out the vertical rows of tiles at each side. Again, if the border tiles are less than half a width, move the rows sideways by half a tile.

CUTTING

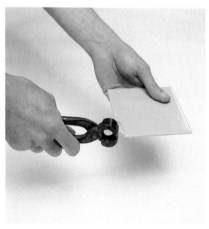

TILE-CUTTING JIG

This is a very worthwhile investment if you are planning on tiling a large area. Not only do they cut tiles, but they also incorporate a mechanism to measure and score them accurately. Jigs speed up tile cutting and reduce wastage.

PINCERS

Cutting very thin strips off tiles is best done with pincers – sometimes called Japanese nippers. Basically, you 'nibble' away at the tile edge to reduce its size, or 'score' and 'pinch' to remove a thin strip along an edge.

TILE SAW

Sometimes, to fit a tile around a light switch or socket, you'll have to cut away a corner or cut a notch. This is easiest if a saw file is used. Score, cut and then snap out the corner or notch.

CUTTING BORDER TILES

Whole tiles – or 'field tiles' – are laid in their rows first. When these are complete, you'll have to cut the ceramic tiles to fill the gaps at the edges and around obstructions such as window frames, cupboards, light fittings, bathroom fittings, taps and pipework. Cutting straight edges for borders is relatively easy – especially if you invested in a tile-cutting jig (see page 322). It's a very unusual room that has absolutely square walls and, inevitably, the margin will be uneven so you'll have to be prepared to measure and cut each tile individually to fit into position.

The technique for measuring to cut a tile to shape is similar to that used when laying floor tiles (see page 85), but in the case of border tiles, you need to make an allowance for the normal spacing between ceramic tiles that will be filled with grout.

Use a water-soluble felt tip pen to transfer the measurements to the tile, but only mark it at the edges, just in case there is a flaw – a tiny crack, hole or gap in the glaze – that the colour could run into and get trapped under the glaze. Use a straight edge to score a line across the face of the tile, joining up the marks at the tile edges. Wear goggles when you cut tiles to protect your eyes from any flying shards of glazed ceramics, which can cause serious injuries.

SAFETY FIRST

- Whatever method you use to cut or 'nibble' your ceramic tiles, you must always protect your eyes from flying shards with safety goggles.

- Make sure your room is well-ventilated when mixing adhesives and grout and, if necessary, wear mouth and nose filters to protect yourself from noxious fumes.

- Always be sure to use the correct tools for the job.

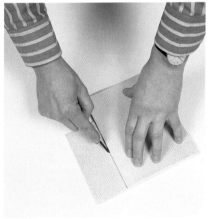

1 Measure and mark
Mark a border tile by placing it face down over its neighbour with one edge against the wall. Remember to allow for the normal spacing between the tiles. Transfer the marks to the edge of the tile using a water-soluble felt tip pen.

2 Score and cut
Using a straight edge, score a line across the face of the tile joining up the marks on the edge. With a proprietary tile cutter, score across the face in one firm stroke to cut through the glaze, then snap the tile over a length of thin wire stretched across a panel of chipboard, pressing down on both sides of the tile to snap it.

3 Position the tile
Smooth off the cut edge of the border tile with a tile sander or small slipstone and then press the tile into position at the edge of the tiled field. Never slide a tile – even a small one – into position: the tile may not bed properly and could come unstuck.

LAYING ADHESIVE

Most ceramic tile adhesives are supplied ready-mixed, although a few types will need to be mixed with water. These have a limited life and you should only mix up as much as you can apply in a given time. While your surface should always be as smooth and level as possible, there are thick bed adhesives available, which will help even out some irregularities. Be warned: these are a little more difficult to apply. A can of 5 litre thin bed adhesive will cover an area of roughly 4 m sq. (a little under 5sq.yds). It should be laid on in sections or areas of about 1m sq. (1sq.yd) with the notched trowel or spreader 3mm (⅛in) thick.

1 Arranging battens

Nail a horizontal batten to the wall with the top edge one tile height above the lowest point to be tiled, then nail a vertical batten at the edge of the area. Check them with a spirit level.

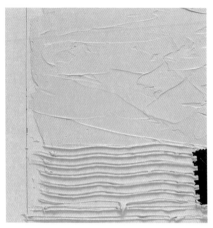

2 Apply adhesive

Using a notched plastic spreader or a notched trowel, apply the adhesive to cover 1m sq. (1sq.yd). Use the notches to form horizontal ridges of the correct depth (about 3mm/⅛in deep).

LAYING TILES

1 Hanging the first tile

With the adhesive applied to the section of wall, press the first tile firmly into place in the angle formed by the two setting-out battens. Begin at the bottom row and work upwards.

2 Complete rows

Butt up tiles on each side of the first tile and build up three or four rows at a time. If the tiles don't have spacer lugs, use thick card or proprietary plastic spacers or even matchsticks to space them evenly for the grout.

3 Check levels

Spread more adhesive and 'build up' more rows until the first rows of whole tiles are complete. Every three or four rows, hold a batten and spirit level across the tile faces and along the top and edges to check for accuracy.

TILING AROUND CORNERS

Tiling around corners and over projecting edges, such as window reveals, is less daunting than you might think. Most of the wall will have been tiled using field tiles, which have straight, unglazed edges.

For edging fields of tiles, you can buy special RE (round edge) tiles, which have one edge rounded and glazed for a neat edge; REX tiles, which have two adjacent edges rounded and glazed; and mitred tiles, which are rounded 'strips' used for 'turning' corners. There are also plastic edging strips available in a range of colours to blend or contrast with the tiles. These are held in place while the last row of tiles is pressed into position.

When you tile around a corner or around a window, tile up to the edge, then use RE tiles on the reveal so they lap the edges of the surrounding tiles. Fitting into a corner may involve cutting a tile down to size. Keep any cut tiles for the back of the reveal.

Follow the instructions on page 322 and remember to wear safety goggles when you cut the tiles to protect your eyes from flying shards. If you have a lot of tiles to cut, it's worth investing in a tile-cutting jig (see page 322) to save time and reduct the amount of wastage.

TILING

- When fixing battens, leave the nail heads protruding so that they can easily be removed when the adhesive has dried.

- Take care to ridge your adhesive to the correct depth, as the ridges are essential for strong tile adhesion.

- Keep checking with a spirit level every three or four rows.

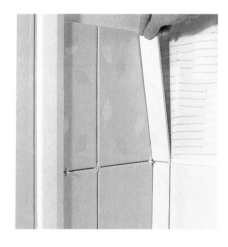

1 Measure and mark
Tiling into a corner will invariably mean cutting a tile to size. Don't assume the edge is straight and true; each tile must be measured and cut individually. Remember also to allow for the normal spacing between tiles. If spacers weren't supplied with your tiles, you can use matchsticks or pieces of thick card.

2 Projecting corners
The edges of projecting corners such as around window reveals should be finished with RE (round edge tiles), keeping any cut border tiles to the back of the reveal. REX tiles can be used where two adjacent edges protrude.

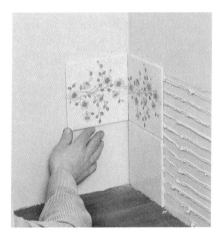

3 Feature tiles
Where patterned tiles are used as feature tiles, avoid cutting them. You will need to spend a little more time planning their position at the setting-out stage – especially if you want full-patterned tiles to meet at corners. Interest can also be added by tiling one wall plain in one colour and the other using patterned tiles or tiles in a contrasting colour.

TILING IN BATHROOMS

Always choose non-slip ceramic tiles for bathrooms or other rooms where the floor is likely to get wet. Bathrooms can be tricky to tile because of the fixed objects like wash basins, WCs and plumbing that you need to fix tiles around. Often you will have to cut odd shapes from tiles so they fit snugly around the obstacles. The other problem is getting access to work in an all-too-often very small area.

Tile around the trickier areas after you have hung all the main field tiles. It's a lot easier, and you'll waste fewer tiles, if you take the time to cut some thin sheets of cardboard – empty cereal boxes are ideal – to exactly the same size as the tiles you are using. This way you can make an accurate template for each tile you need to cut. Where tiles have to fit around curved edges, use a cardboard template with 'fingers' cut along the edge. These can be pressed and creased against the obstacle and the creased, curved outline transferred to the tile. You will then have to nibble away at the tile with pincers.

Tiling around a thin-diameter water pipe is best achieved using two half tiles with matching curved notches cut in the edges so when the two halves are hung, the tiles fit appropriately spaced.

If you have a number of awkward shapes to tile around, you may wish to measure the distances between your bathroom fittings and transfer them onto a scale plan drawn on graph paper to work out how to make the most efficient use of your tiles.

1 Measure and mark
Use a card template to find the angle or curve and then transfer this to the tile using a water-soluble felt pen to indicate the area to be removed.

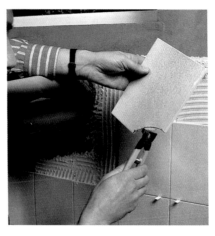

2 Score and cut
Score the line freehand – or, if you can, find a cup or plate edge that matches the curve so you can score around this. Then using the pincers – and wearing protective goggles – carefully nibble away at the 'waste' area.

3 Hang the tile
Where limited access makes spreading adhesive directly onto the wall difficult, especially at the edges against pipes and basins, 'butter' the back of the tile with the adhesive and a notched spreader and press it – never slide it – into position.

TILING AROUND A WINDOW

If there is a window in the area you are tiling, it can be helpful to start planning there first so that you can make sure the tiles on each side of the window are about the same width. It could look odd if they are not, especially on a small window. Start by placing a row of whole tiles at the level of the sill and position cut tiles behind them to reach the back of the window reveal.

Tiling around the architrave of a window requires exactly the same method as fixing any border tiles, except that at the four corners you will have to cut an angle into the tile so it fits snugly. Use RE or REX tiles as appropriate (see page 325). Once again, a cardboard template is extremely useful to get an accurate fit, and the cut edges will need to be

smoothed off. Make your template and transfer the outline to be cut onto the face of the tile using a water-soluble felt pen, making sure you allow for the appropriate spacing between the tiles. Score the cutting line and either nibble away at the tile with pincers or cut the straight lines with a saw file. Always wear protective eye wear whatever method you use to cut tiles.

If you are also tiling along the top of the window, nail a temporary horizontal batten in place just beneath them to support them as the adhesive dries. If you have to use a ladder to reach the top of the window, make sure that it is stable and remember never to over-stretch; just work on the area directly in front of you (see pages 40–1).

TILING AROUND ELECTRICAL SOCKETS

• Whenever you decorate near or around an electrical fitting, always turn off the mains power at the consumer unit, and identify and remove the fuse supplying power to that circuit. It is not enough just to turn off the power at the switch. Wallpaper paste, paint and tiling adhesive are all wet and can make a lethal combination if they come into contact with electricity.

• Once the power is safely off, tiling around switches simply means measuring and marking tiles that need to be cut to size. Use the method that suits you best – hold the tile over its neighbour and mark the cutting lines, or make a cardboard template.

1 Measure and mark
At the four corners of the window frame, you will need to cut away squares or rectangles of tile so they fit neatly. Measure and mark the area to be cut away. Score the lines and nibble with pincers or cut with a saw file.

2 Hang the tile
Position the cut tile and then firmly press it into the adhesive. Don't slide tiles into place; this moves the adhesive around and can affect the adhesion. Complete the tiling around the window and allow the adhesive to set firmly.

GROUTING AND POLISHING

The gap between tiles is filled with a paste called grout. This is a cement-based powder, which is mixed with water and is available in standard colours – white, grey and brown – as well as in a range of colours, so you can add interest to a plain field of tiles by matching or contrasting the coloured grout. Coloured grout is available 'ready-made' but you can also mix dry, powdered pigments into it yourself. Where tiles are exposed to running water, such as around showers, baths, basins and sink splashbacks, it is essential to use an epoxy-based waterproof grout so that these surfaces remain 'stuck' and the grout can be easily cleaned to keep it germ free.

Using a sponge or squeegee, the grout is rubbed firmly into the tile joints and any surplus is removed immediately with a damp sponge. Grouting should be left until the tiles have firmly set in their bed of adhesive – at least 24 hours, but check with the manufacturer's instructions and guidelines, as setting times do vary. Any grout that has dried onto the surface of the tiles will need to be polished off with a soft cloth. Professional decorators use a special tool to finish the joints, but a slightly round-pointed stick – an ice-lolly stick is ideal – can be run between the joints to make a neat joint line before the tiles are given one final polish.

1 Using plastic edging
The top edges of a field of tiles that runs halfway up a wall can be sealed off with a plastic edging strip instead of grout. The smooth coping strip, which comes in a range of colours, is held in place while the tiles are hung.

3 Making good the joins
The grouted joins between the tiles are made neat by using a small stick with a pointed, but slightly rounded tip. The pointed tip is carefully pressed into the grout and run along the join – a little like the pointing on a brick wall – to neaten the finish.

2 Grouting
After the tiles have firmly set – about 24 hours – use a sponge or rubber squeegee to fill the joins between the tiles with grout, using waterproof grout where appropriate. There are also specialist grouts available for use in food-preparation areas and for exterior use.

4 Polished finish
When the excess grout has been removed from the tile surfaces with a damp sponge, the joins finished and the grout dried, polish the tiles to a sheen with a clean dry cloth. A piece of hessian is ideal: while coarse in texture it is still quite soft and won't scratch the glaze.

SEALING

When you need to seal the joins between a wall and a basin, shower tray, bath, or sink unit, you can't use grout or an ordinary filler. This is because these fittings move and flex and a rigid seal would crack even under the slightest pressure. Cracks in the grout or seal would then allow water to seep in and create stains, and any hidden build-up of moisture could cause damp and mould growth to occur. Instead, it's best to use a silicone rubber caulking compound, which, even when dry, remains a little flexible. These compounds come ready-mixed in tubes or in cartridges (applied using a 'gun' mechanism or a finger trigger) and in a range of colours to match your tiles. The compounds will easily fill a gap of up to 3mm (⅛in) wide, but if your gap is wider, then it will need packing out: use lengths of soft rope or even twists of soaked newspaper. Cut off the nozzle end of the tube or cartridge at 45 degrees – this makes it easier to apply, and remember the amount of nozzle you cut off will determine the size of the 'worm' of sealant that is extruded. If you don't achieve a perfectly smooth line when you squeeze out the sealant into the crack, don't worry: smooth out any ripples or irregularities with the back of a wet teaspoon. Don't try smoothing with your finger – it always ends up worse than when you started. Caulking compound isn't the only way to seal gaps: you can also use ceramic coving. These are rounded quadrant tiles and there are also bull-nose tiles – with a nicely rounded finished end – used for the final end of a straight run. You can also seal joins with plastic coving, which you cut to length and glue on using a proprietary adhesive.

REMOVING SEALANT

If old sealant round a bath or sink has become stained or discoloured, brush on a proprietary sealant remover, leave for 15 minutes, then scrape the old sealant off. Thoroughly clean the area then apply new sealant.

1 Mask off

In order to guide your hand and eye – and keep the 'worm' of sealant in a straight line – mask off above and below the area where the sealant is to be laid. Use a low-tack tape and run it in continuous strips where possible at each side of the fitting.

2 Apply the sealant

Cut the nozzle at 45 degrees – don't cut too much off the end of the nozzle or you'll get too thick a 'worm'. Using even pressure, squeeze the sealant from the tube (or use the cartridge gun or finger trigger). Work carefully along the join applying the sealant.

3 Remove masking tape

Smooth out any irregularities in the sealant with the back of a wet teaspoon, and remove the masking tape. Don't rip the tape off: remove it slowly and evenly so you don't pull the sealant away as well. Allow the sealant to dry thoroughly, according to the maker's instructions.

REPAIRING A CRACKED TILE

A well-tiled surface – one that has been correctly prepared, hung, grouted and sealed – should give many years of service. Occasionally, though, a surface will be spoiled by discoloured grouting or a chipped tile. Both of these are very easy problems to solve.

Old grout can be quickly renovated with a renovation kit: liquid colourant, available in a range of colours can be brushed onto the existing clean and dry grout. Wash the tiles with sugar soap first and leave them to dry overnight. Paint on the colourant liquid and leave it for about an hour, then wet it with a sponge and wipe the excess colour away from the tiles. (The colour will

adhere to the grout but not to the glazed tile surface.) These grout kits not only brighten up old grout but are also water-resistant once dry.

A tile that has a missing corner – often because it has been hit or has had something dropped on it – can be repaired by cutting a matching piece from a replacement tile. It's always a good idea to keep and store any leftover tiles from the batch just for this purpose.

SAFETY FIRST

When you cut, chip or drill into ceramic tiles, always wear protective goggles and gloves to prevent injury from flying shards.

1 Making a template
Use a piece of tracing paper – or kitchen greaseproof paper – to make a template of the missing piece of tile. Hold the paper flat against the tile surface and carefully mark the exact shape using a pen or pencil.

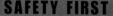

2 Score and cut the tile
Transfer the template shape to the face of the new tile and score around the outline. Using pincers or Japanese nippers – and wearing protective goggles to shield your eyes from flying shards – carefully nibble away until you have made the new tile piece.

3 Hang the piece
Make sure the wall area is clean and dry – scrape out the old grout around the corner and vacuum out any loose material if possible. 'Butter' the back of the piece of tile rather than trying to apply adhesive to a small space. Make sure you apply enough adhesive and ridge it horizontally with the notched spreader. Press the new piece into place.

4 Finishing
Allow the adhesive to dry completely, then touch up the surrounding grout. Use a cotton bud – or a small stick with the end wrapped in a clean cotton rag – to apply a very little grout to the join between the main part of the tile and the new piece. This will mask the join between the two. Remove excess grout, leave to dry and then polish.

REPLACING A CRACKED TILE

Where a tile is badly cracked, it's probably better to remove it and replace it with a new one. This involves drilling and chipping away the tile, so you must wear protective goggles, as shards of tile will fly everywhere. It's also a good idea to wear some stout gloves as these shards can cut the skin. If the offending tile is in a bathroom, make sure when you drill into it that there are no water pipes behind. Scrape out the grout from around the tile, and to avoid damaging the surrounding ones, mask them off with tape to protect them from scratches and chips. Use tape in the centre of the tile to stop the drill bit slipping on the smooth tile surface. Put a towel in the bath so the debris doesn't chip or scratch the enamel.

1 Remove old grout and mask off
Scrape out the grout from around the cracked tile. To protect surrounding tiles, use tape to 'mask' them off. Place some tape in the centre of the tile to stop the drill bit slipping and drill two or three holes in the centre of the tile.

2 Chip out the tile
Use a fine cold chisel – or an old woodworking chisel – and a club hammer to cut away the tile. Work from the centre of the tile outwards so you don't damage or dislodge the neighbouring tiles.

DRILLING TILES

- Use a masonry bit at a slow speed when you drill through the tile.

- To stop the tip of the bit from slipping, place tape on the tile face.

- Don't use a hammer action to drill or you'll shatter the tile and may even damage the surrounding ones as well.

- Don't drill too deeply into the wall, and remember to watch out for hidden water pipes.

3 Chisel out the old adhesive
In order for the new tile to lie flush and stick to the wall securely, chisel out all of the old adhesive. Brush away the debris – if possible, vacuum it out as any dust or debris will impair adhesion.

4 Position the new tile
'Butter' the back of the replacement tile with adhesive and press it into place. Leave to dry and then renew the grout around it.

DECORATING TILES

You don't have to live with patterns, colours and cracks in tiled surfaces thanks to the newly developed ranges of paint products, which make it possible to renovate old tiled surfaces without the trouble and expense of having to remove and replace them.

Of the number of ways to liven up old tiles, the simplest method is to paint them using one of the special tile paints available. You'll need to sand the tiles first so the surface is 'keyed'. These paints are a little more expensive than ordinary paints, but they don't require a primer or a final varnish to seal them. Alternatively, there are primers for use on tiles,

which make it possible to use ordinary emulsion paint on top, which can then be sealed with a tough clear coating to make it long-lasting or waterproof. A third way to

'jazz up' old tiles is to apply some decorative transfers: these are available in a range of styles and colours and are ideal for covering the odd cracked or discoloured tile while adding a little extra interest.

NEW TILES ON TOP OF OLD

If old tiled surfaces are sound but dull, or even 'downright offensive' to your sense of style, it is possible to tile over them in exactly the same way as if you were tiling a plain wall. Always make sure that the old tiled surface is clean and grease-free before you start. If any of the tiles are loose, re-fix them with adhesive, having first cleaned off the old adhesive from the wall and the back of the tile. This way, when re-fixed, they will lie flush with their neighbours. Where you tile a full height over a previously tiled half height, you can disguise the 'step' – the difference in level – by adding a 'mini shelf' or dado effect using a strip of finished hardwood.

1 Clean the old tiles
Clean the old tiled surface. Check that it is flat by using a spirit level against the horizontal and the vertical planes. Apply the adhesive using the notched spreader to create horizontal ridges.

2 Hang the new tiles
Using the old tile layout as your guide, press, don't slide, the new tiles into position. When the adhesive has dried, grout, 'point' with a rounded end stick in the joints to neaten them, and polish.

MOSAIC TILES

For thousands of years, mosaics have been used to create luxurious and hard-wearing surfaces. Mosaic tiles come in a range of shapes, sizes and colours – including silver and gold leaf. You can use them to create continuous 'fields' of a single colour, or insert individual tiles in different colours to make simple patterns, or even design a large mosaic picture. To calculate how many tiles you'll need, draw out the shape of the surface you want to tile (using some small-squared graph paper) and design your pattern first on paper. Mosaic tiles are usually sold in packs of five or ten sheets of 250 tiles attached to a backing paper, which is soaked off. These sheets, about 30 cm sq. (12in sq.), will cover roughly the equivalent of five 108mm sq. tiles and have a paper facing, which is soaked off with a damp sponge before grouting. Other tiles are attached to a mesh backing, which is simply pressed into the bed of tile adhesive. This backing scrim can be cut easily with a sharp knife, and individual tiles detached and cut to fit around awkward shapes. Hang

mosaic tile sheets exactly as if you were hanging an individual ceramic tile – but give them a little help by tapping them in gently with a mallet applied to a board covered with a piece of old carpet.

When you buy mosaic tiles, make sure you buy enough – and all at the same time as the colours can vary from batch to batch. It's a good idea to shuffle the sheets so that any colour 'imperfections' are evened out. Watch out for any odd, delicately coloured tiles, which could be inserted in random places for added effect.

The tiles can be grouted in the same way as standard tiles: you can use coloured grout if you want, but make sure it is waterproof where necessary. Traditionally the tiles – were bedded in with concrete. If you do use concrete, wear heavy-duty rubber gloves and wait for at least two whole days, keeping the concrete damp under a sheet of polythene while it 'cures' before it is allowed to dry off and then the surface cleaned with hydrochloric acid – or patio or path cleaner.

TILING IDEAS

- Don't rush tiling jobs, and be patient: give the adhesive and the grout the correct amount of setting and drying time before you proceed between steps.

- Coloured grout is the simplest way to give old tiles a new face lift.

- Use waterproof adhesive and grout where necessary – in kitchens and bathrooms. You can also get grout designed specially for more hygienic food-preparation areas.

- Use leftover tiles and tesserae to make pot stands for resting hot dishes on. Use a water-resistant adhesive and grout to bed the tiles onto a square of MDF cut to size.

- Be adventurous with tiles: take a look at the works of the Spanish architect Antonio Gaudí, for example, and make use of beautiful but broken pieces of tiles.

- When you have bought your tiles, keep your eyes open for any odd, delicately coloured ones that could be inserted in random places for extra effect.

- Take the time to draw out the pattern of surface you want to tile (using small-squared graph paper) and plan your design first on paper.

OUTDOORS

6

TOOLS & MATERIALS

To undertake the projects in this section you will need most of the tools in your basic tool kit, as well as a few more specialized ones, some of which can be hired.

• Measuring and marking accurately always play a vital role in DIY. Outdoors, often because of the scale of most projects, large measures are inevitable. A builder's square is useful for this type of DIY work. Always use the same measuring tool throughout and write measurements down clearly. Then double check everything by measuring again.

• To get levels even for bricklaying, concrete laying and for erecting fence posts you'll need a spirit level, while, to make sure everything is in a straight vertical line, use some string to make builder's lines (see page 342).

• Some outdoor DIY projects such as building a shed, a carport or garage, a garden wall, laying a paved area such as a patio or path, or erecting fences will require you to do a certain amount of excavating. You can break up the ground or existing paved areas with a pick axe or sledgehammer, or you could hire a power tool – and even an operator too – to do it for you. Don't forget that you'll have to make arrangements to dispose of the waste material when you've finished.

• Other specialized equipment that can be hired includes brick cutters (or you can cut them yourself with a bolster and club hammer), levelling machines for tamping down blocks and bricks on paths and driveways, heavy rollers for compacting the ground, and circular saws for cutting through paving slabs.

• While ready-mixed cement is good for small jobs, it's too expensive to use extensively. To mix your own, you will need: two 9-litre buckets (keep one for cement only); a firm, level base for mixing on (a piece of 19 or 25mm/1in plywood is ideal); and two shovels, one for handling the cement and the other for sand, aggregate and mixing. You could hire a mini cement mixer, if you like. You'll also need some brooms, both for finishing the surface of concrete paths and to tidy up the areas after you've finished.

• For brickwork you'll need a hawk, a brick-laying trowel and a pointing trowel. For a perfect professional finish, you could use a Frenchman, which is simply a metal strip bent and filed to a point at one end and used to skim off excess mortar and leave a neat finish. Make your own 'dressing tool' from a piece of iron rod about 10mm (⅜in) in diameter.

• Some types of fence posts can be erected using metal spikes; in other instances, a hole has to be dug or drilled with an auger, into which the post is placed and then cemented or concreted into position. Augers are basically large corkscrews. You can hire hand-operated ones that you twist into the ground by sheer arm strength alone, but if your ground is very hard, or you have a large number of holes to drill, then it's worth hiring a power-driven auger. Some companies hire out such machinery with the option of hiring someone to operate the machinery as well. If you decide on this, you will have to prepare your site in advance, clearly marking the positions where you want the drilled holes.

• Once erected, fences and other wooden structures outdoors need to be treated with timber preservatives to extend their life. These come in a range of colours and finishes that you can co-ordinate with your house or garden scheme.

SAFETY FIRST

• Where high-speed drilling and cutting are required, it is vital to wear goggles to protect your eyes and a dust mask to stop you breathing in fine particles. If you are operating power tools for a long time, you should use a pair of ear protectors as well.

• Any power tools used outdoors should be plugged into an RCD adaptor or RCD socket outlet.

• Follow the advice on pages 40–1 when using ladders.

• Seek advice from your local authority on the safe disposal of waste materials. On no account should paints, primers, solvents or any other chemicals be discharged into drains or water courses.

TOOLBOX

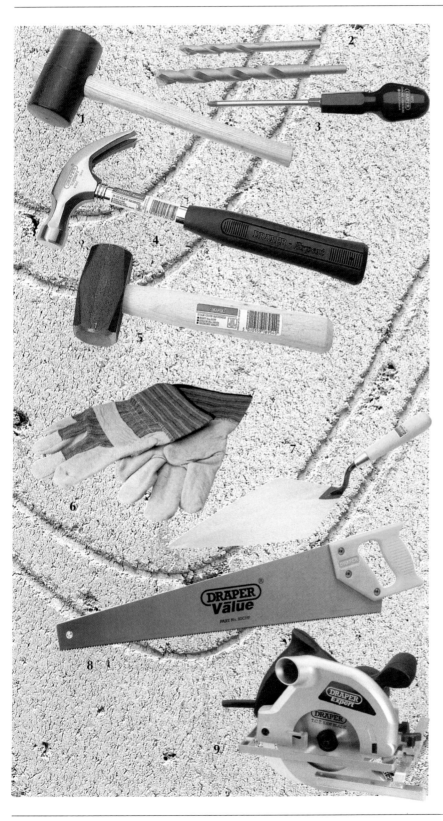

1 Rubber-headed mallet
2 Masonry bits
3 Phillips screwdriver
4 Hammer
5 Mallet
6 Protective gloves
7 Bricklayer's trowel
8 Saw
9 Circular saw
Builder's square
Spirit level
Pick axe
Sledgehammer
Brick cutters
Hawk
Frenchman
Auger

PLANNING A GARDEN

No matter how big or how small, a garden is a very personal space. The best garden design for you, therefore, is one you have conceived and put into practice yourself.

PLANNING YOUR GARDEN

To make the most of your outdoor space, start off by thinking about its physical characteristics. It's useful to have a compass so that you know where north is and can plan your scheme around the sunniest and shadiest areas. Fin out what the local climate is like and what type of soil there is; clay, peat and silty soils tend to need drainage while sandy and chalky soils dry out quickly. Steep slopes are difficult to maintain but you could create a terrace or series of terraces linked by paths or steps.

When you plan your garden, think about the features you have already, as well as the features you'd like to add. Start by listing the features you must include: perhaps a clothesline, a shed, or a gate to stop children and dogs running into the road. Draw up a list in order of priority of the items you'd like to include: hard surfaced areas such as patios, paths and driveways; a garage or carport; or an area of lawn.

A water feature is not only attractive but is also a way to increase the range of wildlife in your garden. A small pool will attract birds, frogs and insects, which will help to devour any pests. Remember that any water, no matter how shallow, is dangerous if you have small children. It might be better to stick to a birdbath instead, until the children have grown up. If you want flowing water, you will have to provide electricity. As with garden lighting, you will need to plan an underground electricity supply before you lay out paths and lawns. The alternative to this is to use solar power. Small solar panels for collecting and storing sunlight will power small fountains during the day or provide power for small lanterns at night; solar panels are available from many garden centres and DIY stores.

Once you've compiled your list, plan how you will carry the work through to completion. Measure the boundaries and draw the area out onto graph paper to scale. Plot the existing features, such as trees or other structures. Lay a piece of tracing paper over this scale drawing and start experimenting with ideas and locations. This gives you an opportunity to work out your ideas and various designs without spoiling the 'master drawing'.

PATHS AND PATIOS

Decide the position of hard surfaces like paths, drives and patios before you do anything else because they will determine the level and position of many other garden features. Paths should be wide enough to walk on and must be kept free of wet leaves and moss, which can make them slippery and dangerous. In a small space, stepping stones are a good way to make a path. Space them sensibly for easy stepping: not too close and not so far apart that you have to jump.

You don't have to build a patio against the house, but this is often the most convenient place. Remember to

Your ideal garden elements may include a patio or paving, fences that afford privacy and a variation in levels.

look carefully at the level of the damp-proof course or position of any air bricks on your house. Paving slabs must finish no less than two courses of bricks below this level or you risk damp creeping into the house. If the back of your house faces north, it could be a bleak area to sit in but you may decide you prefer to have the shade in summer.

Have fun with the shape of paved areas: square and triangular areas can be more useful than long narrow strips. There are paving stones and bricks in a variety of colours to blend in with the style of your house and garden. Slates, cobbles and grit add colour and texture. You could choose 'natural' materials like wooden decking, or go for a modern approach with industrial steel and glass.

Whatever style of garden you have, it is worth adding some lighting. A clever garden lighting scheme will allow you to use your garden well into the night and make an interesting feature when viewed from indoors (see page 212).

Once you have finalized your plan, you can start work. Transferring your ideas from paper to the actual ground can be tricky, so it's a good idea to set a 'datum line'. This is simply a line down the middle of your garden from which you can take all your measurements. You can mark it out using string and some pegs knocked into the ground, or you can use sand trickled from a bottle – but this will blow away in time. Curves can be marked out using canes and for circles, attach a length of string to a fixed post in the ground and use it like a big compass.

BOUNDARIES

Boundaries in gardens are usually marked by hedges or fences: before you alter either of these, you'll need to find out whose fence or hedge it is – yours or your neighbour's. The title deeds to your home should state this. There are many types of fences available, so choose one that suits your needs: do you want it to add privacy, for plants to climb up and over, or to act as a windbreak? If your garden slopes, putting up fencing requires a little thought. Choose a fence type that can be made to follow the slope and make sure that the fence posts are perfectly upright. Don't try to follow every little rise and fall in the level of the ground or the top of your fence will go up and down like a rollercoaster track. Try to aim for one 'overall' and even slope. Panel fencing is harder to put up on a slope than post and rail or post and

Even the smallest outdoor space can become a relaxing garden.

wire link fencing. On a gentle slope, you can put panel fencing in making a series of 'steps'. Make sure you take this into account when you buy your materials because you may need to order more panels and longer fence posts than normal. If your garden slopes steeply then panel fencing is no good, unless you want a big gap underneath the end of each panel.

HEDGES

Hedges can make good garden boundaries and windbreaks. You can

choose from formal 'clipped' hedges or informal ones – those that come into flower each year. Hedges take up a lot of space, so be prepared to sacrifice some of the ground alongside the length of the hedge. Remember also that they will compete with other plants for water and nutrients in the soil. You'll need to keep the area underneath the hedge cleaned out to allow air to circulate freely and also to stop unwanted pests using the debris as their winter homes.

BUILDING A PORCH

Adding an external porch to the front or back door can stop draughts entering the house. It also provides useful space for coats and shoes – so mud and dirt is not tracked through the house – and can double as a mini-greenhouse for delicate or even tropical blooms. A part-glazed porch will allow you to keep the outer access locked until you have identified callers. You won't need planning permission – unless the floor area exceeds 2m sq. (2½sq.yds) – or any part is more than 3m (9ft) high, or less than 2m (6ft) from a boundary adjoining a public highway or foot-path. You can buy ready-made porches in kit form in a range of styles that are easy to erect, and don't require masonry foundations or supporting walls, but you will need a solid foundation.

1 Erecting the side panels
Offer up the first panel to the wall and mark the position of the fixing holes. You may need help to hold the panel in place while you check its vertical levels with a spirit level. Use a masonry bit on a low speed to drill into the wall. Avoid drilling into mortar joints. Then plug the holes.

2 Attaching additional panels
Subsequent panels of the porch are joined using the manufacturer's fittings; some systems simply 'slot and lock' together. You will need to support the panels while they are being positioned and secured, making sure you don't break any glazed sections.

3 Adding the door
Before you buy your porch, make sure you check whether the new front door is to open in or outwards and whether it is to be hung on the left or right-hand side. Also ensure that it locks securely and that there is a letterbox.

4 Securing to the base
Many modern porches are constructed so that the panels slot into a grooved channel at the base and are then secured with the supplied fixings. Follow the instructions regarding number and spacing so that panels are well secured.

5 Adding the seals
To make the joins between the panels neat and weatherproof, strips of plastic or plastic-coated sealant are inserted into the grooves. Depending on the system you have chosen, these may require pinning to secure them.

6 Adding the roof

While porches may appear to have flat roofs, they are designed to slope away from the neighbouring walls so that rainwater doesn't collect on the roof but is channelled and shed off away from the walls. Use a spirit level to ensure the required angle of fall.

7 Securing the roof

The roof, the fascia boards and the internal supporting cross-members of the roof are secured to the panels, often through pre-drilled holes. Finish with roofing felt or transparent PVC roofing, depending on your choice.

ADDING A CONSERVATORY

A conservatory adds both light and additional space to your home, but constructing one is not really a job for an amateur. A conservatory is essentially an extension and, like any other extension, you will need planning permission. Ideally, to make the best use of the space, a conservatory should face the direction that enjoys the best possible light. Construction can be complicated and this depends on the design you have selected – what type of foundations you will require and what types of services (power, light, water and drainage) you choose to have inside the conservatory. A good, reputable conservatory construction company will be able to advise you and should be able to deal with planning applications as well. Always ask for the contact details of at least three previous clients – don't rely on the salesman's pitch or on glossy brochures. Find out if the company actually delivers its promises. If you have neighbours with a conservatory you like, get details from them. Get written quotes and check them carefully to see exactly what's included. Look at your budget – size and materials such as PVC or double glazing will affect the costs – and then add on extra for a contingency fund to cover decoration. Don't forget the floor covering for this new space and any shades or blinds to reduce the glare of the sun. A well-constructed and designed conservatory will be a joy and add significantly to the value of your home. A poorly constructed, leaky and sunless conservatory won't.

BUILDING A SHED

LAYING A CONCRETE PAD

As with all buildings, a shed needs a firm and level base if it is to remain sound, serviceable and safe. Without it, the shed will quickly deteriorate: the walls and roof will sag and the doors (and windows) will jam. The lower timbers in the walls will remain wet while the floor will rot because it is in contact with the ground. Not only will your shed smell, but also tools or materials stored in it will rust and get mouldy. Make sure that your shed will have adequate access because once you have laid the base it is very difficult to change the site. If a shed base is too big, rainwater will form puddles at the edges then seep under the wall, wetting and rotting the structure. If slabs are used to make a base, these must be spaced to suit

the floor size and must be laid on a firm sub-base and then bedded onto a sand and cement mix. The slabs must be level across the whole site. The best solution is to make a solid base, firm and level and the right size to suit the floor. To get the exact size of the shed floor, deduct 20mm (¾in) from the length and width and use these dimensions to set out the floor. Select the location of the shed and mark out the base using nails and string. Then mark 150mm (6in) all round outside this area for the overall size of the 'dig'. Clear all vegetation and remove the topsoil to the required depth: for a garden shed, a base thickness of 73mm (3in) is enough, but on soft clay soils, a 100mm (4in) concrete base laid onto a 50mm (2in) well-compacted hardcore base is essential.

1 Constructing the formwork

Setting-out strings are used to position the concrete formwork made of 25mm (1in) thick timber, which should be as wide as the thickness of the slab. The timber is nailed onto pegs driven into the ground but don't let them protrude above the formwork. Check them with a try square, tape and level.

2 Sub-base

On very soft or clay soils, you will need to add a 50mm (2in) layer of finely broken and well-compacted hardcore. Take care not to leave air gaps in the hardcore layer – if possible use a heavy roller to flatten and compact it. Now it's time to mix your concrete. See page 346 for some extra tips.

3 Adding concrete

Add water gradually to your concrete mix. Place a layer into the formwork and compact it down with a levelling board and tap the sides of the formwork to help produce a solid edge to the slab. Keep adding layers into the formwork until it is full, then smooth the surface with a wooden or plastic float.

4 Cover concrete pad

Concrete must not be allowed to dry out too quickly, or be damaged by frost while it is still wet. Cover the concrete pad with clear plastic sheeting until the concrete is hard and keep spraying it with water to allow it to dry out slowly and thoroughly. Then remove the form-work, leaving the base ready for use.

ERECTING A SHED

You won't need planning permission to erect a small shed or outbuilding as long as it is within the boundaries of your property and is not more than 3m (9ft 9in) high and does not project beyond the foremost wall of the house if facing a highway.

Like many other garden structures, sheds – as well as summerhouses and children's playhouses – are available in a range of different styles and sizes. They also come almost ready-made, as pre-fabricated and self-assembly components. Before you erect the shed, apply liberal coats of timber preservative – especially to the base and where the panels join.

1 Position the floor

Lay out the wooden shed floor onto a pre-prepared concrete base. A roofing felt or damp-proof course 'skirt' incorporated into the shed base while it is being erected helps to keep the bottom timbers dry and stops fallen leaves accumulating under the floor.

2 Secure the side panels

Erecting a shed is pretty straight-forward, but it is always useful to have a helper to support panels while you fix them securely into place. Shed manufacturers will provide full assembly instructions and the fixings to secure the shed.

3 Roof cross members

To support the roof, timber cross-members are secured to the side panels using screws and brackets. In most cases, the timbers are not pre-drilled so you will have to do this yourself. Make sure the screws are galvanized, so they won't rust.

4 Nail on roofing boards

The first 'layer' of the roof is made of sheets of roofing boards. These should also be treated with timber preservative prior to construction. Nail the boards to the shed roof and to the supporting cross-members. Where possible, work from either side of the shed to avoid over-reaching.

5 Secure the roof felt

To make the shed and roof both weatherproof and waterproof, it needs to be covered with a suitable finish such as roofing felt. This is available in standard-width rolls, which can be cut to length then secured to the roof with galvanized nails.

BUILDING A GARAGE

1 Lay the concrete base

Prepare a suitable concrete base for the garage. The floor should be 100mm (4in) thick but the edges built up to 200mm (8in) thick to support the walls, and built on a sub-base of a minimum of 100mm (4in) well-compacted and levelled hardcore.

2 Support the lower sections

While the lower sections of the garage wall are being assembled, they will need to be supported outside by 'buttresses'. These can be made using lengths of stout timber, angled (but not pushing) against the walls. These will hold the structure securely while other components are being added.

3 Erect second level

The second level of wall panels are erected and fixed to the first. Make sure you have safe and level access as you will be working at a height, and work from the inside of the structure. Once the roof cross members are in place, the structure will become more stable.

4 Raise roof sections

On a large-span roof, you will need the assistance of at least one assistant to help you raise and slide the roof into position across the members. Position ladders inside the garage and work slowly and carefully.

5 The last roof section

The final roof section will need to be lifted and positioned from outside and from above. Never stand on the roof of any structure or you could fall through. Instead, use crawl boards to evenly distribute your weight.

6 Hang the door

Lastly, hang the door or doors. If you have selected double-hinged doors that open outwards, then these are hung as you would hang an external door (see page 116). See opposite for advice on installing an up-and-over door.

HANGING A GARAGE DOOR

Traditional hinged doors require a substantial clearance area for them to open properly. An up-and-over door, on the other hand, retracts inside the garage and is ideal for use where a garage forms a boundary and where a door must not swing out.

Up-and-over doors are always counterweighted and they are available as either tracked or untracked, or can be partially or fully retracting. The manufacturers of up-and-over doors produce them in a range of standard sizes that are quite specific in terms of the garage opening – this means the distance between the frame posts and the height measurement from the floor to the head member. Most doors will require a solid wooden frame to provide a strong fixing, but some

manufacturers produce door systems complete with a metal frame that simply needs to be screwed into the surrounding brickwork. When a frame is included in the kit, the openings and the overall frame dimensions will be specified.

Note that if you are replacing old and worn hinge-hung doors with an up-and-over door, your old frame may not be a standard size and in this case you will need a made-to-measure replacement.

Up-and-over doors can be bought with a remote control opening and closing system that you can operate from inside your car. These are best installed by the manufacturer. See page 351 for advice on buying automatic gates; the same principles apply to garage doors. Get a spare remote control for emergencies.

UP-AND-OVER DOOR KITS
Self-assembly, up-and-over doors are readily available in kits from auto accessory and DIY superstores. Each kit comes with the required fixings and full assembly instructions, but you must know your exact key dimensions before you buy one.

1 Attach the mechanism
Follow the individual manufacturers' instructions to attach the counterweight mechanisms to the sides of the garage door.

2 Position door
The most difficult step in fitting the door is raising it into position in the frame and then temporarily holding it there with props and wedges. If possible, get one or two helpers to assist you.

3 Fit the tracks
Once the door is propped and wedged securely in position and then fixed to the frame, the tracks (if your door system requires them) are fixed securely along the interior walls of the garage at the appropriate height.

BUILDING A CARPORT

CONSTRUCTION

- Concrete must be mixed on a firm, level and clean base and make sure that all drains are covered to stop concrete running into them and setting hard.

- Don't make your concrete too wet or you will weaken it – add the water gradually to your mix.

- Make sure that any timber you use is pre-treated with a wood preservative. Treat any sawn, cut or notched areas with additional preservative before assembling the structure.

- Cut roofing sheets without cracking them by sandwiching the sheet between two long timber cut-offs and clamp them into place alongside the cutting line. Cut using a saw with the blade running against the edges of the off-cuts.

- Don't leave fitting the flashing strip until all the roof sheets are in place or you'll have to climb onto the roof to apply it and PVC corrugated roofing will not support your weight. You will probably crack the roof and could even fall through it.

- As an alternative to running waste water from the downpipe into a gully on your finished carport, it is a good idea to set up a water butt so that you can collect any waste water and use it in the garden.

If there is a space off-road for your car, a carport is an inexpensive way to shelter it, and will, at the same time, double as a canopy over a side door providing undercover access and additional storage. The basic structure could also be used as a drying area for laundry, a children's play area, or even an outdoor dining area.

A carport is classed as an outbuilding – regardless of where it is actually sited. It will not require planning permission unless it projects out in front of the local building line (usually determined by the front wall of your house); is not more than 3m (10ft) high; and as long as it does not end up covering more than half of your garden area. You won't need approval from the Buildings Regulator provided the floor area does not exceed 30m sq. (325sq.ft) and the structure is open on at least two sides. If you are in any doubt as to whether your proposed structure needs consent, check first with the planning department of your local authority.

A carport is a simple structure that requires only basic DIY skills. The most important things to bear in mind are that the supporting posts must be absolutely vertical and that the roof needs a slight slope so that rainwater is shed away from the walls of your home. If the drainage runs from one end of the roof to the other, it will be easier to seal the join between the roof and the house as the flashing tape will run parallel to the corrugations in the roofing sheets.

1 Fix the wall plate
The roof is supported by two main beams of 100 x 50mm (4 x 2in) timber, which can run the length of the carport. One beam is used as a wall plate and is fixed to the house wall with masonry bolts while the other is screwed to support posts erected at the outer edge.

2 Position the posts
You can excavate holes and then bed the posts in concrete, but by far the simplest method – especially if there is an existing concrete base – is to use bolt-down fence support sockets fixed into place with small masonry bolts set into holes drilled into the concrete.

3 Fit the main bearer and joists

With the supporting posts securely in their sockets and truly vertical, drill clearance holes for the screws in the face of the outer edge beam. Hold the beam in position and clamp it to the outer faces of the posts, then slot a joist into the notches cut into the beams across the higher end of the roof and use a spirit level to check it is horizontal. When the joist is level, tighten the clamps, and screw the end of the beam to the first post. Repeat the process at the lower end of the roof and then fit the joists.

4 Add the roofing sheets

Lay the first roofing sheet at the down-hill end of the roof with one long edge butted against the house wall and the other overhanging the fascia board at the lower end by about 50mm (2in). Drill 3mm (⅛in) clearance holes in the first ridge above the wall plate and in every fourth ridge above each of the joists. Slip a sealing ring over each screw, insert into the hole and drive into the wood below. Snap on a plastic cover to conceal the screw head. Lay subsequent sheets against the house wall so that the lower end overlaps the sheet you have just fixed by 300mm (12in), and repeat.

5 Sealing the junction between wall and roof

Once the first row of roof sheets has been installed, seal the junction between it and the house wall with self-adhesive flashing tape. First, apply flashing primer to the wall and allow it to become tacky, then peel back the paper backing from the tape and bed one edge against the house wall and let the rest lap onto the roof surface. Work your way along the roof, peeling back the backing on the tape as you go. Cut the tape to length at the end, then go back and press the tape firmly into the roof surface.

6 Check the levels

Throughout the construction process, it is vital that the supporting posts remain truly vertical. Each time you descend from your ladder, check them with a spirit level and make the necessary adjustments. To complete the carport, you could fit gutter brackets and a length of 100mm (4in) wide guttering to the fascia board at the downhill end of the roof; attach a downpipe to the gutter outlet and run it to a nearby gully.

SAFETY FIRST

- Make sure any power tools are plugged into an RCD adaptor or RCD socket outlet.

- Set up stepladders and other access equipment on level ground and take care not to over-reach when working at heights.

ERECTING FENCES

You won't need planning permission to erect a fence unless it is higher than 2m (6ft 6in), your boundary adjoins a highway (when you may be limited to a 1m/3ft 3in high fence), or where your area has been designated as 'open plan' (in this case you may be allowed to erect low 'decorative' ranch-style, or post-and-rope fencing). Short term, a fence will be cheaper than a masonry wall, but you can argue that long term, the cost of maintenance and eventual replace-ment will cancel out any savings made. Nevertheless, a wooden fence that has been treated with preserva-tive regularly should last for years.

Picket fencing (pictured top left) is low level and 'see through' and is good for boundaries or at the front of a cottage-style garden. Narrow, vertical 'pales' with a rounded or pointed top are spaced evenly at 50mm (2in) centres. Picket fences are difficult to make by hand but fortunately are available as prefabricated panels constructed of softwood – or even plastic.

Trellis (top centre) is lightweight but does make a good windbreak and can

offer privacy when climbing plants have grown over it. The concertina fold of trellis, formed from thin lathes of cedar or other softwood will only be as strong as the posts and rails that support it.

Close-boarded fencing (top right) is ideal for screening off a garden or

boundary from an unsightly road or neighbouring plot. A close-board fence is made by nailing overlapping featherboard strips to horizontal rails. Featherboards are sawn planks that 'feather' or taper across their width from 16mm (⅝in) in the middle, down to around 3mm (⅛in) at the edges.

1 Setting out
With all fencing, careful setting out is perhaps the most important part of the job. Set out the line of the fence by stretching strong string between stakes positioned at intervals along the proposed run.

2 Post supports
Post supports are available in different types and sizes. Spiked post supports are driven into the ground with a sledge-hammer. To avoid damaging or distorting the support rim, buy a special driving tool or 'dolly' that fits into the socket.

3 Check verticals

Drive in the spike until the base of the socket is level with the ground, checking regularly that the support is going in straight. If it begins to twist out of line, use the handles on the dolly to realign it. If you don't succeed in setting the support correctly, you'll need to lever it out and start again.

4 Fix the first post

The base of the post slots into the support and is then secured by screwing through the side of the socket or by tightening clamping bolts, depending on the design of the spike. Check that the post is vertical with a spirit level.

5 Positioning subsequent posts

Offer up the first fence panel but do not nail it to the post. Instead, use this panel as a guide to position the next support. When this post support and post is in place, you can secure the first panel. Continue to erect posts and panels alternately along the boundary.

6 Checking levels

Lay a spirit level along the top of each fence panel to check that it is level. When all the panels have been adjusted and secured, fix gravel boards at the base of the fence and nail post caps or finials to the top of each post.

FENCES

- If you bed fencing posts into concrete, shape the top of the concrete to slope away from the posts so rainwater is shed cleanly away.

- Remember that all of the fence posts must be on your side of the boundary. Check the deeds of your house to be sure you know exactly where the boundary lies and avoid future disputes.

- Maintain the appearance and prolong the life of your fence by regularly treating panels and posts with wood preservative.

- Most fence posts and panels are factory treated to prevent vermin and insect attack. If you are setting posts into concrete, soak their cut ends with preservative overnight to prolong their life.

- To save time and energy, rather than lift a large fence panel into position every time you want to position a post, cut a batten to match the width of the panel and use this to mark the position.

- Take care when lifting and carrying heavy sections of fence.

ERECTING GATES

When you first start looking for a gate, you will find that they are generally organized in sales catalogues according to their intended location – side gates, entrance gates, drive gates, for example. It is the location of gates that influences their design, and a complimentary gate and fence makes a property appear well cared for.

Gates can be expensive if they are made to last: wooden gates are often made of softwoods for economy but, for such a focal point of your home, it's worth investing in oak or cedar types. Wrought-iron gates are, in fact, made from mild steel, which must be primed and painted to protect them from rust and decay. Whatever type or style of gate you choose, it is vital that they are mounted on sturdy posts or masonry piers.

1 Lay out the posts and gate

Place the posts and the gate on the ground, making sure the posts are parallel and the correct distance apart and allowing enough space to accommodate the hinges and the latch.

2 Dig trench

Dig a 300mm (1ft) wide trench across the entrance and long enough to contain the gateposts. Where the post holes are to be sited, dig holes 450mm (1ft 6in) deep (for a low gate) or 600mm (2ft) deep (for a tall gate). Make sure that any sawn ends of timber have been treated with wood preservative.

3 Set posts into holes

Set the gate posts into the holes and fill with hardcore and concrete and use temporary cross battens to support them vertically until the concrete has set. Fill the trench with concrete at the same time and level it flush with the pathway.

4 Fit hardware

When the concrete has set completely, the gates can be hung and their hardware – e.g. latches, house number – attached. Use hardware designed for gates, as these are made to withstand both wear and tear and the weather.

5 Finishing

Wooden gates can be finished with varnish or primed and painted with an exterior-grade paint to match the paintwork of your house. Place newspaper under the gates and cover any plants to protect them from paint splashes.

AUTOMATIC GATES

If you are fortunate enough to live in a property with a long driveway, or if you live on a busy road where pulling over, getting out and opening drive gates can cause a traffic jam, or even in a small house or flat where you want to restrict access to welcome visitors only, then installing automatic gates can be a good idea. A simple system would lock and unlock the gate – to a garden flat, for example – by operating it from inside your home, like an entry-phone system.

More elaborate systems are available that allow you to drive in and out without getting out of your car, because the gates have been operated by a hand-held or in-car remote control device, or by specially installed sensors – pads located in the driveway or sensors mounted on gate- or fenceposts.

While all of these offer advantages, they can be very costly to install – and will need a back-up system in case of interruption in the mains power supply. For advice on security aspects, it's a good idea to contact your local Crime Prevention Officer, and for the latest car accessories, check out auto dealers and specialist car magazines. These systems can also be installed on garage doors, allowing you to open and close them from your car.

Elaborate alarm systems are operated by hand-held or in-car remote control devices (above), or by sensors such as pads installed in the drive or mounted on posts (above left and top).

SAFETY FIRST

- Power tools used outdoors must be fitted with an RCD plug or connected to an RCD socket outlet.

- Avoid getting concrete on your skin when you mix and pour it, as it can cause serious irritation: wash off immediately using plenty of water.

DECKING

Decking – areas of wooden planking – have long been features of American and Continental European gardens where the climate allows extended periods of outdoor living and a timber deck can be put to many different uses. In Britain, decking has become increasingly popular – even though it may be frequently rain-soaked or even snow-covered in winter – as an attractive method of surfacing a garden or making a steep or uneven plot more accessible.

TYPES OF DECKING

There are three main types of decking: low-level decking is the simplest and is an alternative to terracing. Usually it is supported by concrete piers (proprietary precast concrete piers can also be bought) or short timber or metal posts. In towns, this type of decking is the most common, as it forms an attractive and useful transition between the house and the garden, and it is possible to buy decks in kit form that you can assemble yourself.

The second type, the hillside deck, creates a level space where none

existed before, and can provide a platform for spectacular views. This type of deck is much more costly to erect and will normally require the skills of an architect and need to take account of planning regulations.

The third type is timber decking used to provide a surface for a flat roof. Again, converting a roof space into a roof garden will require a structural survey so that the maximum load the roof can bear is established. A timber surface alone will be heavy, and when you add on plant containers, the soil they contain, garden furniture and people, the weight increases significantly.

A good deck will depend on the quality of wood used – and on its maintenance. Red cedar is highly durable but expensive; pines, larches and spruces are also used for decking but require regular preservative treatment. It is important that the wood used can be sawn without splintering and will accept galvanized nails easily.

DECKS WITH A DIFFERENCE

There are alternatives to a large, constructed deck. Imaginatively used and placed duck boards on a gravel surface can make an attractive decked area, which can be moved around as you like and stored away during the winter months.

Or why not experiment with old railway sleepers set between cobbles, or even 'slices' of tree trunks? You can also use these to make a 'stepping stone' path – but do remember that, when wet, these and any other timber surfaces will be slippery. Decking should be cleaned with a power hose or careful wire brushing.

TIMBER DECKING

- The simpler the pattern of timber you devise for your deck, the simpler the supporting structure needs to be. Decking timbers laid in parallel lengths on the diagonal needs quite a simple framework, while fancy patterns will need greater support.

- Suppress weeds under low level decking by spreading black plastic sheeting (available from garden suppliers) between the deck-supporting posts.

- See pages 228 and 373–4 for advice on buying wood.

BUILDING GARDEN WALLS

TYPES OF WALLS

Retaining walls are those designed to 'hold back' a bank of earth, usually a terrace or steep slope of ground. However, low retaining walls can also be constructed to provide raised planting beds. Boundary walls mark out the limits of your property, provide security and privacy but also form a solid background to trees and shrubs and support for climbing and rambling plants.

Many gardens also have dividing walls, forming a break between areas of lawn and a patio or vegetable garden, for example. Dividing walls are a great way of providing visual interest in featureless gardens and are a good way to create 'rooms' in the garden. They need not be high: a dividing wall of say 750mm (2ft 6in) in height is easy to build and is a good structure on which to practice your building techniques.

Walls can be constructed from brick, stone or concrete blocks, or even concrete poured on site – although this is normally used to make strong retaining walls within gardens. Different walling materials are used in different ways, and the thickness of them will depend on their height. The thickness of a wall will also determine the number and spacing of piers and buttresses that are built to support the wall. You can avoid building piers and buttresses if you stagger a wall in a zigzagging manner, while curving or 'serpentine' walls – also called 'cringle-crangle' – will support themselves, although they will take up much more space.

CAPPING WALLS

The way you finish – or 'cap' – a wall will make an enormous difference to its final appearance. Stone walls often have a traditional capping, depending on the region, while concrete blocks – now available in a variety of attractive sizes and finishes – can be finished with concrete slabs or even brick. Concrete has suffered a great deal of bad press in the recent past; we associate it too much with grim inner city tower blocks instead of looking at its great design potentials. Concrete is in fact available in a range of colours and textures from the dull, grey aggregate finish of the early material, to colours matching local

DIVIDING WALLS
Dividing walls are a good way to provide visual interest in otherwise featureless gardens.

CORNERS
Use alternate headers and stretchers (see page 50) to form corners and check your angle carefully.

brick and stone, or brightly rendered or painted. You could even tile over concrete with mosaic tiles or brightly coloured broken shards of pottery. Different regions also produce different local stone – or bricks – crushed and used as the aggregate in the composition of reconstituted stone blocks. These, and concrete blocks, are considerably larger than bricks so building a wall is much faster – and cheaper – than using bricks or stones. But, whatever material you use, the finished wall will only be as sturdy and attractive as you build it.

SCALE, TEXTURE AND PATTERN

Consideration of these factors at the planning stage will help you make some decisions as to the type of wall you want. Open-screen walling units, available in a range of patterns and materials – including precast concrete and terracotta units – are useful for piercing solid walls and adding a decorative element. These pierced units are also useful as wind baffles – slowing down the wind over large areas – rather than creating a barrier that causes wind resistance.

The shape of most of our gardens tends to be regular – mostly a long narrow strip at the rear of the house and possibly a small square at the front. The most common mistake is surrounding a regular site with some structure that emphasizes this regularity. The simplest way to provide relief to the visual monotony of a site is to vary the materials used. Use brick or stone nearest to your house, and perhaps timber or concrete blocks for the rest. Alternatively, use one material, but vary the height of the wall at different points along its length.

BRICK WALLS

- Whatever materials you decide to use, the basic techniques for laying stone, brick or concrete blocks remain the same. If you have had experience of laying bricks and pointing then you should find the process straight-forward (see pages 50–1 for bricklaying advice). If, however, you need a high wall, or one that is complicated in design and function in any way, then it's probably best to hire a professional to do the job for you.

- Whatever wall you build, it will require solid foundations: generally, the depth of the foundations will depend on the height of the finished wall, the type of soil – especially if there is a high moisture content present, such as in clay soils – and the level at which frost occurs or the movement of ground moisture. In most cases, a depth of 600mm (2ft) will be sufficient, but if there are difficult site conditions, it's best to seek expert advice.

- When digging a trench for foundations, make sure you avoid any tree roots or drainpipes. Avoid ground that has recently been filled in, which will be too loosely packed, and make sure the soil is well drained or you may get subsidence. If the trench fills with water while you are digging, it's time to call in professional advice.

LAYING A BLOCK DRIVEWAY

1 Marking out

Mark out the drive with pegs leaving an extra 75mm (3in) on each side for the formwork. Excavate the ground, level it and add a 125mm (5in) level layer of hardcore. Rake and shovel concrete on top, then tamp down with a stout plank on edge. When the concrete has dried, add a 75mm (3in) layer of sharp sand.

2 Layout blocks

Lay an area of bricks or blocks, tapping them gently into the sand with a mallet handle. Keep the sand bed dry: if it rains before you finish, let the sand dry out or add new. Start by laying whole bricks or blocks only – leave any gaps at the edges for cut bricks or blocks after you have laid about 2m sq. (2sq.yds) of blocks.

3 Kneeling board

Work from one end of the site and never stand on the bed of sand or on the brick or block paving or you will set them too deep or raise them out of level. Use a long board spread over the drive so that your weight is distributed evenly. Continue to lay bricks or blocks in your chosen pattern.

4 Using a brick cutter

If you are paving a drive, you will need to cut a number of bricks to fit and fill the edges. It's worth hiring a hydraulic brick cutter to speed up the job and cut down on wastage. Follow the operating and safety instructions at all times.

5 Tamping down with a plate vibrator

Fill the surface joints with a dry mortar mix, then sweep it into the cracks. You can tamp down with a club hammer and a piece of stout timber, but it's better to hire a plate vibrator and pass it two or three times over the new paved area.

HIRING TOOLS

Many jobs around your home will need specialized equipment. Tool-hire shops will be able to supply many of the necessary tools such as electric cement mixers, hydraulic brick cutters, and plate vibrators. Spring and summer will be the most popular times to undertake exterior work, so you may need to pre-book at these times. Check whether the hirer will deliver and collect – otherwise you'll need a suitable vehicle to do this yourself. Ask for a demonstration to see how the equipment works and make sure any safety wear is included, as well as an operating manual.

TARMAC

Cold-cure tarmac is a simple way to resurface an old tarmac drive or path. It comes ready to lay from a sack and can be rolled level with a heavy garden roller. Cold-cure tarmac comes in two colours – red or black – and is sold in 25kg (55lb) sacks. One sack will cover just under 1m sq. (1sq.yd) at a thickness of about 12mm (½in). Each sack also contains a separate bag of decorative stone chippings for embedding in the soft tarmac as an alternative finish.

It's easiest to spread tarmac on a warm, dry day. If you are planning on working in the cold, store the materials in a warm place the night before so they are easier to work with. A couple of days before you lay the new cold-cure tarmac, pull up any

● ● ● ┃ ● ● ● ┃ ● ● ● ┃ ● ● ● ┃ ● ● ●

PROTECTING TARMAC

• You can walk on cold-cure tarmac as soon as it's laid – but don't wear high heels or stilettos for a couple of days and wait two or three days before you drive or park a car on cold-cure tarmac so it sets firm.

• Always protect tarmac from chemical spillage – especially oil and petrol from cars and power tools.

• Although its not essential, edging the tarmac with a brick or concrete block 'kerb' will improve the appearance and prolong the life of these often vulnerable areas.

weeds and grass growing through the old surface and apply a good, strong weed killer. Sweep the area clean and level out any potholes: cut the sides of holes vertically, clean out the debris, paint the inside with bitumen emulsion then fill with 18mm (3/4in) layers of tarmac, compacting each layer until the surface is flush with the surrounding level. To make a firm bond between the old surface and the new, on a dry day, apply a tack coat of bitumen emulsion to the entire surface to be covered. Mask off edges and areas to protect from splashes. Stir the emulsion well first, and then pour it on. You can pour direct from the container, but you may find it easier to control if you decant the emulsion into an old watering can – but don't use a 'rose' sprinkler on the end. Use an old stiff-bristled broom to

Laying cold-cure tarmac is straightforward; the only special equipment is a heavy garden roller.

spread the emulsion. Try to avoid splashing surrounding surfaces and avoid leaving puddles.

Let the tack coat set – this usually takes about 20 minutes. While this is setting, wash the broom in hot, soapy water. Shovel on and then rake the tarmac to a layer about 18mm (¾in) thick. Use a straight edge – or the flat side of the rake – to scrape the surface and press down lumps with your foot. Spread three sacks of tarmac and then roll. Keep the roller wet to stop specks being picked up. Spread and roll the next three sacks of tarmac. Scatter the chippings and then roll the whole area in different directions to compact it evenly.

LAYING A PATIO

A paved patio area offers a useful and attractive area for eating and relaxing outdoors. Normally a patio is laid right next to the house but other factors might determine its location. If the bottom of the garden is sunnier for longer periods than the area next to the house, construct a patio there instead but, if shade is important to you, then at least part of the patio must provide for this.

Start the project by making a scale plan on graph paper, and then make some photocopies of it so you can draw out different 'arrangements' within the designated areas. You could pave the area with bricks but it's quicker and easier to lay larger square or rectangular paving slabs – although you'll need someone to help you lift and move them into place.

1 Marking out the patio

Transfer your plans to the ground using nails, a try square, some strong string and pegs. Measure accurately to ensure adequate space for the slabs – allow up to 10mm (⅜in) between each slab for mortar, and to avoid cutting slabs, choose a chequerboard layout or paving that includes half-slabs.

2 Prepare the site

Start by levelling the site: remove all vegetation and at least some of the topsoil. If your patio will be next to your house, it must slope away from the building to shed rainwater. The ideal 'fall' is 1:60 – or 16mm (⅝in) drop in level for every 1m (3ft) distance from the house wall.

3 Ensuring good drainage

With a plate vibrator, compact the excavated ground; if the digging is deep, add a good layer of hardcore. Never reuse topsoil to make up height. If your patio requires a concrete base, see page 342; otherwise, mortar and slabs can be laid on the compacted surface.

4 Checking depths

Check the depth, level and angle of fall. Your excavations must be deep enough so that the top of the paving slabs will be a minimum of 150mm (6in) below the level of the damp-proof course, allowing for the slab thickness. Never cover or block up an airbrick.

5 Laying paving slabs

If your subsoil is well-compacted, lay a 50mm (2in) layer of sharp sand on top, roll it flat and then lay the slabs directly on this. Alternatively, you can lay a 25mm (1in) compacted layer of sand over a hardcore sub-base and bed the slabs on fist-sized dabs of mortar.

6 Tap slabs into place

Start laying slabs in one corner. Put down five dabs of mortar, one at each corner and one in the middle, then lay the first slab and tap it into place using the handle of a club hammer. Use a spirit level to check that the slab is flat and slopes at the required angle away from the house.

7 Continue laying slabs

Working out from the corner, lay the paving slabs using off-cuts of hardboard as spacers. Leave to settle for a couple of days, then fill the joints with a fairly dry mortar mix. Compact this into the joints and brush off surplus. Leave for 24 hours, protecting from rain and frost.

CUTTING A SLAB

Before you start cutting paving slabs, make sure you have the correct safety equipment on hand. To cut a slab, first use a straight edge to draw a line in pencil marking the position of the cut on both sides of the slab. Lay two slabs on a flat bed of sand and place the slab to be cut at an angle against them with the cut line on the edge of the top slab. Chisel a groove 2–3mm (⅛–¼in) deep along the line using a bolster and club hammer. Turn the slab over and then repeat the chiselling on the other side. If the groove is chiselled deep enough, the slab will break easily and cleanly after you give it one or two blows along the chiselled groove. You can also put a block above the chiselled line and give that a couple of hammer blows until the slab splits along the line.

If you have a large number of slabs to cut, consider hiring an electric angle grinder with a stone cutting disc to save time and energy. Follow the manufacturer's instructions carefully and always wear protective eye goggles and stout gloves.

SAFETY FIRST

- Paving slabs are heavy; the main dangers come from lifting and placing them, so take care not to strain your back – or drop slabs on your feet.

- Always wear protective goggles, protective gloves and steel-toed caps or sturdy boots when chiselling and cutting paving slabs.

LAYING PATHS

Laying paths does not require a great deal of skill. Nevertheless, it can still be hard work: 1 cubic meter of wet concrete – roughly 1⅓ cu. yds, or enough for a path about 15.25m (50ft) long – weighs about 2.32t (2 tons). If you are hand-mixing concrete, you'll be picking up those 2 tons a shovelful at a time, so, for a large area, consider hiring a mixer or buying ready-mixed concrete.

If you are laying a path on a new site, leave the area alone and watch which way people – and pets – make their own paths. It may be easier to lay a path there than persuade them to walk another route. If you are cutting a path through a lawn, calculate your levels so that the paving lies about 18mm (¾in) below the level of surrounding turf so you can mow the grass right over the edge without damaging your mower.

Decide on the route and proportions of your path and mark out the perimeter edges with pegs and lengths of string. Excavate the site: remove the topsoil and any vegetation down to a level that allows for the combined height of the sand layer and the paving itself. Compact and level the soil.

A path – whether concrete or paving stones or blocks – does not require a hardcore sub-base since it is just for pedestrian traffic. Instead, lay a well-compacted 25mm (1in) layer of sharp sand. Use a garden roller to compact the sand, spreading it with a rake and levelling it by scraping and tamping with a length of timber.

Lay an area of paving on the sand, working from one end of the site to the other. Lay whole bricks first, leaving cutting and filling spaces until you have completed about 2m sq (2 sq yds). A simple pattern of parallel lines of bricks will require the least amount of cutting.

When the paving is complete, tamp the paving into the bed of sand by laying a stout batten on top and striking it with a heavy club hammer. Brush in a dry mix of sand and cement (4:1) between the joints. This will gradually take up moisture from the ground and slowly set.

Sweep off any excess mortar and pass a heavy garden roller along the path. Add more dry mortar mix, sweeping it well into the joints. Clean off any excess mortar, then use a watering can with a rose sprinkler to lightly wet the surface. Allow the mortar joints to dry thoroughly before the path is used.

Edging stones laid at each side and bedded into the mortar add a final touch. These can be bricks set on their ends and at an angle, or you could use the traditional 'rope' top glazed ceramic panels that were popular in Victorian gardens.

GARDEN PATHS

A well-laid path through a garden makes an attractive feature and provides easier access to work on flowerbeds and borders.

MAKING STEPS

Many homes have gardens that slope away from the house and often these are simply grassed over. A gradient of 30 degrees to the horizontal is about as much slope as a cylinder mower will cope with, although a hover mower will tackle a 45-degree gradient; in either case, it will be hard work maintaining a beautiful lawn. A practical solution is to build a run of steps, which can also provide an interesting feature, a vantage point and a temporary resting place.

Plan your steps as a means of getting from level A to level B. Ideally, steps in a garden should be low, gentle and wide, but the materials you choose will, to a certain extent, dictate their form. Also, bear in mind the safety aspects when you build steps. Treads that are too smooth will be slippery when wet or frosty; materials that wear quickly or an unstable surface will be dangerous, and, if moss is not removed, they can be lethal. Treads on steps outdoors must not be absolutely level because they won't shed rainwater quickly: puddles will develop that, in winter, will ice over.

The proportion of the tread (the area you stand on) to the riser (the vertical 'back' or height of the step) is also important. As a rough guide, construct steps so that the depth of the tread (from front to back) plus twice the height of the riser, equals 650mm (2ft 2in). For safety's sake – and for aesthetics – never make your treads less than 300mm (1ft) deep or risers higher than 175mm (7in). Leave an overhang as the shadow cast will help to define the tread edge.

1 Prepare the site

Measure the difference in height from the top of the slope to the bottom and calculate the number of steps required. Mark the position of risers with pegs and roughly cut out the ground. Construct the risers from concrete facing blocks or bricks, allowing the treads to overhang by about 25–50mm (1–2in).

3 Setting the final tread

The final (topmost) tread should be set so that it is flush with the area at the top of the flight of steps. If you have to excavate some of the soil from the top, dig deep enough for a hardcore sub-base and concrete base on which to lay the tread slabs to make this tread secure.

2 Lay the slabs

Lay concrete slabs bedded in sharp sand flush with the ground at the foot of the slope, or dig a trench to hold a sub-base of well-compacted hardcore and a 100–150mm (4–6in) concrete base to support the first riser. Construct the first riser using normal bricklaying methods (see pages 50–1) and check alignment with a spirit level. Fill behind the riser with compacted hardcore until it is level, and then lay the tread on a bed of mortar. Using the spirit level as a guide, tap down the tread so it slopes very slightly forwards to shed water. Measure from the front edge of the tread to mark the position of the next riser on the slabs and construct the step in the same way.

SAFETY FIRST

Where power cables supply outdoor lights, water features, or power to an outbuilding, they should be run through an impact-resistant plastic conduit that is laid in a trench lined with finely sifted soil or sand. Lay the conduit then carefully fill the trench.

INSTALLING A POND IN THE GROUND

No matter how big or small your garden is, a pond adds an extra dimension to it. Not only do ponds reflect light, they also encourage wildlife and offer a wider range of planting opportunities. Still ponds are restful and contemplative, while the 'tinkling' water of a fountain revives the spirits. Nevertheless, a pond – even a very shallow one – can be extremely dangerous to your children and pets. If your children are very young, the pond should be surrounded by a safety fence to prevent accidents.

You can make a pond using a flexible or rigid liner. Rigid, prefabricated ponds are quick and easy to install and they come in a wide choice of shapes and sizes complete with moulded plastic planting shelves to suit most water plants. All you need to do is dig a hole to accommodate the mould, ensure the mould is level, back fill around it with soil and fill it with water and plants. Flexible plastic liners, on the other hand, allow you to design your own individually shaped and sized ponds.

Ponds should be located away from large trees as fallen leaves will collect in them, rot and be harmful to any fish. Instead, choose an open, semi-shaded, level spot, but remember you'll need to be close to a water supply for filling and topping up the pond in summer. Measure and mark out the site with string, or use sand trickled from a plastic bottle.

1 Excavate the site

Mark out your pond's shape and dimensions, including the maximum depth. The top of the pond must be level all the way round. Place level pegs all round the perimeter – check them with a spirit level – then dig out, working to the pegs and adding 50mm (2in) to the depth for a lining of smooth, fine sand.

3 Drape the liner

Drape the liner over the hole, allowing an even overlap. Make sure when you arrange the liner that you do not disturb the sand lining the edges, ledges and sides of the pond. Let the liner sag a little in the middle.

2 Inspect the site

Once the hole has been dug, inspect the sides, ledges, edges and bottom: remove sharp stones, glass and any other debris that could puncture the liner. Coat the bottom, the sides, the ledges and edges of the hole with a 50mm (2in) layer of damp, fine sand, and compact it well to make it stay in place.

4 Weight the edges

Place bricks or blocks around the edge of the liner: allow enough weight to control the liner but not so much that it stops it gliding and stretching gently into the pond as you very slowly fill it with water from a hosepipe.

5 Trim the liner

When the pond has filled with water, trim off the liner around the rim, leaving a minimum of 200mm (8in) pf liner as an overlap. Hold the edge of the liner in place by driving some nails through it into the ground.

6 Finish the edges

The overlap is easily hidden by placing paving stones around the edge. This will also help to anchor the liner. Slabs must overlap the edge of the liner by 150–200mm (6–8in), but not overhang the pond by more than 40mm (1¾in).

POND LIFE

- You can plant a pond as soon as it is complete, but don't put in any fish for at least four weeks.

- Some tree leaves and seeds are poisonous to fish so don't plan a pond anywhere near a willow, poplar or laburnum.

- So the edging stones don't fall off if someone steps on one, they must be carefully bedded down on mortar.

- See page 365 for advice on installing a fountain in your pond.

- Take care not to let any mortar drop in the water – you will contaminate it and it must then be replaced.

- If you are creating your own shape, try laying out a garden hose on the ground in different shapes to inspire the form.

- Make a ramp out of smooth rocks and pebbles leading from the depths of the pond to the ground surface so that amphibians – frogs and newts – can get in and out.

INSTALLING A POND ABOVE THE GROUND

Ponds don't have to be dug in the ground. A formal pond with a raised edge using bricks or concrete facing blocks makes wonderful waterside seating. Raised ponds are also much safer if there are small children around, especially if you construct the edging about 450–500mm (1ft 6in–2ft) high.

The water must also be clear and to achieve this you will need to install a pump to recycle the water, or establish a careful balance of pond life, which includes oxygenating plants (at least 10 per square meter of water surface), snails and fish. A successful balance creates a food chain, which excludes the green algae that stains surfaces, clouds the water and kills pond life.

The best way to construct a raised pond is to use a low, double-skin construction for strength and to make sure it is watertight in case of leaks in the liner. The inner skin can be constructed of plain concrete blocks (decorative bricks or blocks can be saved for the exterior walls). Build the walls with a space between that matches the width of the coping stones used to finish the top of the walls. You will need to lay good solid foundations to support the walls, so lay footings of 100–150mm (4–6in). Raised ponds can be lined using a made-to-measure prefabricated rigid liner, which reduces the number of creases at the corners that you will have if you opt for a flexible plastic liner, but these often don't have overflow or outlet facilities. The top edge of the liner is trapped under coping stones making it invisible.

1 Constructing the pond

The essential feature of a wall is that there is a firm, level, foundation along its entire length consisting of a concrete base, called the footing. Pour concrete into a prepared trench dug to expose firm and stable ground. Use plain concrete blocks inside the pond for the double skin.

2 Adding the liner

You will need a liner large enough to cover the sides and bottom – add a layer of damp, smooth sand at the bottom of the pond to stop the liner from being punctured by stones when the water is added. Let the liner sag into the pond and arrange it so it lies over the edges. Pleat the edges to neaten the corners.

3 Add water

The liner should overhang the edges sufficiently so that when the water is slowly added, its weight pulls the liner gently down and against the sides. Help the liner in – you want it to lie flush against the bottom and sides.

4 Adding the coping

The overlapping edges of liner can be trimmed off leaving a wide overlap. This will be covered and hidden from view by a row of coping stones. Bed the coping onto the wall with mortar, checking constantly that it is level.

INSTALLING A FOUNTAIN

There are a huge number of types and styles of fountains available, ranging from a simple vertical jet of water to complex waterworks either on their own or in combination with lighting effects, or even integrated into attractive sculptures.

If you are worried about powering a pump electrically, you could opt for a solar-powered one instead. Most will, however, be operated by a low-volume submersible pump fitted with a volume regulator and a by-pass valve. All except the smallest pumps will be able to operate a small fountain and a modest waterfall at the same time.

Bubble fountains on the other hand, bring all the attractions of movement and the sound of a waterfall or fountain but without the need to

install a pond. These can be made by sinking a large waterproof container into the ground so the rim is flush with ground level. Install a submersible pump, mount a layer of small-grid, ridged mesh over the rim of the trough, cover it with round pebbles, fill with water, and then adjust the pump output to the flow of your choice – a gentle wetting or a fairly formidable geyser, it's up to you – but don't forget to keep the water level topped up in the trough.

Pumps need to be checked and serviced from time to time, so place them close to the edge of a pond so you can reach them easily to disconnect the hose running to the fountain. Make sure you follow the safety advice (see box) when installing outdoor water features.

1 Fountain kits
There are a large number of fountain and waterfall kits on the market. Consult manufacturers' brochures and check displays in garden centres to help you find the one that best suits your needs.

SAFETY FIRST

- Submersible pumps for fountains can be operated directly by mains electricity, but this is not recommended. It is much safer to operate them through a transformer that reduces the current to 24 volts. A low-voltage pump is perfectly safe and is easy to install and to wire. However, electricity and water can be a lethal combination, so, if you are in any doubt at all you must consult a qualified electrician.

- Remember, electric cables should be run through impact-resistant plastic conduit laid in a trench of fine soil or sand.

2 The pump
Place the pump in the water and run its electrical cable beneath the edging stones to a waterproof connector attached to the extension lead of a transformer.

3 The transformer
The pump transformer must be housed indoors – a dry, secure place in a garage is good. The pump can easily be lifted from the pond to be maintained or serviced while the extension lead and transformer are left undisturbed.

MAKING CONCRETE PLANTERS

On pages 354–5 there are instructions on how to build walls in gardens and ways in which they can be used to divide up spaces. On page 364 there is advice on building a raised pond using a double-skin wall. The project here provides you with the opportunity to combine aspects of both these projects to create raised planters. These low, double-skin walls, which in this example terminate in hollow piers, are filled with soil and can be planted with your favourite specimens. They can be straight or curving 'serpents' through your garden and the piers can be square, rectangular or – if you are feeling particularly inspired – even circular, as it is possible to buy decorative bricks or blocks cast into curved forms.

The low walls of concrete planters will be softened in time as the plants grow and spill over the edges. You could incorporate some decorative metalwork – an obelisk perhaps to add additional height – or even some attractive outdoor lights in the pier ends. As always, the walls will only be as good as their foundations, so careful planning, excavation and preparation are vital to ensure good, strong walls.

Finally, don't forget that as with all 'containers' the plants growing in them will be reliant on you for their food and water, and could easily dry out in summer.

1 'Double wall' construction

The planters are made by building two parallel walls of the same height with a gap between them. If you want a wide gap, say about 600mm (2ft) wide, keep the walls quite low. Taller walls should have a proportionally smaller gap so they remain strong and upright.

2 Adding coping stones

When you have reached the desired wall height, finish the walls with coping stones bedded into mortar tar. Work out the proportions of the piers according to the materials: note here that, rather than having to cut a coping stone to size, the supporting walls have been built to accommodate them with ease.

3 Checking levels

Gently tap the coping into the mortar bed using the handle of a club hammer or mallet and use a spirit level to check it is horizontal. Check the levels all the way around the piers and across them diagonally.

4 The finished planters

The finished planters, filled with soil, are ready for planting up. You can part fill the spaces with rubble to provide good drainage – this also cuts down on the amount of soil or compost you'll need.

MAKING A BARBECUE

1 Solid base

A barbecue can become the centrepiece of a terrace in summer, but a well-designed structure will still be attractive when not in use — and in winter you could also use it for burning garden waste. A barbecue will sit directly on a level, well-constructed terrace, or on its own concrete foundation.

2 Build the walls

Make sure that the overall height of the barbecue unit is convenient for your height. Compare it with the height of your kitchen worktops. You could also add convenient storage space for cooking implements and charcoal. Check levels and the angles of corners as you construct the three-sided shape.

3 Finishing the stonework

Add flat coping stones on the top and check the levels once again with a spirit level. Take time and care over the finishing touches and details, as you would for any other structure.

4 Making grooves for the grill rack

Before the mortar has completely set, run a round-ended stick horizontally along the mortar join on each side to create a groove into which the grill can slide. Do the same at a slightly lower level to accommodate the charcoal tray.

BARBECUES

- Before you build your barbecue, make sure that it is located where prevailing winds won't blow smoke towards your house, your neighbour's house, or the area where you would like your guests to sit.

- So that everyone can be fed at the same time, a good-sized barbecue should have a cooking grill of no less than 1m x 500mm (3ft x 1½ft) in size. A smaller grill will mean some guests will be sitting waiting for their food while others are eating.

- An electricity supply from your house to a sealable socket will allow you to install a portable spotlight or lamp for evening barbecues.

- Make sure you construct a barbecue in an area where there is plenty of space: on chilly evenings, the warm glow of charcoal will draw a crowd.

- When building the walls of your barbecue, don't forget to include some flat surfaces on which you can place plates and drinks.

- Handling food on a barbecue is easier and safer if you use long-handled tongs. Short-handled utensils get hot very quickly. Make sure as well that you have a bucket of water close by to deal with any sudden flare-ups.

PERGOLAS AND ARCHWAYS

In sunny climates, pergolas are traditionally used to give shade to a path. In less sunny climates, such as in the United Kingdom, pergolas are more often used as a roof transition from the inside of the house to the garden or, alternatively, they can act as support for climbing flowers and rambling plants.

In urban areas, where gardens are often overlooked, a pergola can create a measure of privacy, without giving a 'blocked in' feeling. A pergola structure over a terraced area or patio also helps to create the sense of an 'outdoor room'. A well-positioned archway over a path not only breaks up a long, uninterrupted view but, at the same time, also makes a frame for a portion of the garden that can be seen from a distance.

The design of pergolas and archways should be as simple as possible because their true function is to support plants and those should be the stars of the show, not the fancy details in your construction. Arches and pergolas are available as standard-sized kits but in a variety of styles, so with a little research, it should be relatively easy to find a size and design that suits your taste and requirements. Many kits come with trellis side panels. If you are constructing your own archway, you may need to cut them to size and add a supporting framework if you don't construct to 'standard' sizes. Remember to treat all timber with wood preservative prior to construction. This will keep it strong and attractive for longer.

Plant climbing and rambling plants on the outsides of archways – not in the narrow strips between their feet and a path edge – so they can grow and spread over the arch without blocking the passage through and underneath it.

PERGOLAS

• Treat all timber with wood preservative before construction and reapply regularly afterwards to maintain its condition.

• You can attach a pergola directly to the side of your home more easily if you sit the timbers in 'L'-shaped metal shoes plugged into the walls.

• Trained vines or hops over pergolas and arches will give shade in summer and let in light in winter.

• Consider the scale and proportion of pergolas and arches in relation to the garden features – large trees or changes in levels – as well as your house.

1 Measure and mark

Select the location of the archway and measure and mark the position of the supporting verticals. Most kit-form arches are easy to assemble and the verticals are supported in the ground by metal brackets like those used to support fence posts.

2 Drive in the supporting brackets

Drive in the metal supporting brackets – these normally have spiked ends to make it easier. Make sure they are vertical – check with a spirit level. If you use a mallet to drive in the spikes, place a piece of protective wood over the top so you don't damage them.

3 Attach the posts

Slip the posts into the brackets and fix them in place. This is done either by driving in nails or screws or, sometimes, by tightening the special bolt that comes with some brackets. After securing the posts, check again for verticality with a spirit level.

4 Archway joists

Depending on which style of archway you have chosen, the 'roof' may be flat or pointed. If it is the latter, it is better to secure the two sides of the point 'on the ground' rather than try to attach them individually to the supporting posts

5 Fix the 'roof'

Offer up the archway 'roof' joists. You may need some help, depending on the height. If you need to use a ladder, make sure you position it on level ground for safety. It may help to pre-drill holes so you can fix them quickly and easily.

6 Offer up the trellis panels

Trellis side 'panels' are simply fixed to the vertical posts with galvanized nails to protect them from rust.

Contents

APPENDICES

METRIC AND IMPERIAL MEASUREMENTS

In the EU, measurements are given in metres and millimetres. 52cm is written either as 0.52m or 520mm. 2m + 12.4cm is always 2.124m or 2124mm. In this book, we have given imperial conversions in brackets, where appropriate, but many DIY goods on sale will only list the metric measurement.

LINEAR MEASUREMENTS

1 meter (1m) is approximately 3ft 3in (39.37in).

1in, when converted to metric, is 25.4mm.

However, when you go shopping, you will find that there is slight difference between the actual conversion and the manufacturers' conversion, so that 1in items could be manufactured as 25mm. Because the manufacturer's conversion is always fractionally less than the actual conversion from imperial measurements, you should always measure in metric to avoid mistakes.

Useful Conversions

Imperial	Actual	Manufacturers' Conversion
1in	25.4mm	25mm
2in	50.8mm	50mm
3in	76.2mm	75mm
4in	101.6mm	100mm
5in	127mm	125mm
6in	152.4mm	150mm
7in	177.8mm	175mm
8in	203.2mm	200mm
9in	228.6mm	225mm
10in	254mm	250mm
11in	279.4mm	275mm
12in	304.8mm	300mm
2ft	609.6mm	600mm
3ft	914.4mm	900mm
3ft 3⅜in	1000mm	1000mm
4ft	1219.2mm	1200mm
5ft	1524mm	1500mm
6ft	1828.8mm	1800mm
7ft	2133.6mm	2100mm
8ft	2438.4mm	2400mm

If you continue to calculate using imperial measurements, you will have to convert them into metric measurements.

Conversion Factors:

Imperial to metric:	Metric to Imperial:
in x 25.4 = mm	mm x 0.0394 = inch
ft x 0.3048 = m	m x 3.281 = feet
yd x 0.9144 = m	m x 1.0936 = yard

AREA

The same way of working out areas applies to metric measurements: 1m sq. = 1.20sq.yds

Conversion Factors:

Imperial to Metric:	Metric to Imperial:
sq.in x 645.2 = mm sq.	mm sq. x 0.00155 = sq.in
sq.ft x 0.0929 = m sq.	m sq. x 10.764 = sq.ft
sq.yd x 0.8361 = m sq.	m sq. x 1.196 = sq.yd.

VOLUME

Working out volumes in the metric system is much easier than in the imperial system. The word 'litre' is always written in full; this is so that it is never confused with the number 1.

1 litre = 1000 cubic centimetres (1000cc)

1000 litres = 1m

1000 millilitres (ml) = 1 litre

1ml = 1 cubic centimeter (cc)

1cubic m = 1.31cu.yds

Conversion Factors

Imperial to metric:	Metric to Imperial:
cu. ft x 0.0283 = cu. m	cu. m x 35.335 = cu. ft
cu. ft x 28.32 = cu. litres	cu. litres x 0.035 = cu. ft
cu. yd x 0.7646 = cu. m	cu. m x 1.3079 = cu. yd
ml (cc) x 0.035 = fl. oz	fl. oz x 28.413 = ml (cc)
ml (cc) x 0.0017 = pints	pints x 568.000 = ml (cc)
litres x 1.76 = pints	pints x 0.568 = litres
litres x 0.22 = gallons	gallons x 4.5461 = litres

WEIGHT

1000 grams (1000g) = 1 kilogram (1kg)

1000 kilograms (1000kg) = 1 tonne (1t)

1 tonne (1t) = 2205lbs

The old imperial ton = 2240lbs

There are slight differences between manufacturers' approximate weights and actual weights. Again, the best advice is to calculate using metric to avoid shortfalls.

Conversion Factors

Imperial to metric:	Metric to Imperial:
lb x 0.45359 = kg	kg x 2.20462 = lb.
cwt x 50.8 = kg	kg x 0.0197 = cwt
oz x 28.3 = g	g x 0.035 = oz

BRICKS AND BLOCKS

The metric brick is slightly smaller than the old imperial one. New bricks can be bonded into old work by slightly increasing the mortar bed joint.

	length	width	height	typical joint
Metric	225mm	112.5mm	75mm	10 mm
	(8.86in)	(4.43in)	(2.95in)	(0.39in)
Imperial	9in	4½in	3in	⅜in
	(228.6mm)	(114.3mm)	(76.2 mm)	(9.5 mm)

Brick quantities

Area	Quantity
1m sq.	60 bricks
2m sq.	120 bricks
5m sq.	300 bricks
10m sq.	600 bricks

Blocks

One block equals 2 brick lengths and 3 brick heights

Block quantities

Area	Quantity
1m sq.	10 blocks
2m sq.	21 blocks
5m sq.	53 blocks
10m sq.	106 blocks

PLUMBING FITTINGS

Only fittings for copper pipes were affected by metrication. Metric compression fittings are interchangeable with imperial in some sizes, but adaptors are available for others:

Interchangeable sizes		Sizes needing adaptors	
mm	in	mm	in
12	⅜	22	¾
15	½	28	1

GLASS

In the past, glass thickness was determined by weight; now it is determined by mm thickness. Lengths and widths are specified in mm.

Old weight	Metric thickness
18oz	2mm
24oz	3mm
32oz	4mm
¼in plate glass	6mm

BUYING TIMBER

Timber can be purchased sawn, planed all round (PAR), or, planed both sides (PBS) but with the edges left sawn. Sawn wood is very rough and is mostly used for structural work. To make furniture or cupboards, you will need planed wood. Planing timber means that between 3mm to 5mm of wood is removed, so a 25mm piece of planed wood ends up as 22mm. A board measuring 152mm long will end up as 146mm long, as 3mm at each end will have been planed. The annoying thing about buying wood at timber yards or DIY stores, is that the sizes referred to are still sawn wood sizes – even after it has been planed to make it smooth. So a 50 x 100mm PAR wood is actually 47 x 95mm.

When you buy timber, it's a good idea to try and buy the standard sizes as these are cheaper. Allow a little extra on lengths, in particular for cutting, and to compensate for any 'dirty' or damaged edges. A good rule of thumb is to add an extra 13mm for every 610mm. Always reject material with large knots as this is the sign of weak wood. Where there's a

METRIC AND IMPERIAL MEASUREMENTS

knot, there's often a bend or twist in the wood. Timber with bits of bark at the edges – effectively reducing the width because you'll have to cut it away – is called 'waney-edged'. End splits or 'shakes' are another common fault and can sometimes extend right up the board. These are usually caused by too-rapid drying and again you'll lose length because the split wood has to be cut away. Other defects to look out for are 'cupped' boards, where there is a warped curve across the width, and sapwood on the edge of boards (which is a lighter colour than the rest of the board), which is attractive to woodworm.

BASIC LENGTHS OF SAWN SOFTWOODS:
1.80m 2.10m 2.40m 2.70m 3.0m 3.30m 3.60m 3.90m 4.20m 4.50m 4.80m 5.10m 5.40m 5.70m 6.0m 6.30m

For planed softwood timbers, deduct 3mm from sawn sizes. For example, 25 x 50mm PAR (planed all round) is 22 x 47mm in actual size – although you should allow for some slight variations.

HARDWOOD SIZES:
Lengths: as available, due to different sizes of trees. If not available in 100mm increments, it is normally charged to the next 100 mm.

Widths: 50 mm, rising in 10 mm increments. Also depends on species of tree.

Thickness: 19mm, 25mm, 32mm, 38mm, 50mm, 63mm, 75mm, and 100mm, rising thereafter in 25mm increments.

MAN-MADE BOARDS:
Plywood
Thickness: 3mm to 18mm
Standard sheet sizes: 2440 x 1220mm (8 x 4ft)
1220 x 1220mm (4 x 4ft)
1220 x 610mm (4 x 2ft)

Chipboard
Thickness: 9mm, 12mm, 15mm and 18mm
Standard sheet sizes: 2440 x 1220mm (8 x 4ft)

Melamine and timber finished chipboard:
Thickness: 15mm
Plank lengths: 1820mm (6ft), 2440mm (8ft)
Widths: from 150mm (6in) to 600mm (2ft)

Hardboard
Standard sheet size: 2440 x 1200mm (8 x 4ft)
Thickness of standard hardboard: 3.2mm

SCREWS & NAILS

TYPES OF SCREWS

Countersunk head: For general joinery.

Roundhead: For fixing sheet material too thin to be countersunk.

Raised countersunk head: For use with ironmongery and screwcups for high-quality finishes.

Dome heads: For fixing mirrors and plastic/laminated panels. Heads can be drilled and topped to take threaded shank of dome, or snap-on fitting can be used.

Star (or cross) heads: These screws require special screwdrivers, but the recessed cross slots in the heads offer good positive contact with the screwdriver and, therefore, there is less likelihood of damaging a surface with a slipping screwdriver head.

'Twinfast' double spiral thread: Fast to drive home and self-centring with 25% more holding power than ordinary screws. Ideal for use with chipboard, blockboard and fibreboard.

Clutch head: Non-removeable/tamper proof wood screws used for security purposes.

Coach screws: Used for heavy construction. They use washers and are driven into specially prepared holes and given final turns with a spanner.
D. Cut floor brad. All purpose nail, strong and secure.

SCREW SIZES

(Standard wood screws sizes are imperial with metric conversions)
o = slotted head   x = slotted and recessed head

Diameter/Gauge	0	1	2	3	4	5	6	7	8	9	10	12	14	16	18	20
mm	1.6	1.8	2	2.3	2.6	2.9	3.3	3.7	4.1	4.5	4.9	5.6	6.3	7	7.7	8.4
Length in mm																
¼ 6.4	o	o	o	o	x											
⅜ 9.5	o	o	o	x	x	x	x		o							
½ 12.7		o	o	x	x	x	x	x	x	o	o					
⅝ 15.9			o	o	x	x	x	x	o	o	x					
¾ 19.1			o	o	x	x	x	x	x	x	x	o	o			
⅞ 22.2					x	x	x	x	x	o	o	o				
1 25.5			o	o	x	x	x	o	x	x	x	x		o		
1¼ 31.8				o	o	x	x	x	x	x	x	o	o			
1½ 38.1				o	o	x	x	x	x	x	x	x	o	o	o	
1¾ 44.5				o		o	o	x	x	x	x	o	o	o		
2 50.8				o		o	o	x	x	x	x	x	o	o	o	
2¼ 57.2						o	o	x	o	x	x	x	o			
2½ 63.5						o	o	x	x	x	x	x	o			
2¾ 69.9						o		o		o	o	o	o			
3 76.2						o		x	o	x	x	x	o	o	o	
3¼ 82.6											o	o	o			
3½ 88.9								o		o	o		x	o	o	
4 101.6						o		o		o	o	o	o			
4½ 114.3										o	o	o	o	o		
5 127										o	o	o	o	o		
6 152.4												o	o	o	o	

THE RIGHT NAIL FOR THE JOB

Job	Nail
Wood sheet materials (hardboard, plywood,blockboard)	F, G, H
Plasterboard	J
Fixings to masonry	M, N
Fixing metal to wood	H
Hard roof coverings	I, K, L
Roofing felt	L
Wire to timber or brickwork	Q
Holding glass to wooden frames	P
Rough woodwork & heavy joinery	A, B, C, D, E
Light joinery & cabinet making	B, C, F
Carpet fixing	O

A. Round wire nail (or French nail). Strong fixing, large head. Good for general carpentry and carcass making

15mm	20mm	25mm	30mm	40mm
⅝in	¾in	1in	1¼in	1½in
45mm	50mm	60mm	65mm	75mm
1¾in	2in	2¼in	2½in	3in
90mm	100mm	115mm	125mm	150mm
3½in	4in	4½in	5in	6in
180mm	200mm			
7in	8in			

B. Oval wire nail (oval lost or brad head). Good for joinery: won't usually split wood if section follows the grain and head can be punched into wood.

20mm	25mm	30mm	40mm	45mm
¾in	1in	1¼in	1½in	1¾in
50mm	60mm	65mm	75mm	90mm
2in	2¼in	2½in	3in	3½in
100mm	125mm	150mm		
4in	5in	6in		

C. Round lost head. Good for joinery; head can be punched below surface, leaving only a small hole.

15mm	20mm	25mm	30mm	40mm
⅝in	¾in	1in	1¼in	1½in
50mm	60mm	65mm	75mm	
2in	2¼in	2½in	3in	

D. Cut floor brad. All purpose nail, strong and secure.

20mm	25mm	30mm	40mm	45mm
¾in	1in	1¼in	1½in	1¾in
50mm	60mm	65mm	70mm	75mm
2in	2¼in	2½in	2¾in	3in
90mm	100mm	115mm		
3½in	4in	4½in		

E. Cut clasp. Good all-purpose carpentry nail with strong grip.

25mm	30mm	40mm	50mm	65mm
1in	1¼in	1½in	2in	2½in
75mm	90mm	100mm	115mm	125mm
3in	3½in	4in	4½in	5in
150mm	180mm	200mm		
6in	7in	8in		

F. Panel pin. Good for light joinery. Fine gauge and small head easily driven below surface.

10mm	15mm	20mm	25mm	30mm
½in	5/8in	¾in	1in	1¼in
40mm	50mm	65mm	75mm	
1½in	2in	2½in	3in	

G. Hardboard (deep-drive or diamond point) pin. Head is self-countersinking.

20mm
¾in

H. Screw nail. For securing sheets of ply, hardboard or metal to timber, e.g. floors.

10mm	15mm	20mm	25mm	30mm	40mm
½in	⅝in	¾in	1in	1¼in	1½in
45mm	50mm				
1¾in	2in				

I. Helical threaded nail. For corrugated sheet roofing. Helical thread gives extra-secure hold and is usually used with shaped washers.

40mm	45mm	50mm	60mm	65mm	75mm
1½in	1¾in	2in	2¼in	2½in	3in
90mm	100mm	115mm	125mm	150mm	180mm
3½in	4in	4½in	5in	6in	7in
200mm					
8in					

J. Plasterboard nail. Has jagged sides to help secure it.

30mm	40mm
1¼in	1½in

K. Clout nail (slate nail). For fencing, roofing and fixing slates.

15mm	20mm	25mm	30mm	40mm	45mm
½in–⅝in	¾in	1in	1¼in	1½in	1¾in

50mm	65mm	75mm	90mm	100mm
2in	2½in	3in	3½in	4in

L. Extra large head clout (felt) nail. For securing roofing felt and external fabrics.

15mm	20mm	25mm	30mm	40mm
⅝in	¾in	1in	1¼in	1½in

M. Pipe (chisel point) nail. For fixing drainpipes and gutters into masonry.

50mm	65mm	75mm	90mm	100mm
2in	2½in	3in	3½in	4in

N. Masonry nail. Made of hardened steel, it will penetrate masonry and concrete but must only be driven in using a hardened engineers' hammer.

20mm	25mm	30mm	40mm	45mm	50mm
¾–⅞in	1in	1¼in	1½in	1¾in	2in

60mm	65mm	70mm	75mm	90mm	100mm
2¼in	2½in	2¾in	3in	3½in	4in

O. Cut tack. For fixing carpets. Can also be used for upholstery.

5mm	10mm	12mm	15mm	20mm	25mm	30mm
¼in	⅜in	½in	⅝in	¾in	1in	1¼in

P. Sprig. A headless tack for holding glass in wooden frames.

10mm	15mm	20mm
⅜in	½in	¾in

Q. Staple. Made of galvanized wire and used for fixing wire to timber. Tenterhook staples have one longer 'leg' for easy fixing.

10mm	15mm	20mm	25mm	30mm	40mm	50mm
½in	⅝in	¾in	1in	1¼in	1½in	2in

USEFUL ADDRESSES

Association of Plumbing and
Heating Contractors
Ensign House
Westwood Way
Coventry CV4 8JA
02476 470626

British Decorators Association
32 Coton Road
Nuneaton CV11 5TW
01247 6353776

Federation of Master Builders
14 Great James St
London WC1N 2BB
020 7242 7583

Glass and Glazing Federation
44 Borough High Street

London SE1 1XB
020 7403 7177

Guild of Master Craftsmen
166 High Street
Lewes, BN7 2NZ
01273 478449

Institute of Plumbing
64 Station Lane
Hornchurch RM12 6ND
01708 472791

National Association of
Plumbing, Heating and
Mechanical Services Contractors
6 Gate Street
London WC2A 3HX
020 7405 2678

National Federation of Builders
Catherine House
56–64 Leonard Street
London EC2A 4LT
020 7608 5150

National Federation of Roofing
Contractors
24 Weymouth Street
London W1N 3FA
020 7436 0387

National Inspection Council for
Electrical Installation
Connecting
237 Kennington Lane
London SE11 5QJ
020 7405 2678

Royal Institute of British
Architects
66 Portland Place
London W1N 4AD
020 7580 5533

Royal Institute of Chartered
Surveyors
12 Great George Street
London SW1P 3AD
020 7222 7000

See page 18 for details of
CORGI, the Council for
Registered Gas Installers.

GLOSSARY

ABRASIVES Materials used for grinding or rubbing down to fine surfaces such as sand, glass, wet and dry paper or wire wool.

AIR BRICK Perforated bricks placed in a wall to assist ventilation.

ARCHITRAVE Mouldings surrounding doors and windows.

BALUSTER Vertical members of a stair handrail.

BALUSTRADE Handrail supported by balusters.

BEADING Small timber or plastic moulding used as decoration or finish.

BOND Way in which courses (layers) of bricks are laid to give strength to a wall.

BONDED Pipes and other metalwork connected together electrically, especially to the Earth.

BUTT JOINING Joining wallpaper and coverings edge to edge with no overlap.

CAPILLARY JOINT Method of joining copper pipe by soldering.

CASEMENT Windows hinged on one vertical edge.

CEILING JOISTS Wooden ties from walls, from which ceilings are suspended.

CAVITY WALLS Walls made of two leaves separated by a continuous air space 50mm (2in) wide

CIRCUIT BREAKER Switch adapted for automatic closing in the event of overload or short circuit.

CISTERN a) Storage: stores water for indirect, low-pressure services in home. Normally located in roof space. b) Flushing: used with a WC. There are two types: old style 'ball' and modern 'piston' action flushing cisterns.

COMPRESSION JOINT Method of joining two pipes that does not require soldering.

CONDUCTOR Single wire or group of wires in continuous contact with each other.

CONSUMER UNIT Consumer's fuse board, usually with an On/Off switch.

CORE Conductor of a cable, including insulation but not the protective covering.

COVE Shaped cornice.

CROSS LINING Method of hanging lining paper horizontally in order to disguise joins when final paper is applied.

CYLINDER Hot water tank.

DADO The lower part of a wall when decorative treatment is different to upper portion.

DISTEMPER An obsolete paint based on coloured pigment, finely ground chalk and size (glue).

DOUBLE HUNG Sash windows suspended by ropes or chains and counterweights over pulleys.

DOUBLE POLE Switch in which circuit is broken at live and neutral poles simultaneously.

DOWEL Straight-sided circular section pin, used to hold together two pieces of timber.

DRYING OUT TIME The time taken for new plaster and brickwork to dry out. During this time, paint finishes should not be applied.

EAVES The lowest overhanging part of a sloping roof.

EFFLORESCENCE Natural salts in bricks, mortar and plaster, which appear on the surface as they dry. Can cause paint to blister or flake off.

ELBOW Pipe fitting for connecting two lengths at an angle to each other.

ESCUTCHEON Metal plate surrounding or lining a keyhole.

FEATHER EDGE Boards cut to a thin wedge shape used for fencing, cladding sheds and exterior walls.

FIGURED The pattern in timber caused by the grain.

FLOOR JOISTS Structural (load bearing) timbers suspended between supporting walls on which floorboards are laid.

FOOTINGS Concrete foundation or base on which walls are built.

FORMWORK Temporary structure made to act as a mould for concrete.

FUSE The (deliberate) weak link to protect an electrical circuit. Consists of thin wire, which melts when excessive current flows.

GROUT Decorative, waterproof filler used to seal joins between mosaic and ceramic tiles.

HORNS Also called joggles, the waste portion of timber left on top and bottom of door stiles to give protection in transit, which are removed when door is hung.

INSPECTION CHAMBER 'Manhole' method of access to underground drainage system, usually where two drains meet.

KERF The cut made by a saw.

KEY Condition of work piece enabling paint to adhere to surface.

JAMB Vertical support for a door or window.

JUNCTION BOX Box that forms part of wiring installation, used where three or more conductors join together.

KNOTTING Shellac-based treatment painted onto knots in new wood to stop resins bleeding through subsequent layers of paint.

LAGGING Protecting water pipes and tanks by surrounding them with insulating materials.

LAYING OFF Action of final paintbrush strokes that give a smooth finish.

MARBLING Imitation of marble by a paint technique.

MASKING OFF Using a shield, or masking tape stuck to a surface to stop paint adhering.

MATT Dull (not glossy) in finish.

NEWEL Main supporting post for stairs and bannisters.

NOGGINS Horizontal structural members within a stud wall.

NOSING Overhanging portion of a stair tread.

OILSTONE Fine-grade stone used with a lubricant to sharpen tools.

PARQUET Wooden flooring made or hardwood blocks or veneers laid in geometrical patterns.

POINTING Raking out soft mortar joints and filling them with a hard or decorative mortar mix.

PRIMER First coat of sealing paint or varnish applied to wood or metal in order that subsequent coats will adhere.

PURLIN Horizontal roof member running at right angles to the rafters along their midpoint.

RADIAL CIRCUIT System of electrical distribution where circuit cables radiate from consumer unit.

RAFTERS Sloping timbers in a roof framework.

RAILS Horizontal members of a door or table.

RENDER Cement mortar applied as protective screed to external brickwork.

REVEAL Side of window/door opening.

RUST INHIBITOR Paint primer for iron, which excludes oxygen and thus prevents rust forming.

SCREED Thin layer of plaster on a wall, or a thin layer of concrete on a floor used for levelling the surface.

STILES Vertical members of a door, window frame or staircase.

STIPPLE Dragging the surface of tacky paint (or plaster) to decorative effect.

STRING Side member of a staircase or step ladder.

TAMP To ram down.

TEMPLATE Metal, wood or card mould or outline used as a guide when shaping materials.

TESSERAE Individual tiles in mosaics.

INDEX

PICTURE CREDITS AND ACKNOWLEDGEMENTS

All pictures are from the DIY Picture Library, with the following exceptions:

tl - top left   tr - top right

ml - middle left   mr - middle right

bl - bottom left   br - bottom right

Elizabeth Whiting Associates supplied images on pages 23, 25, 27, 31, 135 (tl), 146, 173, 213, 215, 248, 279, 295, 296, 299, 302 (ml), 303 (tl), 315, 320, 321, 338, 339.

Courtesy of Draper: images on pages 13 (tools), 37 (tools), 38, 145 (tools), 165, 189 (tools), 227 (tools), 277 nos 1-6 (tools), 337.

Courtesy of Bosch: images on pages 180, 181 (tr), 192, 193.

Courtesy of Alexanders: image on page 220.

Photographed by Gary Ombler: images on pages 11, 34, 37 (background), 42, 142, 145 (background), 149, 186, 189 (background), 216, 218 (tr), 219 (tr), 224, 227 (background), 239 (bl), 274, 277 (background), 277 nos 7-8 (tools), 282 (tr), 292 (tl), 322 (bl), 334, 337 (background), 346 (tl).

Photographed by Nick Carter: image on page 206.

All illustrations by Chris Lyon.

Special thanks to Melanie Charles.